BRIEFCASE FULL OF BABY BLUES®

HOWLIN' BABY PRODUCTIONS

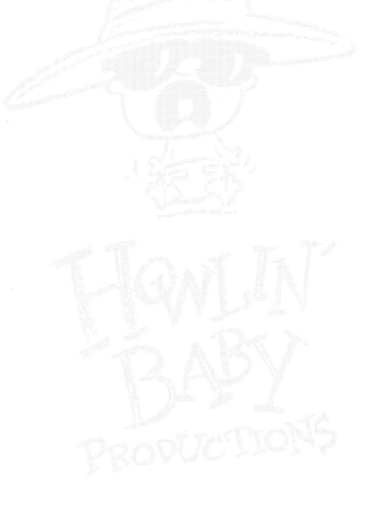

Other *Baby Blues*® Books from Andrews McMeel Publishing

Guess Who Didn't Take a Nap?
I Thought Labor Ended When the Baby Was Born
We Are Experiencing Parental Difficulties . . . Please Stand By
Night of the Living Dad
I Saw Elvis in My Ultrasound
One More and We're Outnumbered!
Check, Please . . .
threats, bribes & videotape
If I'm a Stay-at-Home Mom, Why Am I Always in the Car?
Lift and Separate
I Shouldn't Have to Scream More Than Once!
Motherhood Is Not for Wimps
Baby Blues®: Unplugged
Dad to the Bone
Never a Dry Moment
Two Plus One Is Enough
Playdate: Category 5
Our Server Is Down
Something Chocolate This Way Comes

Treasuries

The Super-Absorbent Biodegradable Family-Size Baby Blues®
Baby Blues®: Ten Years and Still in Diapers
Butt-Naked Baby Blues®
Wall-to-Wall Baby Blues®
Driving Under the Influence of Children
Framed!

BABY BLUES® 22 SCRAPBOOK

BRIEFCASE FULL OF BABY BLUES®

KIRKMAN & SCOTT

Andrews McMeel
Publishing, LLC

Kansas City

07 08 09 10 11 BBG 10 9 8 7 6 5 4 3 2 1

ISBN: 978-0-7407-6355-7
ISBN: 0-7407-6355-5

Library of Congress Control Number: 2006937454

www.andrewsmcmeel.com

Find *Baby Blues*® on the Web at
www.babyblues.com.

──── **ATTENTION: SCHOOLS AND BUSINESSES** ────

Andrews McMeel books are available at quantity discounts with bulk purchase for educational, business, or sales promotional use. For information, please write to: Special Sales Department, Andrews McMeel Publishing, LLC, 4520 Main Street, Kansas City, Missouri 64111.

BABY BLUES®
BY RICK KIRKMAN / JERRY SCOTT

YOU KNOW... THE KIDS ARE ALL ASLEEP, AND IT'S ONLY 10 O'CLOCK.
IS THAT SO?
YEAH. DOES THAT GIVE YOU ANY IDEAS?
IT SURE DOES.
WILL YOU EXCUSE ME WHILE I GO SLIP INTO SOMETHING MORE COMFORTABLE?
YOU BET
Z
I SHOULD HAVE SEEN THAT ONE COMING.
KIRKMAN & SCOTT

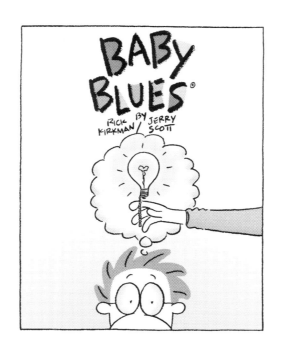

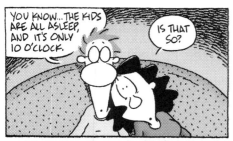

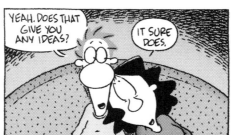

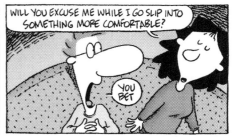

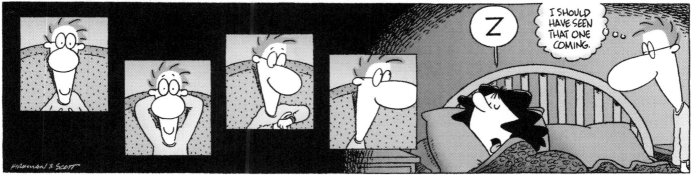

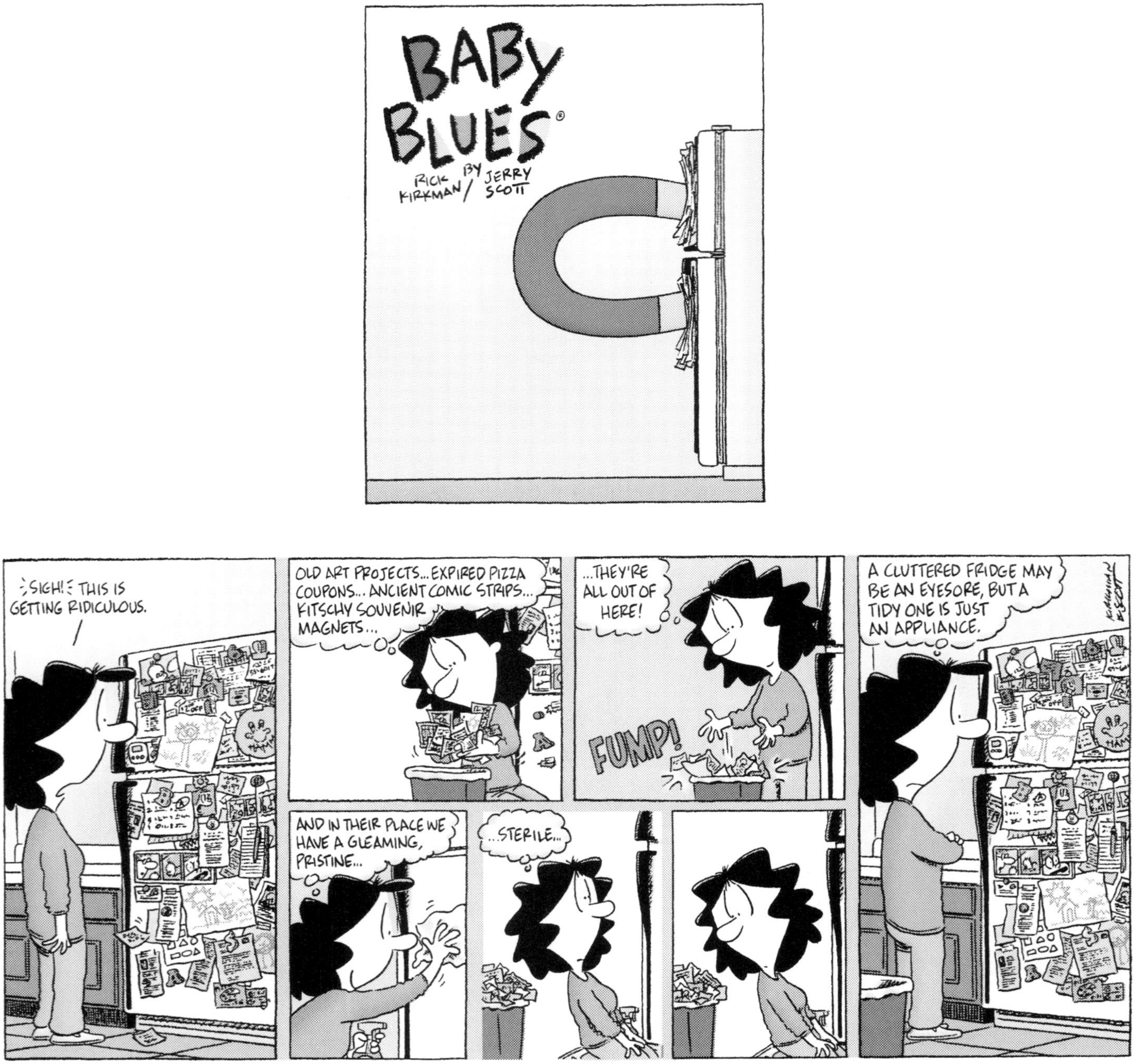
BABY BLUES®
BY RICK KIRKMAN / JERRY SCOTT
¦SIGH!¦ THIS IS GETTING RIDICULOUS.
OLD ART PROJECTS... EXPIRED PIZZA COUPONS... ANCIENT COMIC STRIPS... KITSCHY SOUVENIR MAGNETS...
...THEY'RE ALL OUT OF HERE!
FUMP!
AND IN THEIR PLACE WE HAVE A GLEAMING, PRISTINE...
...STERILE...
A CLUTTERED FRIDGE MAY BE AN EYESORE, BUT A TIDY ONE IS JUST AN APPLIANCE.

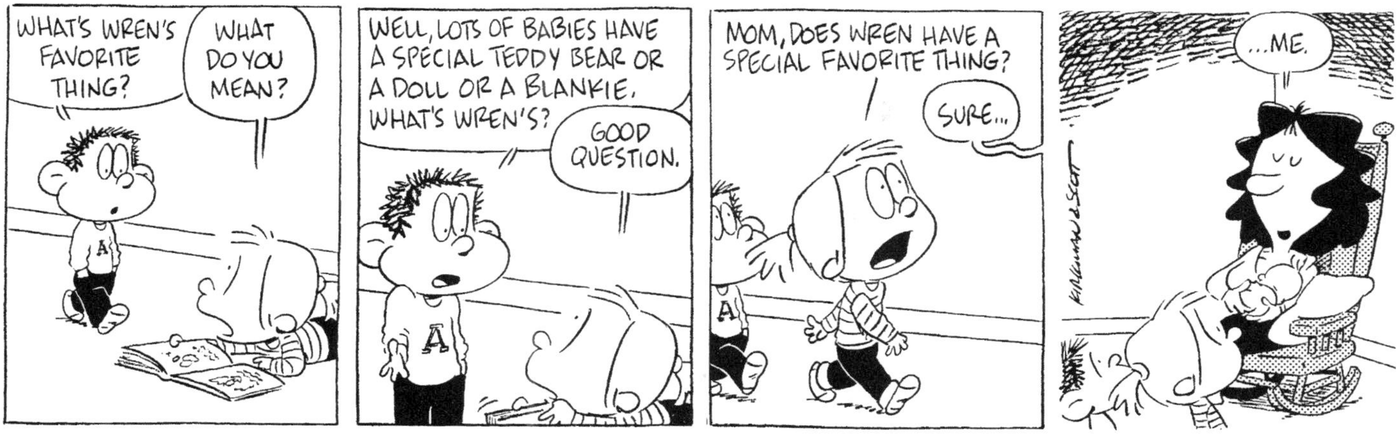
WHAT'S WREN'S FAVORITE THING?
WHAT DO YOU MEAN?
WELL, LOTS OF BABIES HAVE A SPECIAL TEDDY BEAR OR A DOLL OR A BLANKIE. WHAT'S WREN'S?
GOOD QUESTION.
MOM, DOES WREN HAVE A SPECIAL FAVORITE THING?
SURE...
...ME.
KIRKMAN & SCOTT

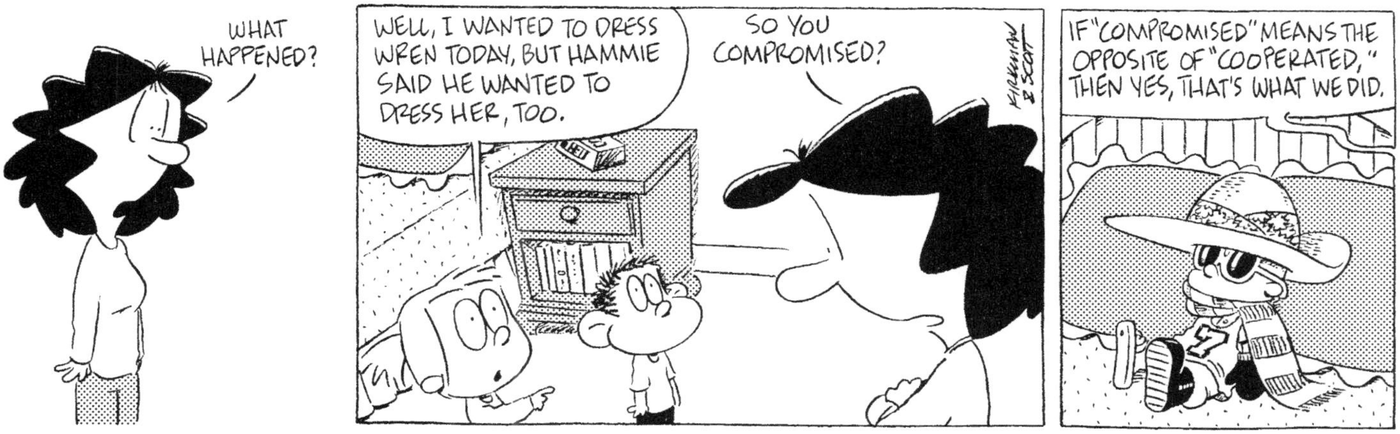
WHAT HAPPENED?
WELL, I WANTED TO DRESS WREN TODAY, BUT HAMMIE SAID HE WANTED TO DRESS HER, TOO.
SO YOU COMPROMISED?
KIRKMAN & SCOTT
IF "COMPROMISED" MEANS THE OPPOSITE OF "COOPERATED," THEN YES, THAT'S WHAT WE DID.

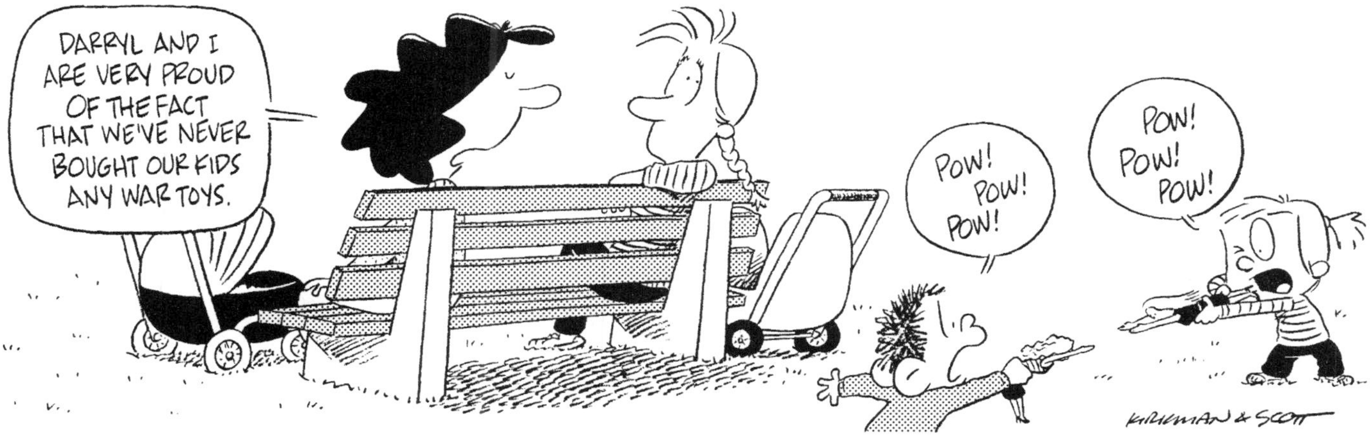
DARRYL AND I ARE VERY PROUD OF THE FACT THAT WE'VE NEVER BOUGHT OUR KIDS ANY WAR TOYS.
POW! POW! POW!
POW! POW! POW!
KIRKMAN & SCOTT

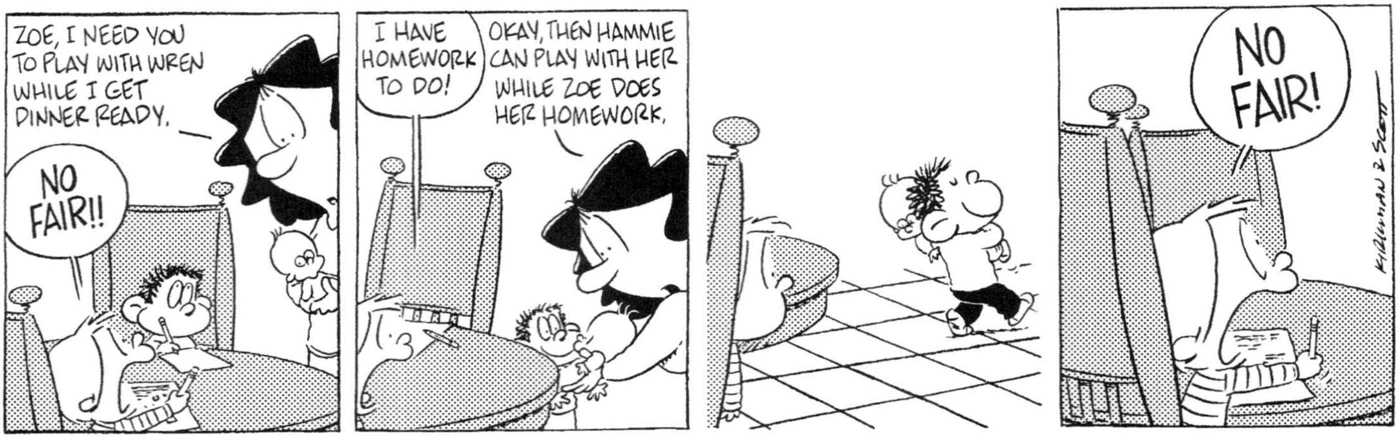
ZOE, I NEED YOU TO PLAY WITH WREN WHILE I GET DINNER READY.
NO FAIR!!
I HAVE HOMEWORK TO DO!
OKAY, THEN HAMMIE CAN PLAY WITH HER WHILE ZOE DOES HER HOMEWORK.
NO FAIR!
KIRKMAN & SCOTT

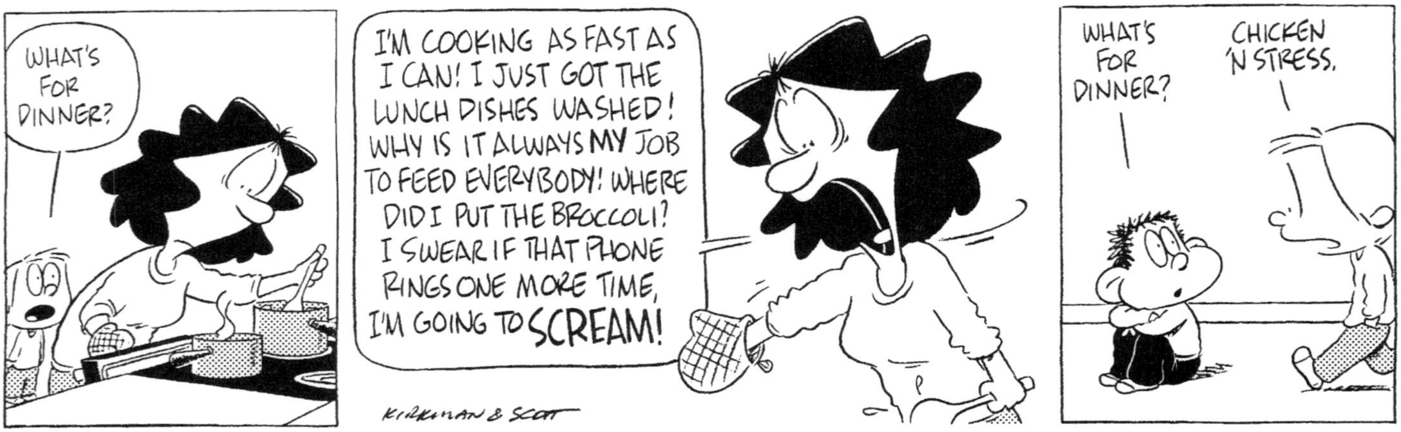
WHAT'S FOR DINNER?
I'M COOKING AS FAST AS I CAN! I JUST GOT THE LUNCH DISHES WASHED! WHY IS IT ALWAYS MY JOB TO FEED EVERYBODY! WHERE DID I PUT THE BROCCOLI? I SWEAR IF THAT PHONE RINGS ONE MORE TIME, I'M GOING TO SCREAM!
KIRKMAN & SCOTT
WHAT'S FOR DINNER?
CHICKEN 'N STRESS.

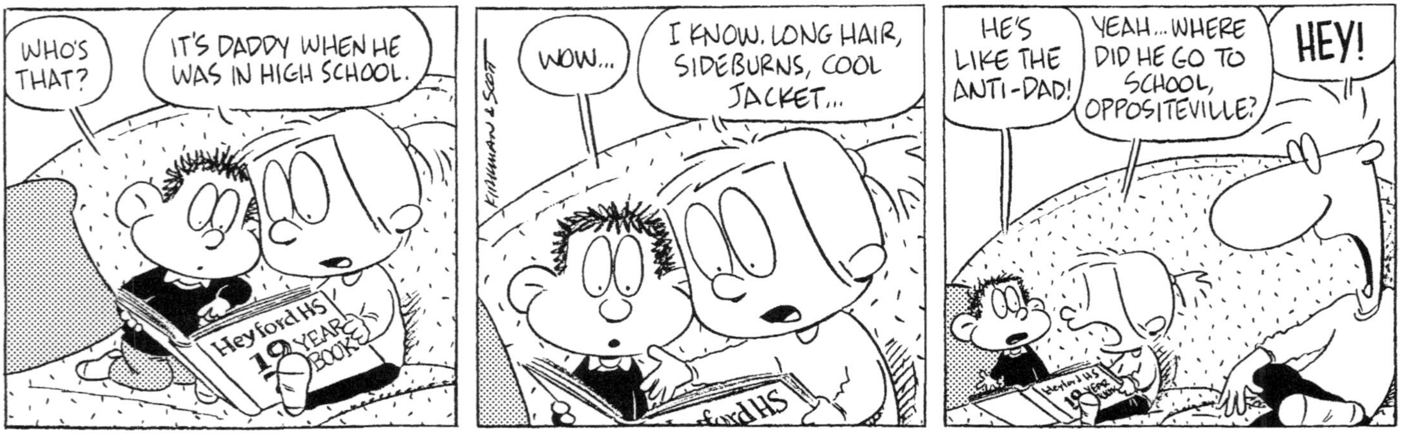
WHO'S THAT?
IT'S DADDY WHEN HE WAS IN HIGH SCHOOL.
Heyford HS 19 YEAR BOOK
KIRKMAN & SCOTT
WOW...
I KNOW. LONG HAIR, SIDEBURNS, COOL JACKET...
HE'S LIKE THE ANTI-DAD!
YEAH... WHERE DID HE GO TO SCHOOL, OPPOSITEVILLE?
HEY!

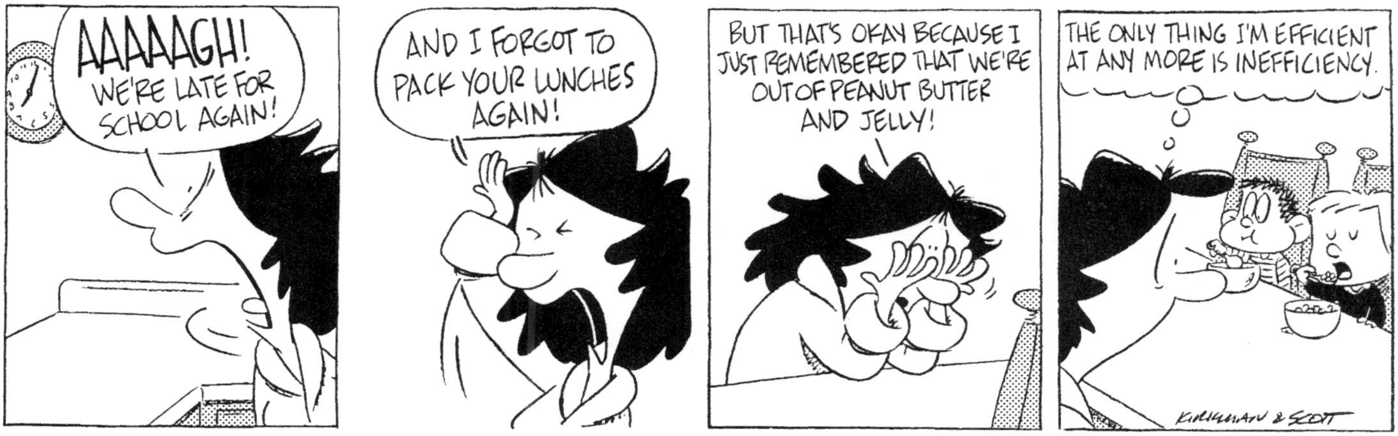
AAAAAGH! WE'RE LATE FOR SCHOOL AGAIN!
AND I FORGOT TO PACK YOUR LUNCHES AGAIN!
BUT THAT'S OKAY BECAUSE I JUST REMEMBERED THAT WE'RE OUT OF PEANUT BUTTER AND JELLY!
THE ONLY THING I'M EFFICIENT AT ANY MORE IS INEFFICIENCY.
KIRKMAN & SCOTT

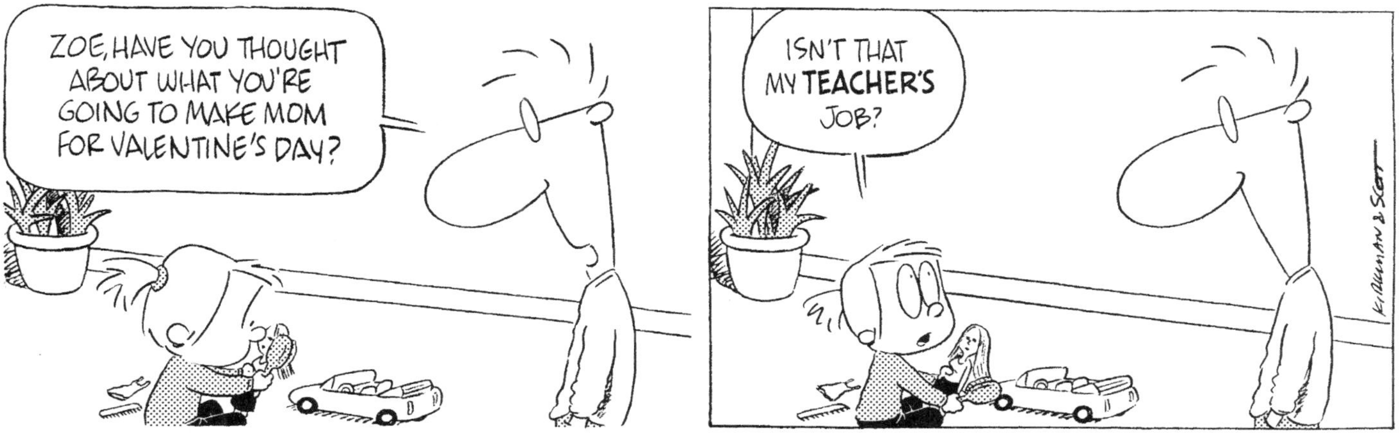
ZOE, HAVE YOU THOUGHT ABOUT WHAT YOU'RE GOING TO MAKE MOM FOR VALENTINE'S DAY?
ISN'T THAT MY **TEACHER'S** JOB?
KIRKMAN & SCOTT

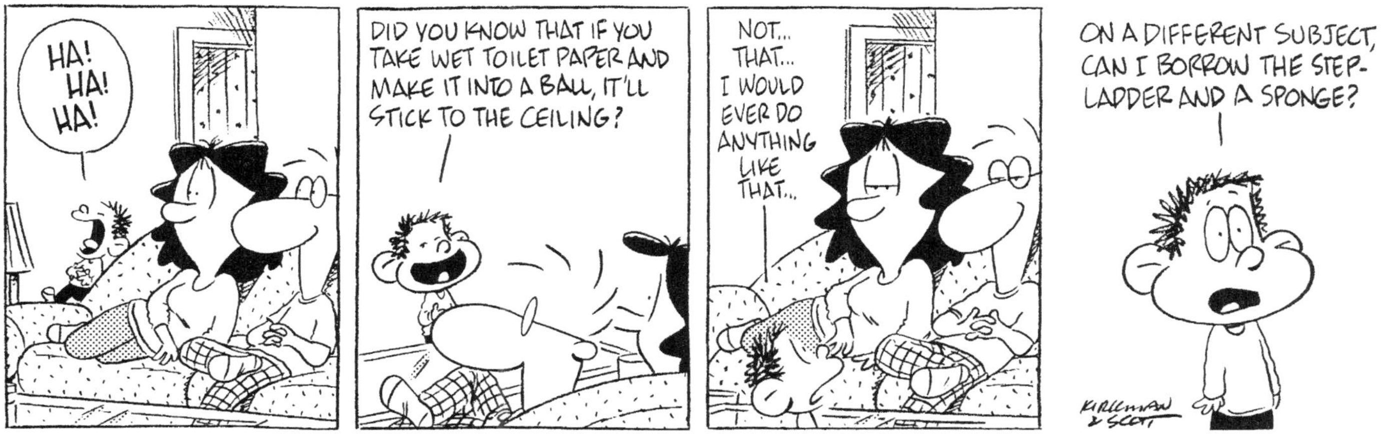
HA! HA! HA!
DID YOU KNOW THAT IF YOU TAKE WET TOILET PAPER AND MAKE IT INTO A BALL, IT'LL STICK TO THE CEILING?
NOT... THAT... I WOULD EVER DO ANYTHING LIKE THAT...
ON A DIFFERENT SUBJECT, CAN I BORROW THE STEP-LADDER AND A SPONGE?
KIRKMAN & SCOTT

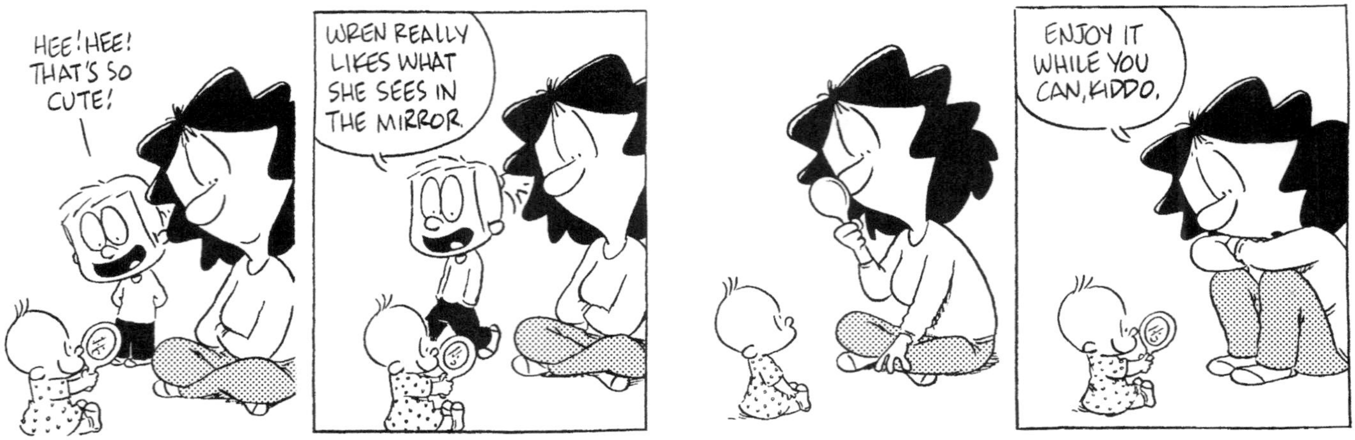
HEE! HEE! THAT'S SO CUTE!
WREN REALLY LIKES WHAT SHE SEES IN THE MIRROR.
ENJOY IT WHILE YOU CAN, KIDDO.

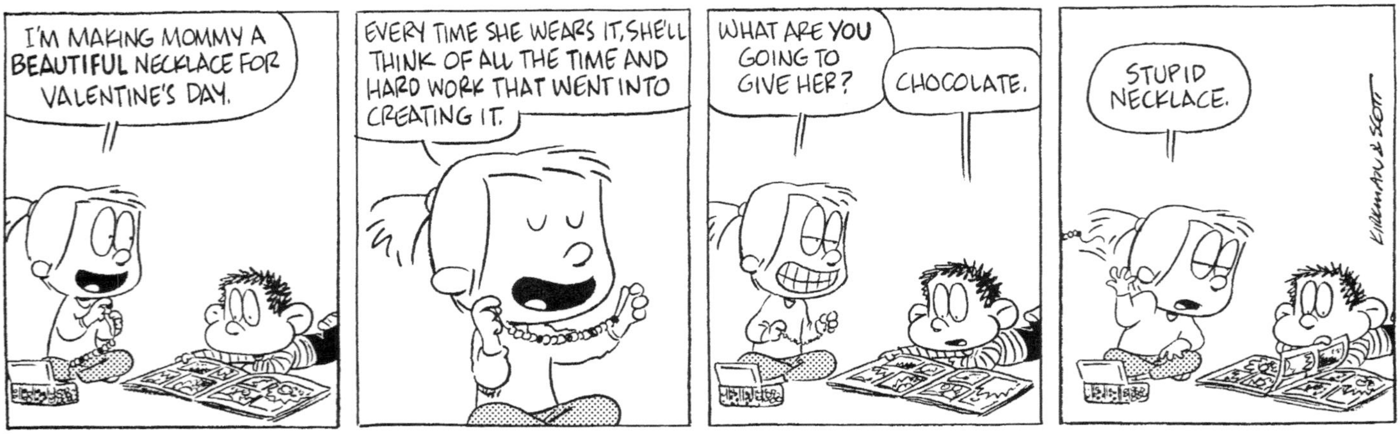
I'M MAKING MOMMY A **BEAUTIFUL** NECKLACE FOR VALENTINE'S DAY.
EVERY TIME SHE WEARS IT, SHE'LL THINK OF ALL THE TIME AND HARD WORK THAT WENT INTO CREATING IT.
WHAT ARE **YOU** GOING TO GIVE HER?
CHOCOLATE.
STUPID NECKLACE.
KIRKMAN & SCOTT

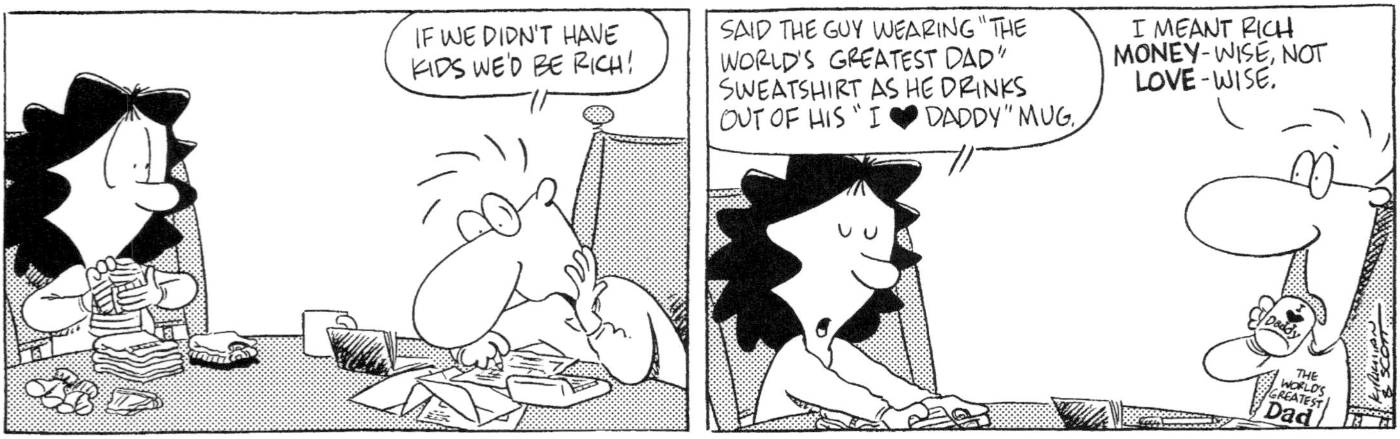
IF WE DIDN'T HAVE KIDS WE'D BE RICH!
SAID THE GUY WEARING "THE WORLD'S GREATEST DAD" SWEATSHIRT AS HE DRINKS OUT OF HIS "I ♥ DADDY" MUG.
I MEANT RICH **MONEY**-WISE, NOT **LOVE**-WISE.
I ♥ Daddy
THE WORLD'S GREATEST Dad

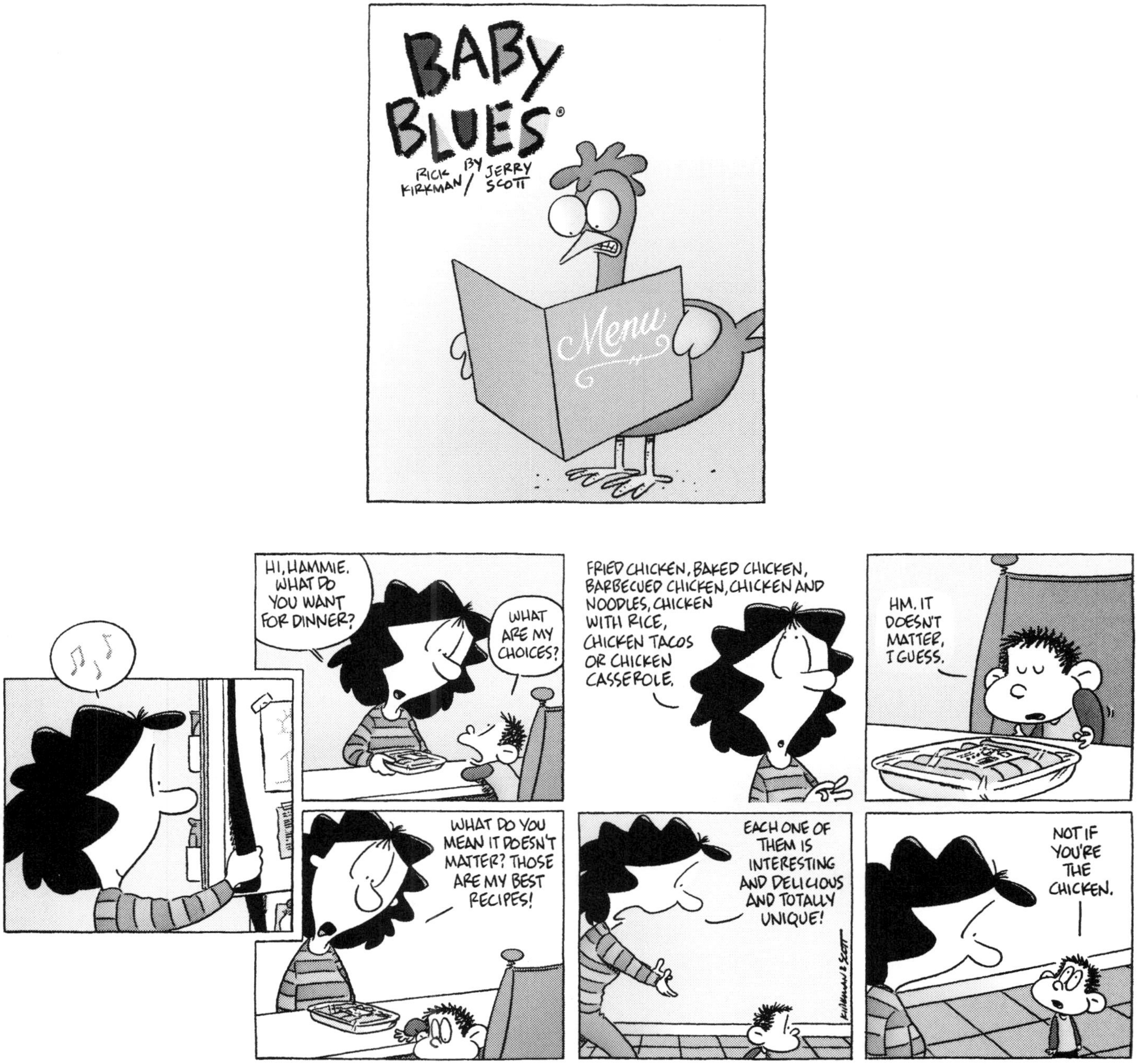
BABY BLUES®
BY RICK KIRKMAN / JERRY SCOTT
Menu
HI, HAMMIE. WHAT DO YOU WANT FOR DINNER?
WHAT ARE MY CHOICES?
FRIED CHICKEN, BAKED CHICKEN, BARBECUED CHICKEN, CHICKEN AND NOODLES, CHICKEN WITH RICE, CHICKEN TACOS OR CHICKEN CASSEROLE.
HM. IT DOESN'T MATTER, I GUESS.
WHAT DO YOU MEAN IT DOESN'T MATTER? THOSE ARE MY BEST RECIPES!
EACH ONE OF THEM IS INTERESTING AND DELICIOUS AND TOTALLY UNIQUE!
NOT IF YOU'RE THE CHICKEN.

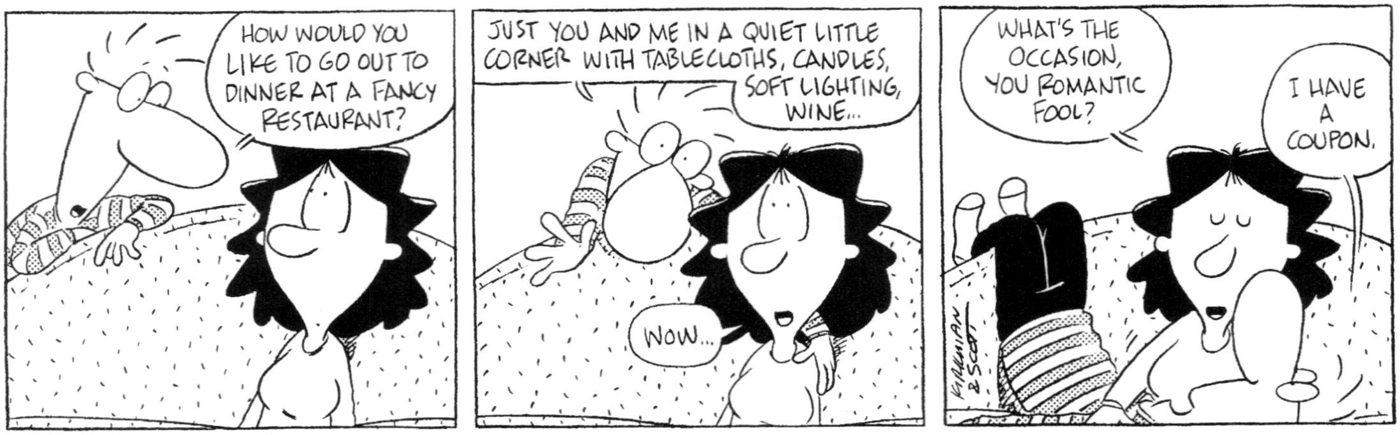
HOW WOULD YOU LIKE TO GO OUT TO DINNER AT A FANCY RESTAURANT?
JUST YOU AND ME IN A QUIET LITTLE CORNER WITH TABLECLOTHS, CANDLES, SOFT LIGHTING, WINE...
WOW...
WHAT'S THE OCCASION, YOU ROMANTIC FOOL?
I HAVE A COUPON.
KIRKMAN & SCOTT

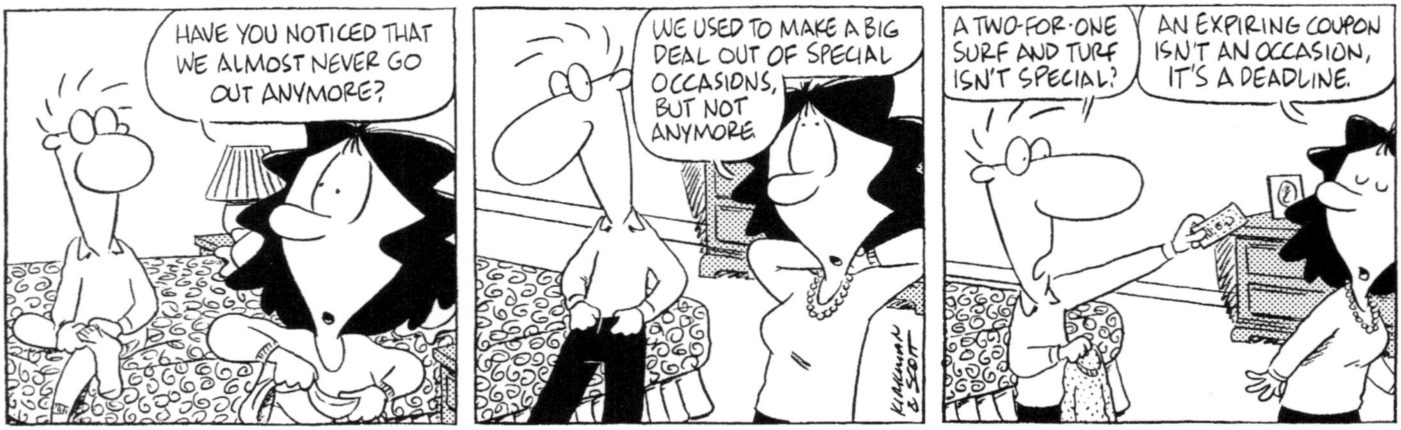
HAVE YOU NOTICED THAT WE ALMOST NEVER GO OUT ANYMORE?
WE USED TO MAKE A BIG DEAL OUT OF SPECIAL OCCASIONS, BUT NOT ANYMORE.
KIRKMAN & SCOTT
A TWO-FOR-ONE SURF AND TURF ISN'T SPECIAL?
AN EXPIRING COUPON ISN'T AN OCCASION, IT'S A DEADLINE.

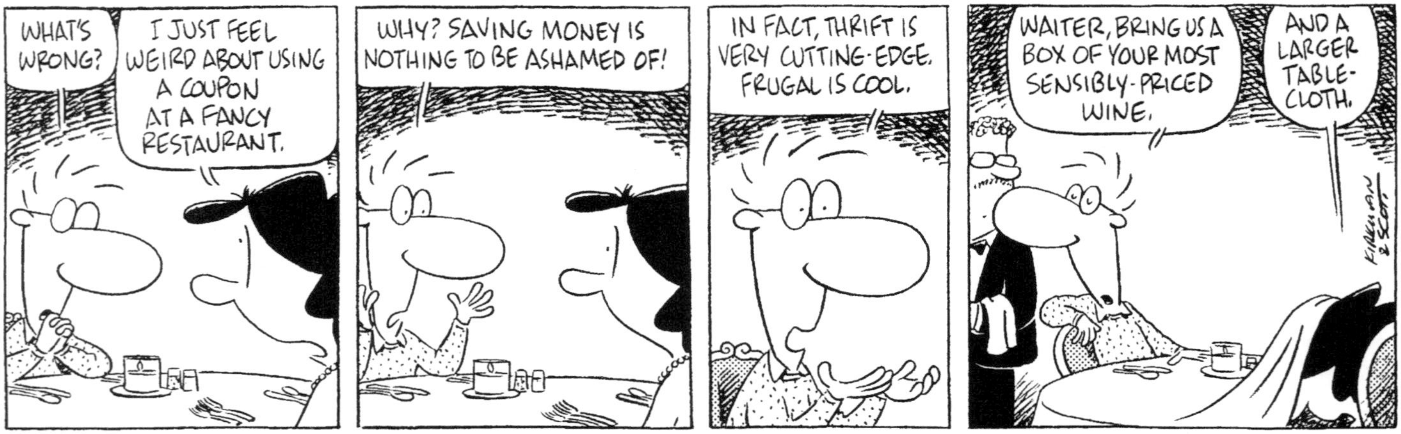
WHAT'S WRONG?
I JUST FEEL WEIRD ABOUT USING A COUPON AT A FANCY RESTAURANT.
WHY? SAVING MONEY IS NOTHING TO BE ASHAMED OF!
IN FACT, THRIFT IS VERY CUTTING-EDGE. FRUGAL IS COOL.
WAITER, BRING US A BOX OF YOUR MOST SENSIBLY-PRICED WINE.
AND A LARGER TABLE-CLOTH.
KIRKMAN & SCOTT

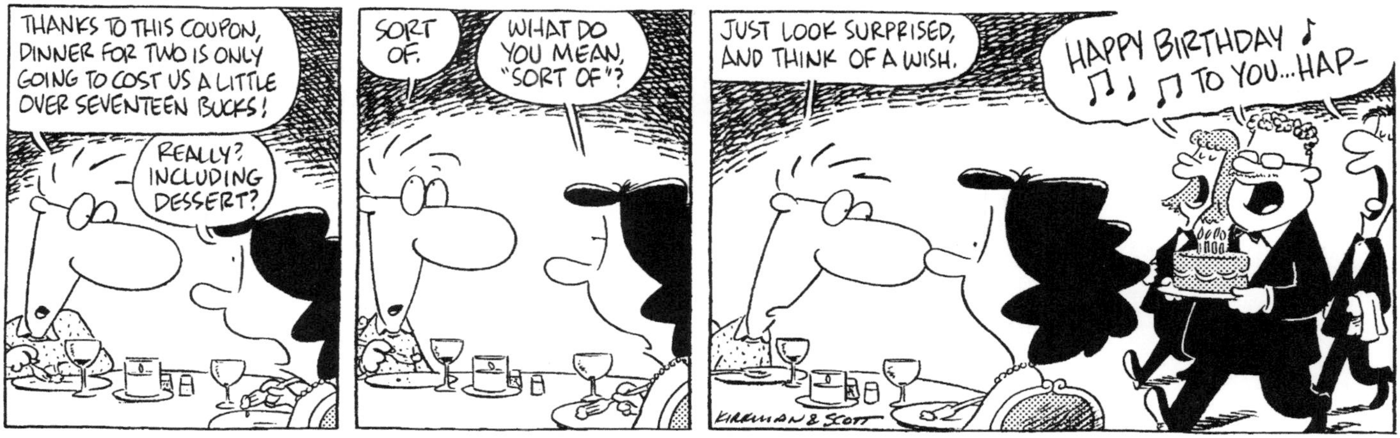
THANKS TO THIS COUPON, DINNER FOR TWO IS ONLY GOING TO COST US A LITTLE OVER SEVENTEEN BUCKS!
REALLY? INCLUDING DESSERT?
SORT OF.
WHAT DO YOU MEAN, "SORT OF"?
JUST LOOK SURPRISED, AND THINK OF A WISH.
HAPPY BIRTHDAY TO YOU...HAP-
KIRKMAN & SCOTT

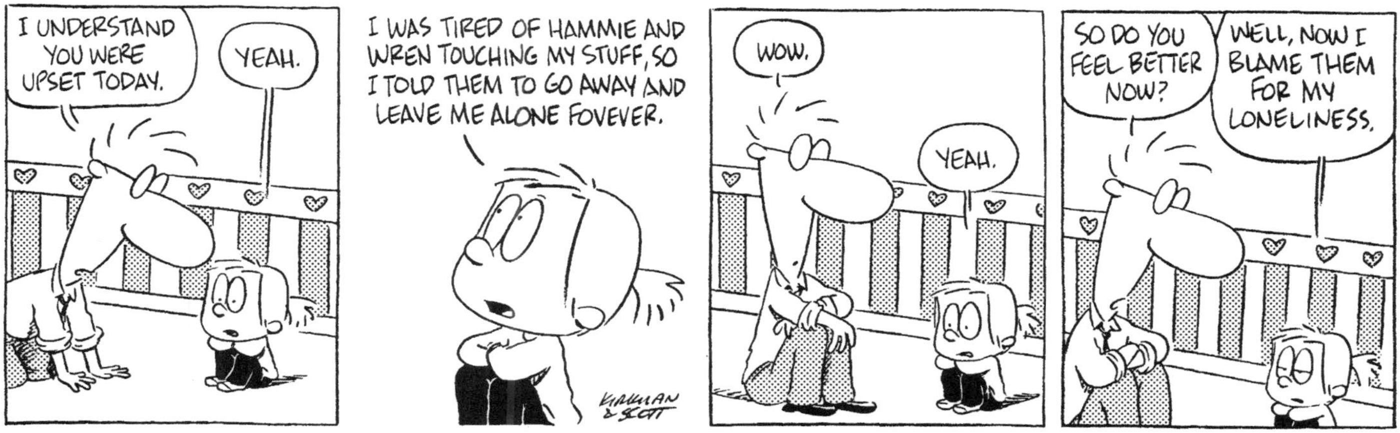
I UNDERSTAND YOU WERE UPSET TODAY.
YEAH.
I WAS TIRED OF HAMMIE AND WREN TOUCHING MY STUFF, SO I TOLD THEM TO GO AWAY AND LEAVE ME ALONE FOVEVER.
KIRKMAN & SCOTT
WOW.
YEAH.
SO DO YOU FEEL BETTER NOW?
WELL, NOW I BLAME THEM FOR MY LONELINESS.

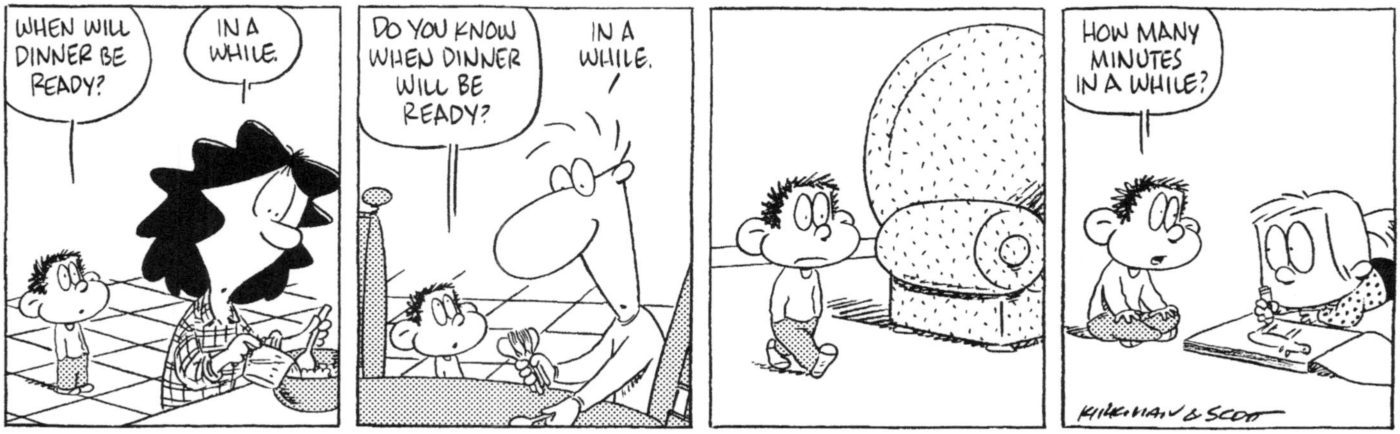
WHEN WILL DINNER BE READY?
IN A WHILE.
DO YOU KNOW WHEN DINNER WILL BE READY?
IN A WHILE.
HOW MANY MINUTES IN A WHILE?
KIRKMAN & SCOTT

BABY BLUES®
BY RICK KIRKMAN / JERRY SCOTT
12:4

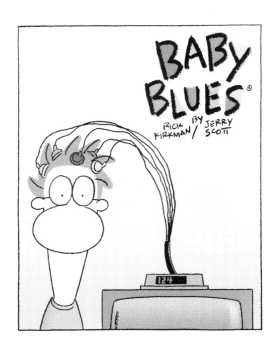

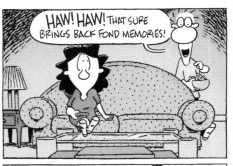

HAW! HAW! THAT SURE BRINGS BACK FOND MEMORIES!
REMEMBER WHEN OUR KIDS DID THE EXACT SAME THING? WHAT A MESS!
YEAH. ONLY WHEN OUR KIDS DID IT, IT COST $800 TO FIX THE CARPET AND REPAINT THE LIVING ROOM, WHICH TOOK US SIX WEEKS BECAUSE THE ONLY TIME WE COULD GET ANYTHING DONE WAS AT NIGHT AFTER THEY WENT TO BED!
OH YEAH.
WHEN STUFF HAPPENS IN A SITCOM, EVERYTHING GETS CLEANED UP AND RESOLVED IN THIRTY MINUTES! IN REAL LIFE, THE PAIN LINGERS!
YOU'RE RIGHT ABOUT THAT.
I SAY FROM NOW ON, WE TAKE ALL OUR MEMORIES FROM TV.

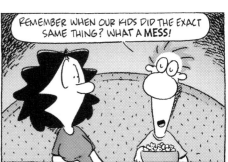

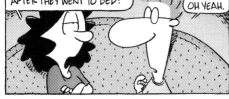

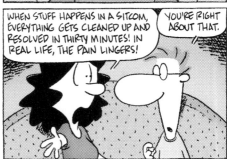

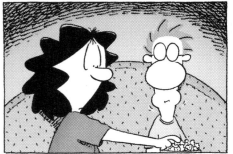

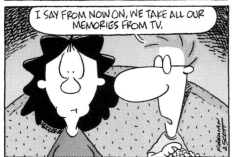

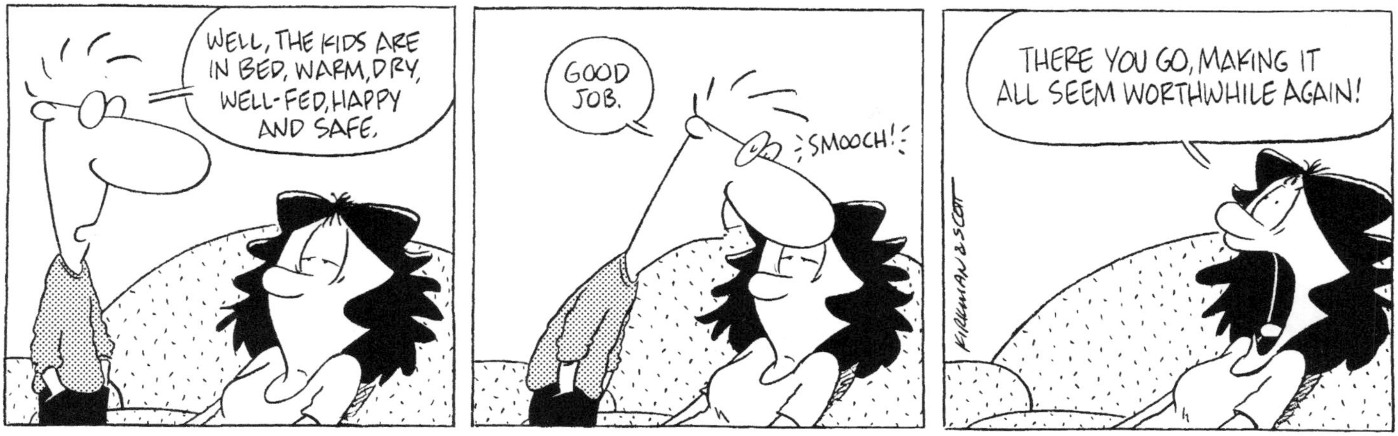
WELL, THE KIDS ARE IN BED, WARM, DRY, WELL-FED, HAPPY AND SAFE.
GOOD JOB.
SMOOCH!
THERE YOU GO, MAKING IT ALL SEEM WORTHWHILE AGAIN!
KIRKMAN & SCOTT

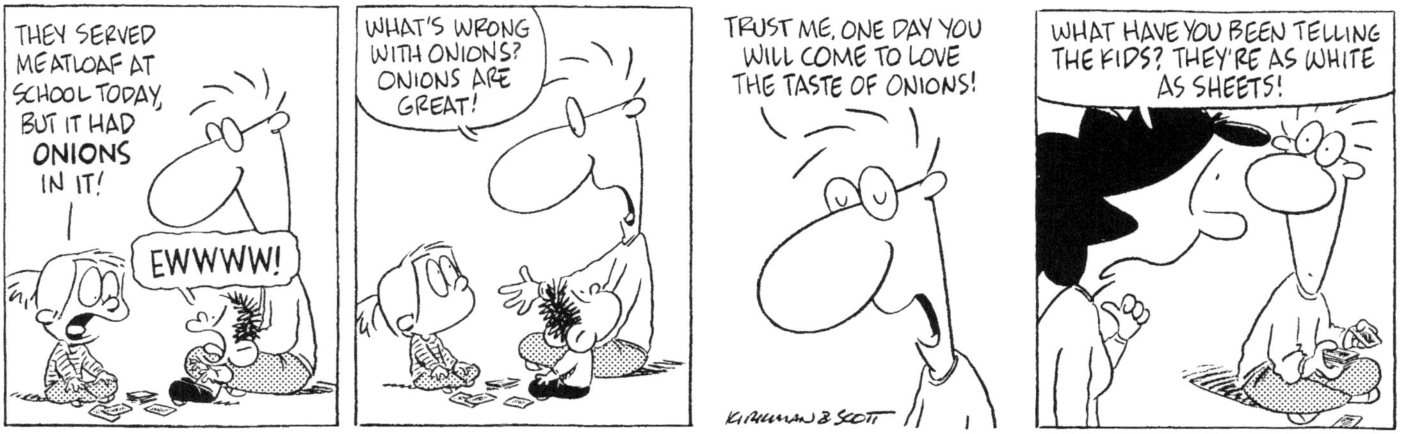
THEY SERVED MEATLOAF AT SCHOOL TODAY, BUT IT HAD ONIONS IN IT!
EWWWW!
WHAT'S WRONG WITH ONIONS? ONIONS ARE GREAT!
TRUST ME, ONE DAY YOU WILL COME TO LOVE THE TASTE OF ONIONS!
KIRKMAN & SCOTT
WHAT HAVE YOU BEEN TELLING THE KIDS? THEY'RE AS WHITE AS SHEETS!

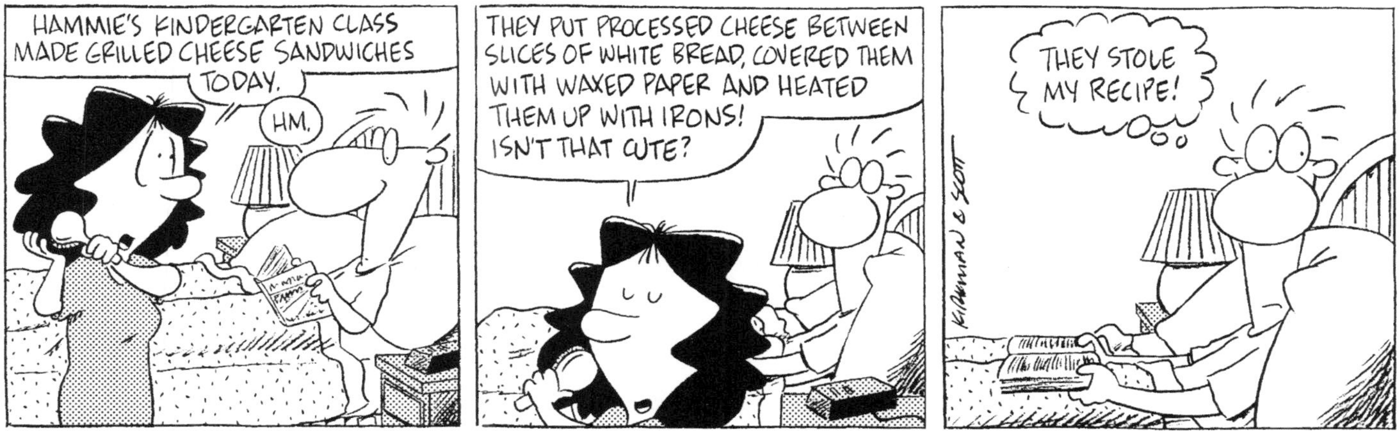
HAMMIE'S KINDERGARTEN CLASS MADE GRILLED CHEESE SANDWICHES TODAY.
HM.
THEY PUT PROCESSED CHEESE BETWEEN SLICES OF WHITE BREAD, COVERED THEM WITH WAXED PAPER AND HEATED THEM UP WITH IRONS! ISN'T THAT CUTE?
KIRKMAN & SCOTT
THEY STOLE MY RECIPE!

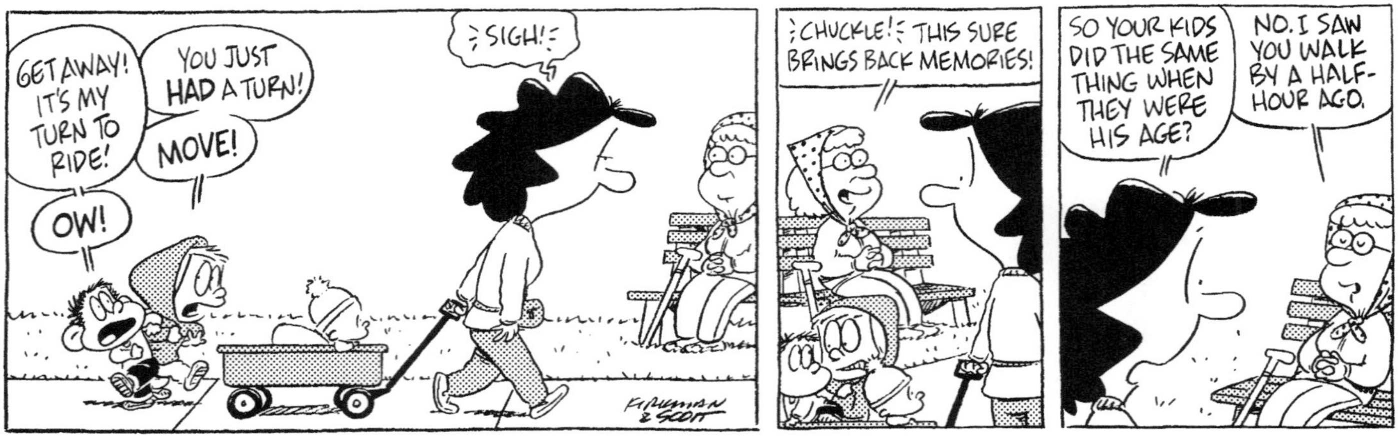
GET AWAY! IT'S MY TURN TO RIDE!
YOU JUST HAD A TURN!
MOVE!
OW!
SIGH!
KIRKMAN & SCOTT
CHUCKLE! THIS SURE BRINGS BACK MEMORIES!
SO YOUR KIDS DID THE SAME THING WHEN THEY WERE HIS AGE?
NO. I SAW YOU WALK BY A HALF-HOUR AGO.

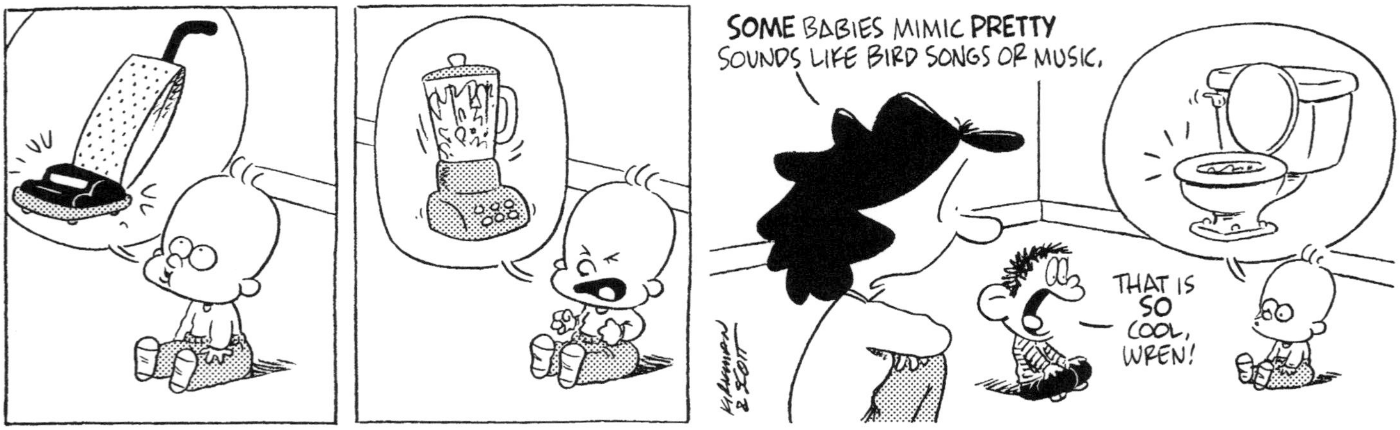
SOME BABIES MIMIC PRETTY SOUNDS LIKE BIRD SONGS OR MUSIC.
KIRKMAN & SCOTT
THAT IS SO COOL, WREN!

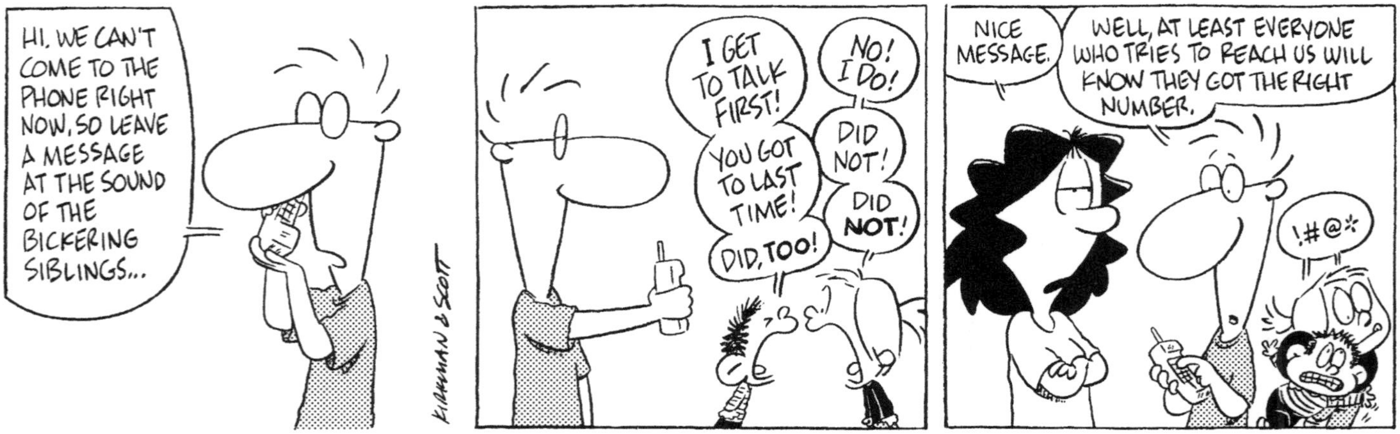
HI. WE CAN'T COME TO THE PHONE RIGHT NOW, SO LEAVE A MESSAGE AT THE SOUND OF THE BICKERING SIBLINGS...
KIRKMAN & SCOTT
I GET TO TALK FIRST!
NO! I DO!
YOU GOT TO LAST TIME!
DID NOT!
DID, TOO!
DID NOT!
NICE MESSAGE.
WELL, AT LEAST EVERYONE WHO TRIES TO REACH US WILL KNOW THEY GOT THE RIGHT NUMBER.
!#@*

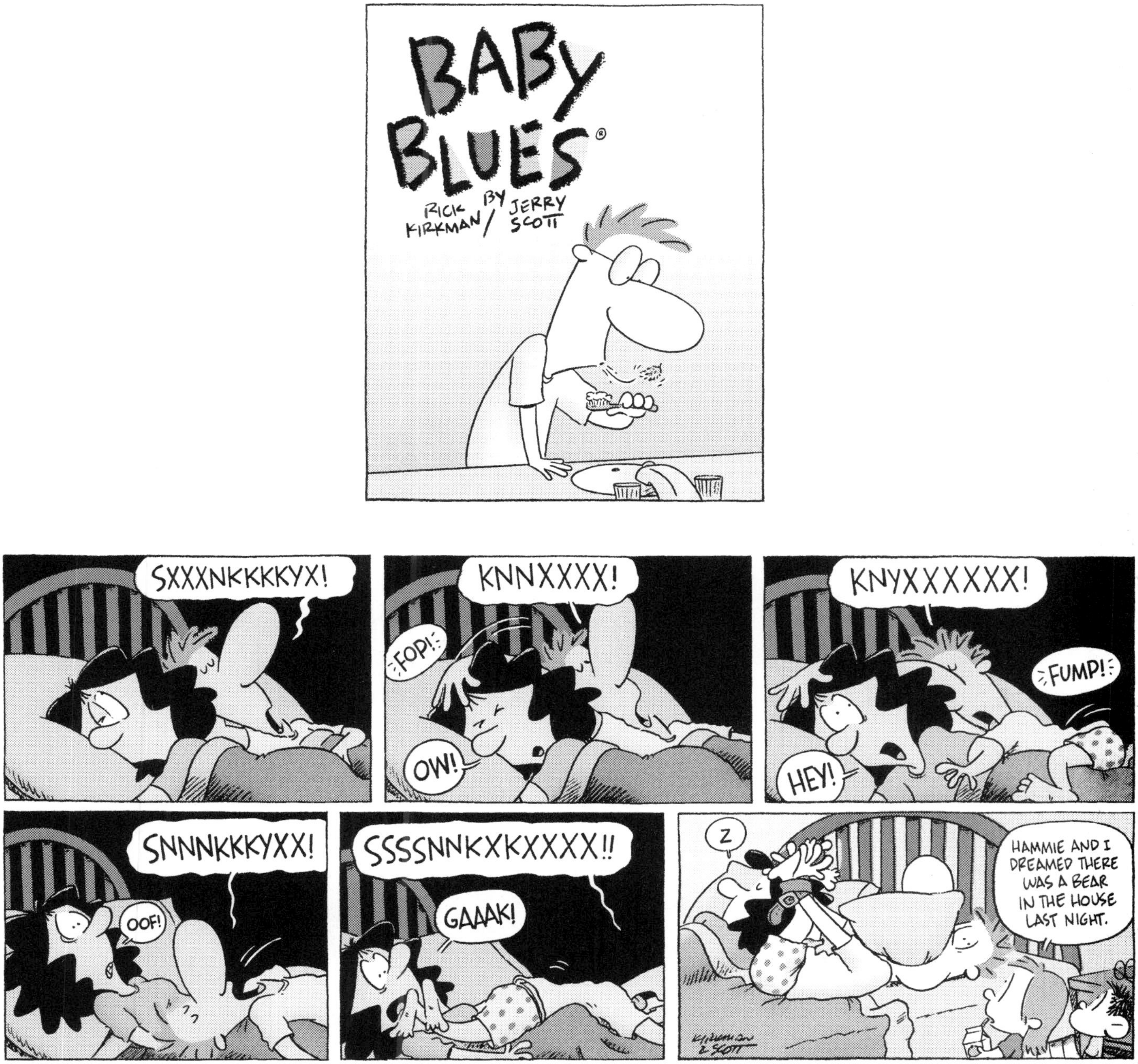
BABY BLUES®
BY RICK KIRKMAN / JERRY SCOTT
SXXXNKKKKYX!
KNNXXXX!
FOP!
OW!
KNYXXXXXX!
FUMP!
HEY!
SNNNKKKYXX!
OOF!
SSSSNNKXKXXXX!!
GAAAK!
Z
HAMMIE AND I DREAMED THERE WAS A BEAR IN THE HOUSE LAST NIGHT.

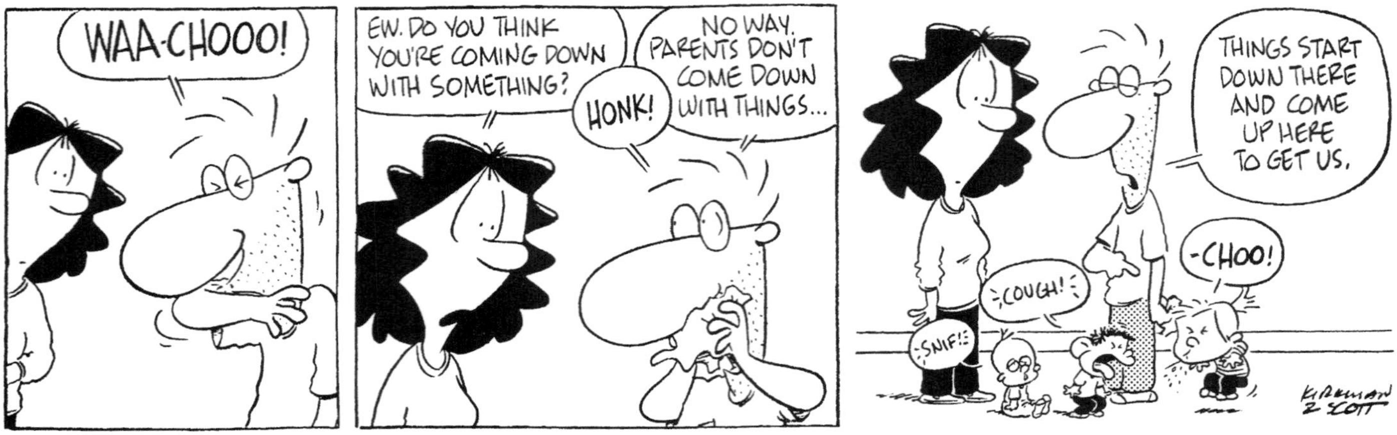
WAA-CHOOO!
EW. DO YOU THINK YOU'RE COMING DOWN WITH SOMETHING?
HONK!
NO WAY. PARENTS DON'T COME DOWN WITH THINGS...
THINGS START DOWN THERE AND COME UP HERE TO GET US.
SNIF!
COUGH!
-CHOO!
KIRKMAN & SCOTT

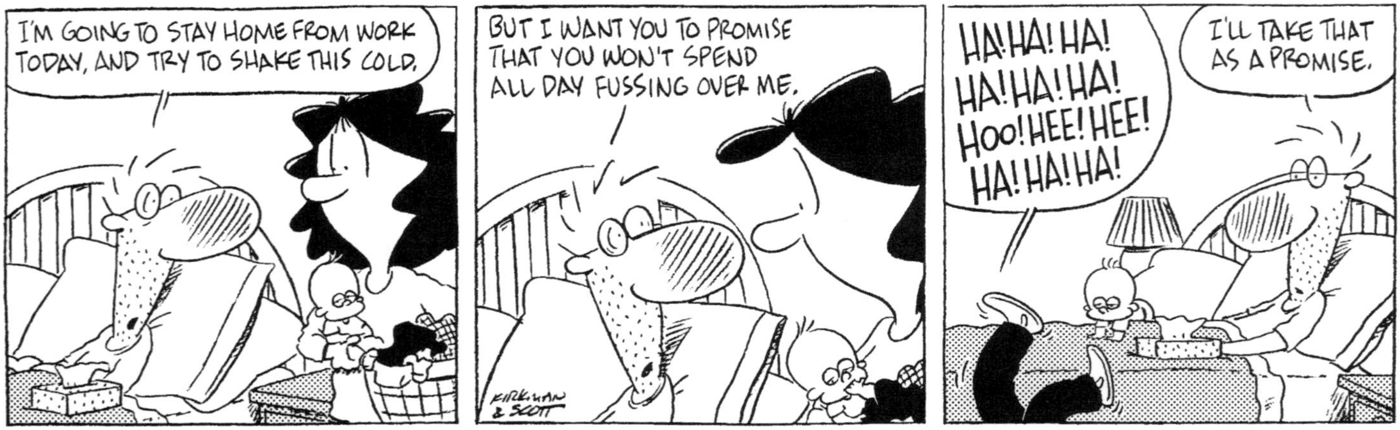
I'M GOING TO STAY HOME FROM WORK TODAY, AND TRY TO SHAKE THIS COLD.
BUT I WANT YOU TO PROMISE THAT YOU WON'T SPEND ALL DAY FUSSING OVER ME.
KIRKMAN & SCOTT
HA! HA! HA! HA! HA! HA! HOO! HEE! HEE! HA! HA! HA!
I'LL TAKE THAT AS A PROMISE.

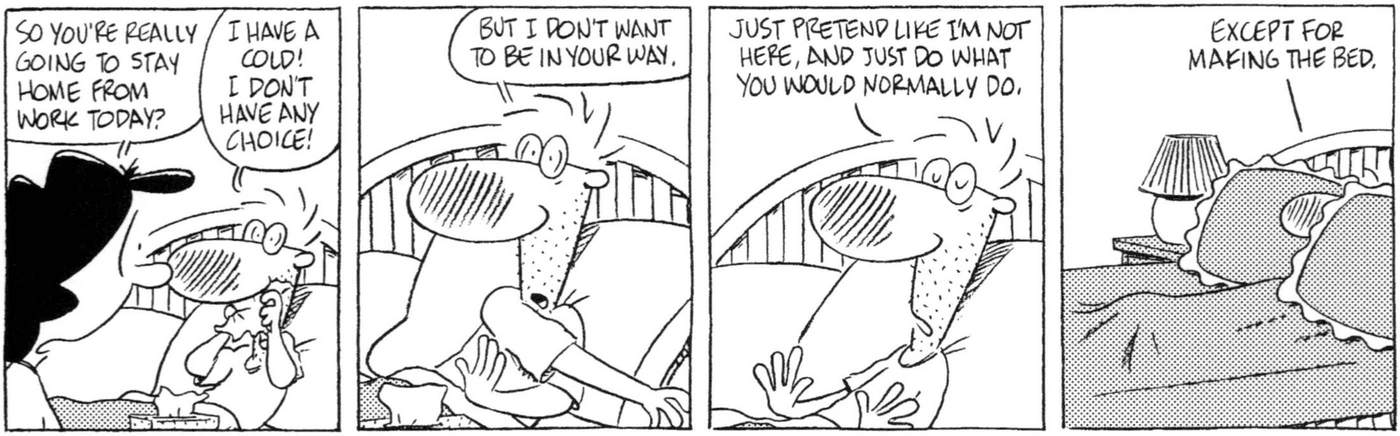
SO YOU'RE REALLY GOING TO STAY HOME FROM WORK TODAY?
I HAVE A COLD! I DON'T HAVE ANY CHOICE!
BUT I DON'T WANT TO BE IN YOUR WAY.
JUST PRETEND LIKE I'M NOT HERE, AND JUST DO WHAT YOU WOULD NORMALLY DO.
EXCEPT FOR MAKING THE BED.

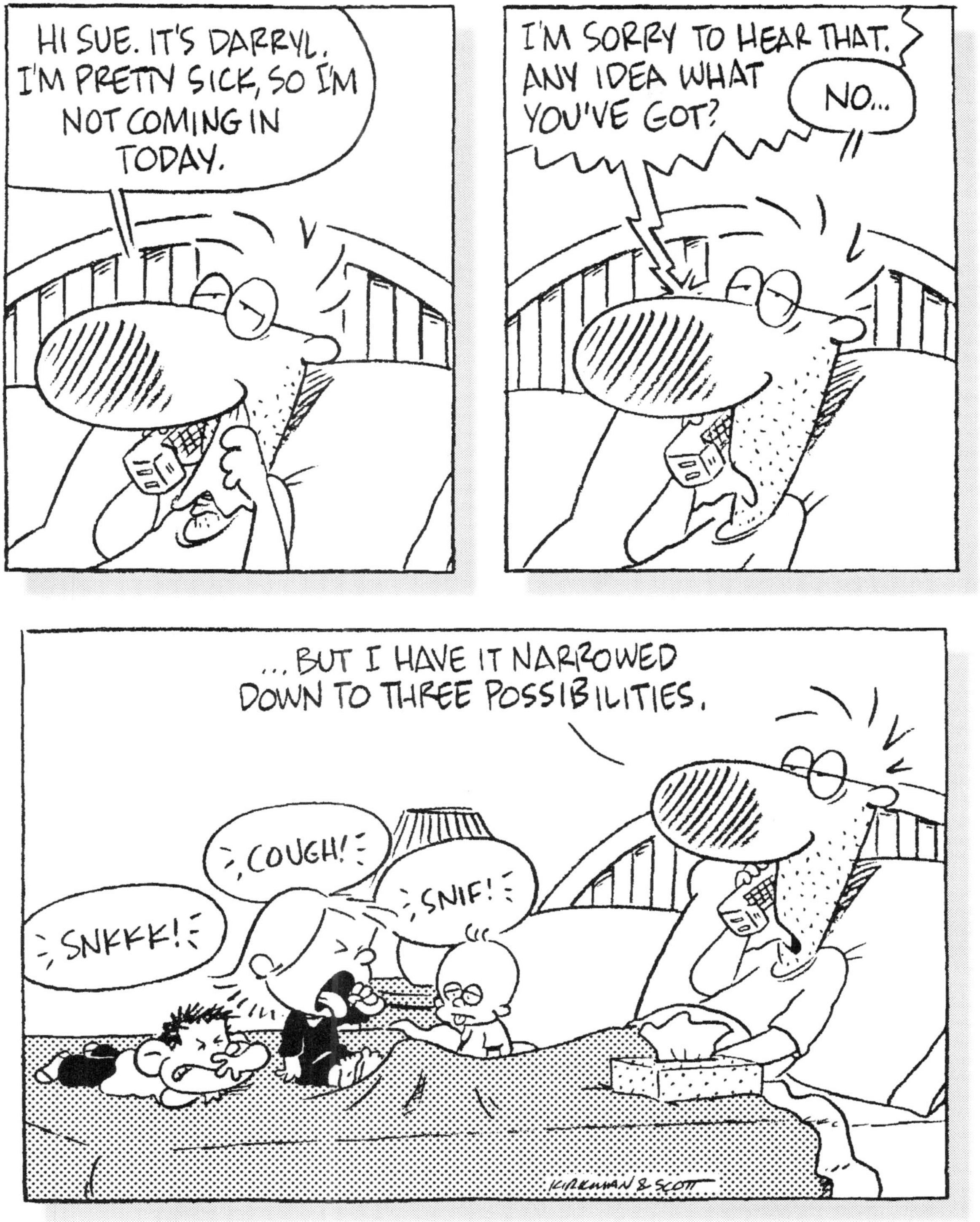
HI SUE. IT'S DARRYL. I'M PRETTY SICK, SO I'M NOT COMING IN TODAY.
I'M SORRY TO HEAR THAT. ANY IDEA WHAT YOU'VE GOT?
NO...
...BUT I HAVE IT NARROWED DOWN TO THREE POSSIBILITIES.
COUGH!
SNIF!
SNKKK!
KIRKMAN & SCOTT

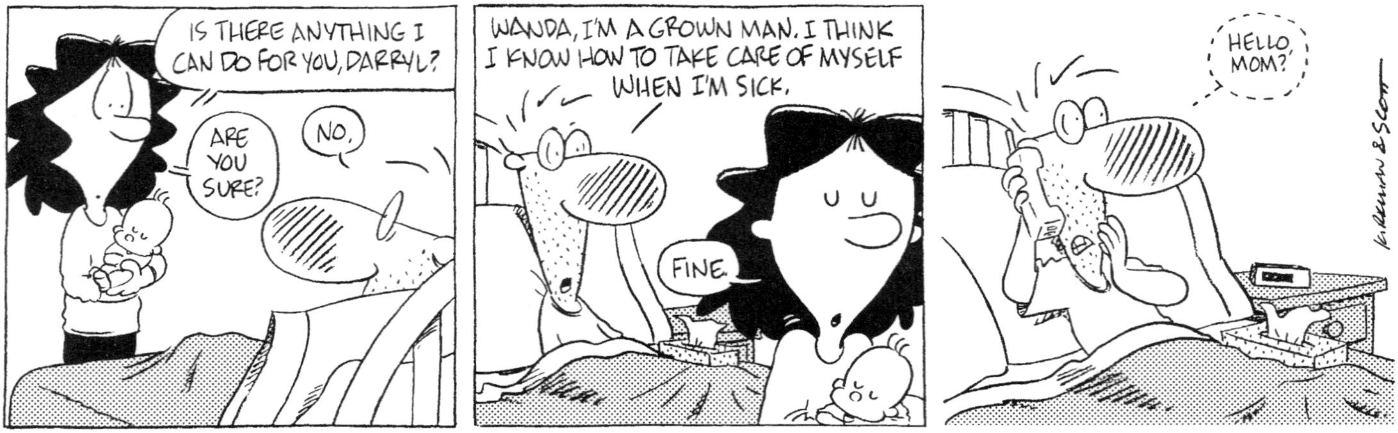
IS THERE ANYTHING I CAN DO FOR YOU, DARRYL?
ARE YOU SURE?
NO.
WANDA, I'M A GROWN MAN. I THINK I KNOW HOW TO TAKE CARE OF MYSELF WHEN I'M SICK.
FINE.
HELLO, MOM?
KIRKMAN & SCOTT

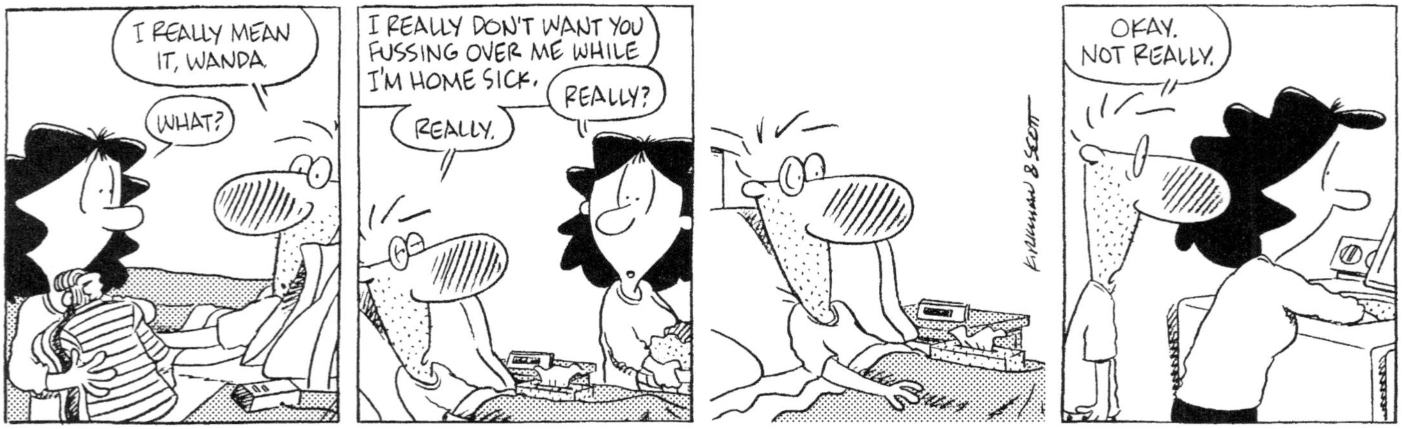
I REALLY MEAN IT, WANDA.
WHAT?
I REALLY DON'T WANT YOU FUSSING OVER ME WHILE I'M HOME SICK.
REALLY?
REALLY.
KIRKMAN & SCOTT
OKAY. NOT REALLY.

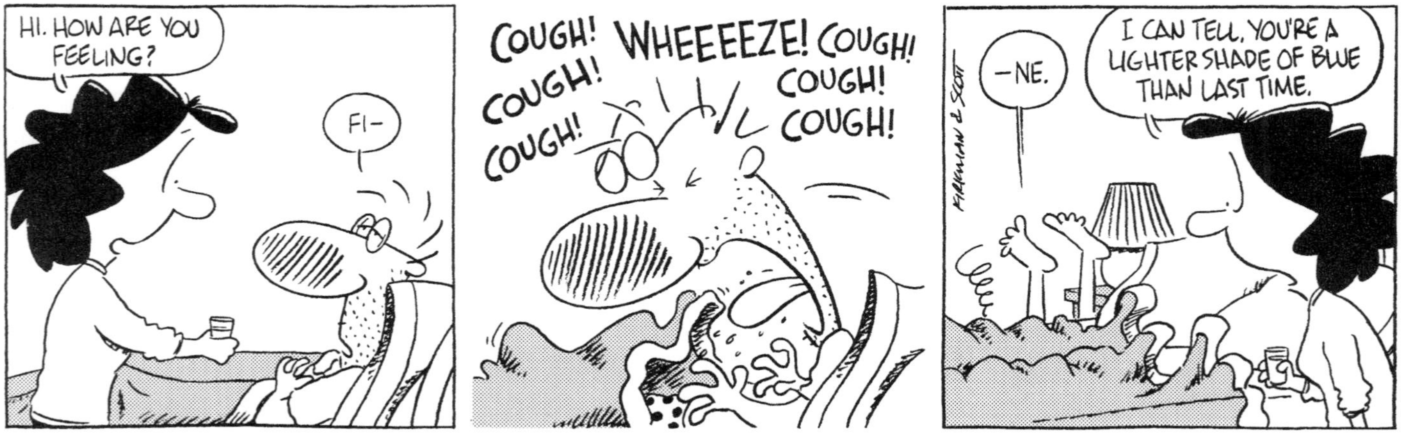
HI. HOW ARE YOU FEELING?
FI-
COUGH! COUGH! COUGH!
WHEEEEZE!
COUGH! COUGH! COUGH!
KIRKMAN & SCOTT
-NE.
I CAN TELL. YOU'RE A LIGHTER SHADE OF BLUE THAN LAST TIME.

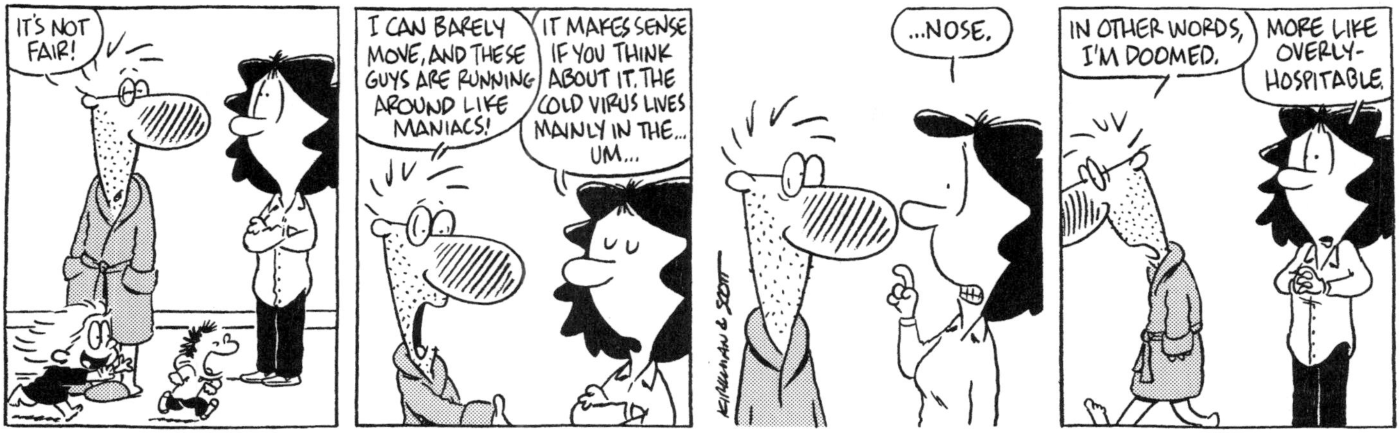
IT'S NOT FAIR!
I CAN BARELY MOVE, AND THESE GUYS ARE RUNNING AROUND LIKE MANIACS!
IT MAKES SENSE IF YOU THINK ABOUT IT. THE COLD VIRUS LIVES MAINLY IN THE... UM...
...NOSE.
IN OTHER WORDS, I'M DOOMED.
MORE LIKE OVERLY-HOSPITABLE.

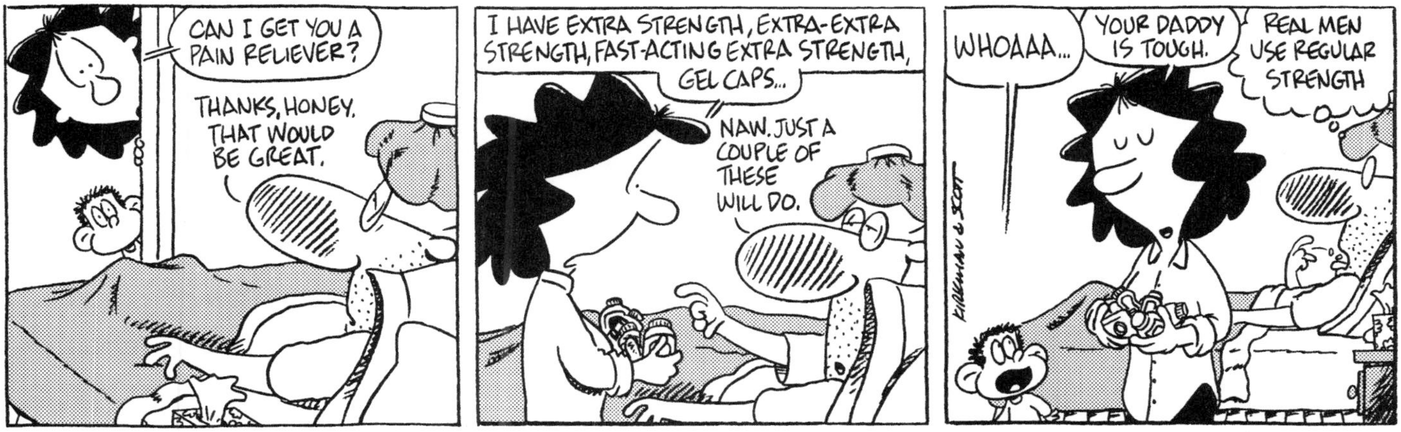
CAN I GET YOU A PAIN RELIEVER?
THANKS, HONEY. THAT WOULD BE GREAT.
I HAVE EXTRA STRENGTH, EXTRA-EXTRA STRENGTH, FAST-ACTING EXTRA STRENGTH, GEL CAPS...
NAW. JUST A COUPLE OF THESE WILL DO.
WHOAAA...
YOUR DADDY IS TOUGH.
REAL MEN USE REGULAR STRENGTH

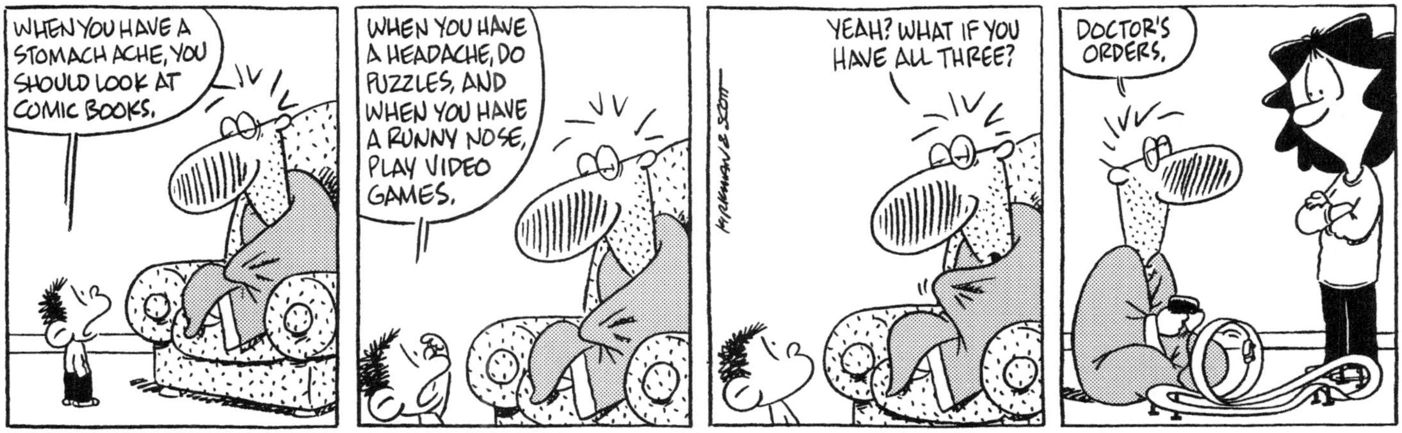
WHEN YOU HAVE A STOMACH ACHE, YOU SHOULD LOOK AT COMIC BOOKS.
WHEN YOU HAVE A HEADACHE, DO PUZZLES, AND WHEN YOU HAVE A RUNNY NOSE, PLAY VIDEO GAMES.
YEAH? WHAT IF YOU HAVE ALL THREE?
DOCTOR'S ORDERS.

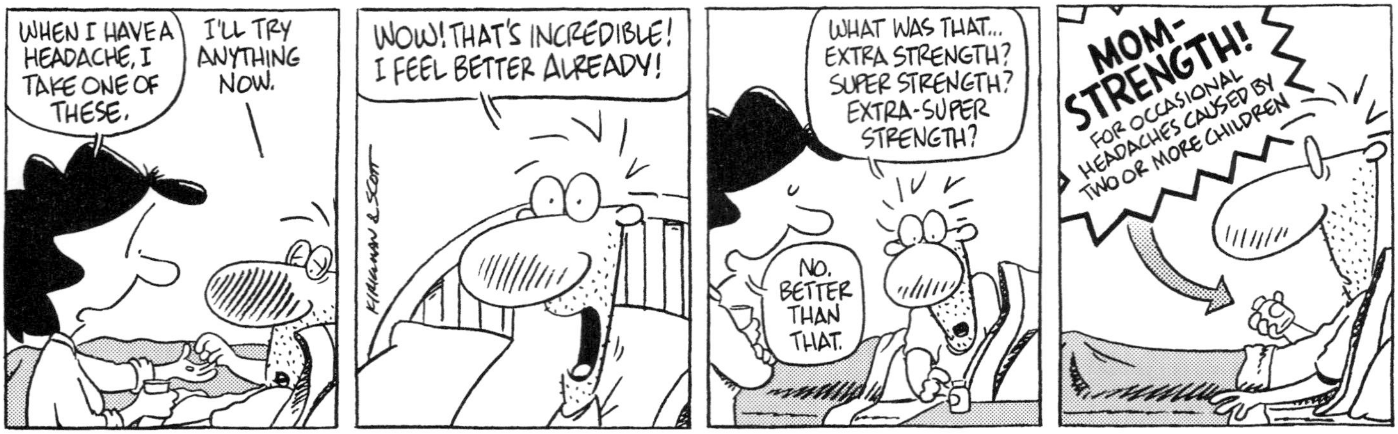
WHEN I HAVE A HEADACHE, I TAKE ONE OF THESE.
I'LL TRY ANYTHING NOW.
KIRKMAN & SCOTT
WOW! THAT'S INCREDIBLE! I FEEL BETTER ALREADY!
WHAT WAS THAT... EXTRA STRENGTH? SUPER STRENGTH? EXTRA-SUPER STRENGTH?
NO. BETTER THAN THAT.
MOM-STRENGTH!
FOR OCCASIONAL HEADACHES CAUSED BY TWO OR MORE CHILDREN

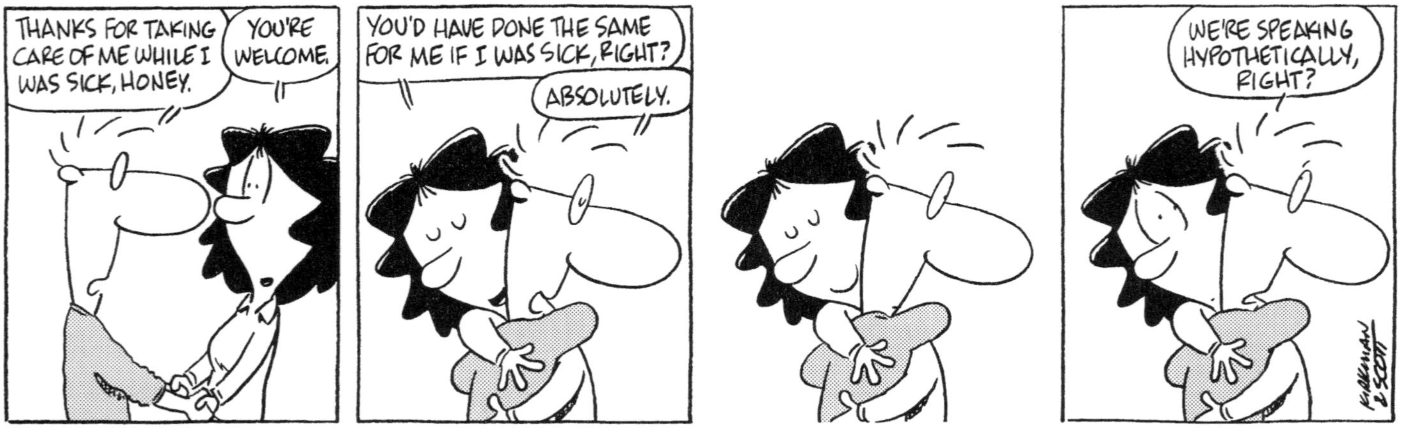
THANKS FOR TAKING CARE OF ME WHILE I WAS SICK, HONEY.
YOU'RE WELCOME.
YOU'D HAVE DONE THE SAME FOR ME IF I WAS SICK, RIGHT?
ABSOLUTELY.
WE'RE SPEAKING HYPOTHETICALLY, RIGHT?
KIRKMAN & SCOTT

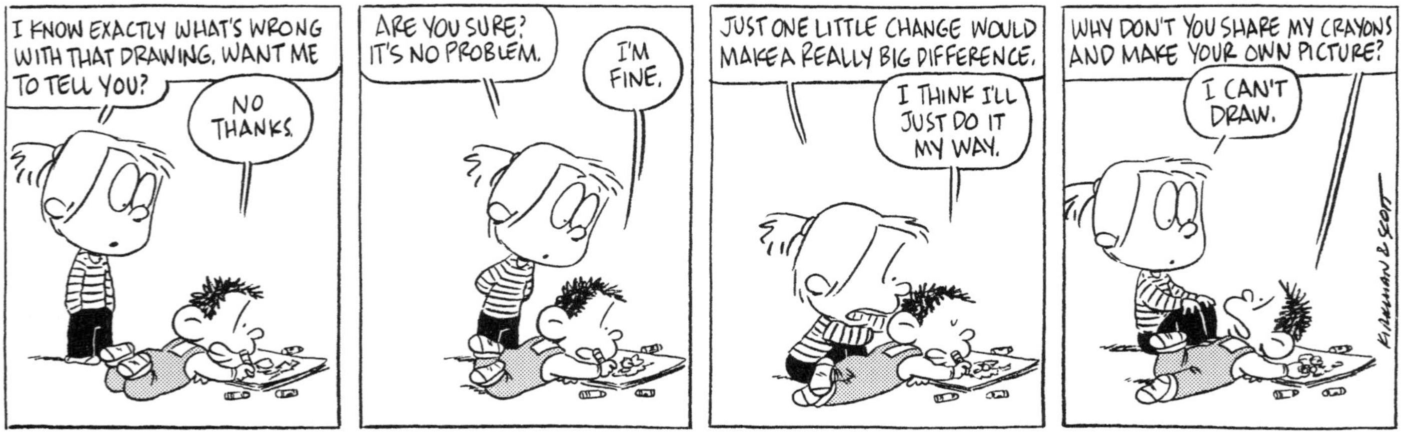
I KNOW EXACTLY WHAT'S WRONG WITH THAT DRAWING. WANT ME TO TELL YOU?
NO THANKS.
ARE YOU SURE? IT'S NO PROBLEM.
I'M FINE.
JUST ONE LITTLE CHANGE WOULD MAKE A REALLY BIG DIFFERENCE.
I THINK I'LL JUST DO IT MY WAY.
WHY DON'T YOU SHARE MY CRAYONS AND MAKE YOUR OWN PICTURE?
I CAN'T DRAW.
KIRKMAN & SCOTT

BABY BLUES®
BY RICK KIRKMAN / JERRY SCOTT
~~ROAD TRIP~~
WH~~ERE'S ODYSSE~~US? MY LONG BORING POEM...
WITH APOLOGIES TO MATT GROENING

KIRKMAN & SCOTT
WHY IS IT WHEN I TAKE THE KIDS TO THE GROCERY STORE, IT'S JUST SHOPPING, BUT WHEN YOU DO IT, IT'S AN ODYSSEY?
GROAN!

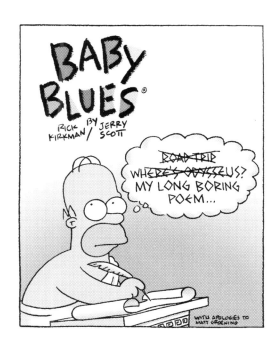

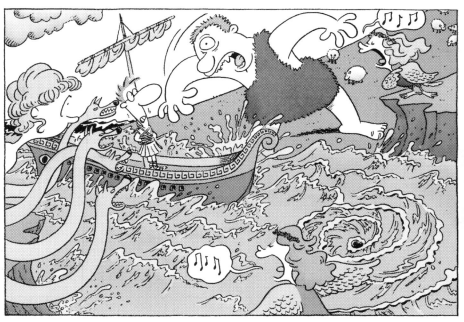

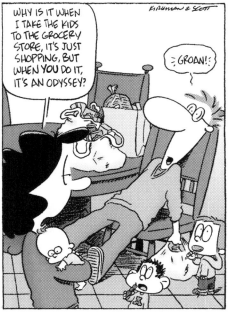

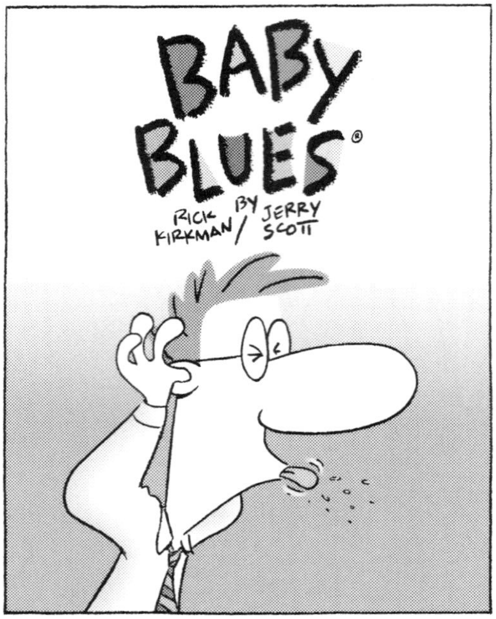
BABY BLUES®
BY RICK KIRKMAN / JERRY SCOTT

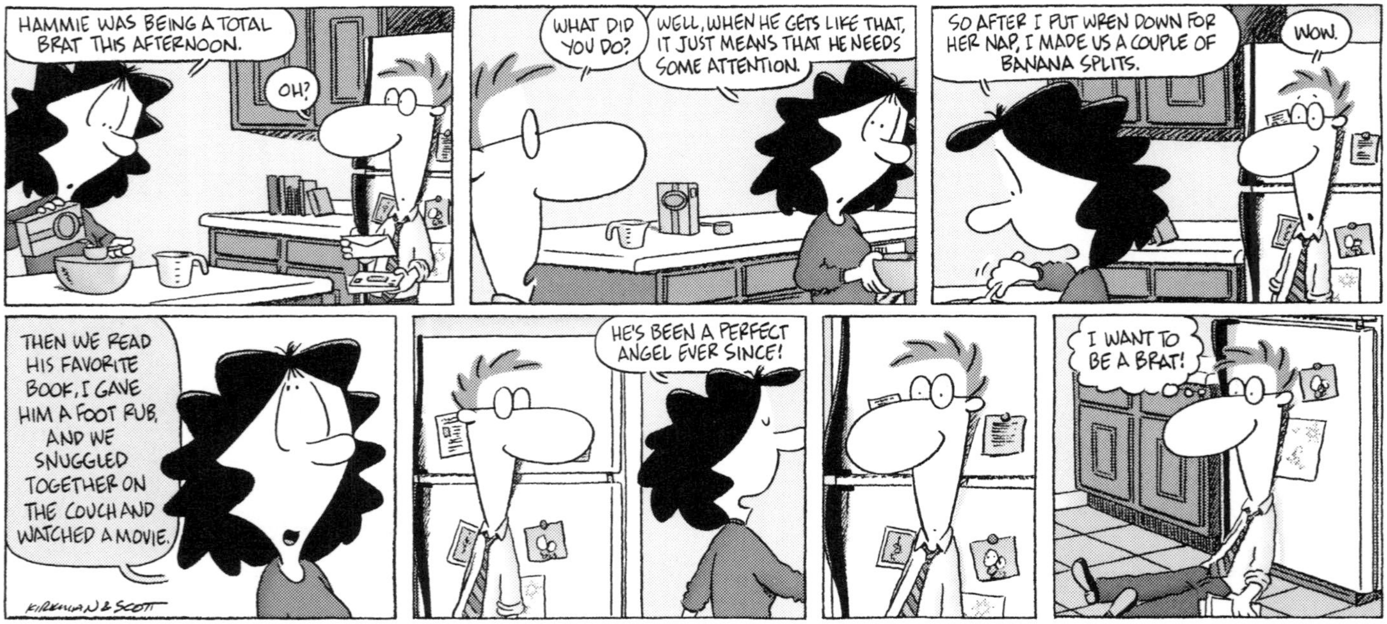
HAMMIE WAS BEING A TOTAL BRAT THIS AFTERNOON.
OH?
WHAT DID YOU DO?
WELL, WHEN HE GETS LIKE THAT, IT JUST MEANS THAT HE NEEDS SOME ATTENTION.
SO AFTER I PUT WREN DOWN FOR HER NAP, I MADE US A COUPLE OF BANANA SPLITS.
WOW.
THEN WE READ HIS FAVORITE BOOK, I GAVE HIM A FOOT RUB, AND WE SNUGGLED TOGETHER ON THE COUCH AND WATCHED A MOVIE.
KIRKMAN & SCOTT
HE'S BEEN A PERFECT ANGEL EVER SINCE!
I WANT TO BE A BRAT!

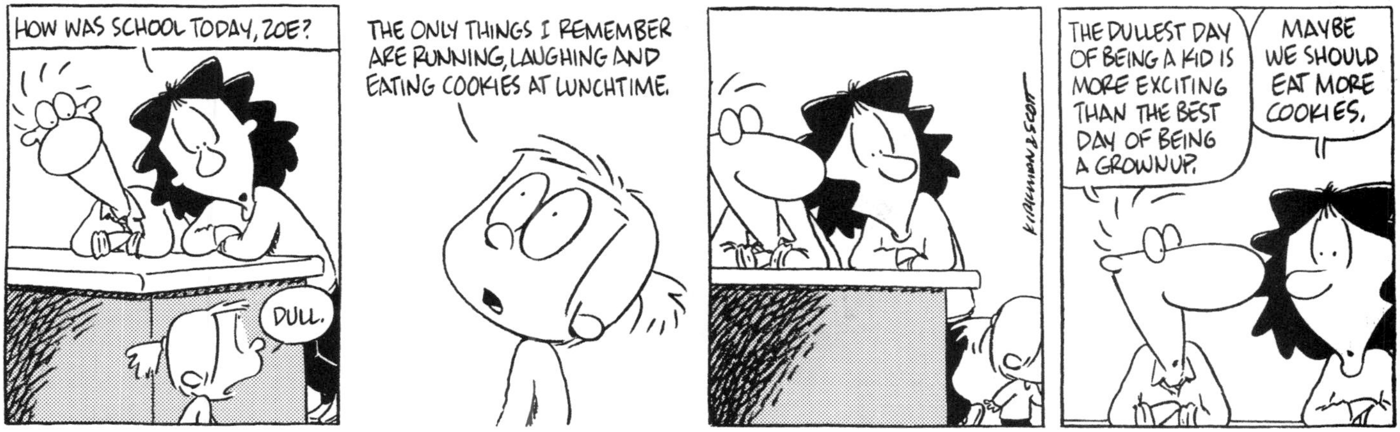
HOW WAS SCHOOL TODAY, ZOE?
DULL.
THE ONLY THINGS I REMEMBER ARE RUNNING, LAUGHING AND EATING COOKIES AT LUNCHTIME.
KIRKMAN & SCOTT
THE DULLEST DAY OF BEING A KID IS MORE EXCITING THAN THE BEST DAY OF BEING A GROWNUP.
MAYBE WE SHOULD EAT MORE COOKIES.

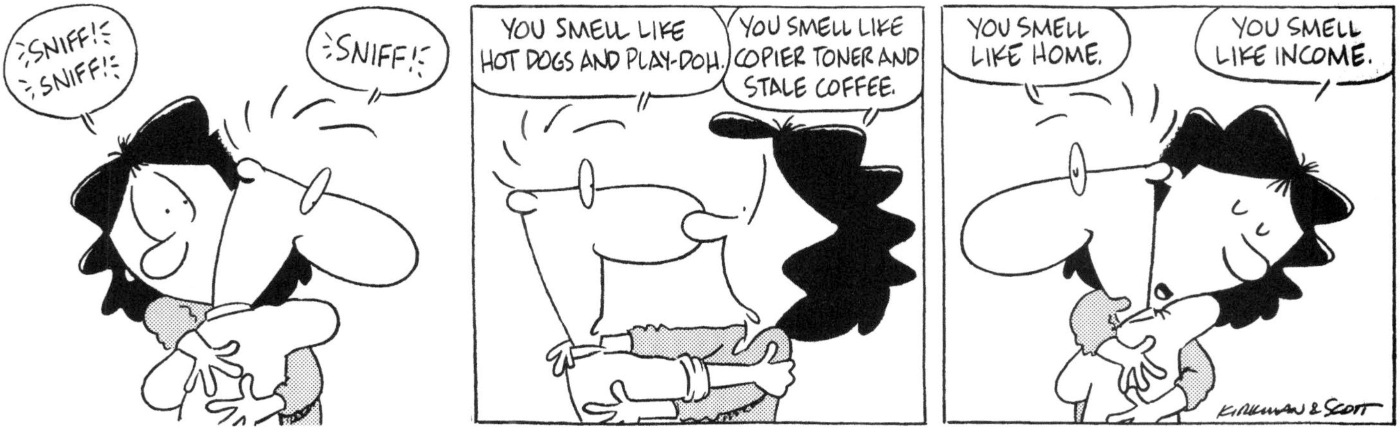
SNIFF! SNIFF!
SNIFF!
YOU SMELL LIKE HOT DOGS AND PLAY-DOH.
YOU SMELL LIKE COPIER TONER AND STALE COFFEE.
YOU SMELL LIKE HOME.
YOU SMELL LIKE INCOME.
KIRKMAN & SCOTT

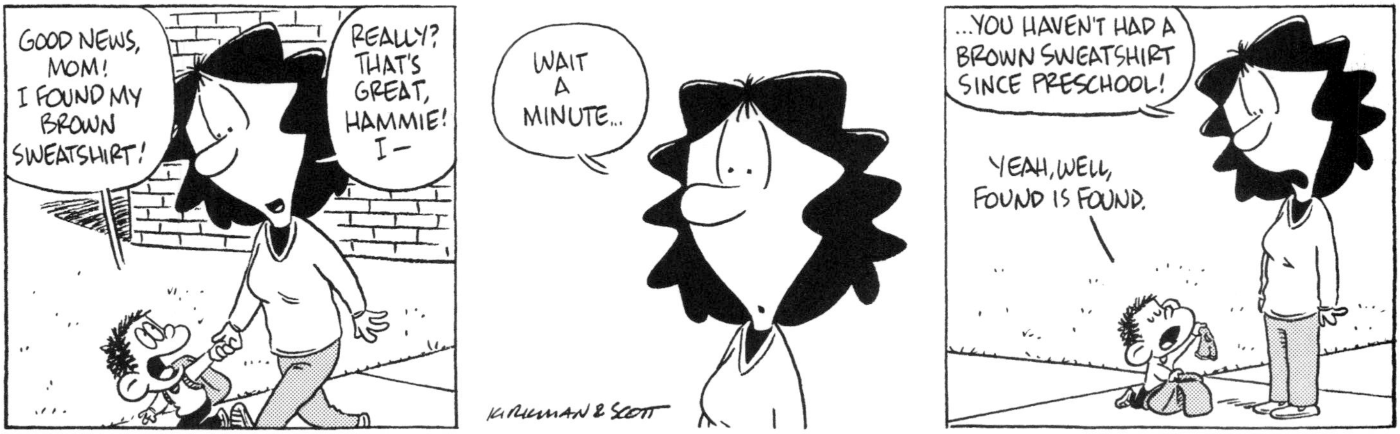
GOOD NEWS, MOM! I FOUND MY BROWN SWEATSHIRT!
REALLY? THAT'S GREAT, HAMMIE! I—
WAIT A MINUTE...
KIRKMAN & SCOTT
...YOU HAVEN'T HAD A BROWN SWEATSHIRT SINCE PRESCHOOL!
YEAH, WELL, FOUND IS FOUND.

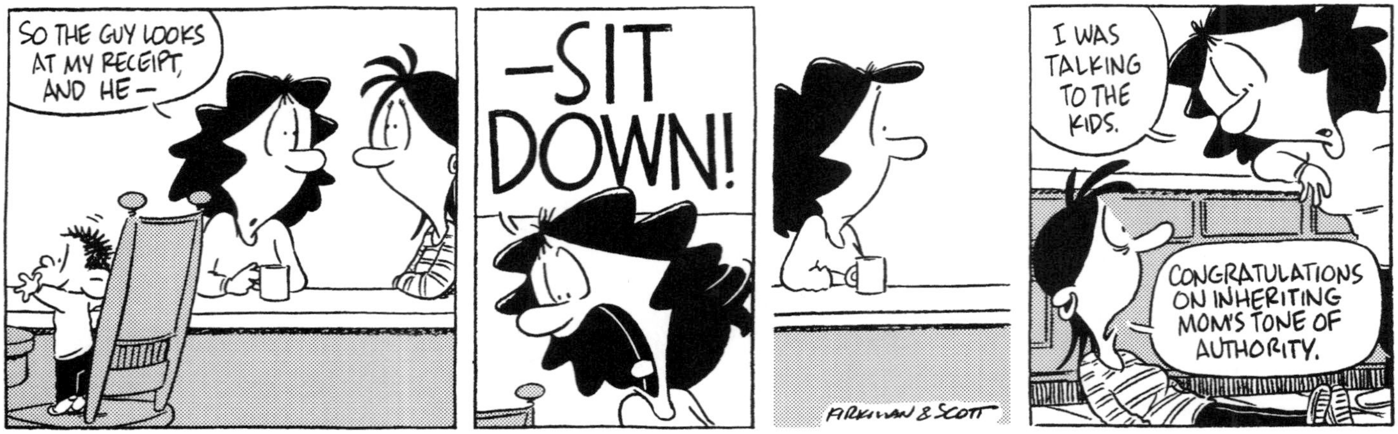
SO THE GUY LOOKS AT MY RECEIPT, AND HE—
—SIT DOWN!
KIRKMAN & SCOTT
I WAS TALKING TO THE KIDS.
CONGRATULATIONS ON INHERITING MOM'S TONE OF AUTHORITY.

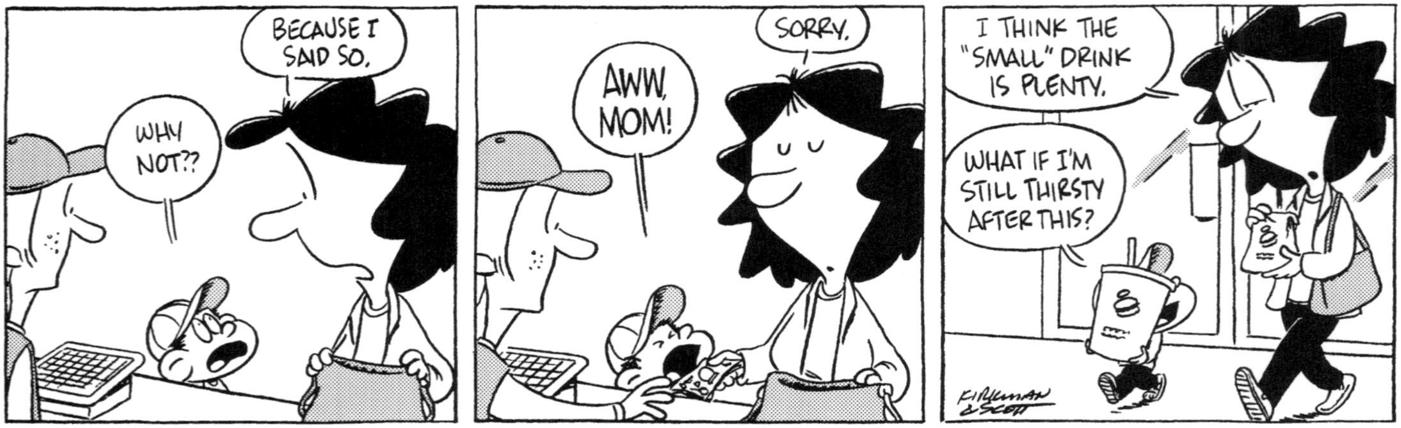
WHY NOT??
BECAUSE I SAID SO.
AWW, MOM!
SORRY.
I THINK THE "SMALL" DRINK IS PLENTY.
WHAT IF I'M STILL THIRSTY AFTER THIS?
KIRKMAN & SCOTT

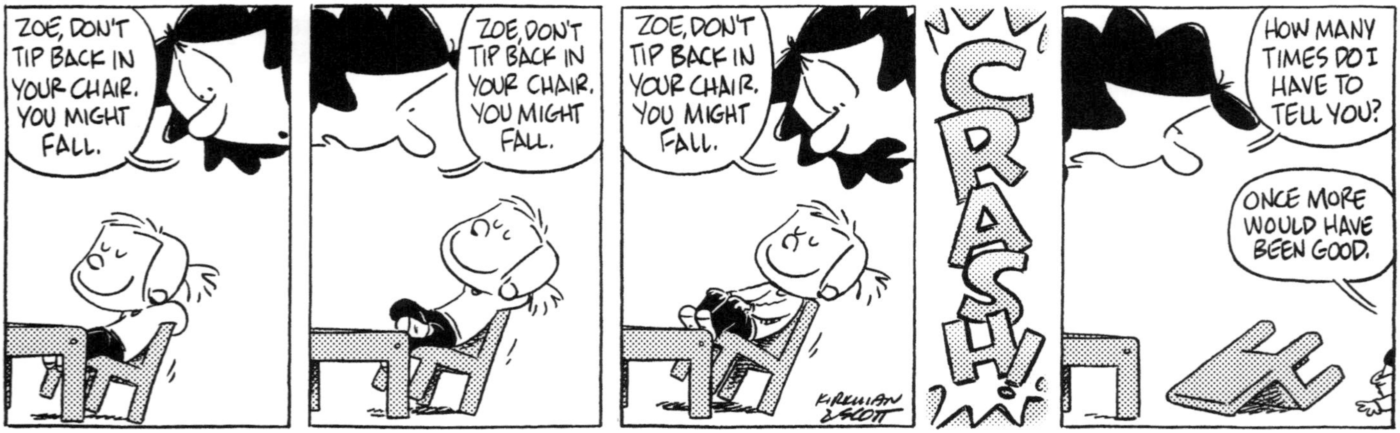
ZOE, DON'T TIP BACK IN YOUR CHAIR. YOU MIGHT FALL.
ZOE, DON'T TIP BACK IN YOUR CHAIR. YOU MIGHT FALL.
ZOE, DON'T TIP BACK IN YOUR CHAIR. YOU MIGHT FALL.
KIRKMAN & SCOTT
CRASH!
HOW MANY TIMES DO I HAVE TO TELL YOU?
ONCE MORE WOULD HAVE BEEN GOOD.

BABY BLUES®
RICK KIRKMAN / BY JERRY SCOTT

SO, YOU'LL TAKE ZOE AND HAMMIE TO THE STORE AND PICK UP THESE THREE THINGS.

RIGHT.

HAVE THE FIRST ONE GIFT-WRAPPED, THEN DROP OFF IT AND HAMMIE AT THE ADDRESS AT THE BOTTOM.

OKAY.

THEN CIRCLE BACK HERE, AND I'LL WRAP THE SECOND ITEM WHILE YOU CHANGE WREN'S CLOTHES,

UH-HUH.

AT THAT POINT, IT'LL BE TIME TO WALK ZOE OVER TO KEESHA'S WITH WRAPPED ITEM #2.

GOTCHA,

BY THE TIME YOU GET BACK, WREN AND I WILL BE AT PHOEBE'S PARTY. YOU'LL HAVE TO PICK UP HAMMIE BY FOUR.

YEAH.

MAKE SURE HAMMIE SAYS THANK YOU, AND I'LL MEET YOU BACK HERE AT 4:30 SO WE CAN ALL GO PICK UP ZOE TOGETHER. ANY QUESTIONS?

NO.

I BET NAPOLEON NEVER DID THIS MUCH STRATEGIZING.

YEAH, WELL, NAPOLEON DIDN'T HAVE THREE KIDS WITH THREE DIFFERENT BIRTHDAY PARTIES ON THE SAME DAY, EITHER.

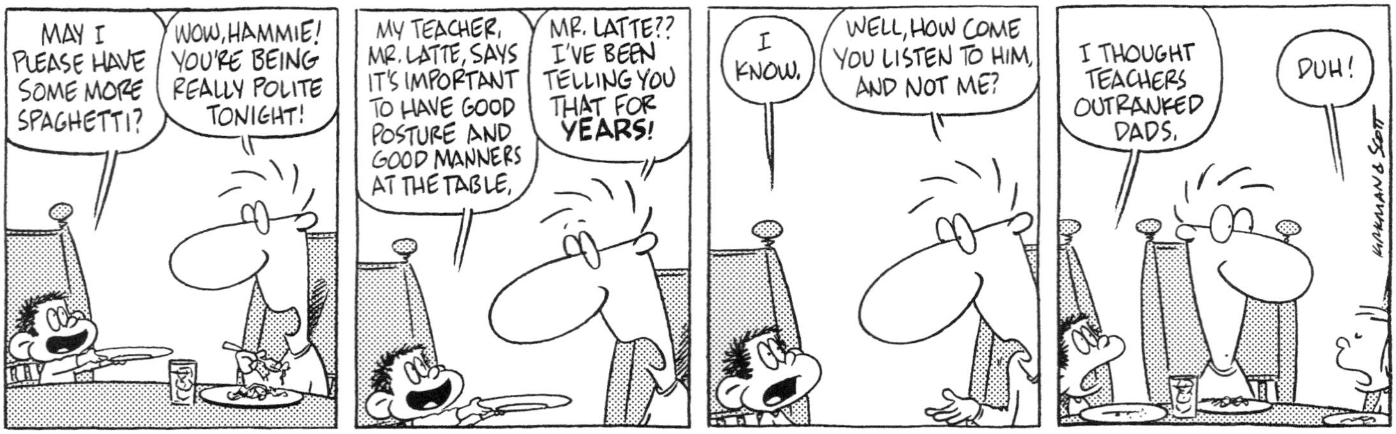
MAY I PLEASE HAVE SOME MORE SPAGHETTI?
WOW, HAMMIE! YOU'RE BEING REALLY POLITE TONIGHT!
MY TEACHER, MR. LATTE, SAYS IT'S IMPORTANT TO HAVE GOOD POSTURE AND GOOD MANNERS AT THE TABLE.
MR. LATTE?? I'VE BEEN TELLING YOU THAT FOR **YEARS!**
I KNOW.
WELL, HOW COME YOU LISTEN TO HIM, AND NOT ME?
I THOUGHT TEACHERS OUTRANKED DADS.
DUH!
KIRKMAN & SCOTT

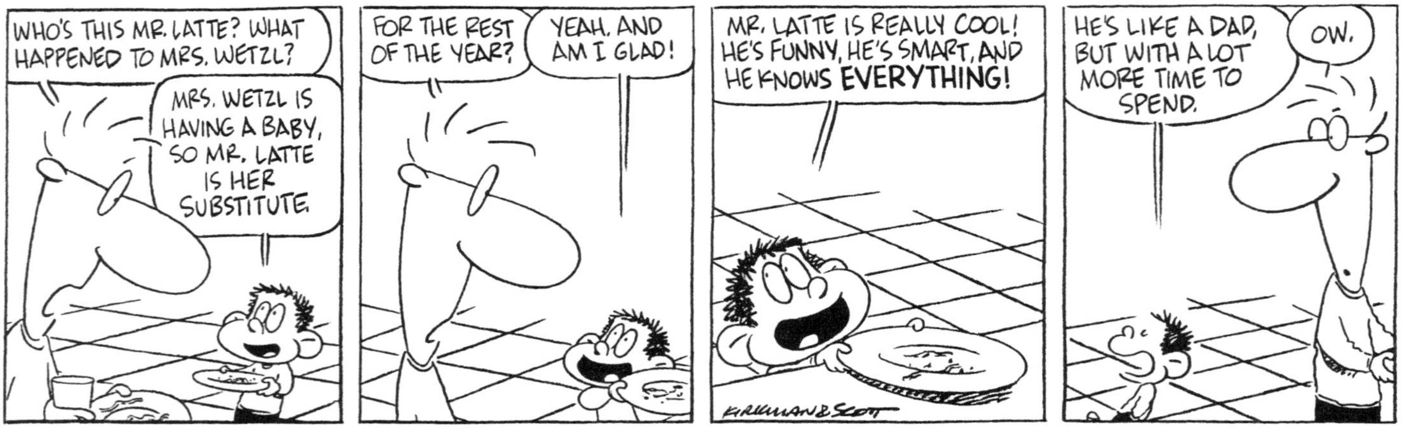
WHO'S THIS MR. LATTE? WHAT HAPPENED TO MRS. WETZL?
MRS. WETZL IS HAVING A BABY, SO MR. LATTE IS HER SUBSTITUTE.
FOR THE REST OF THE YEAR?
YEAH. AND AM I GLAD!
MR. LATTE IS REALLY COOL! HE'S FUNNY, HE'S SMART, AND HE KNOWS **EVERYTHING!**
KIRKMAN & SCOTT
HE'S LIKE A DAD, BUT WITH A LOT MORE TIME TO SPEND.
OW.

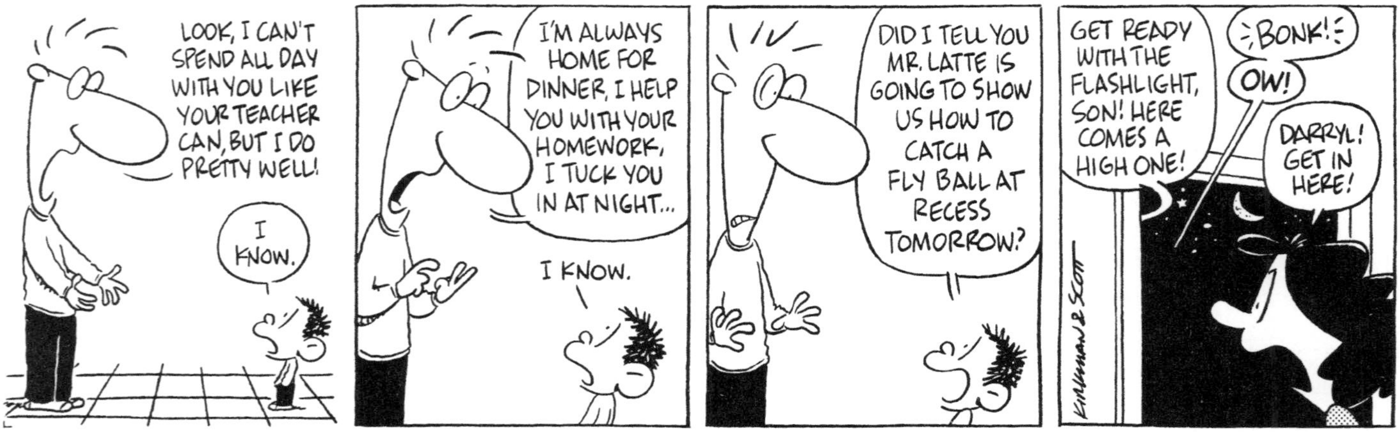
LOOK, I CAN'T SPEND ALL DAY WITH YOU LIKE YOUR TEACHER CAN, BUT I DO PRETTY WELL!
I KNOW.
I'M ALWAYS HOME FOR DINNER, I HELP YOU WITH YOUR HOMEWORK, I TUCK YOU IN AT NIGHT...
I KNOW.
DID I TELL YOU MR. LATTE IS GOING TO SHOW US HOW TO CATCH A FLY BALL AT RECESS TOMORROW?
KIRKMAN & SCOTT
GET READY WITH THE FLASHLIGHT, SON! HERE COMES A HIGH ONE!
BONK!
OW!
DARRYL! GET IN HERE!

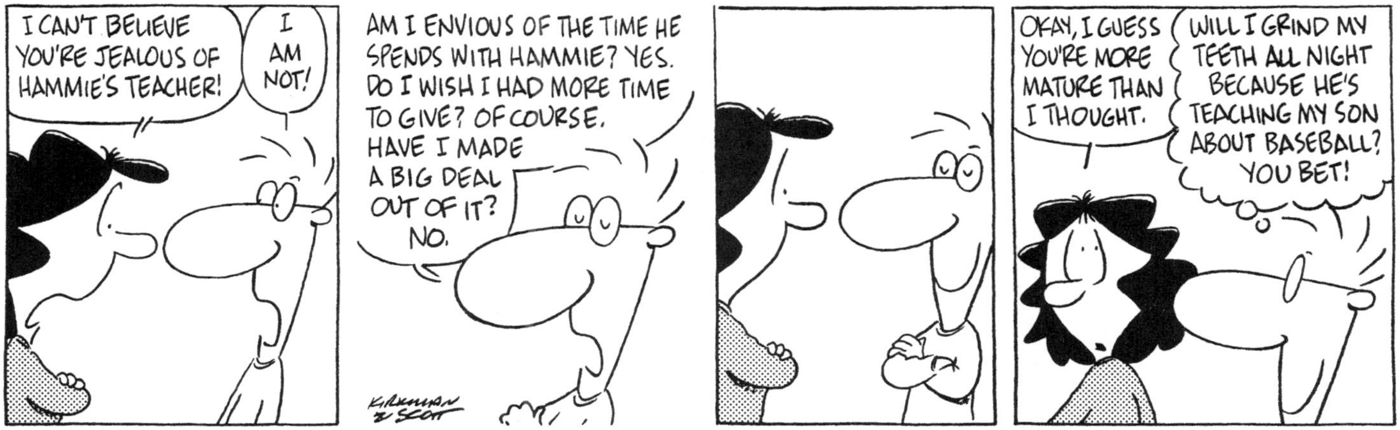
I CAN'T BELIEVE YOU'RE JEALOUS OF HAMMIE'S TEACHER!
I AM NOT!
AM I ENVIOUS OF THE TIME HE SPENDS WITH HAMMIE? YES. DO I WISH I HAD MORE TIME TO GIVE? OF COURSE. HAVE I MADE A BIG DEAL OUT OF IT? NO.
KIRKMAN & SCOTT
OKAY, I GUESS YOU'RE MORE MATURE THAN I THOUGHT.
WILL I GRIND MY TEETH ALL NIGHT BECAUSE HE'S TEACHING MY SON ABOUT BASEBALL? YOU BET!

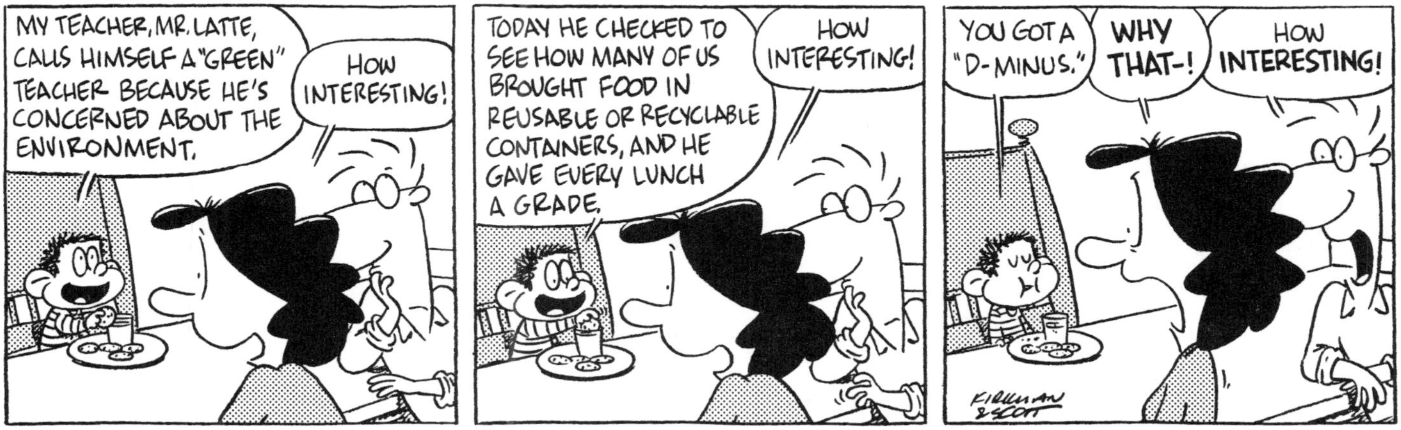
MY TEACHER, MR. LATTE, CALLS HIMSELF A "GREEN" TEACHER BECAUSE HE'S CONCERNED ABOUT THE ENVIRONMENT.
HOW INTERESTING!
TODAY HE CHECKED TO SEE HOW MANY OF US BROUGHT FOOD IN REUSABLE OR RECYCLABLE CONTAINERS, AND HE GAVE EVERY LUNCH A GRADE.
HOW INTERESTING!
YOU GOT A "D-MINUS."
WHY THAT-!
HOW INTERESTING!
KIRKMAN & SCOTT

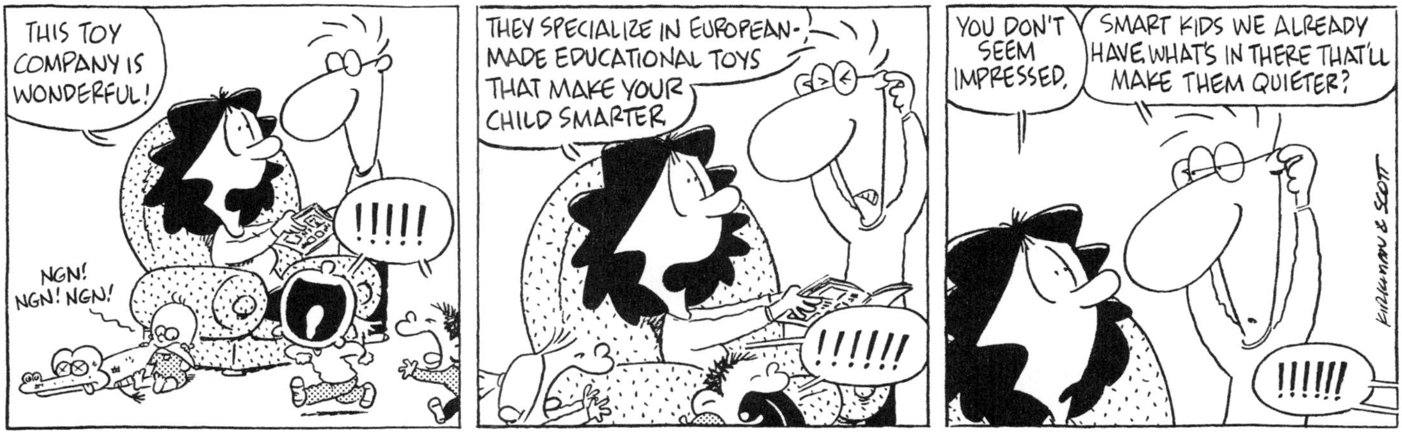
THIS TOY COMPANY IS WONDERFUL!
!!!!!
NGN! NGN! NGN!
THEY SPECIALIZE IN EUROPEAN-MADE EDUCATIONAL TOYS THAT MAKE YOUR CHILD SMARTER.
!!!!!!
YOU DON'T SEEM IMPRESSED.
SMART KIDS WE ALREADY HAVE. WHAT'S IN THERE THAT'LL MAKE THEM QUIETER?
!!!!!!
KIRKMAN & SCOTT

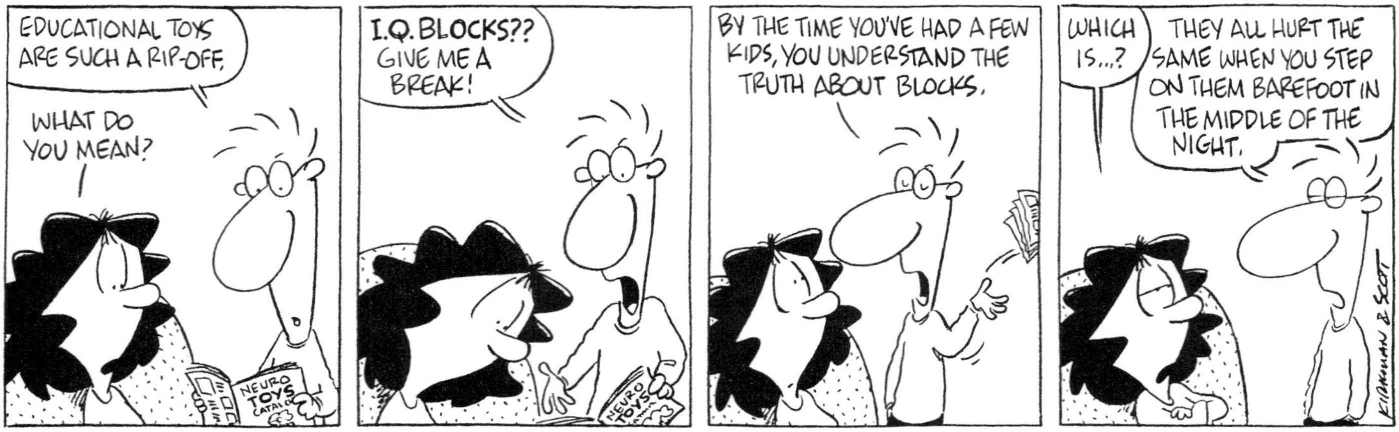
EDUCATIONAL TOYS ARE SUCH A RIP-OFF.
WHAT DO YOU MEAN?
NEURO TOYS CATALOG
I.Q. BLOCKS?? GIVE ME A BREAK!
BY THE TIME YOU'VE HAD A FEW KIDS, YOU UNDERSTAND THE TRUTH ABOUT BLOCKS.
WHICH IS...?
THEY ALL HURT THE SAME WHEN YOU STEP ON THEM BAREFOOT IN THE MIDDLE OF THE NIGHT.
KIRKMAN & SCOTT

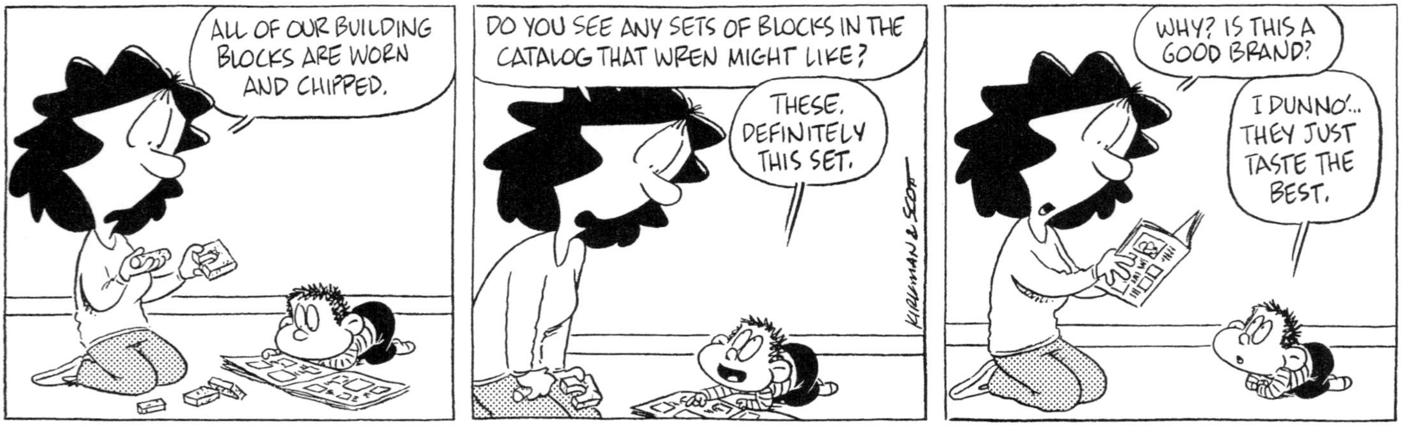
ALL OF OUR BUILDING BLOCKS ARE WORN AND CHIPPED.
DO YOU SEE ANY SETS OF BLOCKS IN THE CATALOG THAT WREN MIGHT LIKE?
THESE. DEFINITELY THIS SET.
KIRKMAN & SCOTT
WHY? IS THIS A GOOD BRAND?
I DUNNO'... THEY JUST TASTE THE BEST.

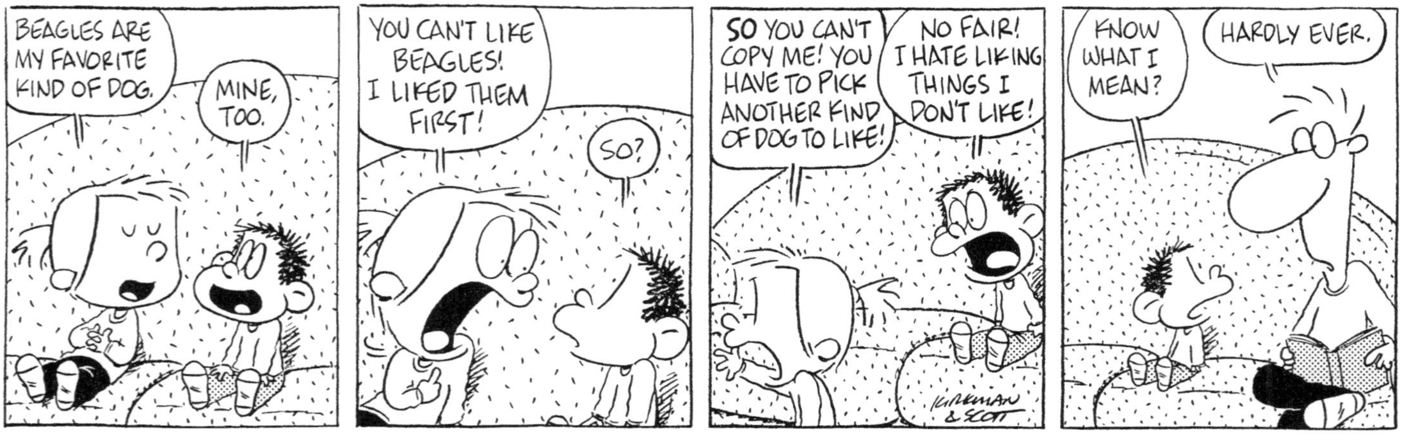
BEAGLES ARE MY FAVORITE KIND OF DOG.
MINE, TOO.
YOU CAN'T LIKE BEAGLES! I LIKED THEM FIRST!
SO?
SO YOU CAN'T COPY ME! YOU HAVE TO PICK ANOTHER KIND OF DOG TO LIKE!
NO FAIR! I HATE LIKING THINGS I DON'T LIKE!
KIRKMAN & SCOTT
KNOW WHAT I MEAN?
HARDLY EVER.

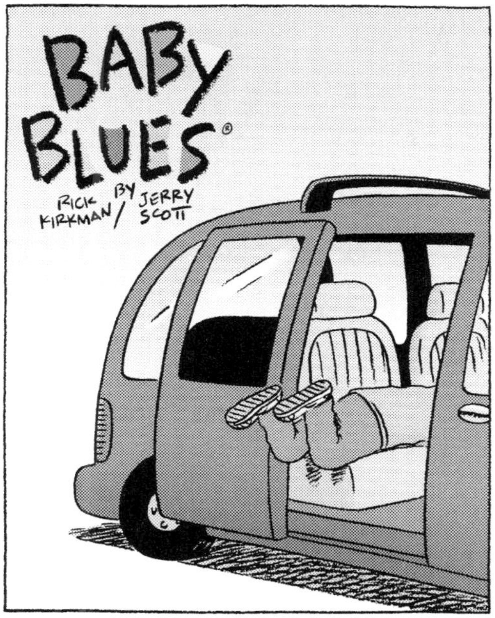
BABY BLUES®
BY RICK KIRKMAN / JERRY SCOTT

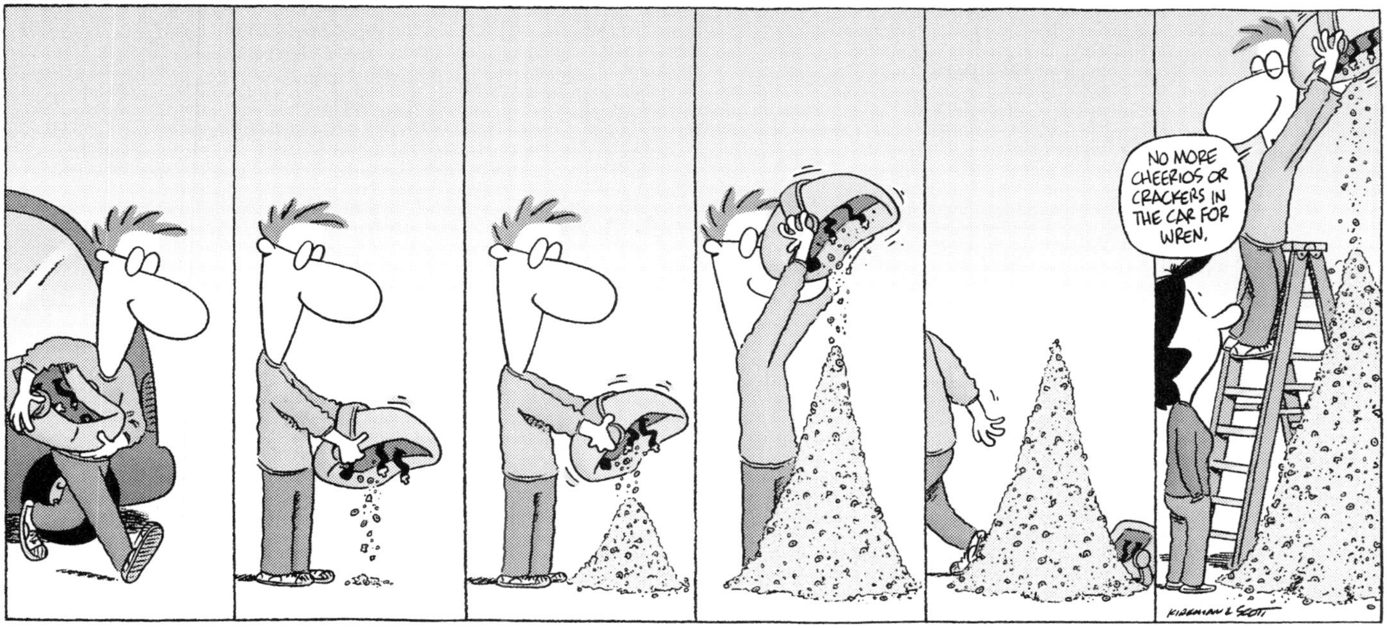
NO MORE CHEERIOS OR CRACKERS IN THE CAR FOR WREN.
KIRKMAN & SCOTT

BABY BLUES®
BY RICK KIRKMAN / JERRY SCOTT

HERE YOU GO.
HEY, THIS ISN'T MY USUAL KIND OF VITAMIN.
WE'RE OUT OF THE CHEWABLE KIND. JUST SWALLOW IT WITH A SIP OF WATER.
OKAY.
www.babyblues.com
GERK!
ORP!
GEEP!
GURP!
GASP!
THIS FROM A KID WHO CAN EAT THREE HAMBURGERS AND A SLICE OF PIZZA WITHOUT CHEWING.
JUNK FOOD AND MEDICINE ARE TWO DIFFERENT THINGS!
KIRKMAN & SCOTT

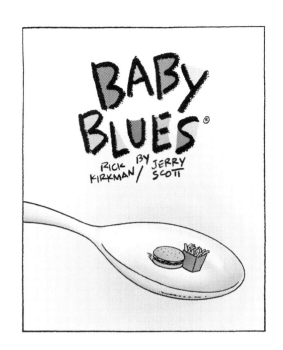

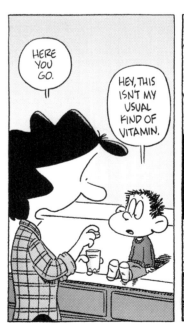

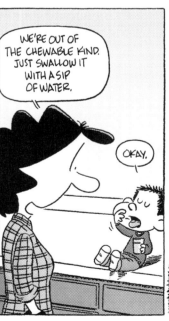

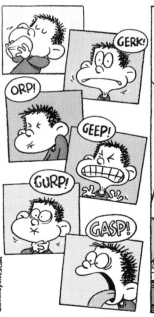

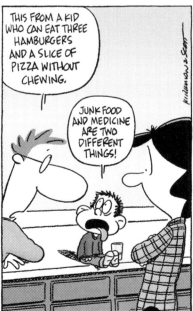

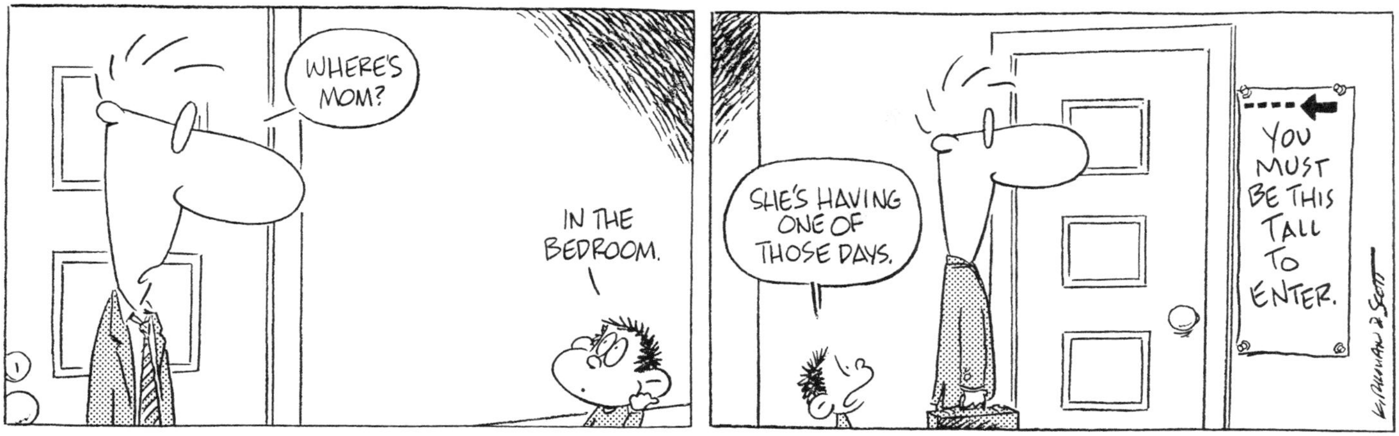
WHERE'S MOM?
IN THE BEDROOM.
SHE'S HAVING ONE OF THOSE DAYS.
YOU MUST BE THIS TALL TO ENTER.
KIRKMAN & SCOTT

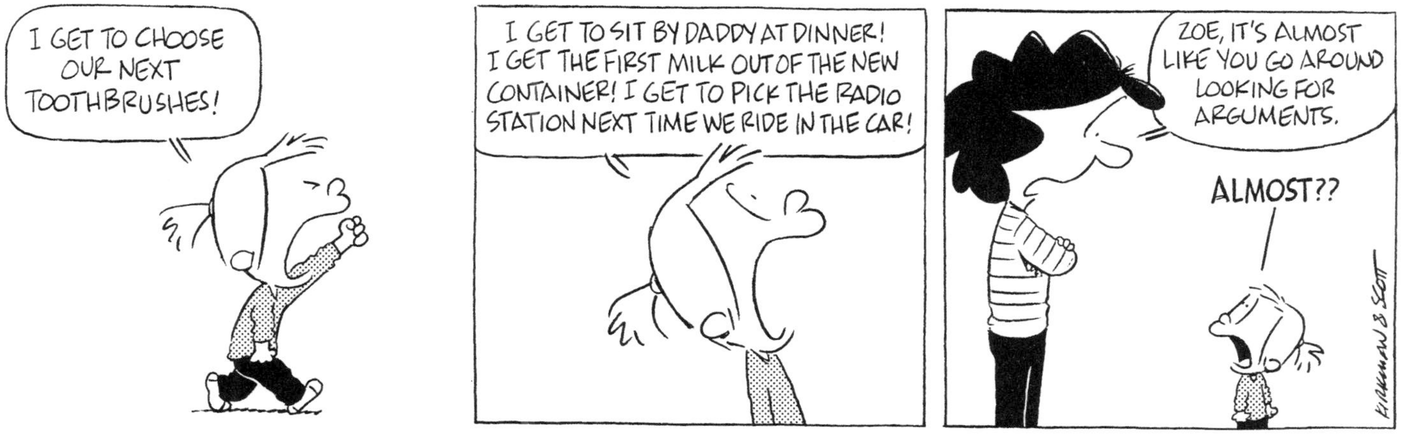
I GET TO CHOOSE OUR NEXT TOOTHBRUSHES!
I GET TO SIT BY DADDY AT DINNER! I GET THE FIRST MILK OUT OF THE NEW CONTAINER! I GET TO PICK THE RADIO STATION NEXT TIME WE RIDE IN THE CAR!
ZOE, IT'S ALMOST LIKE YOU GO AROUND LOOKING FOR ARGUMENTS.
ALMOST??
KIRKMAN & SCOTT

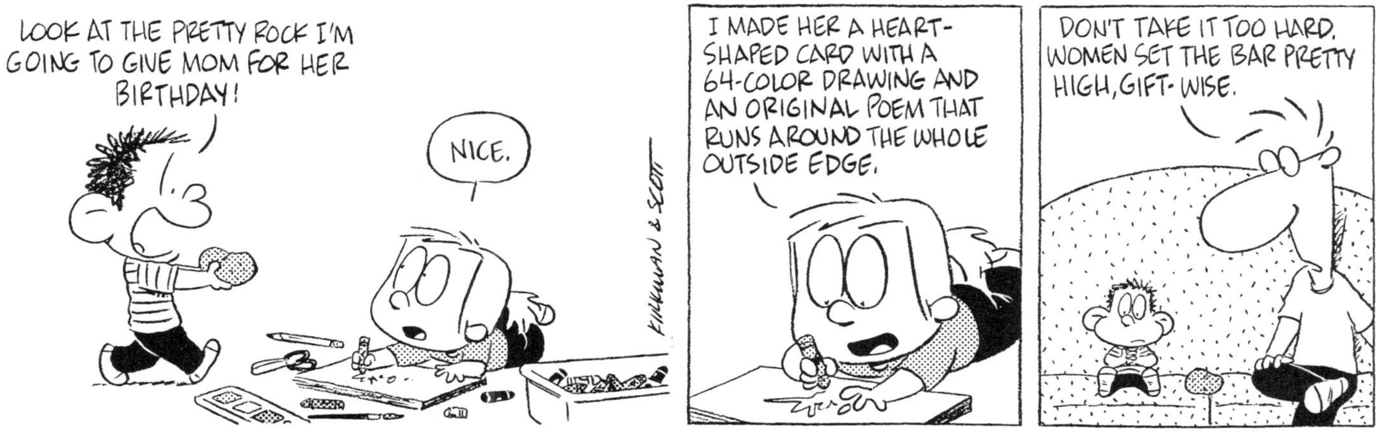
LOOK AT THE PRETTY ROCK I'M GOING TO GIVE MOM FOR HER BIRTHDAY!
NICE.
KIRKMAN & SCOTT
I MADE HER A HEART-SHAPED CARD WITH A 64-COLOR DRAWING AND AN ORIGINAL POEM THAT RUNS AROUND THE WHOLE OUTSIDE EDGE.
DON'T TAKE IT TOO HARD. WOMEN SET THE BAR PRETTY HIGH, GIFT-WISE.

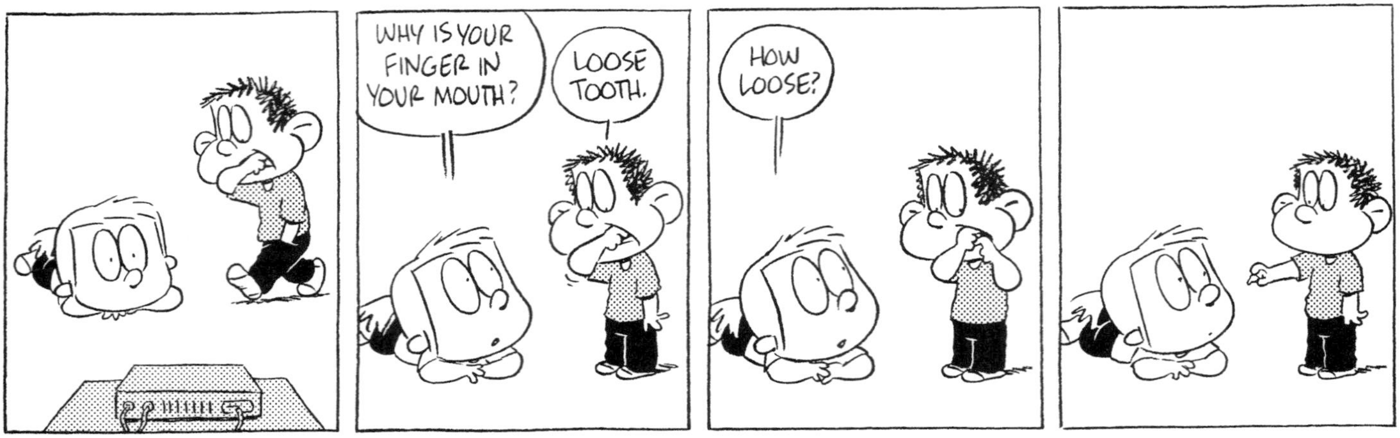
WHY IS YOUR FINGER IN YOUR MOUTH?
LOOSE TOOTH.
HOW LOOSE?

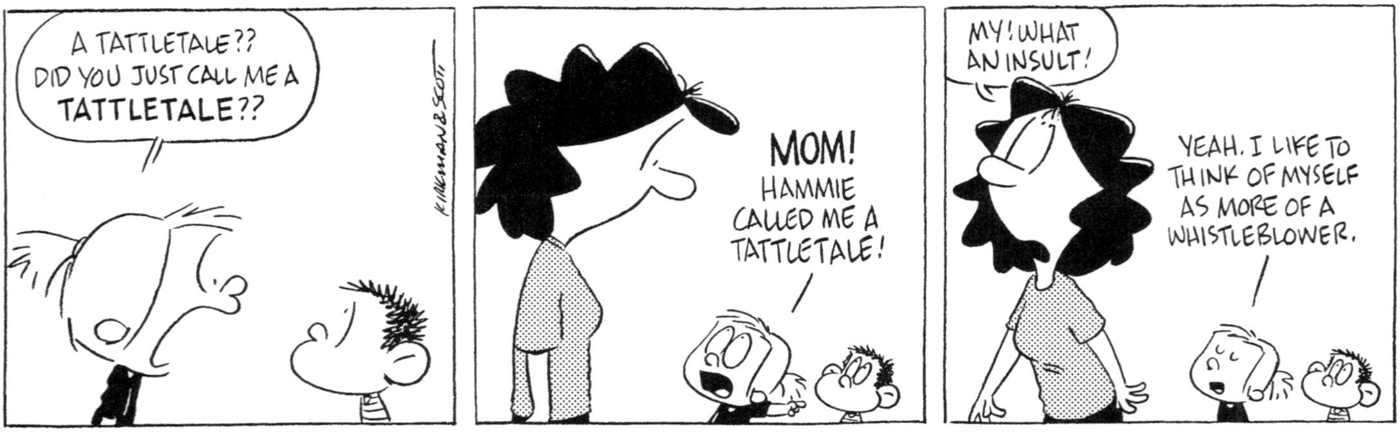
A TATTLETALE?? DID YOU JUST CALL ME A TATTLETALE??
KIRKMAN & SCOTT
MOM! HAMMIE CALLED ME A TATTLETALE!
MY! WHAT AN INSULT!
YEAH. I LIKE TO THINK OF MYSELF AS MORE OF A WHISTLEBLOWER.

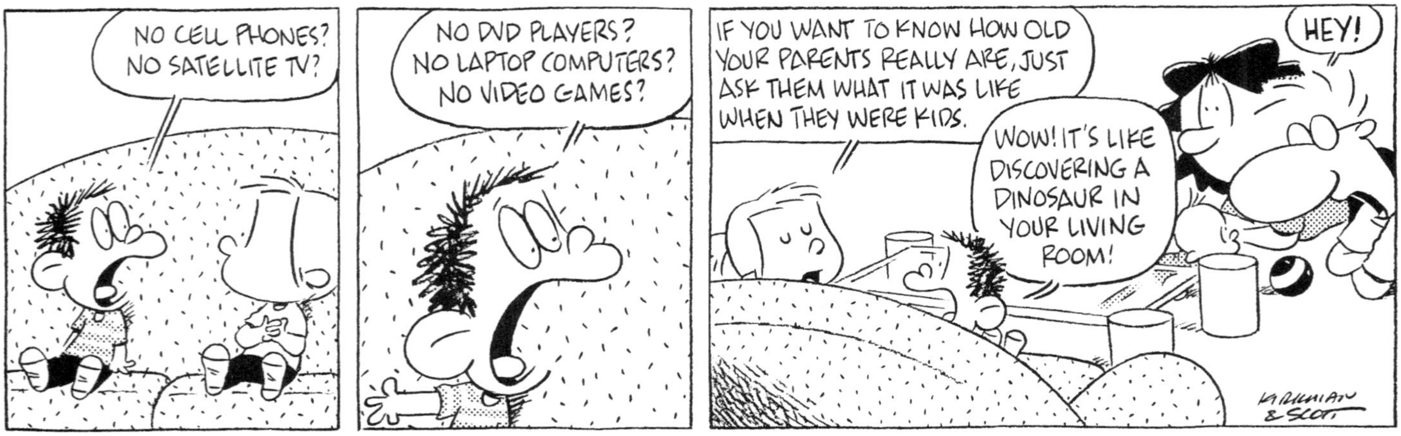
NO CELL PHONES? NO SATELLITE TV?
NO DVD PLAYERS? NO LAPTOP COMPUTERS? NO VIDEO GAMES?
IF YOU WANT TO KNOW HOW OLD YOUR PARENTS REALLY ARE, JUST ASK THEM WHAT IT WAS LIKE WHEN THEY WERE KIDS.
HEY!
WOW! IT'S LIKE DISCOVERING A DINOSAUR IN YOUR LIVING ROOM!
KIRKMAN & SCOTT

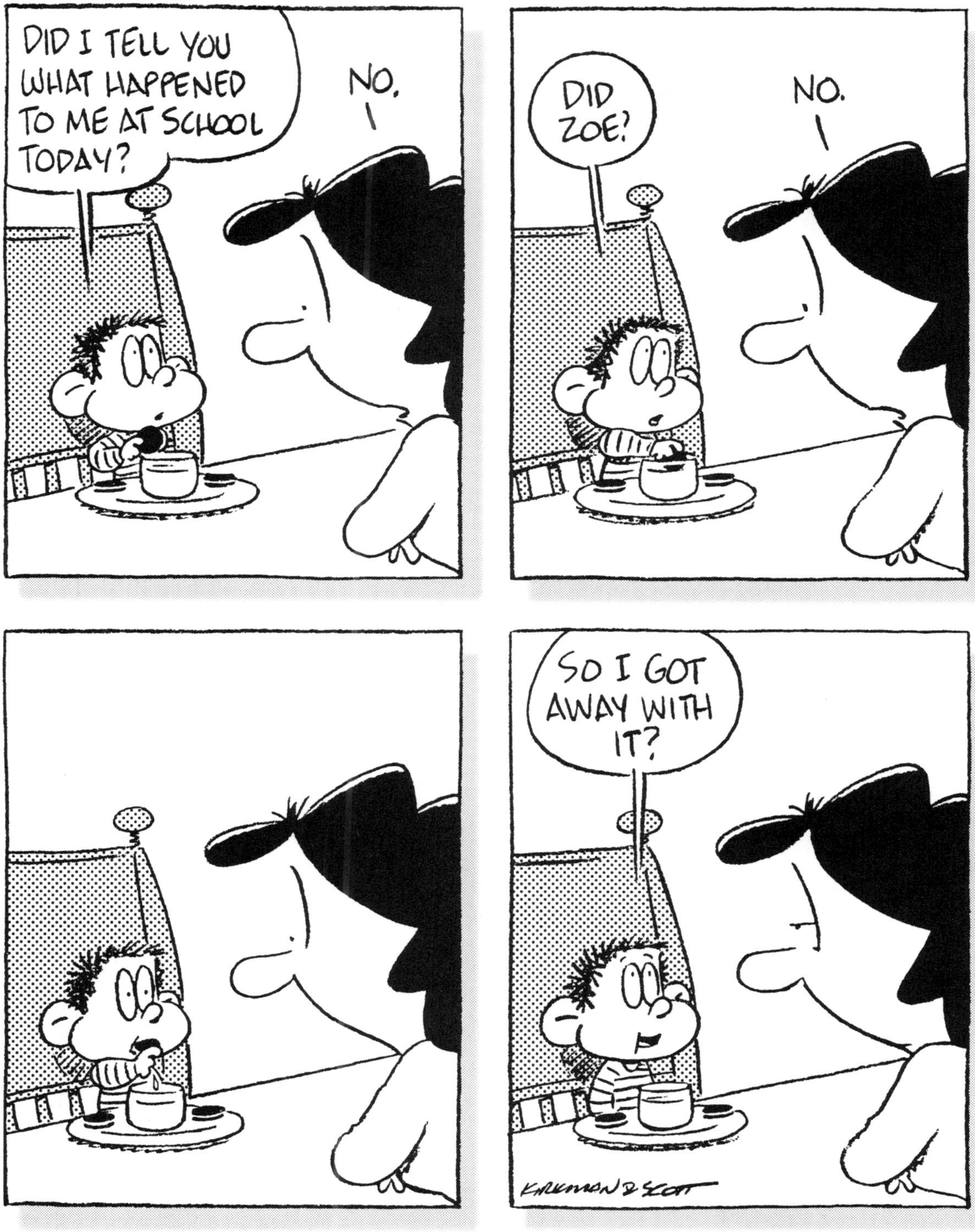
DID I TELL YOU WHAT HAPPENED TO ME AT SCHOOL TODAY?
NO.
DID ZOE?
NO.
SO I GOT AWAY WITH IT?
KIRKMAN & SCOTT

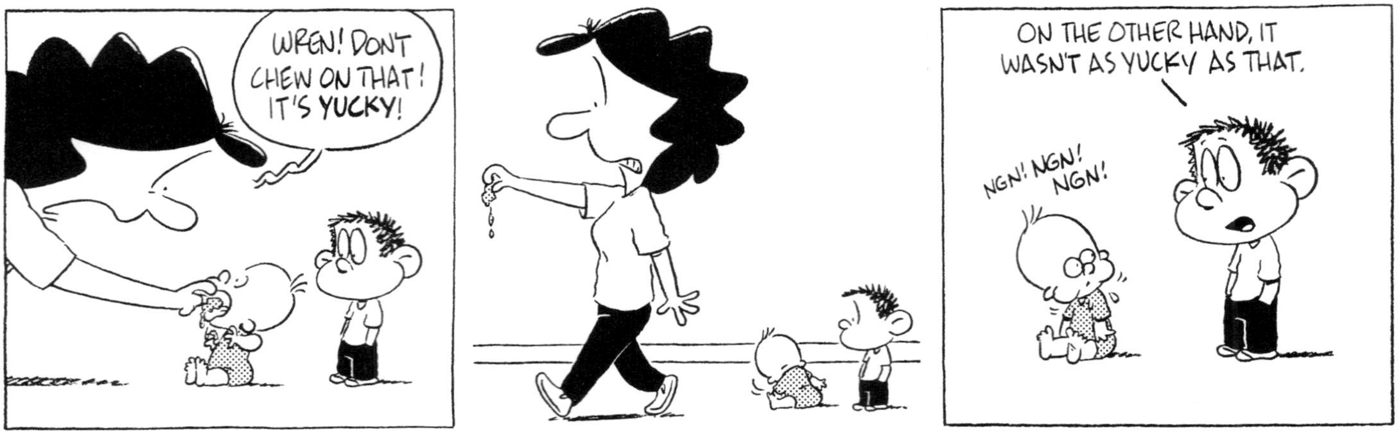
WREN! DON'T CHEW ON THAT! IT'S YUCKY!
ON THE OTHER HAND, IT WASN'T AS YUCKY AS THAT.
NGN! NGN! NGN!

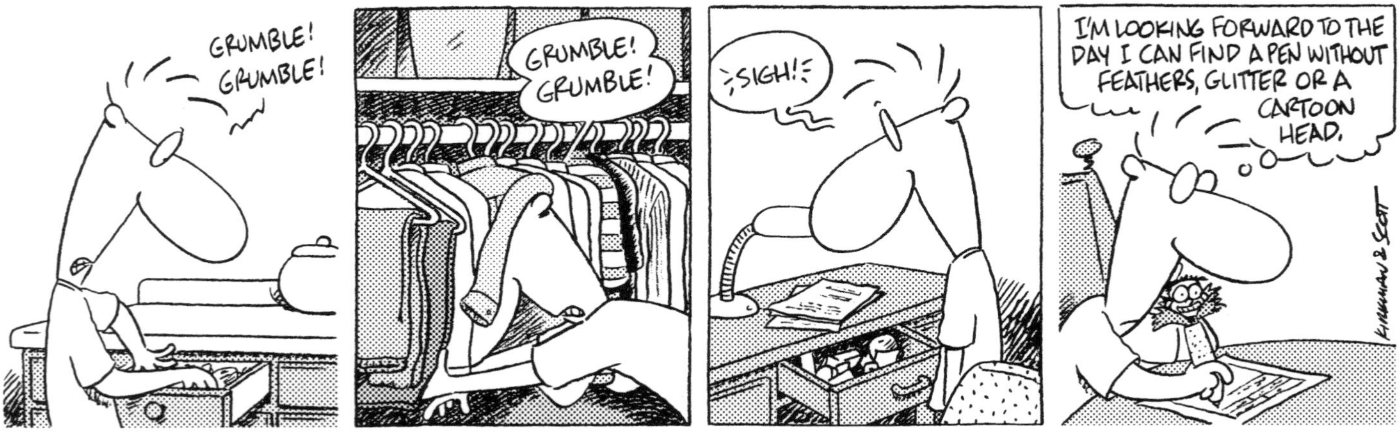
GRUMBLE! GRUMBLE!
GRUMBLE! GRUMBLE!
SIGH!
I'M LOOKING FORWARD TO THE DAY I CAN FIND A PEN WITHOUT FEATHERS, GLITTER OR A CARTOON HEAD.
KIRKMAN & SCOTT

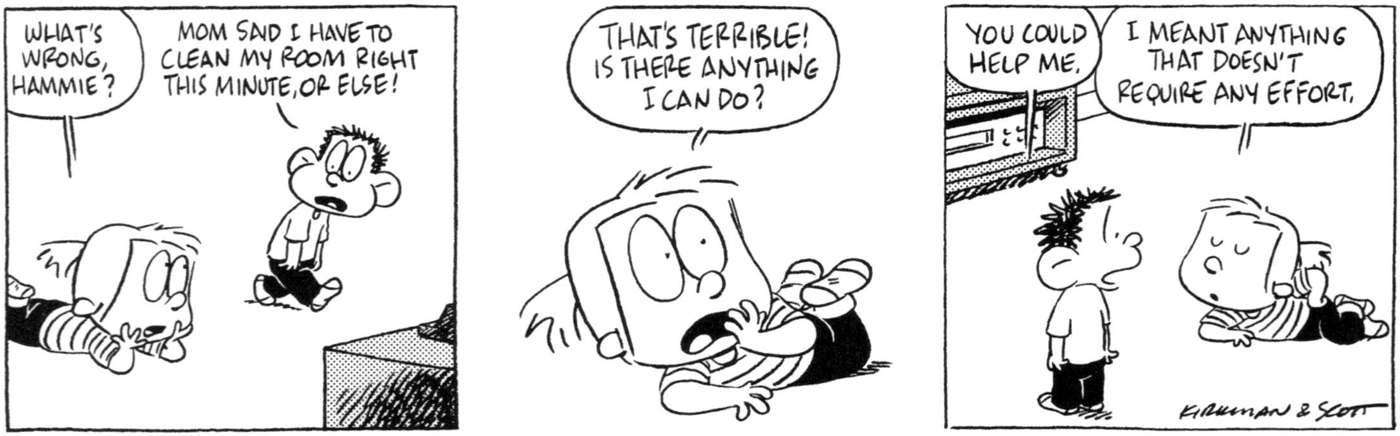
WHAT'S WRONG, HAMMIE?
MOM SAID I HAVE TO CLEAN MY ROOM RIGHT THIS MINUTE, OR ELSE!
THAT'S TERRIBLE! IS THERE ANYTHING I CAN DO?
YOU COULD HELP ME.
I MEANT ANYTHING THAT DOESN'T REQUIRE ANY EFFORT.
KIRKMAN & SCOTT

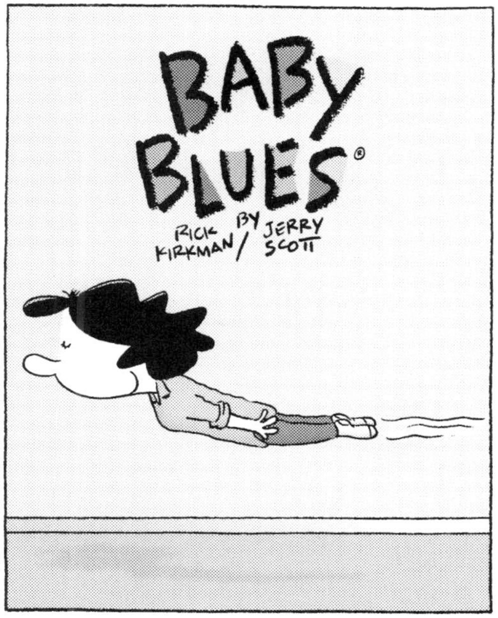
BABY BLUES®
BY RICK KIRKMAN / JERRY SCOTT

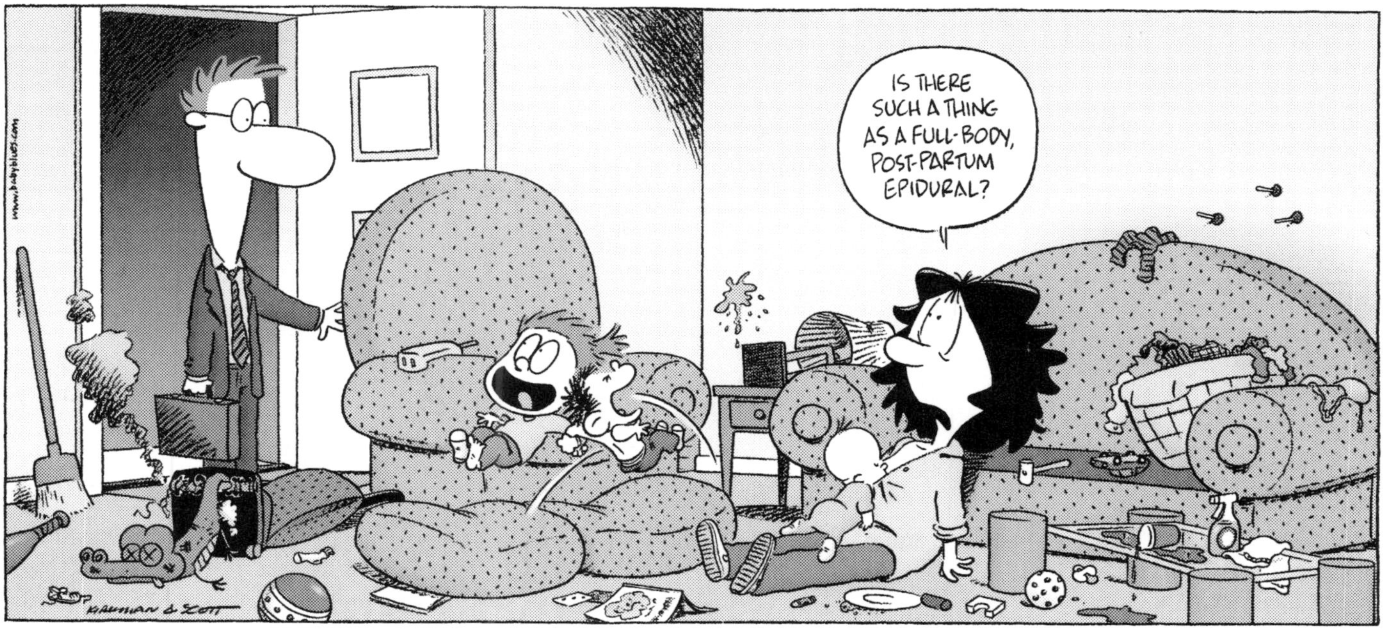
IS THERE SUCH A THING AS A FULL-BODY, POST-PARTUM EPIDURAL?
KIRKMAN & SCOTT

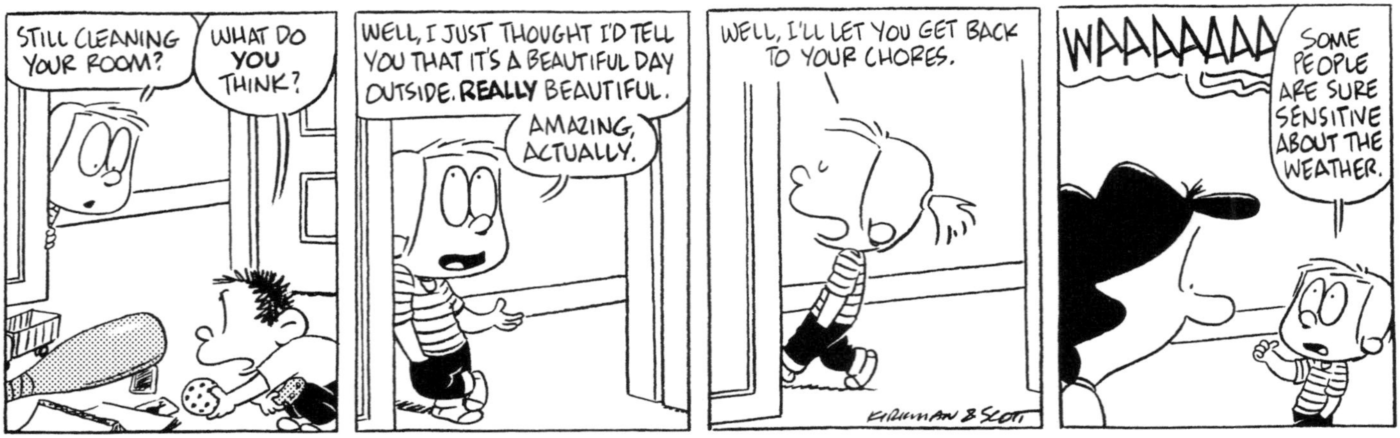
STILL CLEANING YOUR ROOM?
WHAT DO **YOU** THINK?
WELL, I JUST THOUGHT I'D TELL YOU THAT IT'S A BEAUTIFUL DAY OUTSIDE. **REALLY** BEAUTIFUL.
AMAZING, ACTUALLY.
WELL, I'LL LET YOU GET BACK TO YOUR CHORES.
KIRKMAN & SCOTT
WAAAAAAA
SOME PEOPLE ARE SURE SENSITIVE ABOUT THE WEATHER.

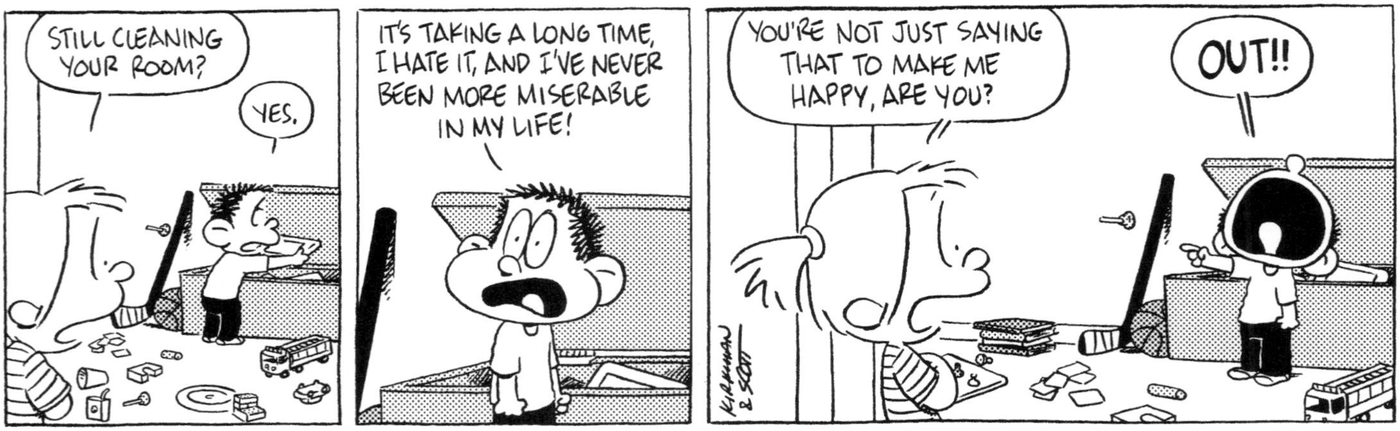
STILL CLEANING YOUR ROOM?
YES.
IT'S TAKING A LONG TIME, I HATE IT, AND I'VE NEVER BEEN MORE MISERABLE IN MY LIFE!
KIRKMAN & SCOTT
YOU'RE NOT JUST SAYING THAT TO MAKE ME HAPPY, ARE YOU?
OUT!!

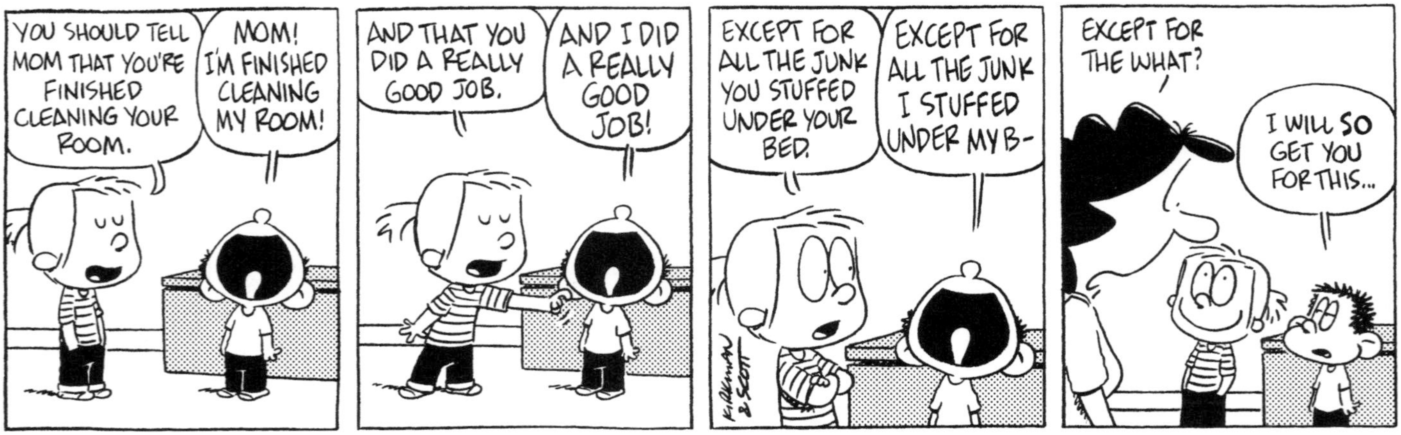
YOU SHOULD TELL MOM THAT YOU'RE FINISHED CLEANING YOUR ROOM.
MOM! I'M FINISHED CLEANING MY ROOM!
AND THAT YOU DID A REALLY GOOD JOB.
AND I DID A REALLY GOOD JOB!
EXCEPT FOR ALL THE JUNK YOU STUFFED UNDER YOUR BED.
EXCEPT FOR ALL THE JUNK I STUFFED UNDER MY B-
KIRKMAN & SCOTT
EXCEPT FOR THE WHAT?
I WILL **SO** GET YOU FOR THIS...

BABY BLUES®
BY
RICK KIRKMAN / JERRY SCOTT

HAMMIE, YOU'RE NOT COLORING INSIDE THE LINES.
SO?
SO— IT LOOKS SLOPPY! COLORING BOOKS ARE SUPPOSED TO BE NEAT AND TIDY, LIKE MINE.
REALLY?
THEN I GUESS I NEED TO BE CAREFUL!
I WOULDN'T WANT TO SPOIL YOUR PICTURE BY—
SWIPE!
JAB! JAB! JAB!
—ACCIDENTALLY MAKING YOU—
COLOR OUTSIDE THE LINES!!
NICE.
YOU SHOULD TRY LOOSENING UP YOUR STYLE A LITTLE, HAMMIE.
KIRKMAN & SCOTT

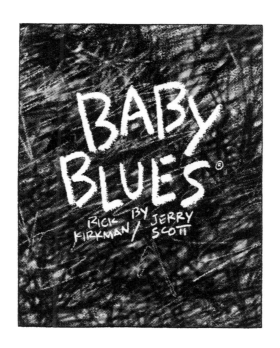

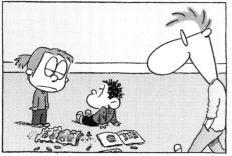

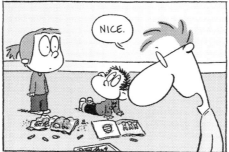

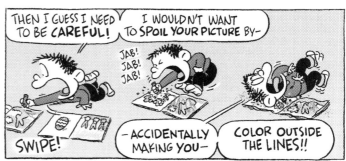

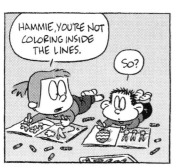

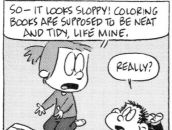

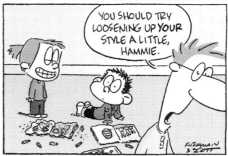

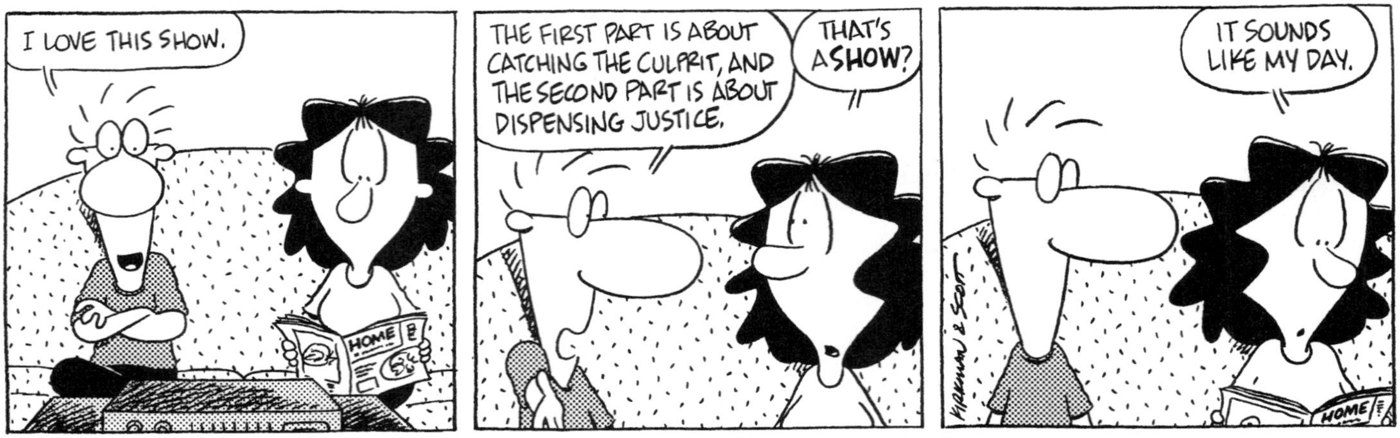
I LOVE THIS SHOW.
THE FIRST PART IS ABOUT CATCHING THE CULPRIT, AND THE SECOND PART IS ABOUT DISPENSING JUSTICE.
THAT'S A **SHOW**?
IT SOUNDS LIKE MY DAY.
KIRKMAN & SCOTT

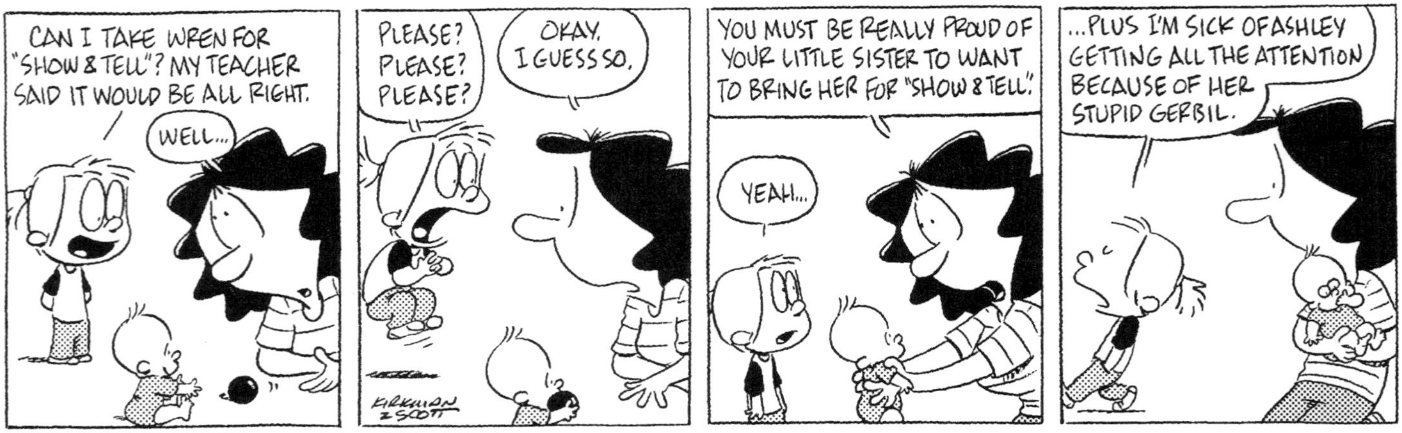
CAN I TAKE WREN FOR "SHOW & TELL"? MY TEACHER SAID IT WOULD BE ALL RIGHT.
WELL...
PLEASE? PLEASE? PLEASE?
OKAY. I GUESS SO.
KIRKMAN & SCOTT
YOU MUST BE REALLY PROUD OF YOUR LITTLE SISTER TO WANT TO BRING HER FOR "SHOW & TELL."
YEAH...
...PLUS I'M SICK OF ASHLEY GETTING ALL THE ATTENTION BECAUSE OF HER STUPID GERBIL.

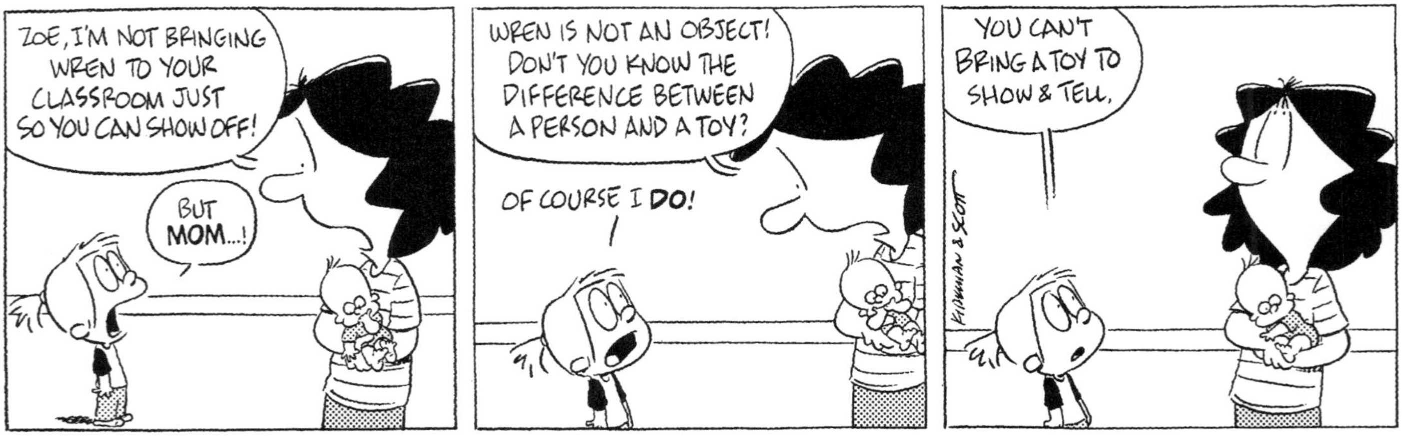
ZOE, I'M NOT BRINGING WREN TO YOUR CLASSROOM JUST SO YOU CAN SHOW OFF!
BUT **MOM**...!
WREN IS NOT AN OBJECT! DON'T YOU KNOW THE DIFFERENCE BETWEEN A PERSON AND A TOY?
OF COURSE I **DO**!
KIRKMAN & SCOTT
YOU CAN'T BRING A TOY TO SHOW & TELL.

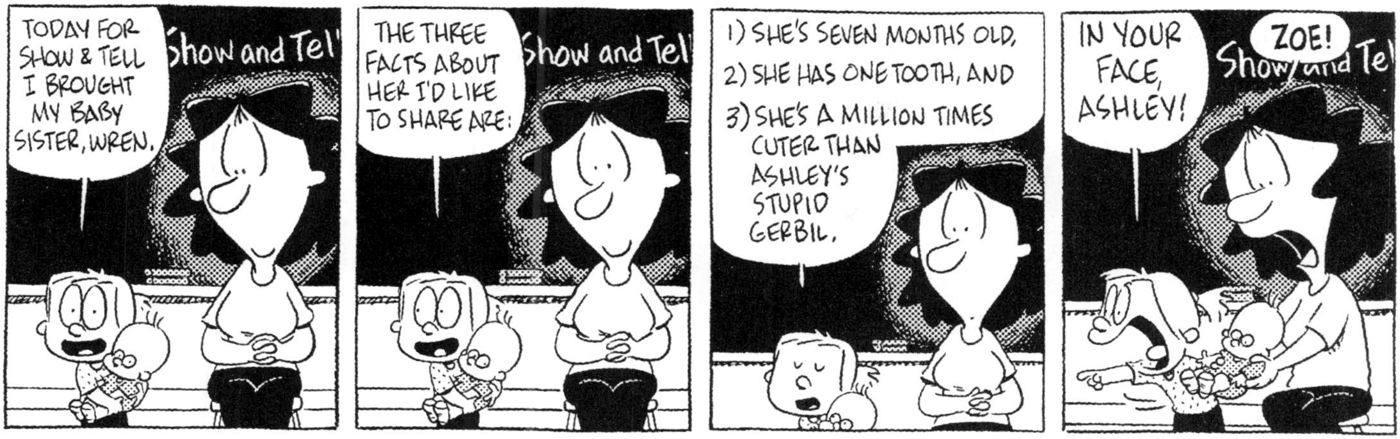
TODAY FOR SHOW & TELL I BROUGHT MY BABY SISTER, WREN.
THE THREE FACTS ABOUT HER I'D LIKE TO SHARE ARE:
1) SHE'S SEVEN MONTHS OLD, 2) SHE HAS ONE TOOTH, AND 3) SHE'S A MILLION TIMES CUTER THAN ASHLEY'S STUPID GERBIL.
IN YOUR FACE, ASHLEY!
ZOE!

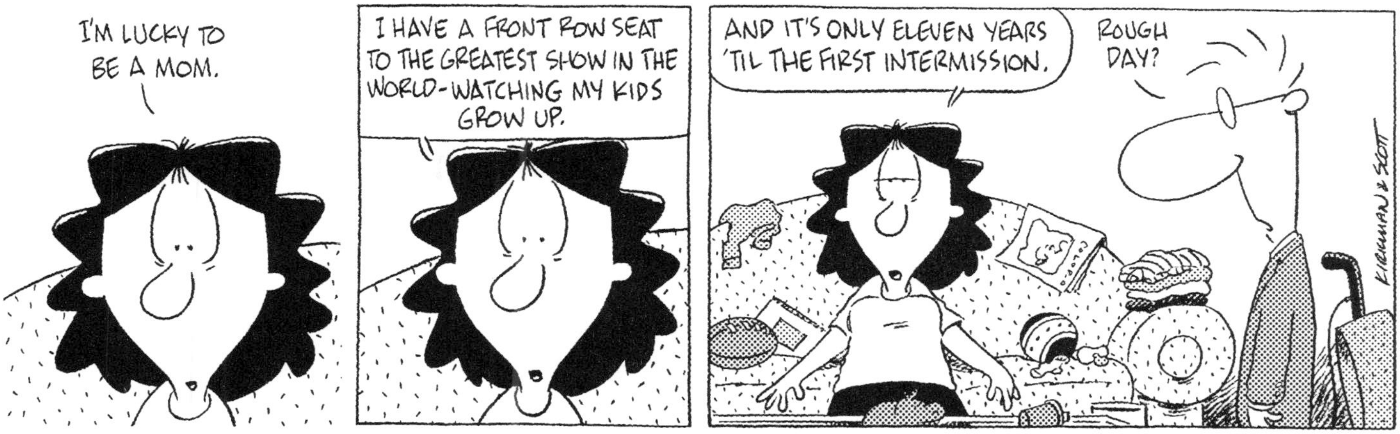
I'M LUCKY TO BE A MOM.
I HAVE A FRONT ROW SEAT TO THE GREATEST SHOW IN THE WORLD-WATCHING MY KIDS GROW UP.
AND IT'S ONLY ELEVEN YEARS 'TIL THE FIRST INTERMISSION.
ROUGH DAY?
KIRKMAN & SCOTT

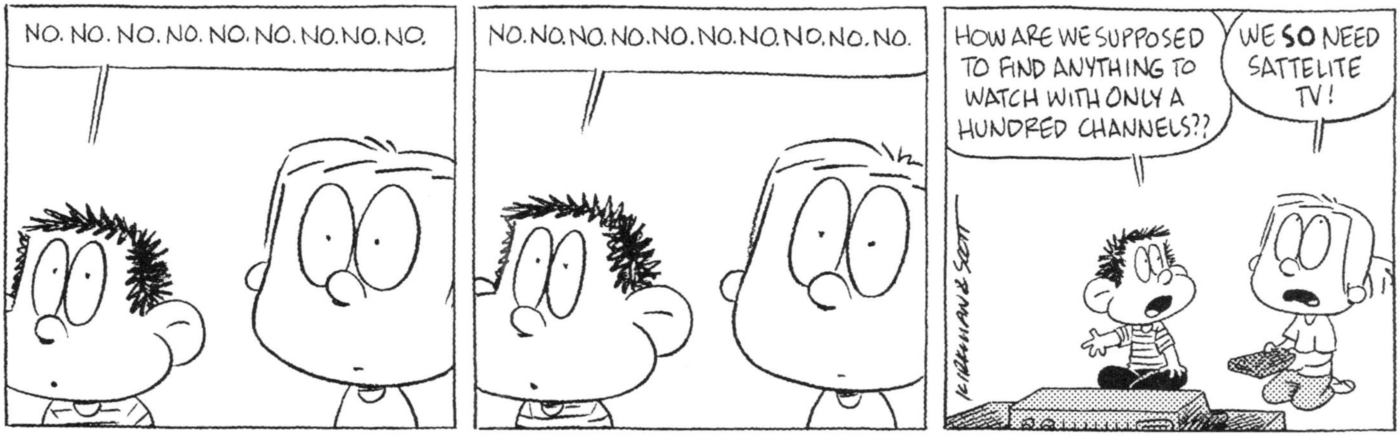
NO. NO. NO. NO. NO. NO. NO. NO. NO.
NO. NO. NO. NO. NO. NO. NO. NO. NO. NO.
HOW ARE WE SUPPOSED TO FIND ANYTHING TO WATCH WITH ONLY A HUNDRED CHANNELS??
WE SO NEED SATTELITE TV!
KIRKMAN & SCOTT

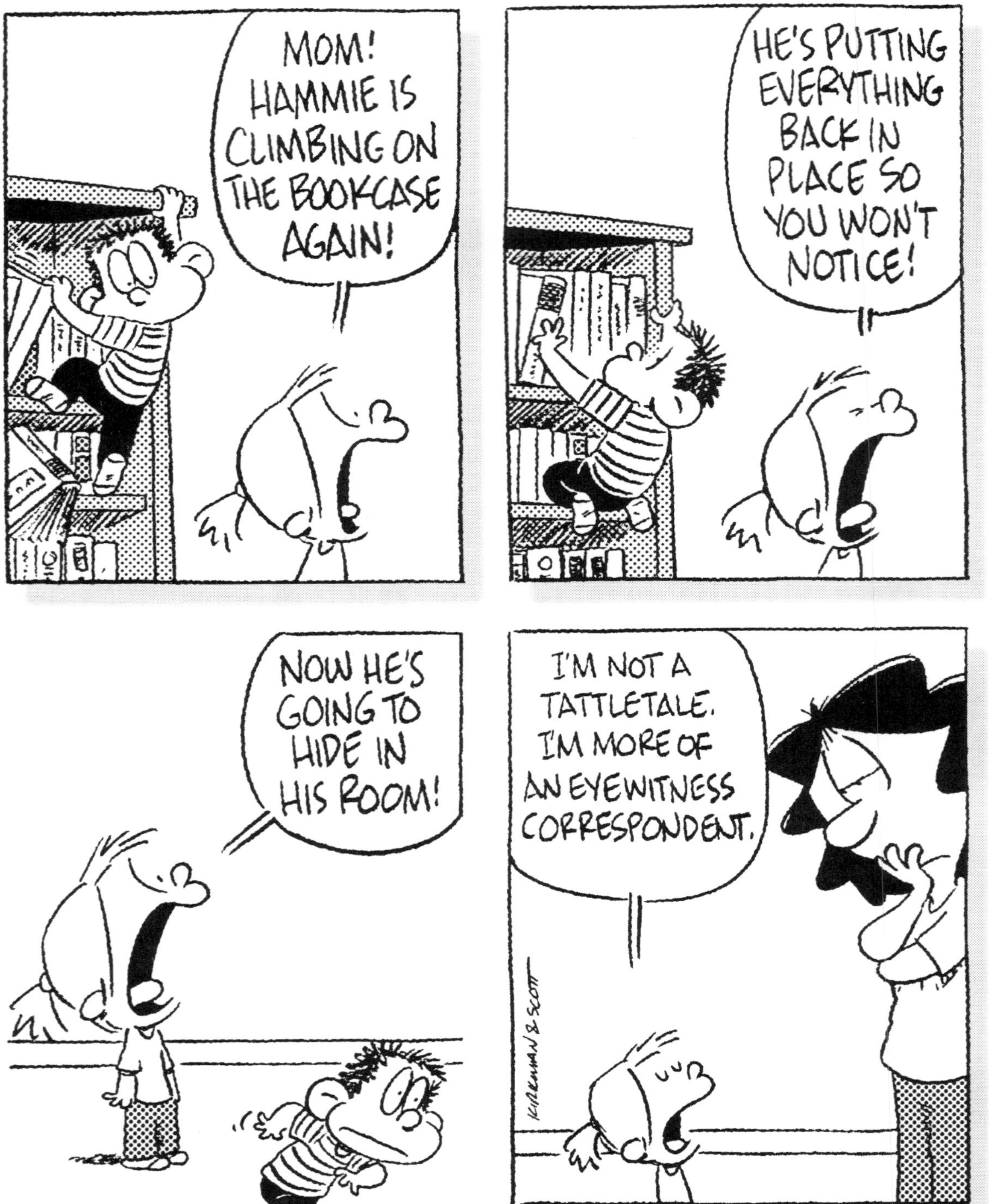
MOM! HAMMIE IS CLIMBING ON THE BOOKCASE AGAIN!
HE'S PUTTING EVERYTHING BACK IN PLACE SO YOU WON'T NOTICE!
NOW HE'S GOING TO HIDE IN HIS ROOM!
I'M NOT A TATTLETALE. I'M MORE OF AN EYEWITNESS CORRESPONDENT.
KIRKMAN & SCOTT

BABY BLUES®
BY RICK KIRKMAN / JERRY SCOTT

HOW TO PLAY A BOARD GAME
1. Fight over which game to play.
2. Argue over who gets which game piece.
3. Discover that the dice are missing.
4. Ransack other games looking for dice.
5. Argue about who gets to go first.
6. Roll dice to see who gets to go first.
7. Loser cries.
8. Game finally starts.
9. Cheating alleged. Cheater cries.
10. Cheater calls Accuser a name, Accuser quits.
11. Cheater apologizes to Quitter, game resumes.
12. Somebody wins. Loser cries.
13. Repeat.
WANNA' PLAY AGAIN?
SURE!
KIRKMAN & SCOTT

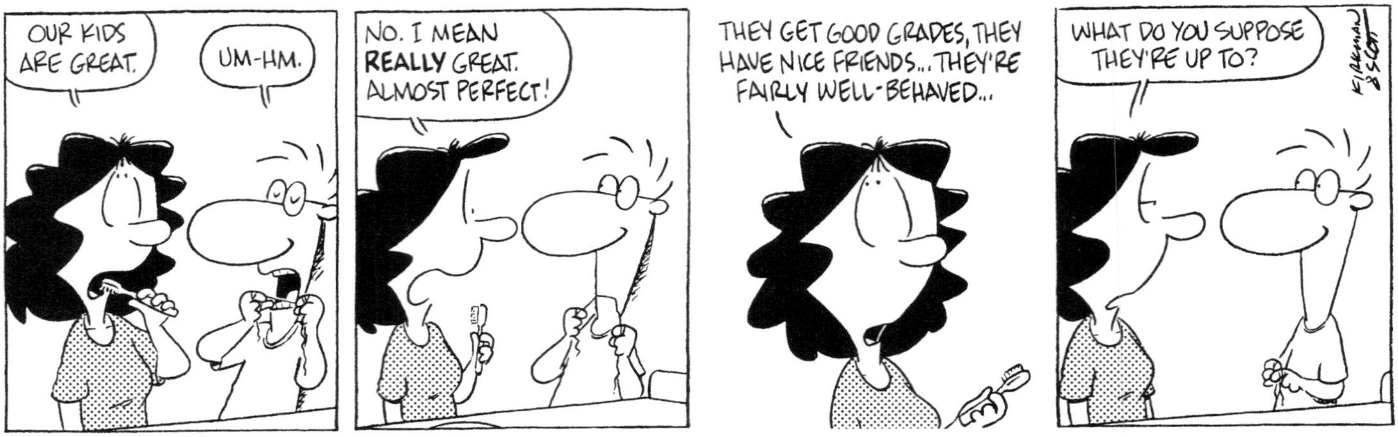
OUR KIDS ARE GREAT.
UM-HM.
NO. I MEAN **REALLY** GREAT. ALMOST PERFECT!
THEY GET GOOD GRADES, THEY HAVE NICE FRIENDS... THEY'RE FAIRLY WELL-BEHAVED...
WHAT DO YOU SUPPOSE THEY'RE UP TO?
KIRKMAN & SCOTT

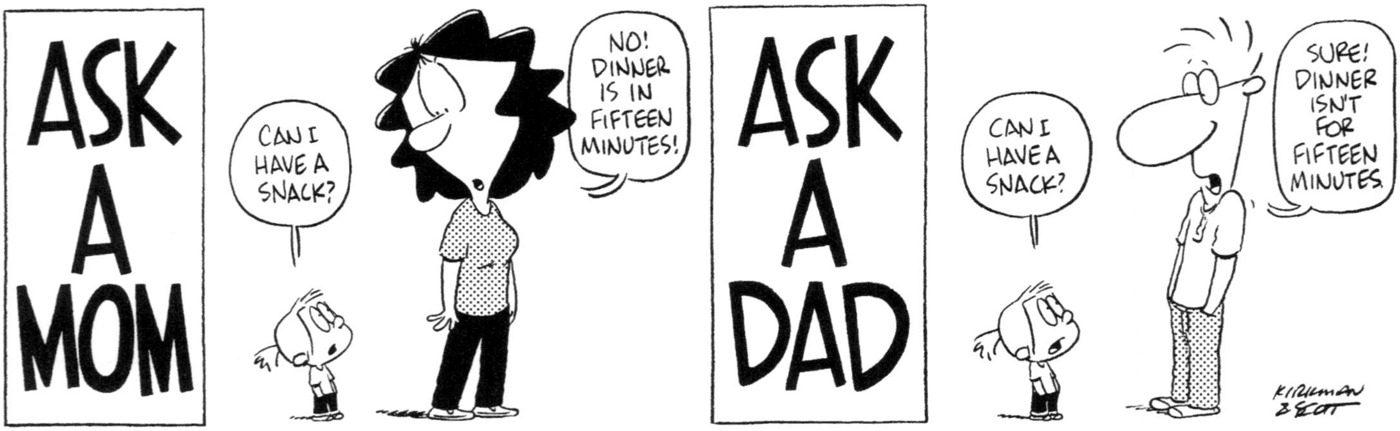
ASK A MOM
CAN I HAVE A SNACK?
NO! DINNER IS IN FIFTEEN MINUTES!
ASK A DAD
CAN I HAVE A SNACK?
SURE! DINNER ISN'T FOR FIFTEEN MINUTES.
KIRKMAN & SCOTT

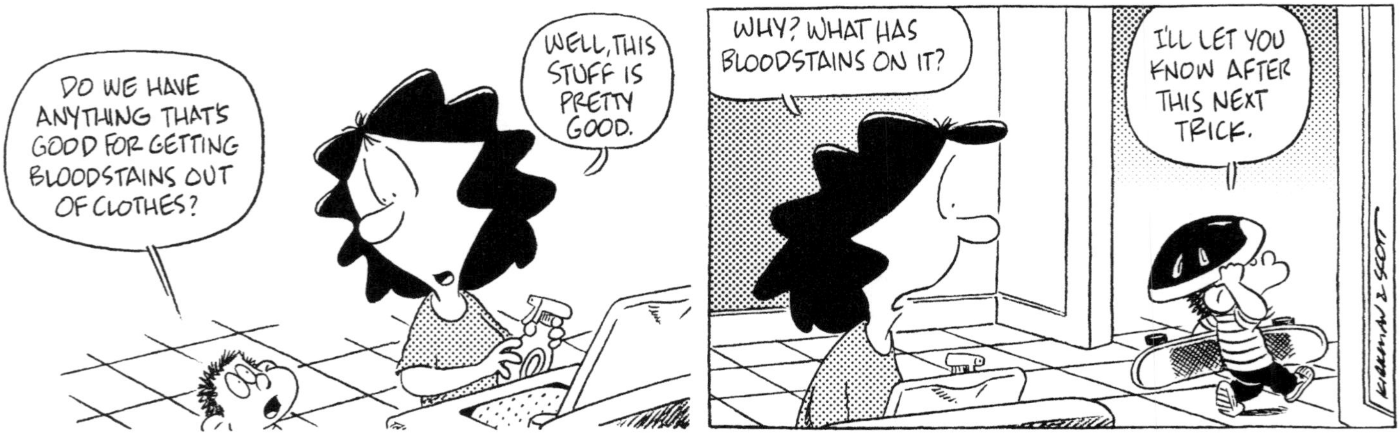
DO WE HAVE ANYTHING THAT'S GOOD FOR GETTING BLOODSTAINS OUT OF CLOTHES?
WELL, THIS STUFF IS PRETTY GOOD.
WHY? WHAT HAS BLOODSTAINS ON IT?
I'LL LET YOU KNOW AFTER THIS NEXT TRICK.
KIRKMAN & SCOTT

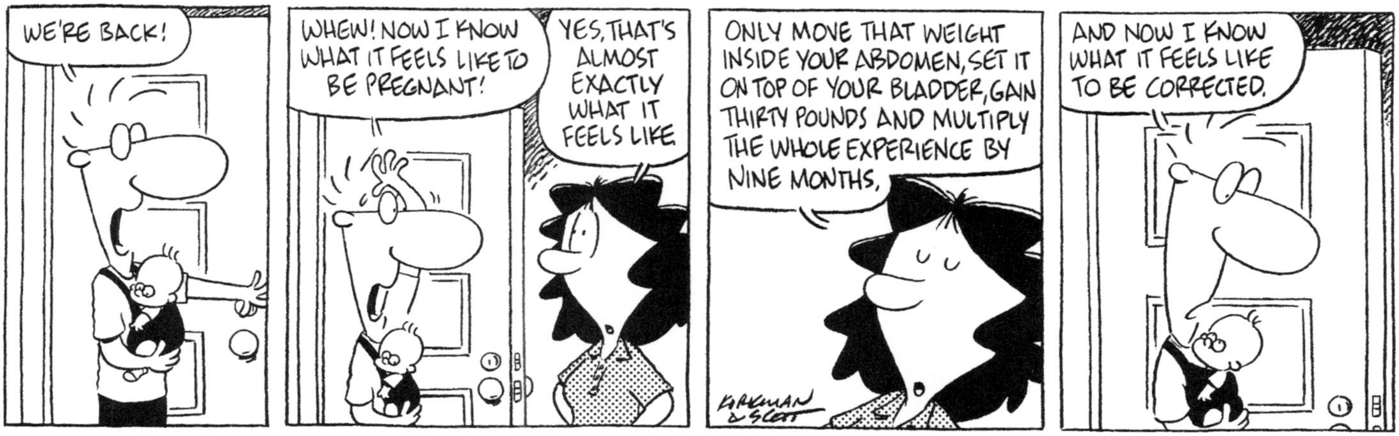
WE'RE BACK!
WHEW! NOW I KNOW WHAT IT FEELS LIKE TO BE PREGNANT!
YES, THAT'S ALMOST EXACTLY WHAT IT FEELS LIKE.
ONLY MOVE THAT WEIGHT INSIDE YOUR ABDOMEN, SET IT ON TOP OF YOUR BLADDER, GAIN THIRTY POUNDS AND MULTIPLY THE WHOLE EXPERIENCE BY NINE MONTHS.
KIRKMAN & SCOTT
AND NOW I KNOW WHAT IT FEELS LIKE TO BE CORRECTED.

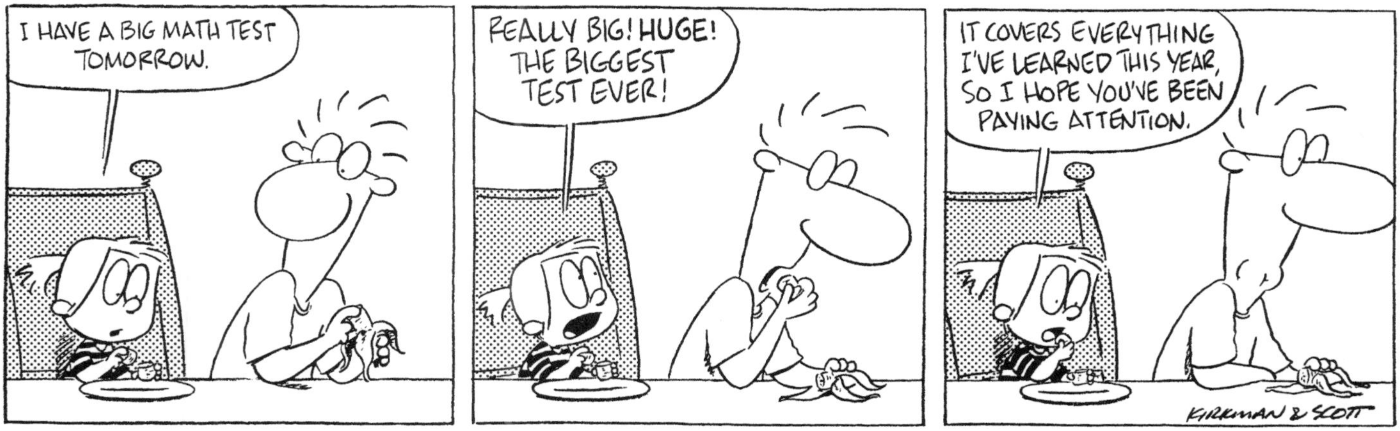
I HAVE A BIG MATH TEST TOMORROW.
REALLY BIG! HUGE! THE BIGGEST TEST EVER!
IT COVERS EVERYTHING I'VE LEARNED THIS YEAR, SO I HOPE YOU'VE BEEN PAYING ATTENTION.
KIRKMAN & SCOTT

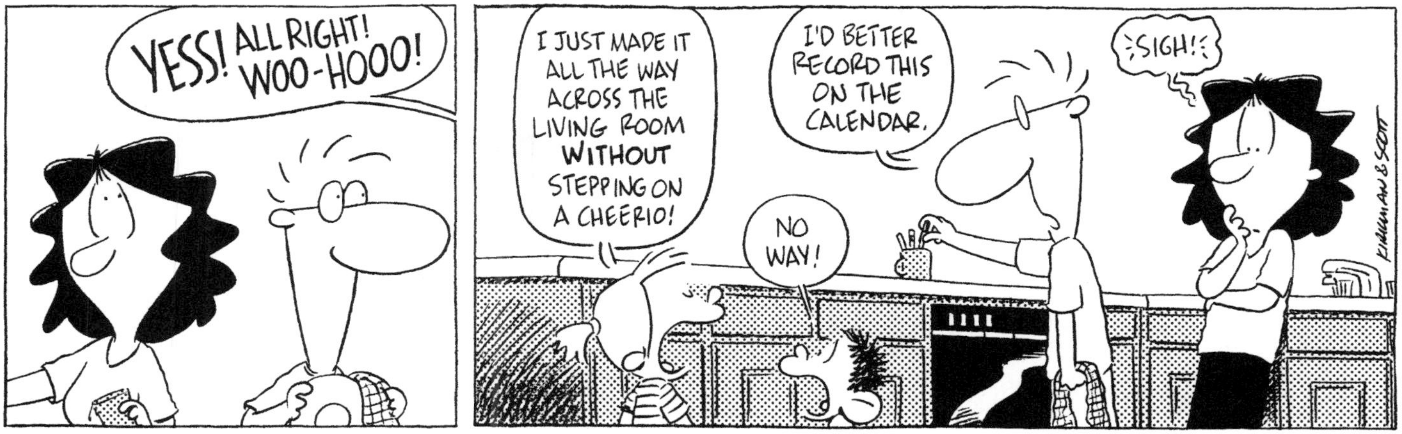
YESS! ALL RIGHT! WOO-HOOO!
I JUST MADE IT ALL THE WAY ACROSS THE LIVING ROOM WITHOUT STEPPING ON A CHEERIO!
NO WAY!
I'D BETTER RECORD THIS ON THE CALENDAR.
SIGH!
KIRKMAN & SCOTT

BABY BLUES
BY KIRKMAN & SCOTT

WOW... LOOK AT ALL THE STARS!
DO YOU LIKE LOOKING AT THE STARS, ZOE?
OH, YEAH!
THAT'S THE BIG DIPPER, RIGHT?
YEP, AND THAT ONE IS ORION, AND THAT MIGHT BE GEMINI.
HOW DID YOU LEARN SO MUCH ABOUT THE STARS, DADDY?
I GOT INTERESTED WHEN I WAS ABOUT YOUR AGE.
AT ONE TIME I WANTED TO BE AN ASTRONOMER.
REALLY? ME TOO!
HEY! WHY DON'T I GET MY STAR MAP SO WE CAN FIND A BUNCH OF STUFF?
YEAH! THAT WOULD BE GREAT!
YOU REALLY WANT TO BE AN ASTRONOMER?
I'LL BE ANYTHING THAT LETS ME STAY UP PAST MY BEDTIME.
KIRKMAN & SCOTT

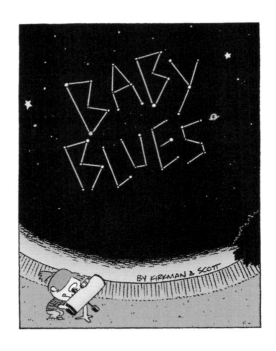

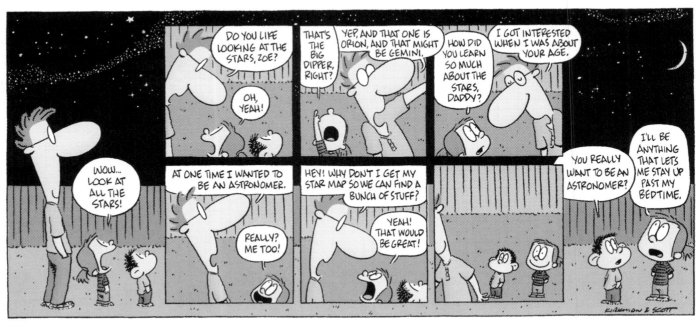

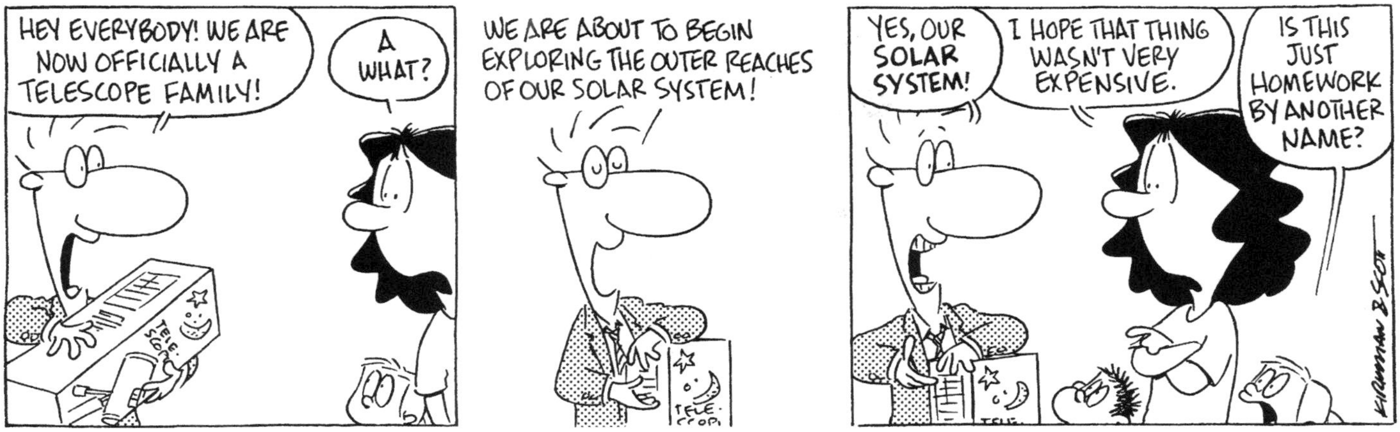
HEY EVERYBODY! WE ARE NOW OFFICIALLY A TELESCOPE FAMILY!
A WHAT?
WE ARE ABOUT TO BEGIN EXPLORING THE OUTER REACHES OF OUR SOLAR SYSTEM!
YES, OUR **SOLAR SYSTEM!**
I HOPE THAT THING WASN'T VERY EXPENSIVE.
IS THIS JUST HOMEWORK BY ANOTHER NAME?

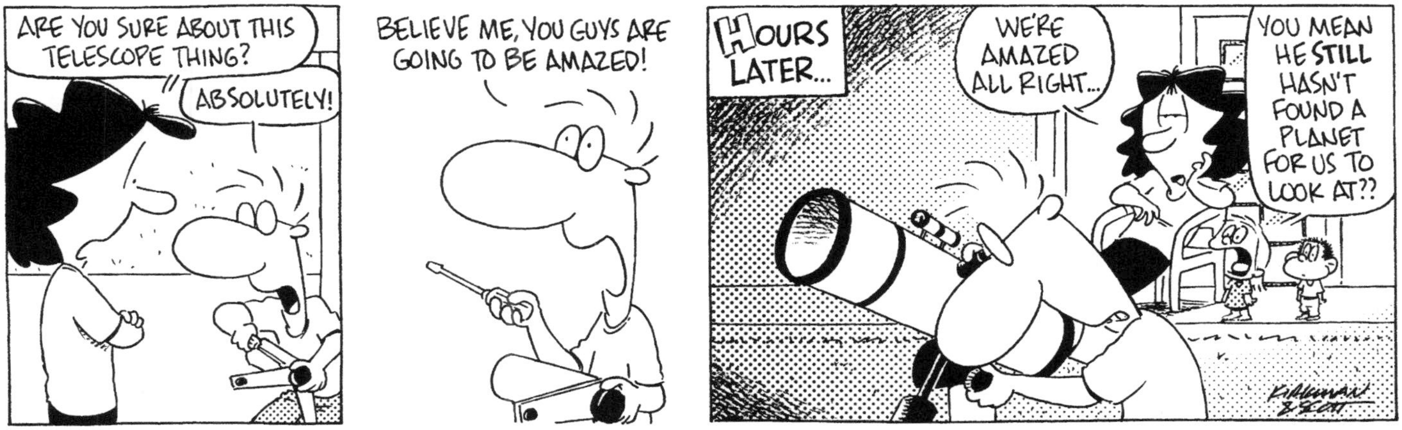
ARE YOU SURE ABOUT THIS TELESCOPE THING?
ABSOLUTELY!
BELIEVE ME, YOU GUYS ARE GOING TO BE AMAZED!
HOURS LATER...
WE'RE AMAZED ALL RIGHT...
YOU MEAN HE **STILL** HASN'T FOUND A PLANET FOR US TO LOOK AT??

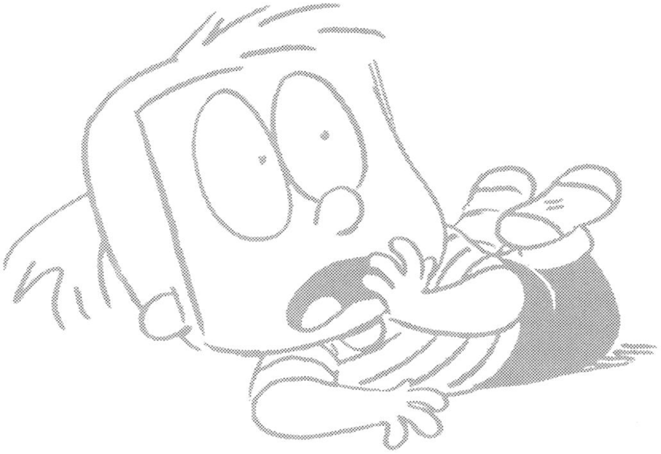

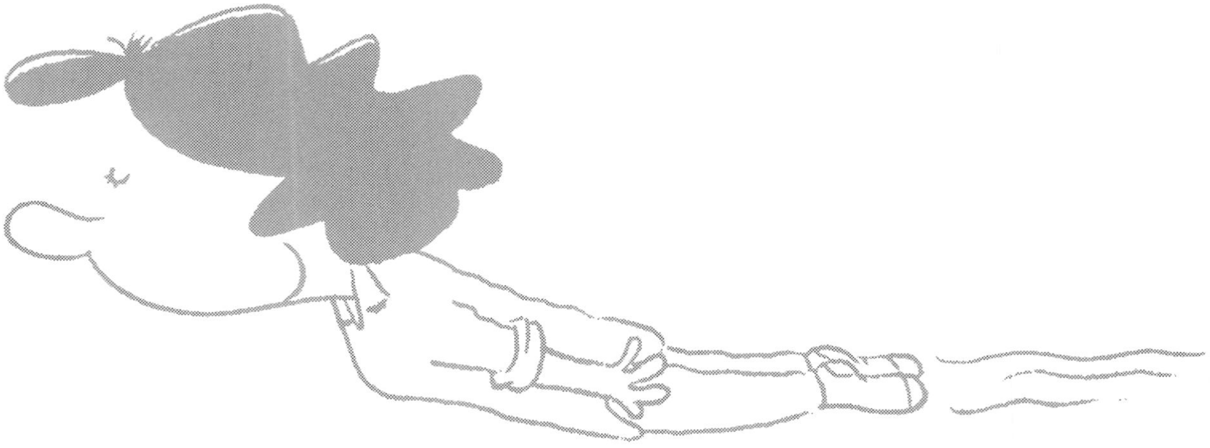

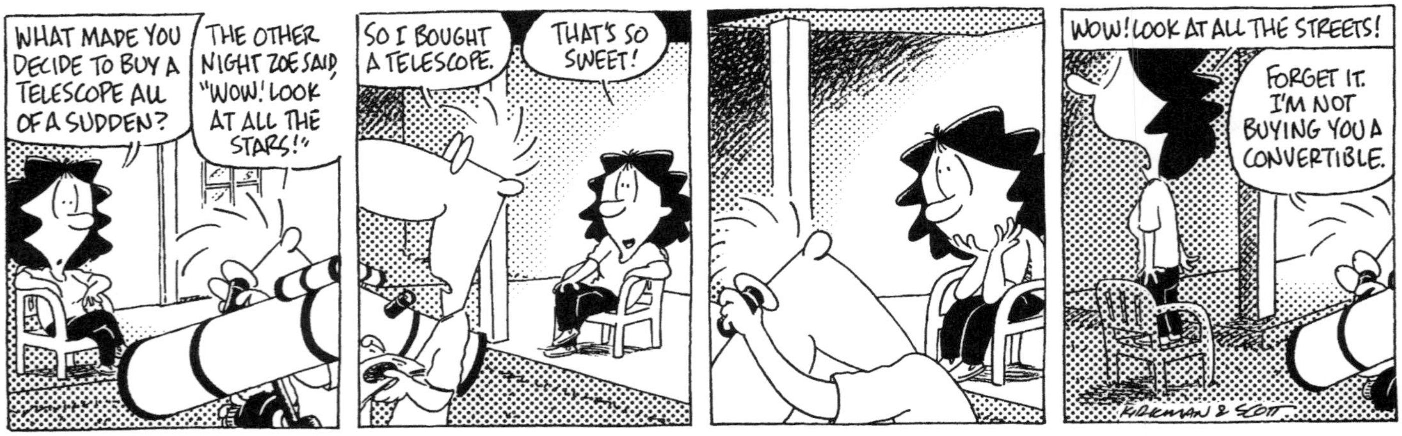

WHAT MADE YOU DECIDE TO BUY A TELESCOPE ALL OF A SUDDEN?
THE OTHER NIGHT ZOE SAID, "WOW! LOOK AT ALL THE STARS!"
SO I BOUGHT A TELESCOPE.
THAT'S SO SWEET!
WOW! LOOK AT ALL THE STREETS!
FORGET IT. I'M NOT BUYING YOU A CONVERTIBLE.
KIRKMAN & SCOTT

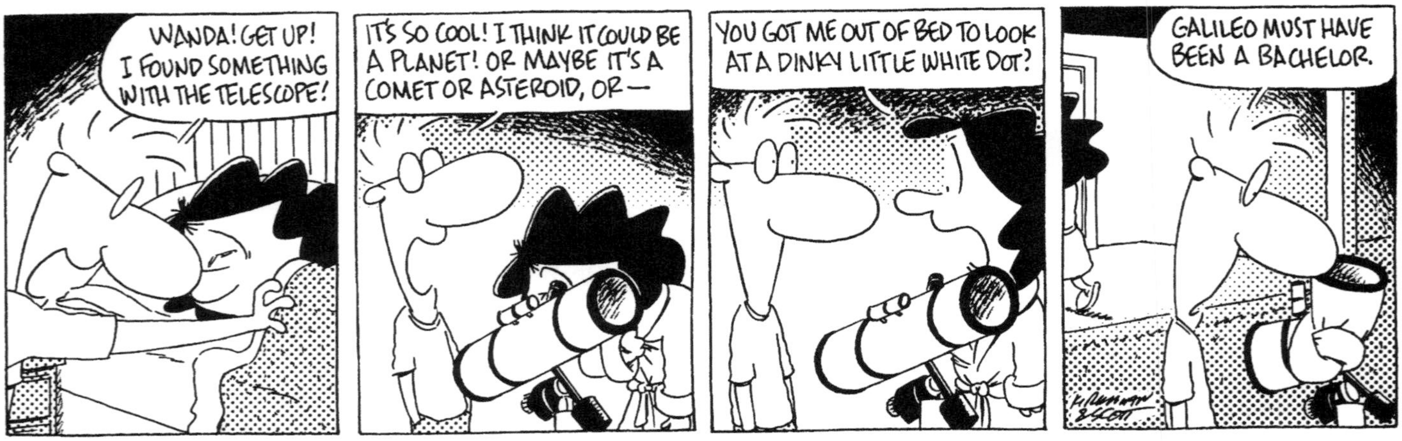

WANDA! GET UP! I FOUND SOMETHING WITH THE TELESCOPE!
IT'S SO COOL! I THINK IT COULD BE A PLANET! OR MAYBE IT'S A COMET OR ASTEROID, OR—
YOU GOT ME OUT OF BED TO LOOK AT A DINKY LITTLE WHITE DOT?
GALILEO MUST HAVE BEEN A BACHELOR.
KIRKMAN & SCOTT

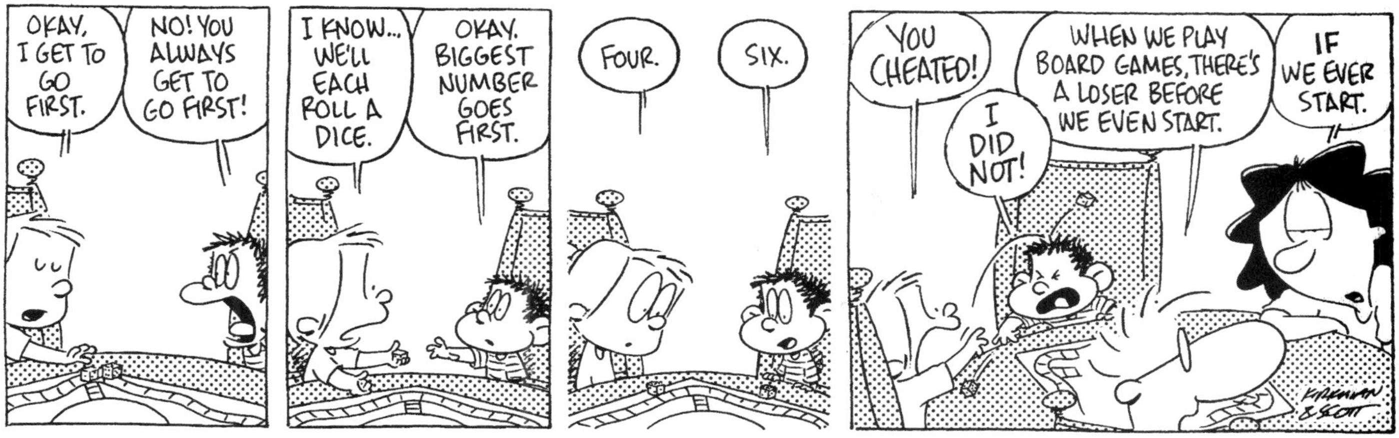
OKAY, I GET TO GO FIRST.
NO! YOU ALWAYS GET TO GO FIRST!
I KNOW... WE'LL EACH ROLL A DICE.
OKAY. BIGGEST NUMBER GOES FIRST.
FOUR.
SIX.
YOU CHEATED!
I DID NOT!
WHEN WE PLAY BOARD GAMES, THERE'S A LOSER BEFORE WE EVEN START.
IF WE EVER START.
KIRKMAN & SCOTT

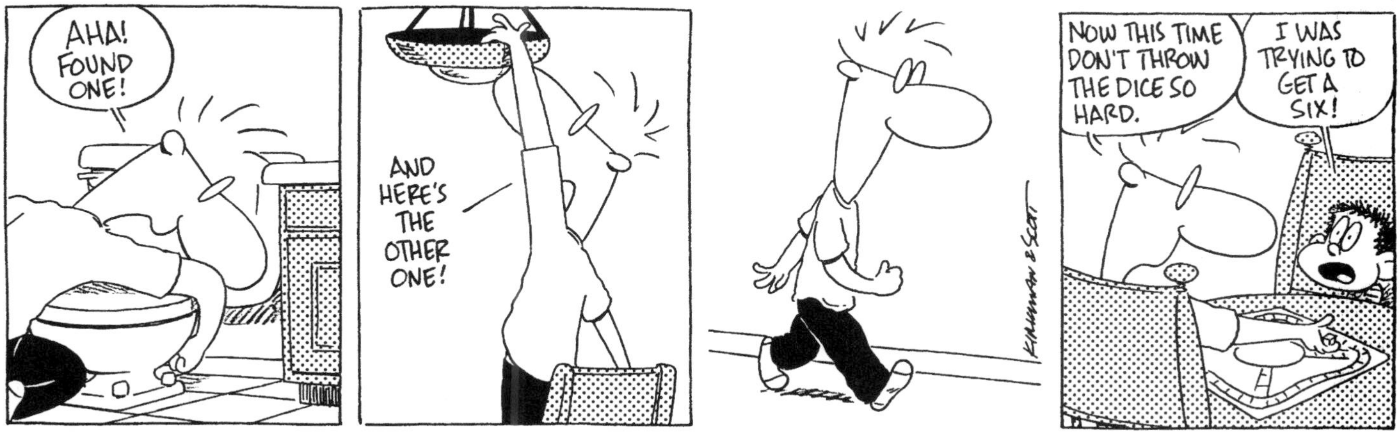
AHA! FOUND ONE!
AND HERE'S THE OTHER ONE!
KIRKMAN & SCOTT
NOW THIS TIME DON'T THROW THE DICE SO HARD.
I WAS TRYING TO GET A SIX!

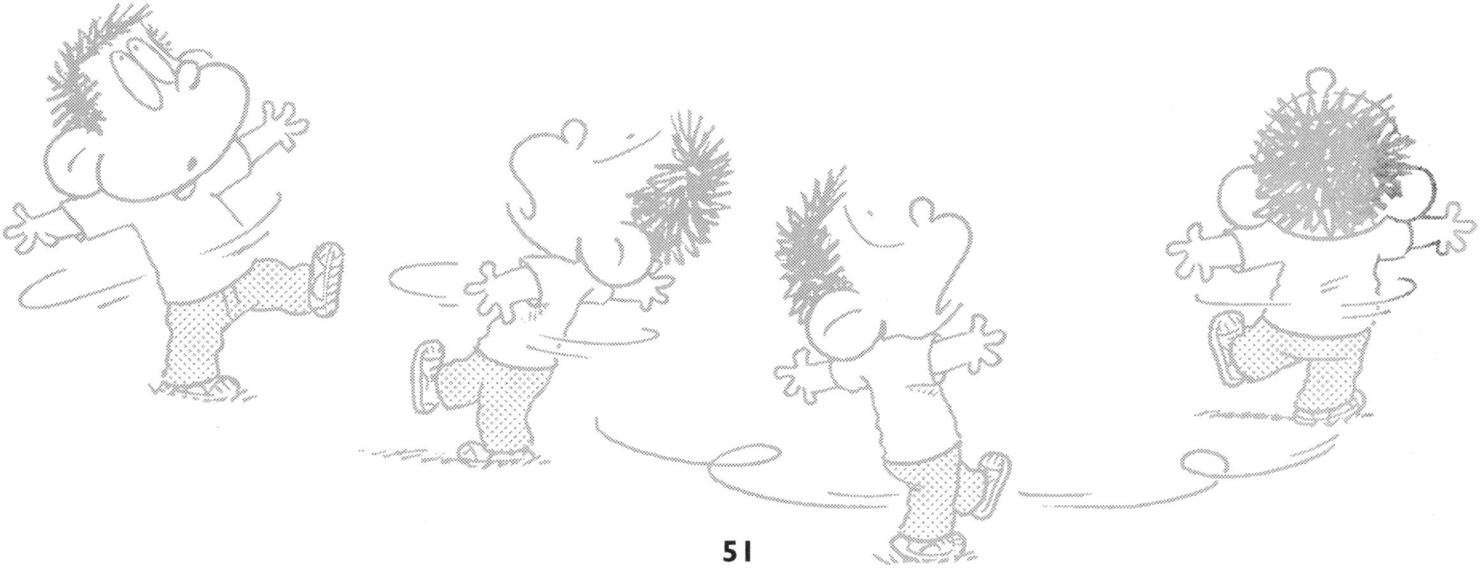

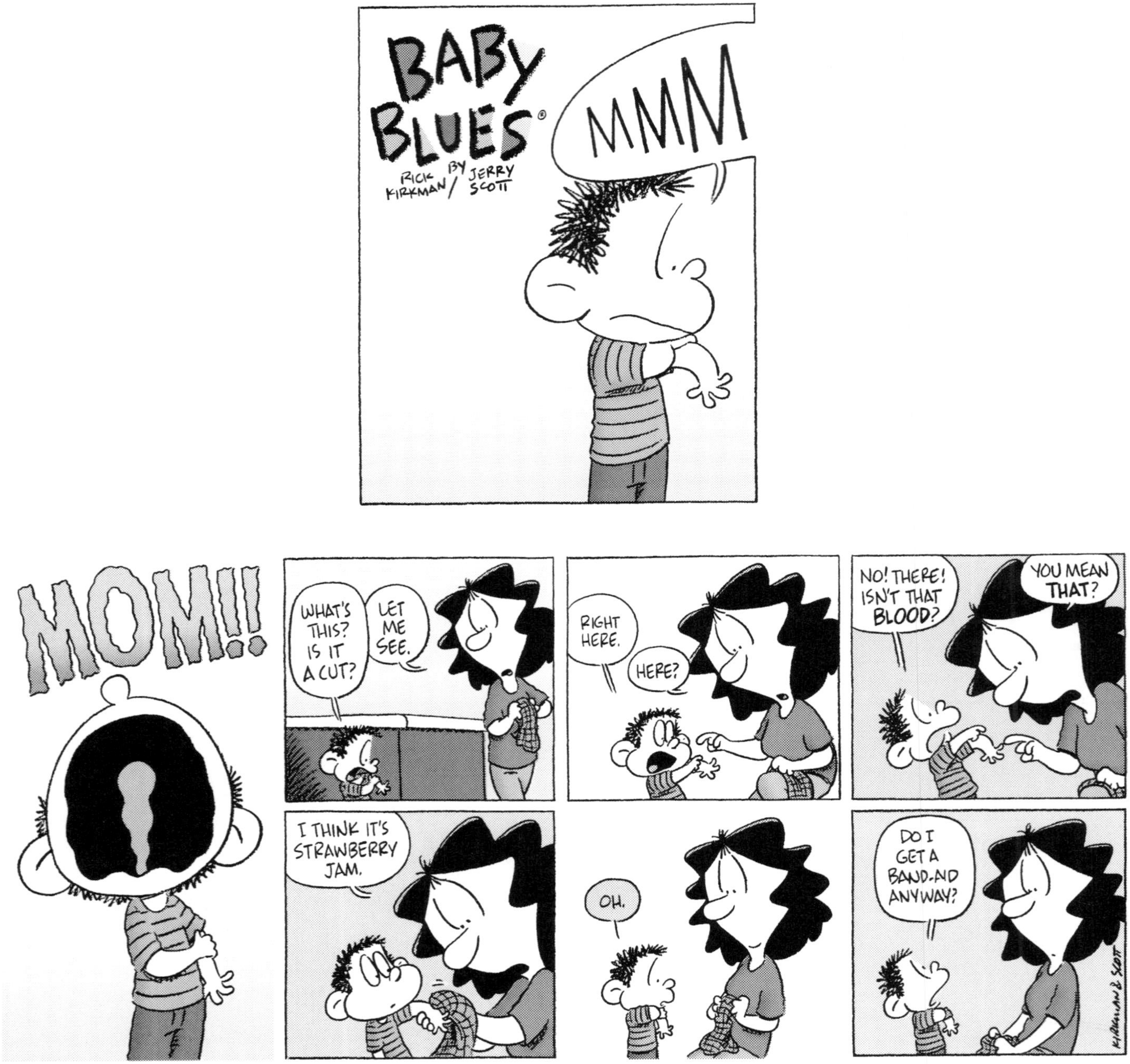
BABY BLUES®
RICK KIRKMAN / BY JERRY SCOTT
MMM
MOM!!
WHAT'S THIS? IS IT A CUT?
LET ME SEE.
RIGHT HERE.
HERE?
NO! THERE! ISN'T THAT BLOOD?
YOU MEAN THAT?
I THINK IT'S STRAWBERRY JAM.
OH.
DO I GET A BAND-AID ANYWAY?
KIRKMAN & SCOTT

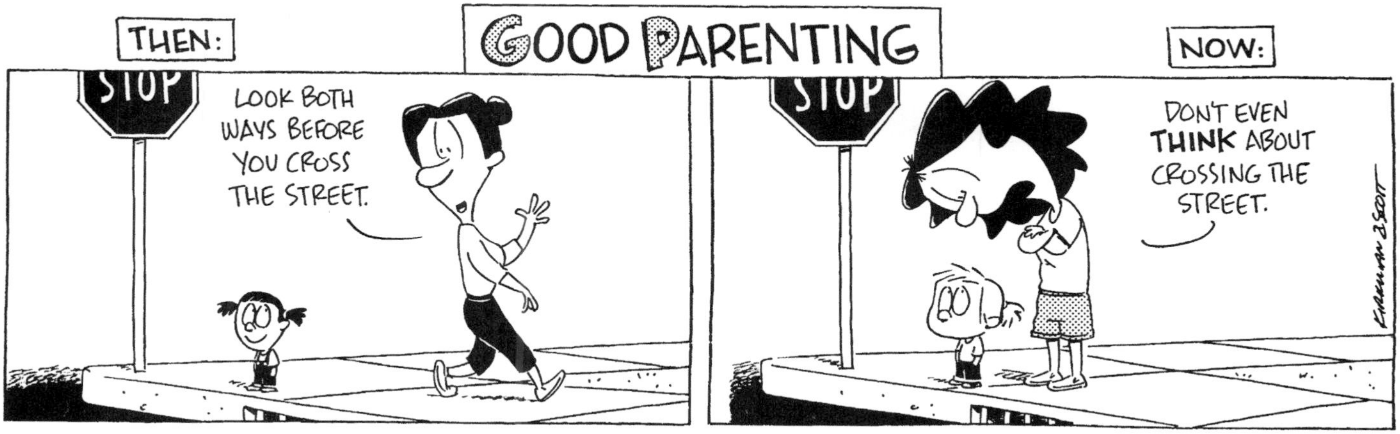
THEN:
GOOD PARENTING
NOW:
STOP
LOOK BOTH WAYS BEFORE YOU CROSS THE STREET.
STOP
DON'T EVEN THINK ABOUT CROSSING THE STREET.
KIRKMAN & SCOTT

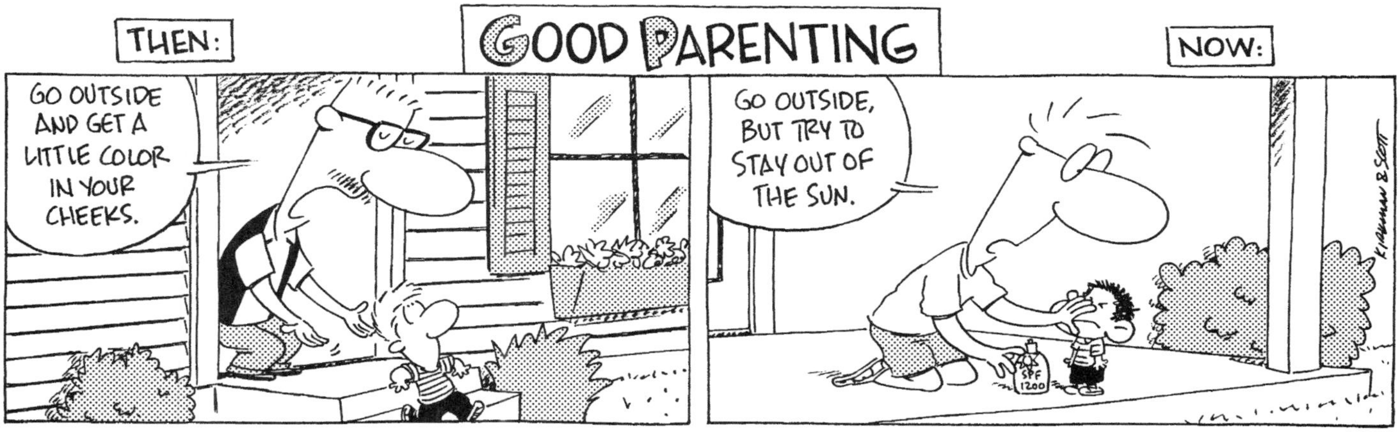
THEN:
GOOD PARENTING
NOW:
GO OUTSIDE AND GET A LITTLE COLOR IN YOUR CHEEKS.
GO OUTSIDE, BUT TRY TO STAY OUT OF THE SUN.
SPF 1200
KIRKMAN & SCOTT

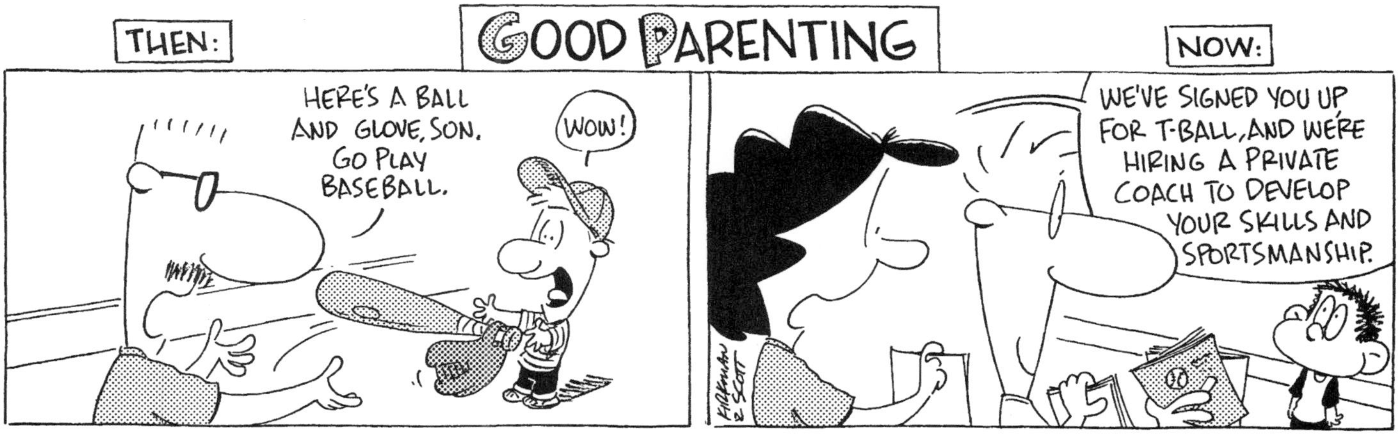
THEN:
GOOD PARENTING
NOW:
HERE'S A BALL AND GLOVE, SON. GO PLAY BASEBALL.
WOW!
WE'VE SIGNED YOU UP FOR T-BALL, AND WE'RE HIRING A PRIVATE COACH TO DEVELOP YOUR SKILLS AND SPORTSMANSHIP.
KIRKMAN & SCOTT

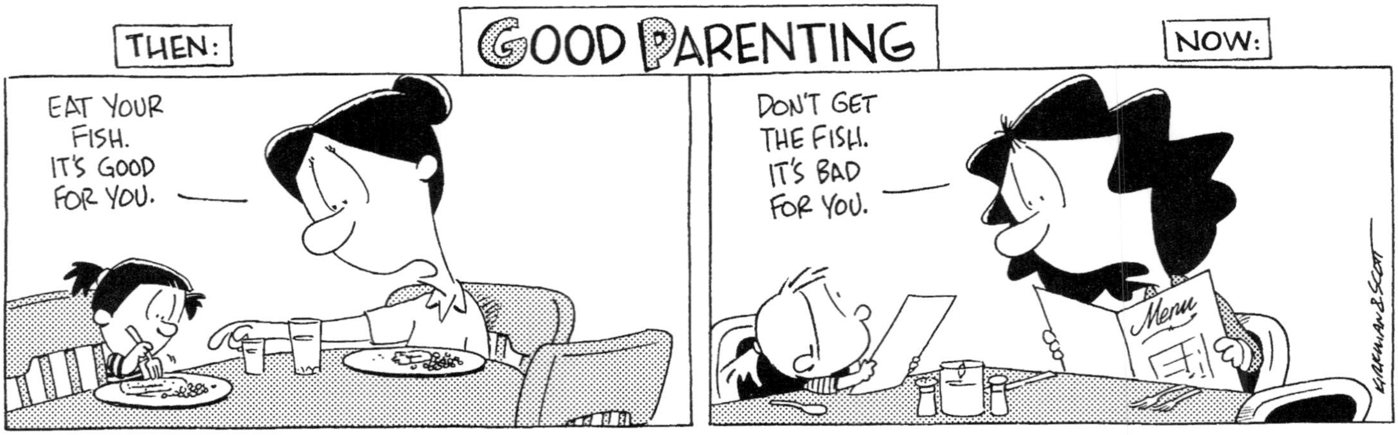
THEN:
GOOD PARENTING
NOW:
EAT YOUR FISH. IT'S GOOD FOR YOU.
DON'T GET THE FISH. IT'S BAD FOR YOU.
Menu

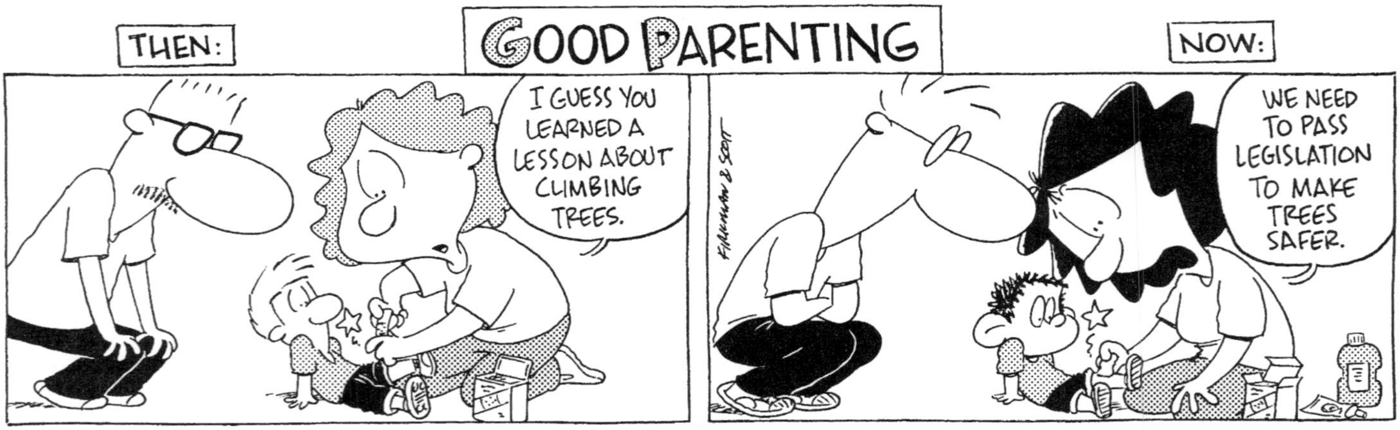
THEN:
GOOD PARENTING
NOW:
I GUESS YOU LEARNED A LESSON ABOUT CLIMBING TREES.
WE NEED TO PASS LEGISLATION TO MAKE TREES SAFER.

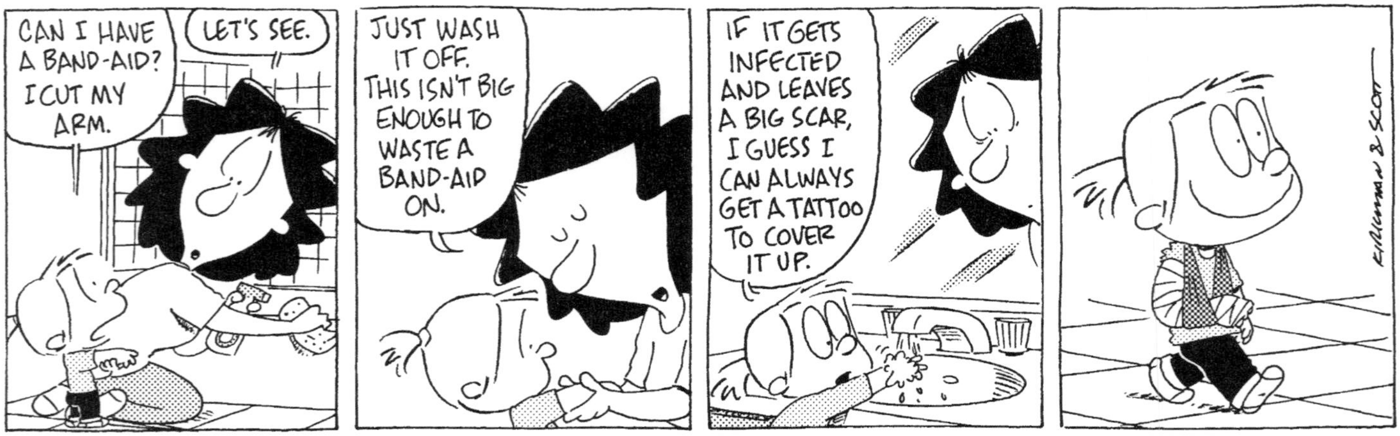
CAN I HAVE A BAND-AID? I CUT MY ARM.
LET'S SEE.
JUST WASH IT OFF. THIS ISN'T BIG ENOUGH TO WASTE A BAND-AID ON.
IF IT GETS INFECTED AND LEAVES A BIG SCAR, I GUESS I CAN ALWAYS GET A TATTOO TO COVER IT UP.

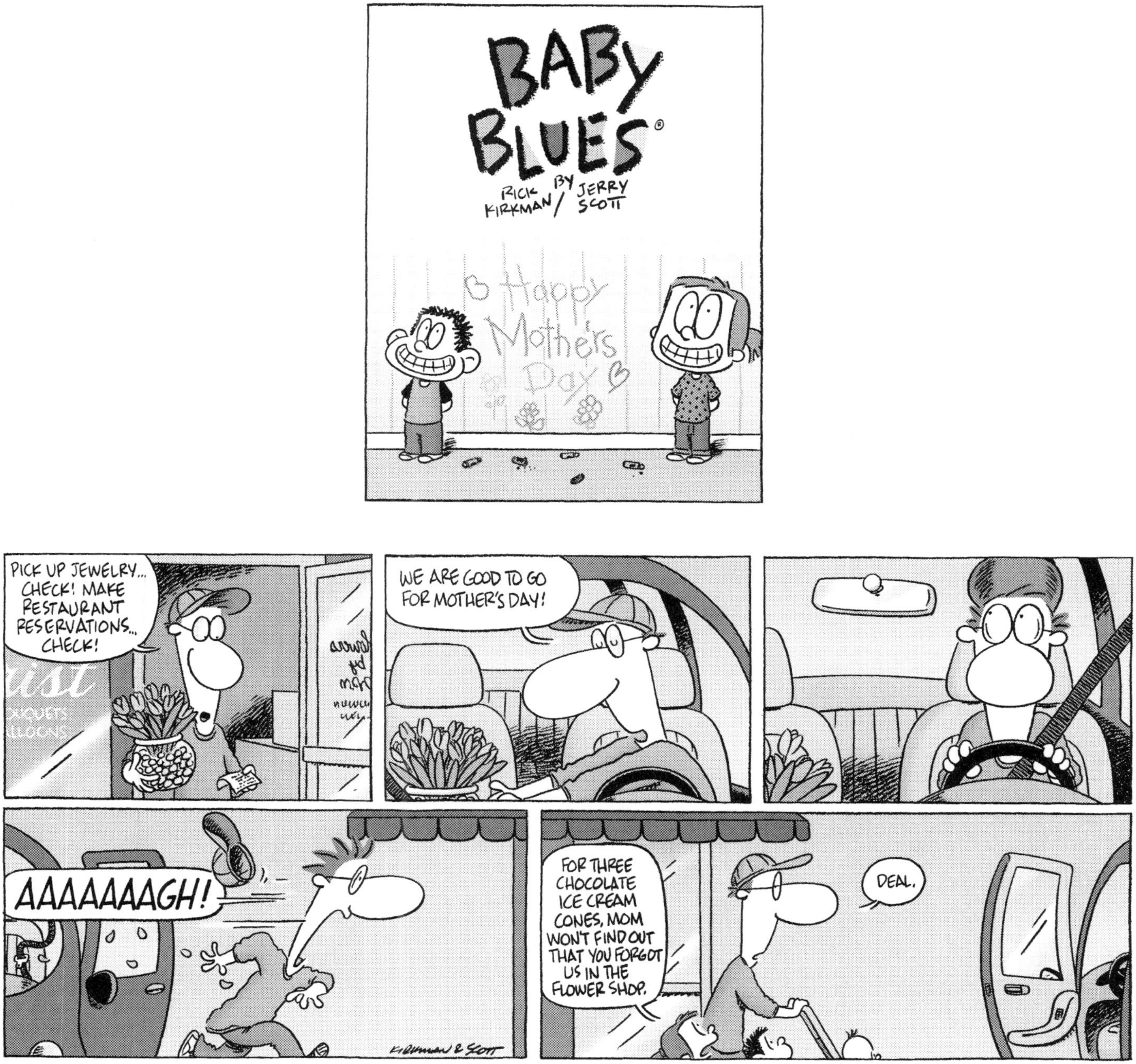
BABY BLUES®
BY RICK KIRKMAN / JERRY SCOTT
Happy Mother's Day
PICK UP JEWELRY... CHECK! MAKE RESTAURANT RESERVATIONS... CHECK!
WE ARE GOOD TO GO FOR MOTHER'S DAY!
AAAAAAAGH!
FOR THREE CHOCOLATE ICE CREAM CONES, MOM WON'T FIND OUT THAT YOU FORGOT US IN THE FLOWER SHOP.
DEAL.
KIRKMAN & SCOTT

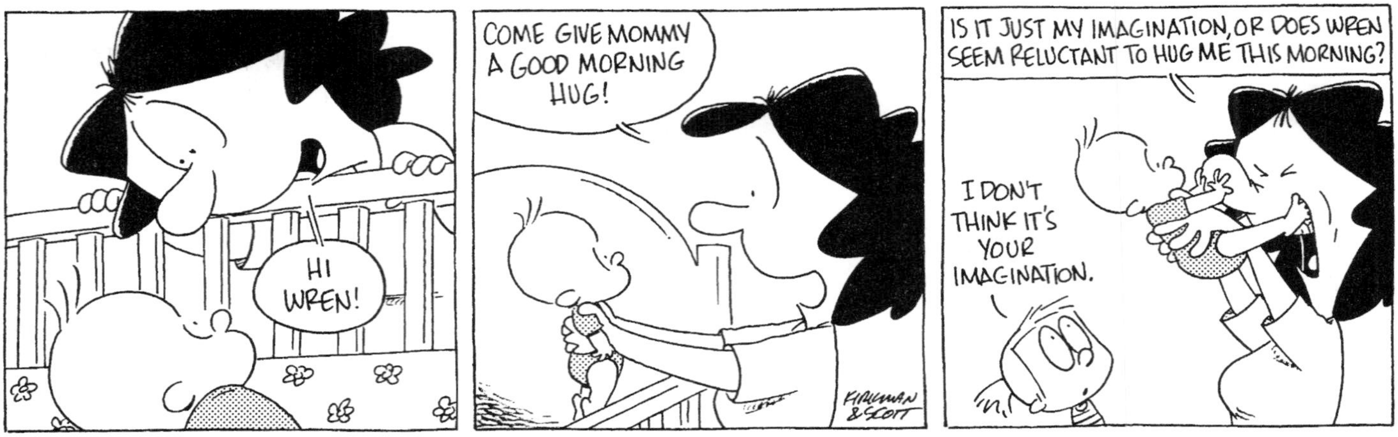
HI WREN!
COME GIVE MOMMY A GOOD MORNING HUG!
KIRKMAN & SCOTT
IS IT JUST MY IMAGINATION, OR DOES WREN SEEM RELUCTANT TO HUG ME THIS MORNING?
I DON'T THINK IT'S YOUR IMAGINATION.

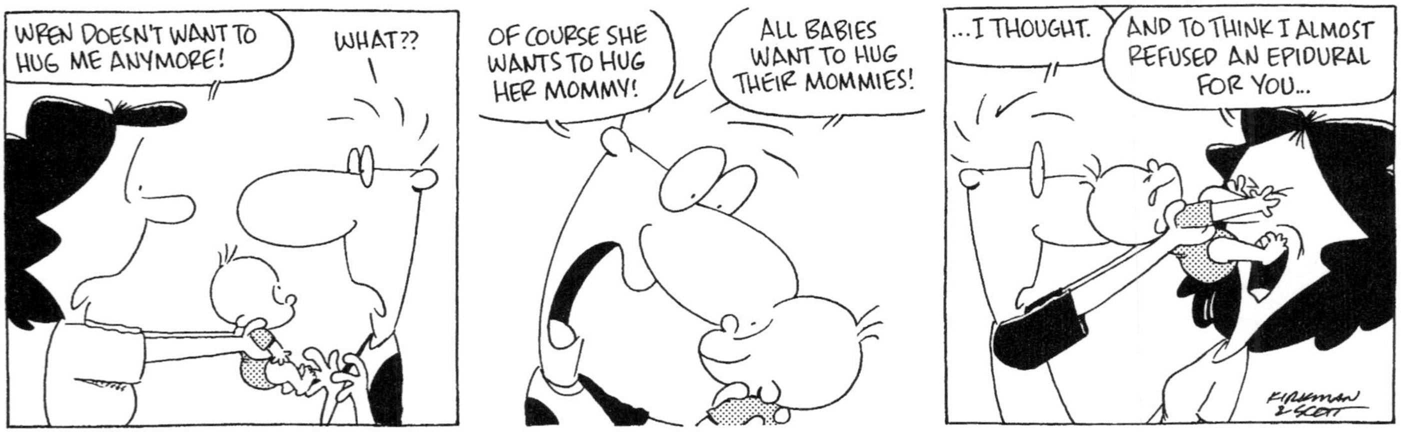
WREN DOESN'T WANT TO HUG ME ANYMORE!
WHAT??
OF COURSE SHE WANTS TO HUG HER MOMMY!
ALL BABIES WANT TO HUG THEIR MOMMIES!
...I THOUGHT.
AND TO THINK I ALMOST REFUSED AN EPIDURAL FOR YOU...
KIRKMAN & SCOTT

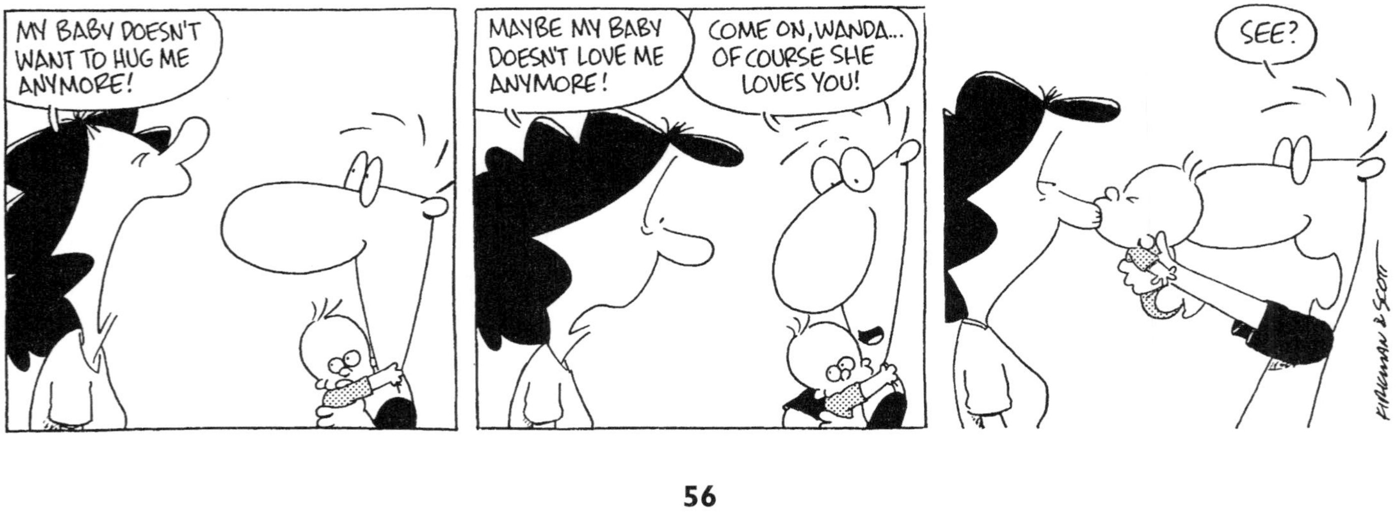
MY BABY DOESN'T WANT TO HUG ME ANYMORE!
MAYBE MY BABY DOESN'T LOVE ME ANYMORE!
COME ON, WANDA... OF COURSE SHE LOVES YOU!
SEE?
KIRKMAN & SCOTT

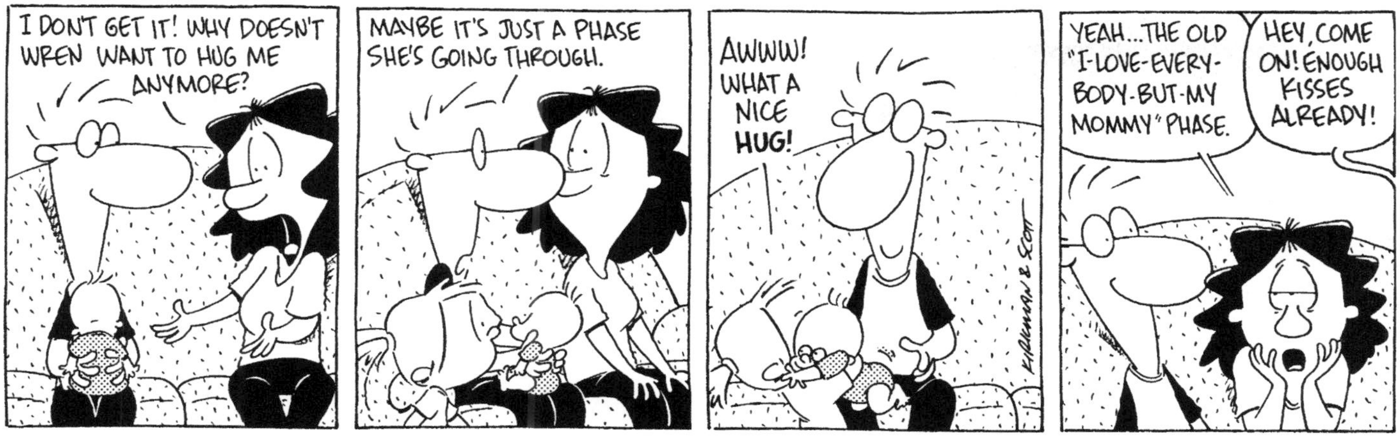
I DON'T GET IT! WHY DOESN'T WREN WANT TO HUG ME ANYMORE?
MAYBE IT'S JUST A PHASE SHE'S GOING THROUGH.
AWWW! WHAT A NICE HUG!
KIRKMAN & SCOTT
YEAH... THE OLD "I-LOVE-EVERY-BODY-BUT-MY MOMMY" PHASE.
HEY, COME ON! ENOUGH KISSES ALREADY!

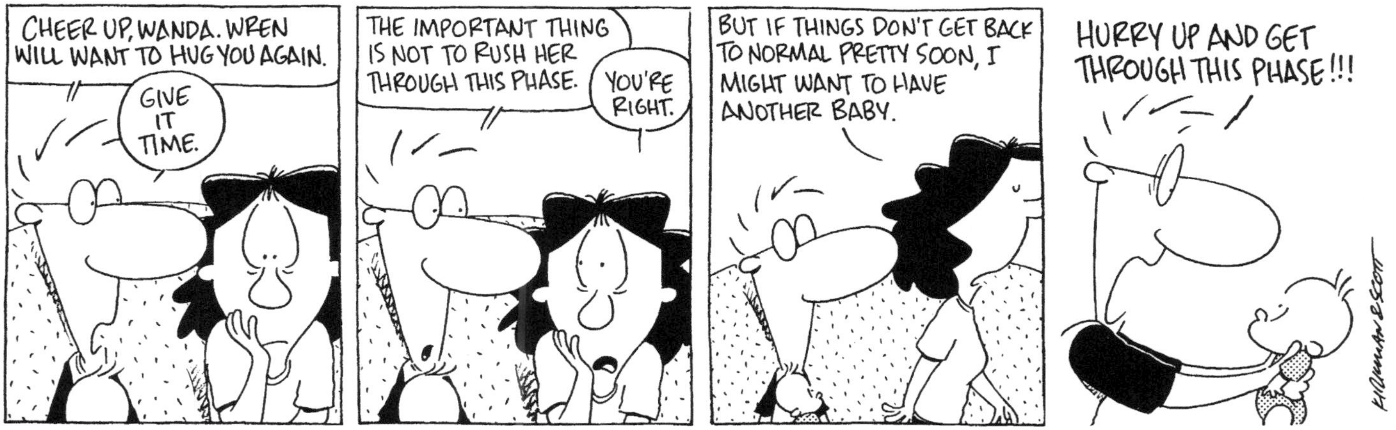
CHEER UP, WANDA. WREN WILL WANT TO HUG YOU AGAIN.
GIVE IT TIME.
THE IMPORTANT THING IS NOT TO RUSH HER THROUGH THIS PHASE.
YOU'RE RIGHT.
BUT IF THINGS DON'T GET BACK TO NORMAL PRETTY SOON, I MIGHT WANT TO HAVE ANOTHER BABY.
HURRY UP AND GET THROUGH THIS PHASE!!!
KIRKMAN & SCOTT

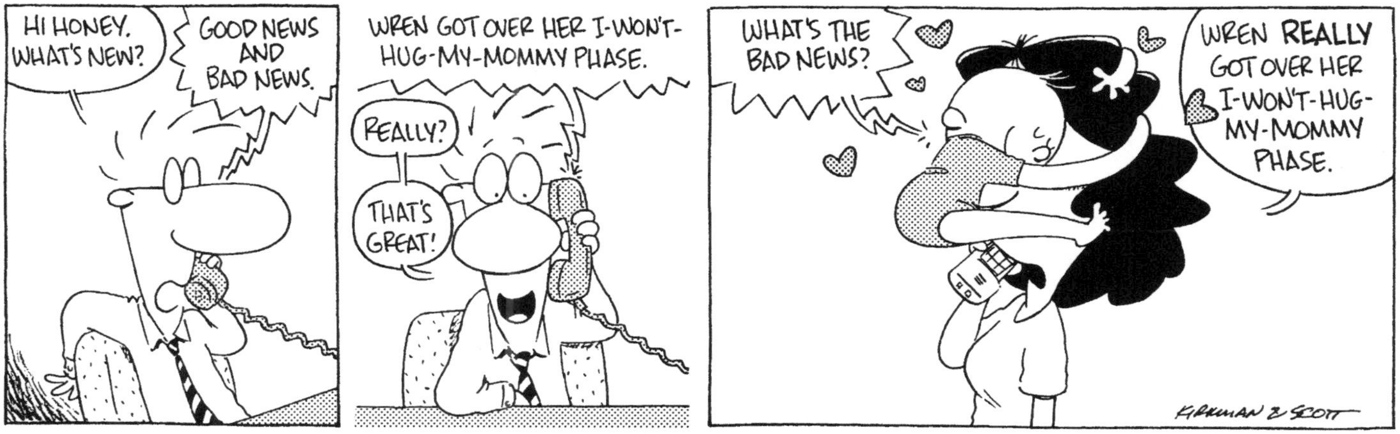
HI HONEY. WHAT'S NEW?
GOOD NEWS AND BAD NEWS.
WREN GOT OVER HER I-WON'T-HUG-MY-MOMMY PHASE.
REALLY?
THAT'S GREAT!
WHAT'S THE BAD NEWS?
WREN REALLY GOT OVER HER I-WON'T-HUG-MY-MOMMY PHASE.
KIRKMAN & SCOTT

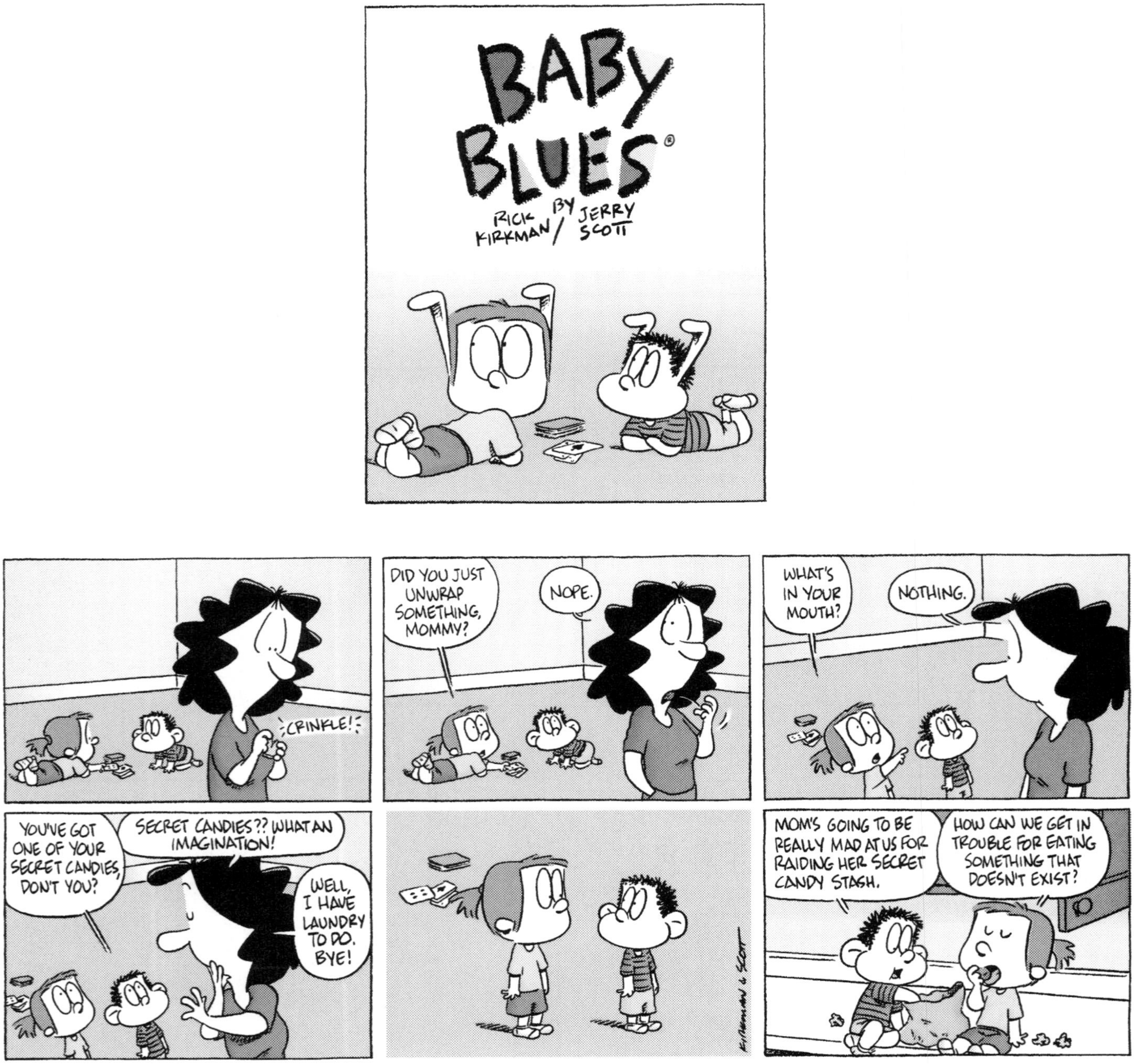
BABY BLUES®
BY RICK KIRKMAN / JERRY SCOTT
CRINKLE!
DID YOU JUST UNWRAP SOMETHING, MOMMY?
NOPE.
WHAT'S IN YOUR MOUTH?
NOTHING.
YOU'VE GOT ONE OF YOUR SECRET CANDIES, DON'T YOU?
SECRET CANDIES?? WHAT AN IMAGINATION!
WELL, I HAVE LAUNDRY TO DO. BYE!
MOM'S GOING TO BE REALLY MAD AT US FOR RAIDING HER SECRET CANDY STASH.
HOW CAN WE GET IN TROUBLE FOR EATING SOMETHING THAT DOESN'T EXIST?

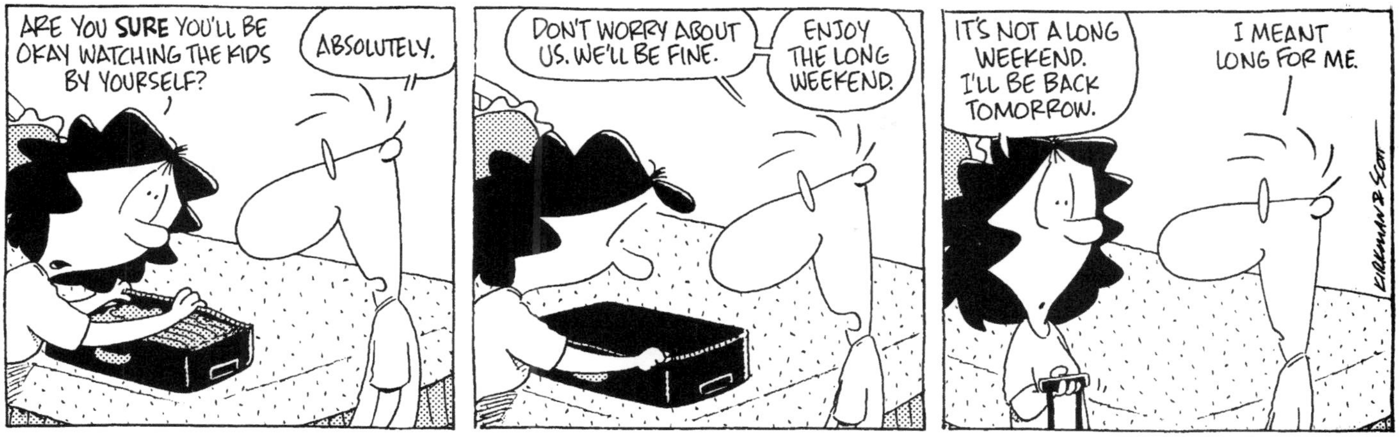
ARE YOU **SURE** YOU'LL BE OKAY WATCHING THE KIDS BY YOURSELF?
ABSOLUTELY.
DON'T WORRY ABOUT US. WE'LL BE FINE.
ENJOY THE LONG WEEKEND.
IT'S NOT A LONG WEEKEND. I'LL BE BACK TOMORROW.
I MEANT LONG FOR ME.
KIRKMAN & SCOTT

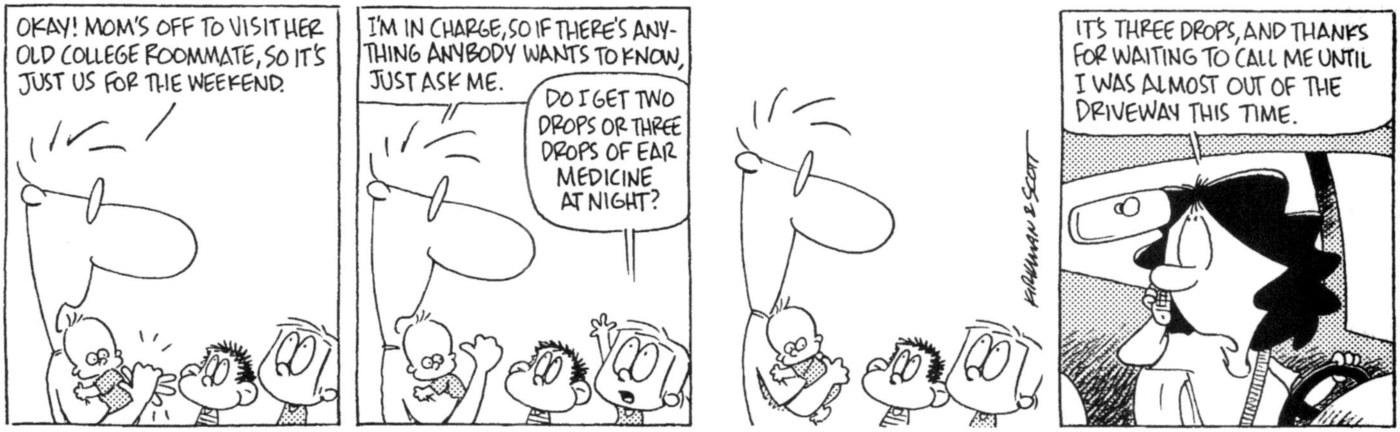
OKAY! MOM'S OFF TO VISIT HER OLD COLLEGE ROOMMATE, SO IT'S JUST US FOR THE WEEKEND.
I'M IN CHARGE, SO IF THERE'S ANYTHING ANYBODY WANTS TO KNOW, JUST ASK ME.
DO I GET TWO DROPS OR THREE DROPS OF EAR MEDICINE AT NIGHT?
KIRKMAN & SCOTT
IT'S THREE DROPS, AND THANKS FOR WAITING TO CALL ME UNTIL I WAS ALMOST OUT OF THE DRIVEWAY THIS TIME.

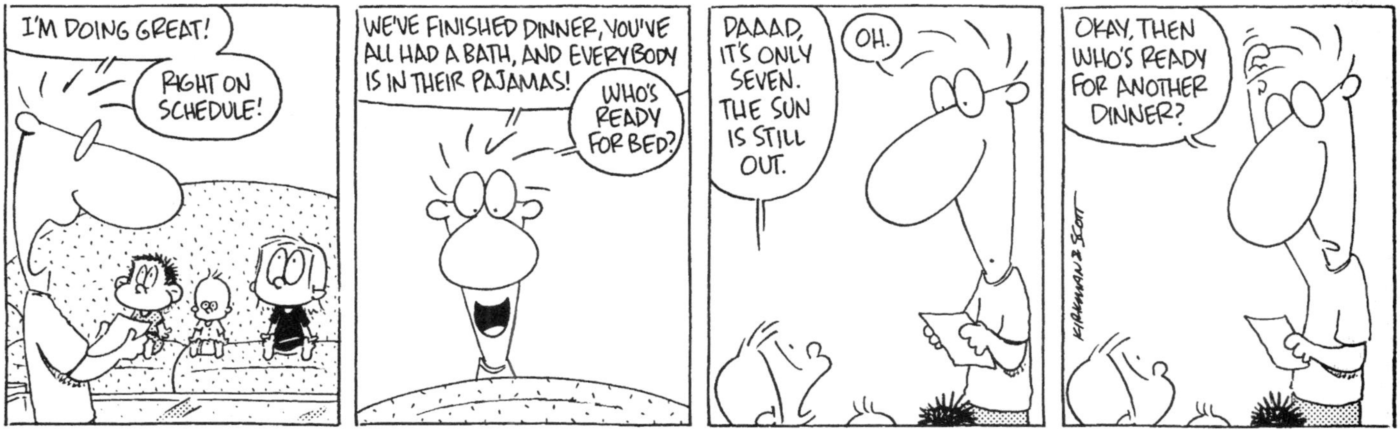
I'M DOING GREAT!
RIGHT ON SCHEDULE!
WE'VE FINISHED DINNER, YOU'VE ALL HAD A BATH, AND EVERYBODY IS IN THEIR PAJAMAS!
WHO'S READY FOR BED?
DAAAD, IT'S ONLY SEVEN. THE SUN IS STILL OUT.
OH.
KIRKMAN & SCOTT
OKAY, THEN WHO'S READY FOR ANOTHER DINNER?

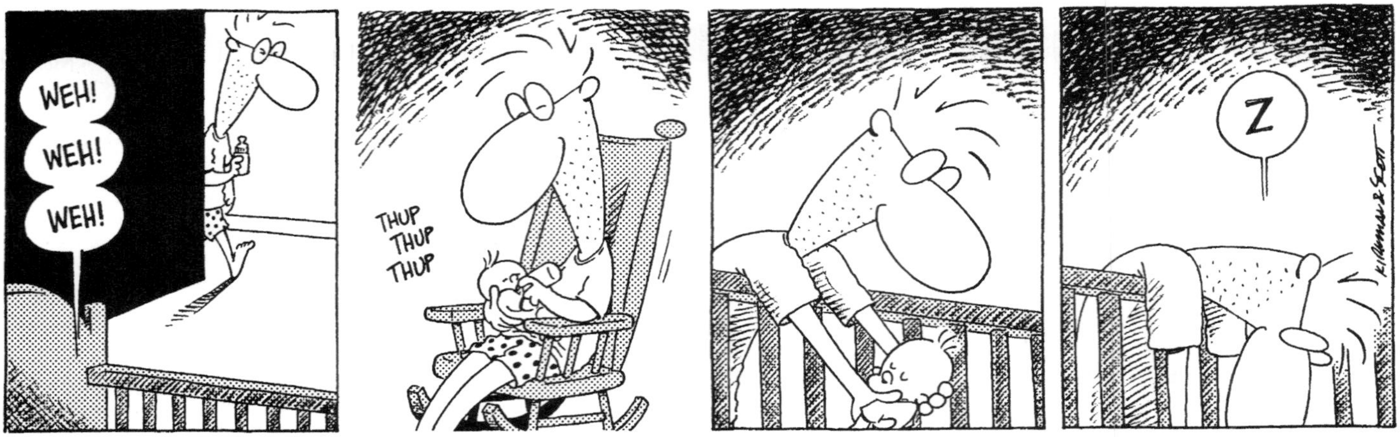
WEH!
WEH!
WEH!
THUP
THUP
THUP
Z

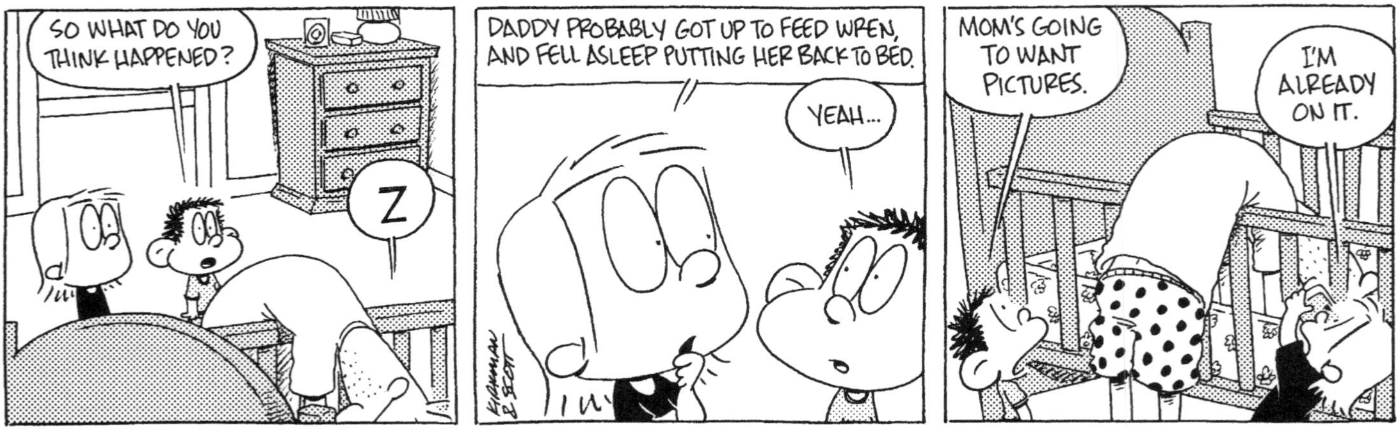
SO WHAT DO YOU THINK HAPPENED?
Z
DADDY PROBABLY GOT UP TO FEED WREN, AND FELL ASLEEP PUTTING HER BACK TO BED.
YEAH...
MOM'S GOING TO WANT PICTURES.
I'M ALREADY ON IT.

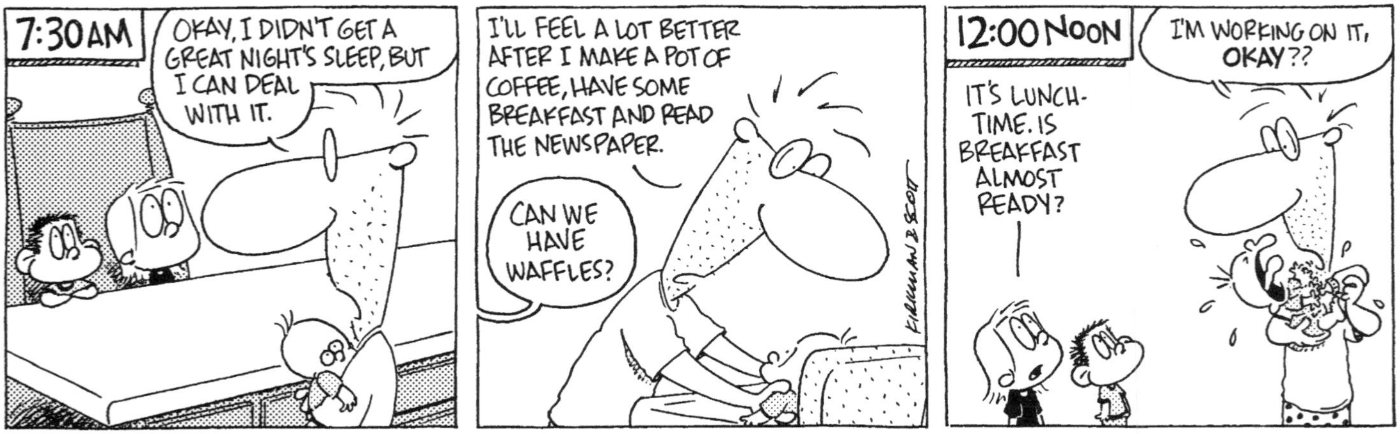
7:30 AM
OKAY, I DIDN'T GET A GREAT NIGHT'S SLEEP, BUT I CAN DEAL WITH IT.
I'LL FEEL A LOT BETTER AFTER I MAKE A POT OF COFFEE, HAVE SOME BREAKFAST AND READ THE NEWSPAPER.
CAN WE HAVE WAFFLES?
12:00 NOON
IT'S LUNCH-TIME. IS BREAKFAST ALMOST READY?
I'M WORKING ON IT, OKAY??

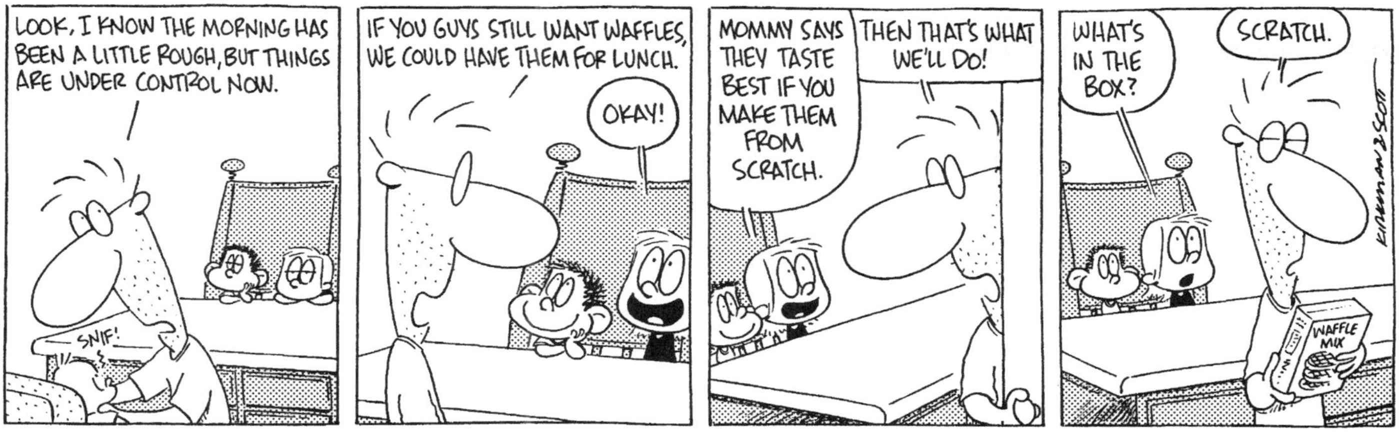
LOOK, I KNOW THE MORNING HAS BEEN A LITTLE ROUGH, BUT THINGS ARE UNDER CONTROL NOW.
SNIF!
IF YOU GUYS STILL WANT WAFFLES, WE COULD HAVE THEM FOR LUNCH.
OKAY!
MOMMY SAYS THEY TASTE BEST IF YOU MAKE THEM FROM SCRATCH.
THEN THAT'S WHAT WE'LL DO!
WHAT'S IN THE BOX?
SCRATCH.
WAFFLE MIX

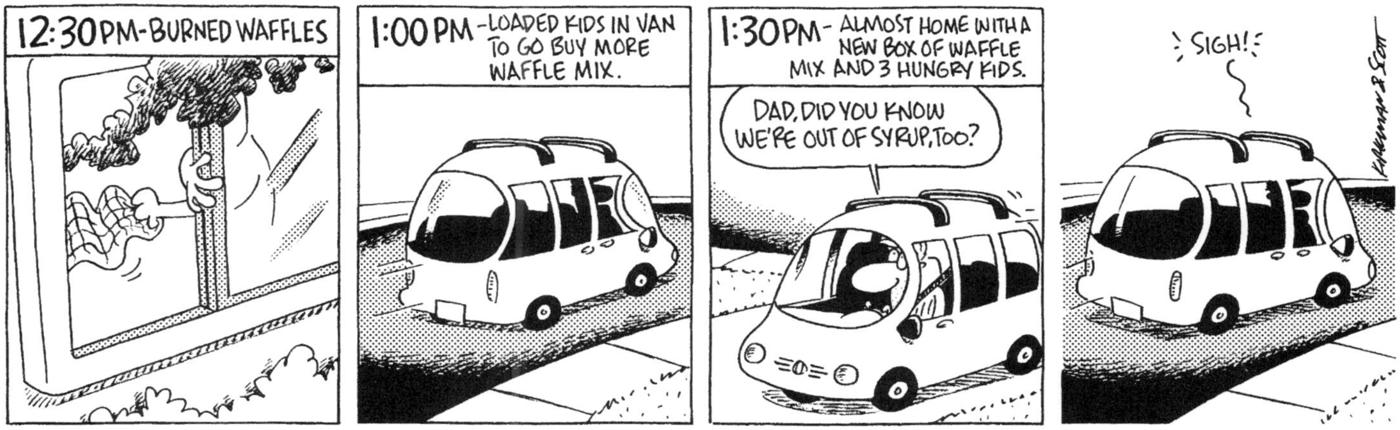
12:30 PM-BURNED WAFFLES
1:00 PM-LOADED KIDS IN VAN TO GO BUY MORE WAFFLE MIX.
1:30 PM- ALMOST HOME WITH A NEW BOX OF WAFFLE MIX AND 3 HUNGRY KIDS.
DAD, DID YOU KNOW WE'RE OUT OF SYRUP, TOO?
SIGH!

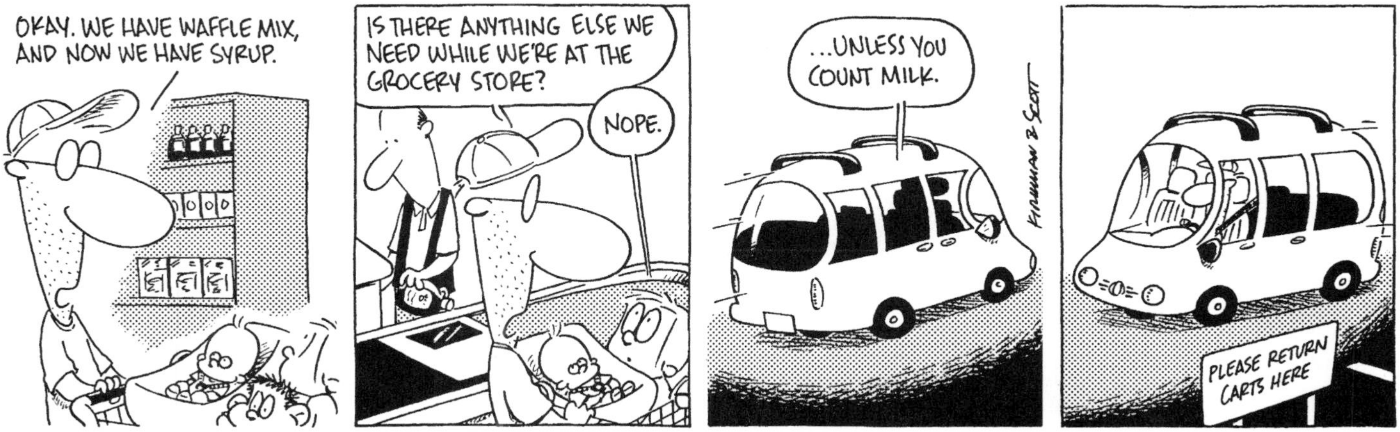
OKAY. WE HAVE WAFFLE MIX, AND NOW WE HAVE SYRUP.
IS THERE ANYTHING ELSE WE NEED WHILE WE'RE AT THE GROCERY STORE?
NOPE.
...UNLESS YOU COUNT MILK.
PLEASE RETURN CARTS HERE

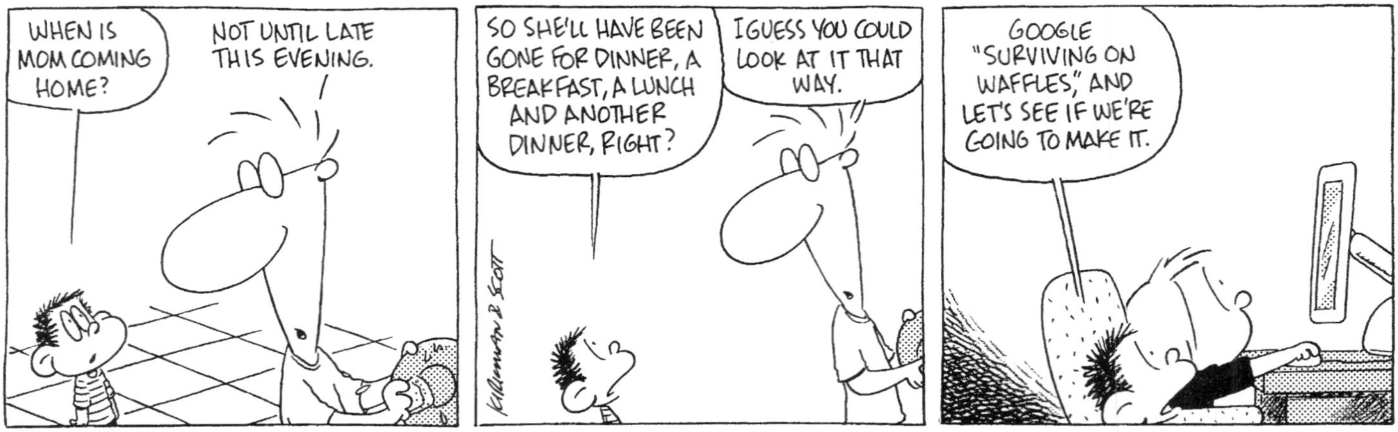
WHEN IS MOM COMING HOME?
NOT UNTIL LATE THIS EVENING.
SO SHE'LL HAVE BEEN GONE FOR DINNER, A BREAKFAST, A LUNCH AND ANOTHER DINNER, RIGHT?
I GUESS YOU COULD LOOK AT IT THAT WAY.
GOOGLE "SURVIVING ON WAFFLES," AND LET'S SEE IF WE'RE GOING TO MAKE IT.

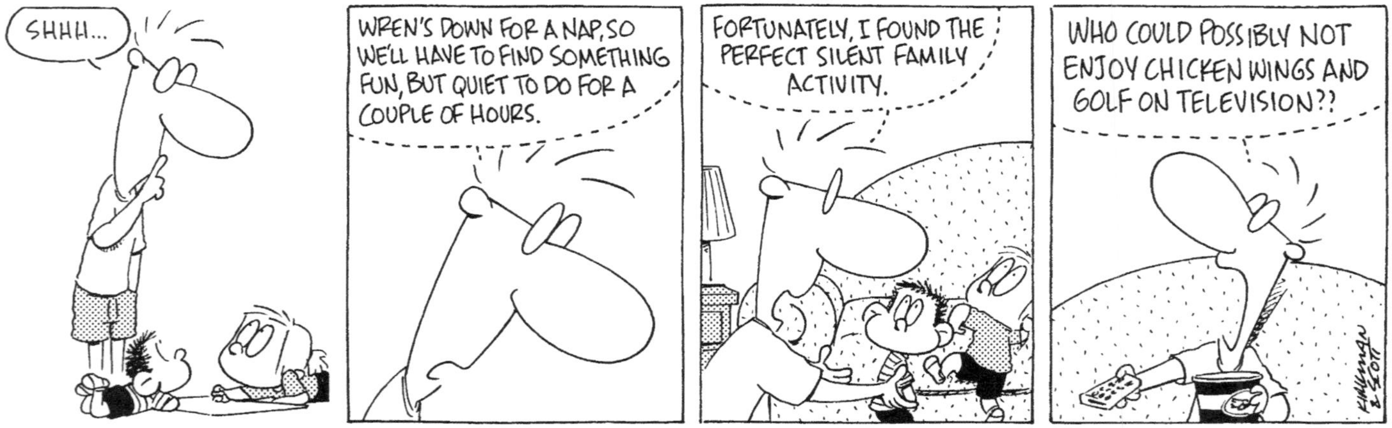
SHHH...
WREN'S DOWN FOR A NAP, SO WE'LL HAVE TO FIND SOMETHING FUN, BUT QUIET TO DO FOR A COUPLE OF HOURS.
FORTUNATELY, I FOUND THE PERFECT SILENT FAMILY ACTIVITY.
WHO COULD POSSIBLY NOT ENJOY CHICKEN WINGS AND GOLF ON TELEVISION??

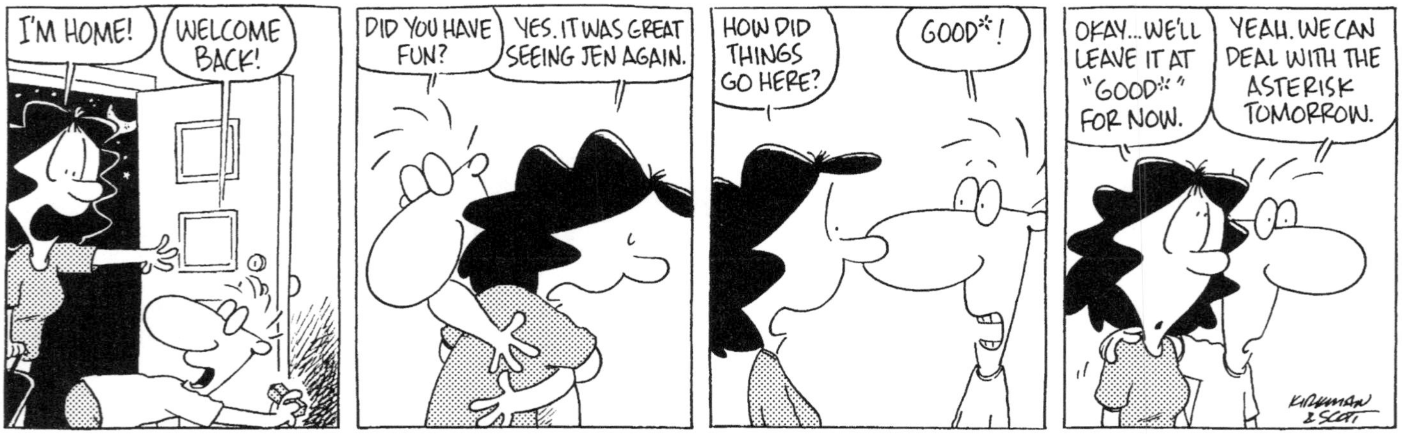
I'M HOME!
WELCOME BACK!
DID YOU HAVE FUN?
YES. IT WAS GREAT SEEING JEN AGAIN.
HOW DID THINGS GO HERE?
GOOD*!
OKAY... WE'LL LEAVE IT AT "GOOD*" FOR NOW.
YEAH. WE CAN DEAL WITH THE ASTERISK TOMORROW.

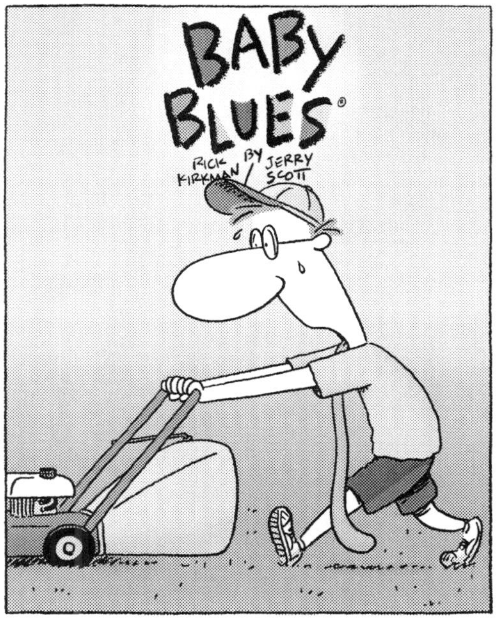
BABY BLUES®
RICK KIRKMAN / BY / JERRY SCOTT

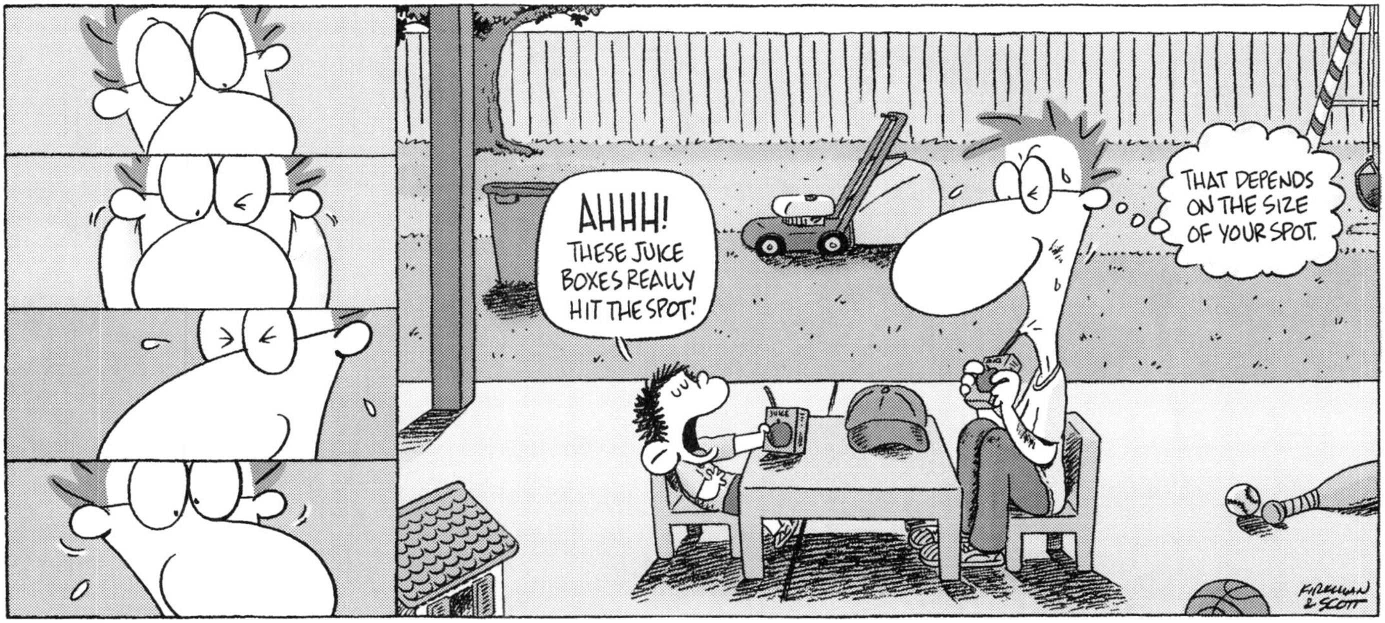
AHHH! THESE JUICE BOXES REALLY HIT THE SPOT!
THAT DEPENDS ON THE SIZE OF YOUR SPOT.
KIRKMAN & SCOTT

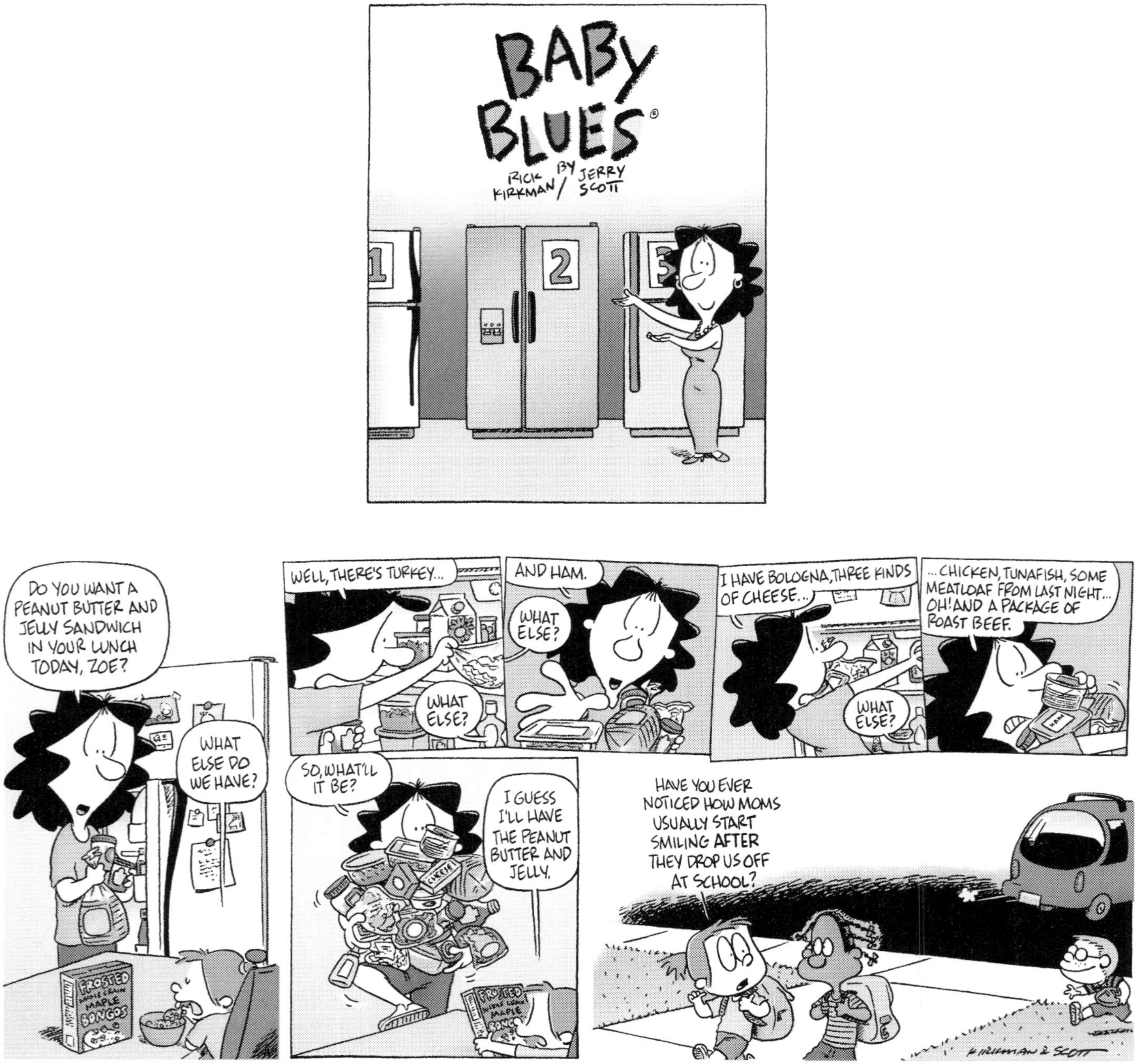
BABY BLUES®
BY RICK KIRKMAN / JERRY SCOTT
1
2
3
DO YOU WANT A PEANUT BUTTER AND JELLY SANDWICH IN YOUR LUNCH TODAY, ZOE?
WHAT ELSE DO WE HAVE?
FROSTED WHOLE GRAIN MAPLE BONGOS
WELL, THERE'S TURKEY...
WHAT ELSE?
AND HAM.
WHAT ELSE?
I HAVE BOLOGNA, THREE KINDS OF CHEESE...
WHAT ELSE?
...CHICKEN, TUNAFISH, SOME MEATLOAF FROM LAST NIGHT... OH! AND A PACKAGE OF ROAST BEEF.
HAM
SO, WHAT'LL IT BE?
I GUESS I'LL HAVE THE PEANUT BUTTER AND JELLY.
CHEESE
HAVE YOU EVER NOTICED HOW MOMS USUALLY START SMILING **AFTER** THEY DROP US OFF AT SCHOOL?
KIRKMAN & SCOTT

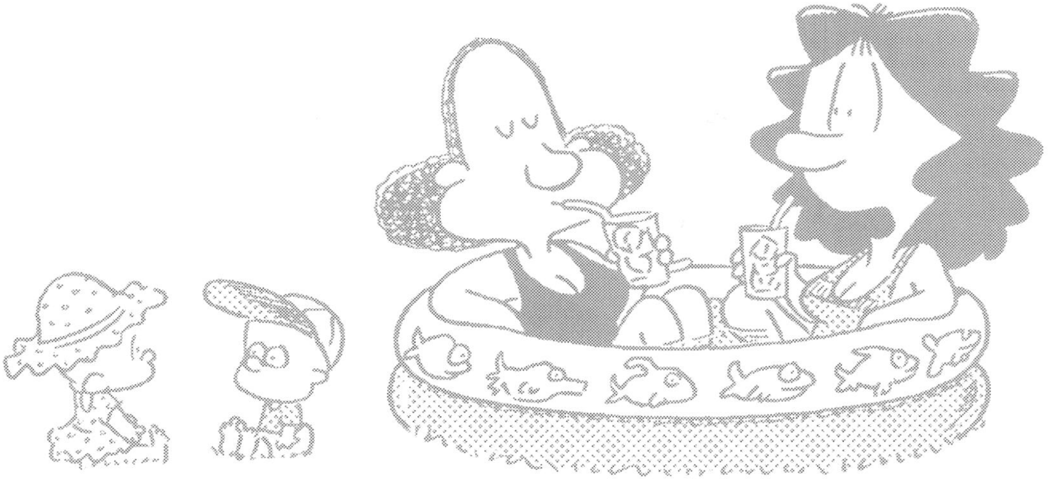

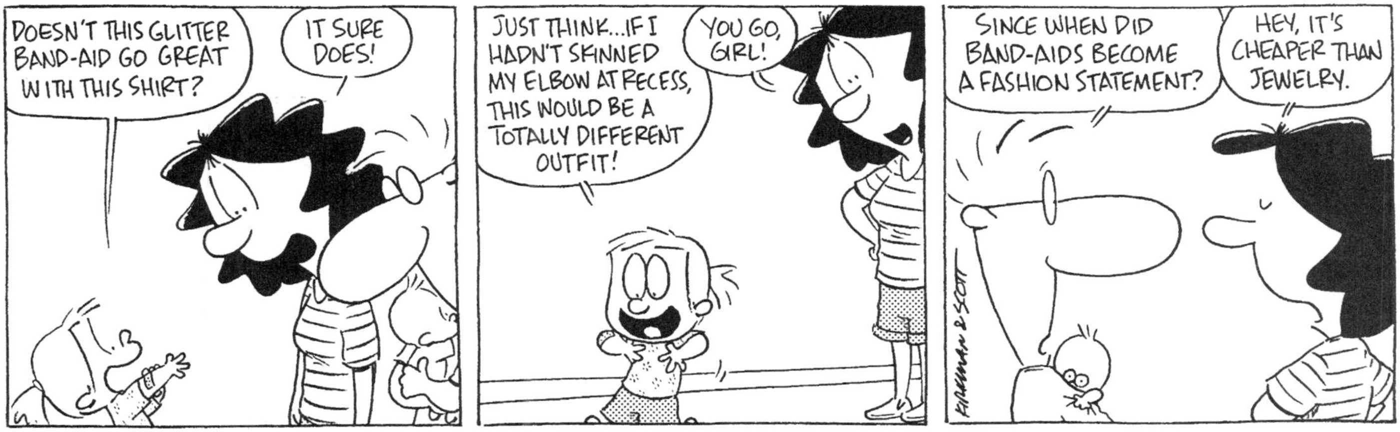
DOESN'T THIS GLITTER BAND-AID GO GREAT WITH THIS SHIRT?
IT SURE DOES!
JUST THINK...IF I HADN'T SKINNED MY ELBOW AT RECESS, THIS WOULD BE A TOTALLY DIFFERENT OUTFIT!
YOU GO, GIRL!
SINCE WHEN DID BAND-AIDS BECOME A FASHION STATEMENT?
HEY, IT'S CHEAPER THAN JEWELRY.
KIRKMAN & SCOTT

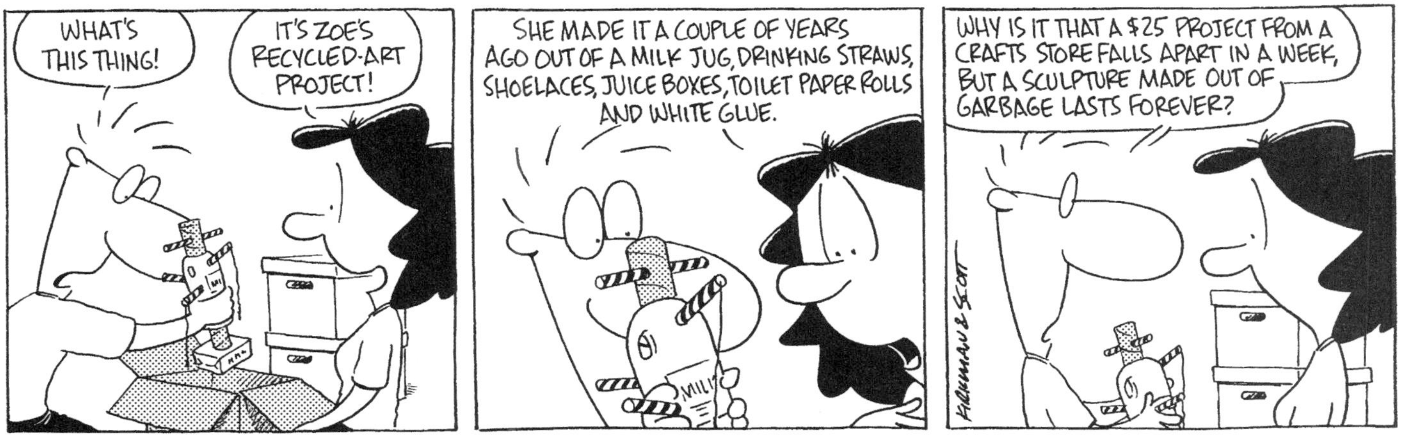
WHAT'S THIS THING!
IT'S ZOE'S RECYCLED-ART PROJECT!
SHE MADE IT A COUPLE OF YEARS AGO OUT OF A MILK JUG, DRINKING STRAWS, SHOELACES, JUICE BOXES, TOILET PAPER ROLLS AND WHITE GLUE.
WHY IS IT THAT A $25 PROJECT FROM A CRAFTS STORE FALLS APART IN A WEEK, BUT A SCULPTURE MADE OUT OF GARBAGE LASTS FOREVER?
KIRKMAN & SCOTT

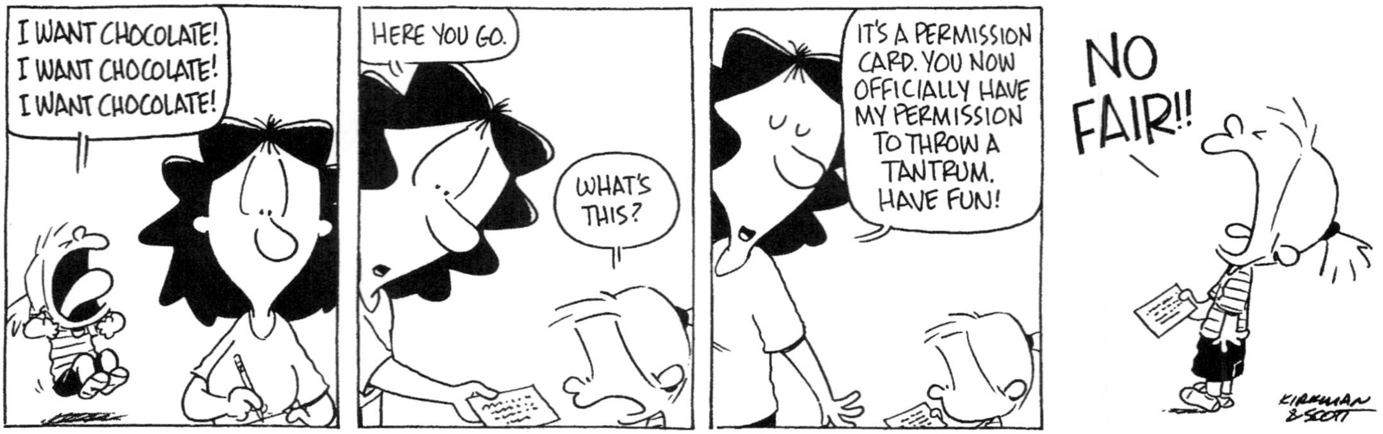
I WANT CHOCOLATE! I WANT CHOCOLATE! I WANT CHOCOLATE!
HERE YOU GO.
WHAT'S THIS?
IT'S A PERMISSION CARD. YOU NOW OFFICIALLY HAVE MY PERMISSION TO THROW A TANTRUM. HAVE FUN!
NO FAIR!!
KIRKMAN & SCOTT

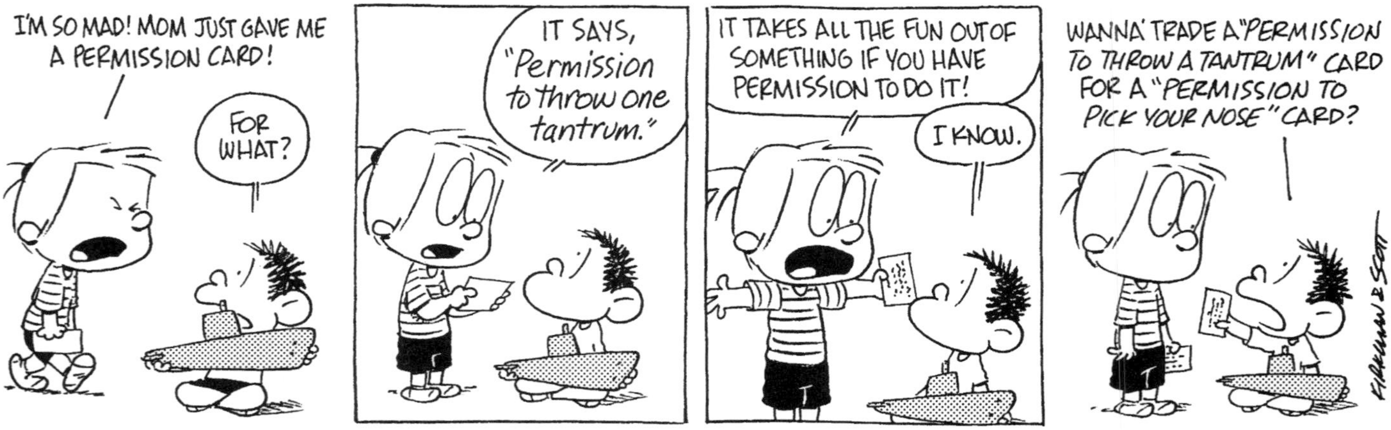
I'M SO MAD! MOM JUST GAVE ME A PERMISSION CARD!
FOR WHAT?
IT SAYS, "Permission to throw one tantrum."
IT TAKES ALL THE FUN OUT OF SOMETHING IF YOU HAVE PERMISSION TO DO IT!
I KNOW.
WANNA' TRADE A "PERMISSION TO THROW A TANTRUM" CARD FOR A "PERMISSION TO PICK YOUR NOSE" CARD?
KIRKMAN & SCOTT

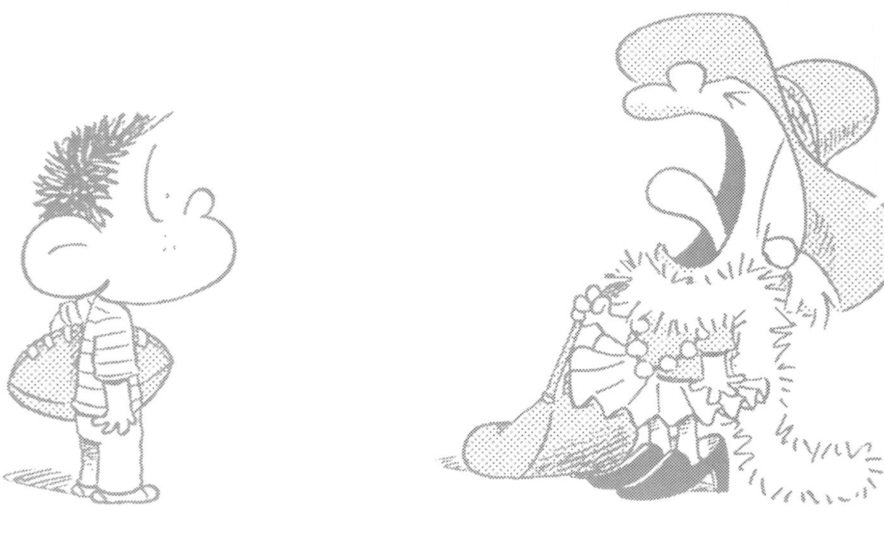

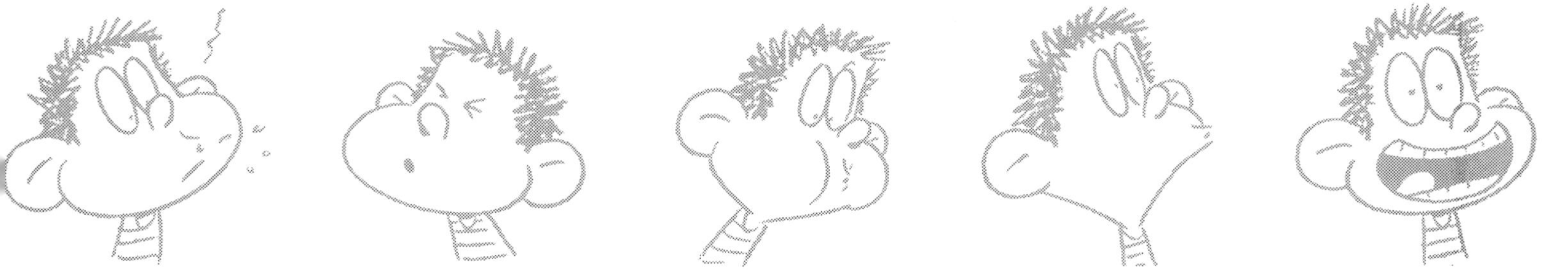

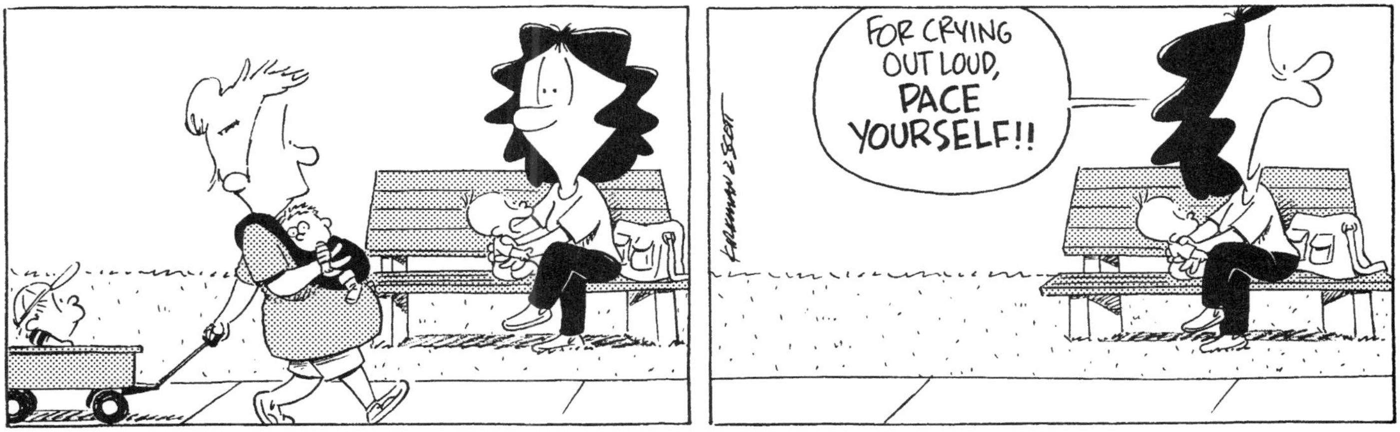

FOR CRYING OUT LOUD, PACE YOURSELF!!

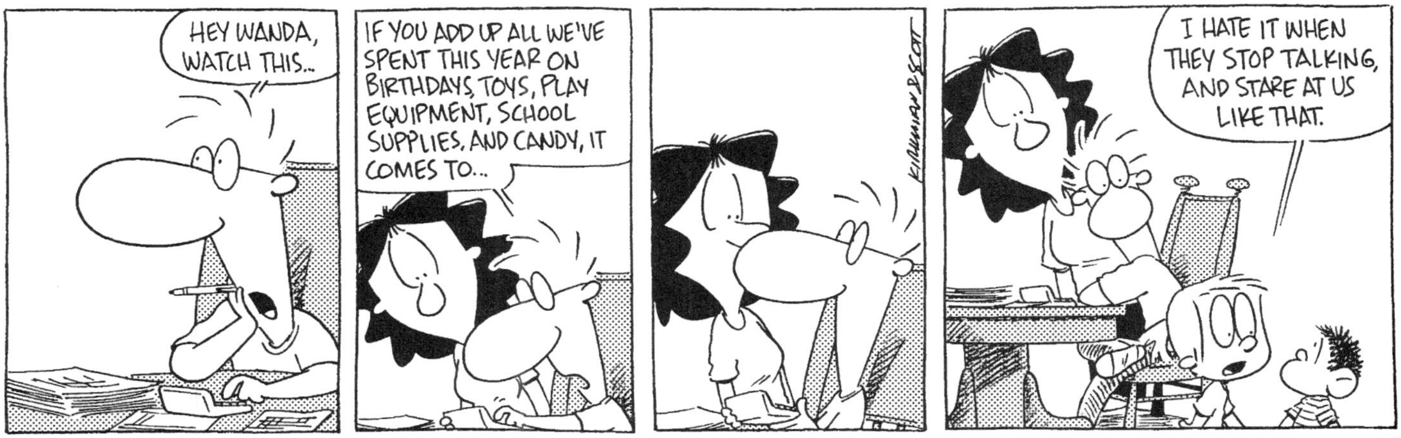

HEY WANDA, WATCH THIS...
IF YOU ADD UP ALL WE'VE SPENT THIS YEAR ON BIRTHDAYS, TOYS, PLAY EQUIPMENT, SCHOOL SUPPLIES, AND CANDY, IT COMES TO...
I HATE IT WHEN THEY STOP TALKING, AND STARE AT US LIKE THAT.

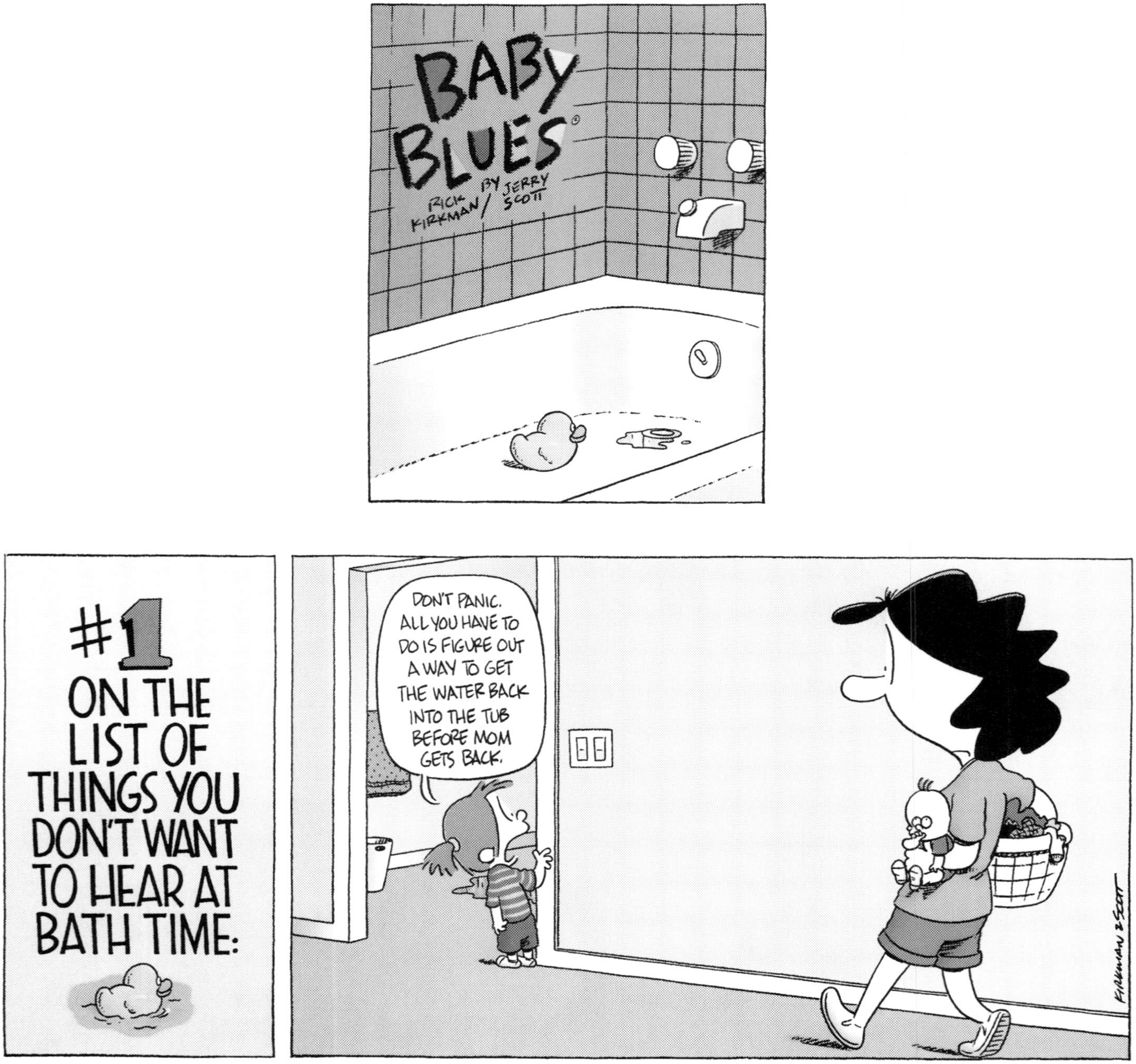
BABY BLUES®
BY RICK KIRKMAN / JERRY SCOTT
#1 ON THE LIST OF THINGS YOU DON'T WANT TO HEAR AT BATH TIME:
DON'T PANIC. ALL YOU HAVE TO DO IS FIGURE OUT A WAY TO GET THE WATER BACK INTO THE TUB BEFORE MOM GETS BACK.
KIRKMAN & SCOTT

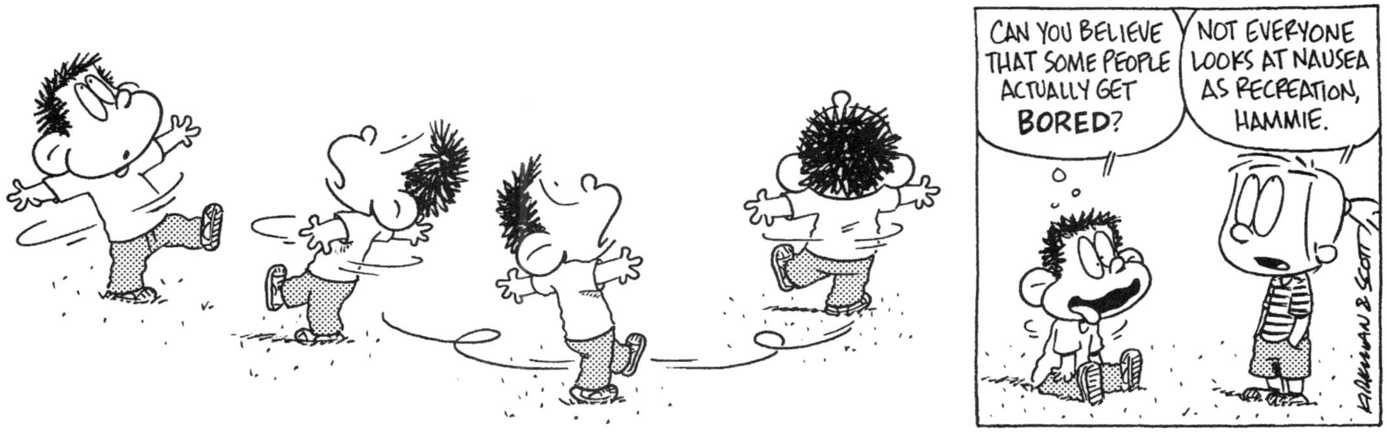
CAN YOU BELIEVE THAT SOME PEOPLE ACTUALLY GET **BORED**?
NOT EVERYONE LOOKS AT NAUSEA AS RECREATION, HAMMIE.

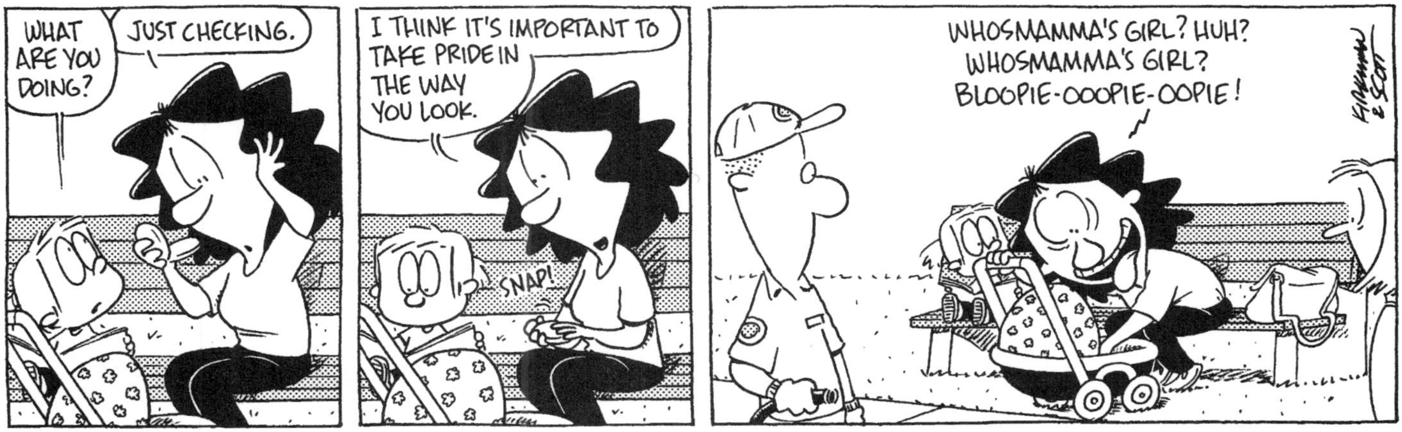
WHAT ARE YOU DOING?
JUST CHECKING.
I THINK IT'S IMPORTANT TO TAKE PRIDE IN THE WAY YOU LOOK.
SNAP!
WHOSMAMMA'S GIRL? HUH? WHOSMAMMA'S GIRL? BLOOPIE-OOOPIE-OOPIE!

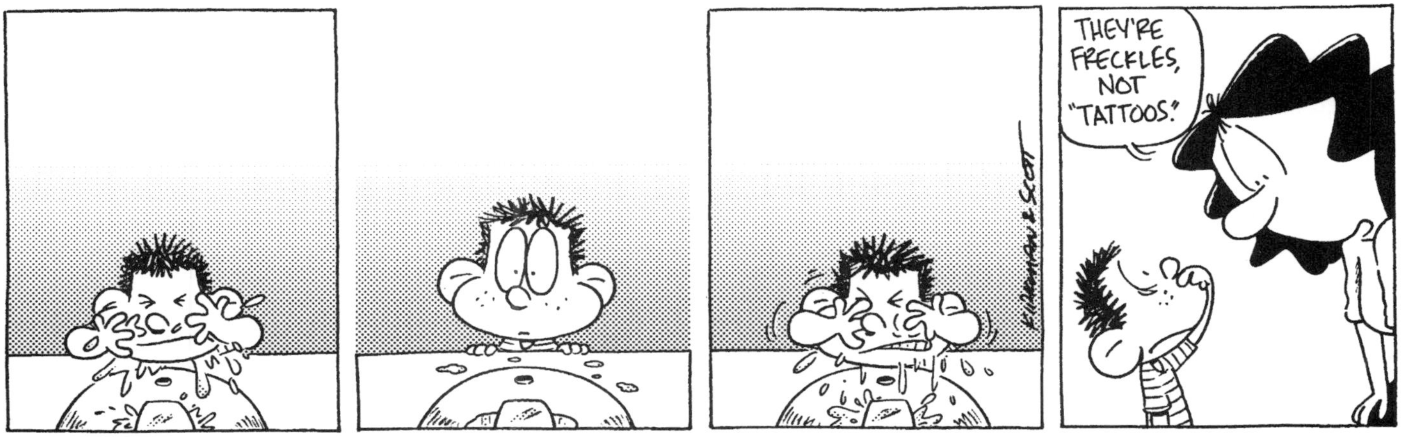
THEY'RE FRECKLES, NOT "TATTOOS."

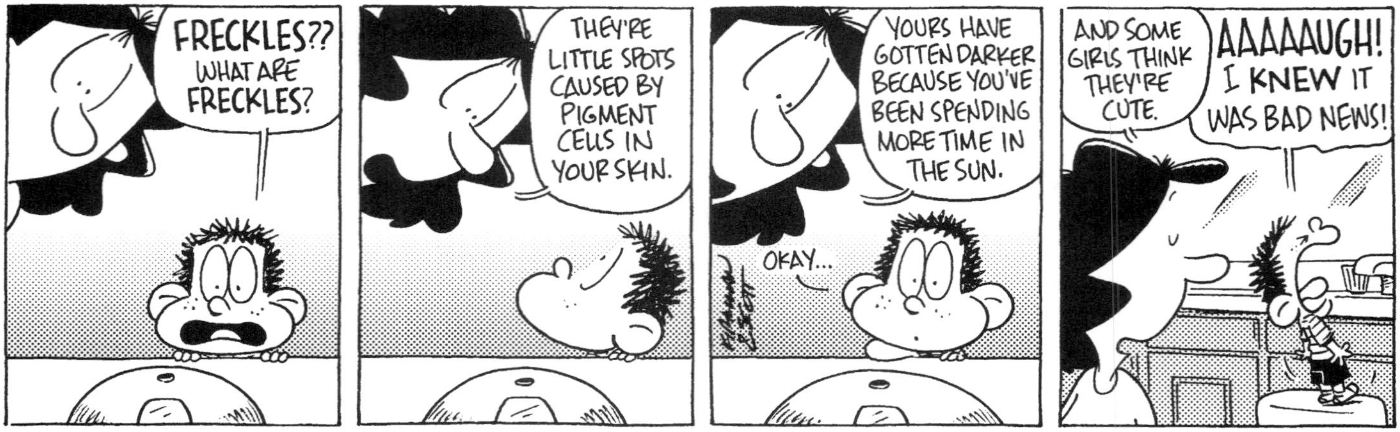
FRECKLES?? WHAT ARE FRECKLES?
THEY'RE LITTLE SPOTS CAUSED BY PIGMENT CELLS IN YOUR SKIN.
YOURS HAVE GOTTEN DARKER BECAUSE YOU'VE BEEN SPENDING MORE TIME IN THE SUN.
OKAY...
AND SOME GIRLS THINK THEY'RE CUTE.
AAAAAUGH! I KNEW IT WAS BAD NEWS!

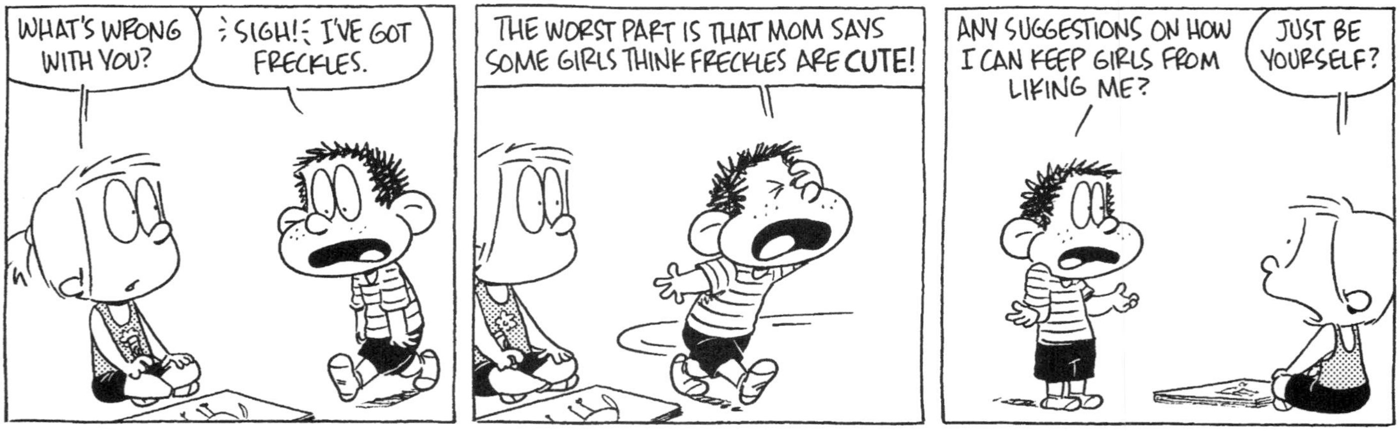
WHAT'S WRONG WITH YOU?
SIGH! I'VE GOT FRECKLES.
THE WORST PART IS THAT MOM SAYS SOME GIRLS THINK FRECKLES ARE CUTE!
ANY SUGGESTIONS ON HOW I CAN KEEP GIRLS FROM LIKING ME?
JUST BE YOURSELF?

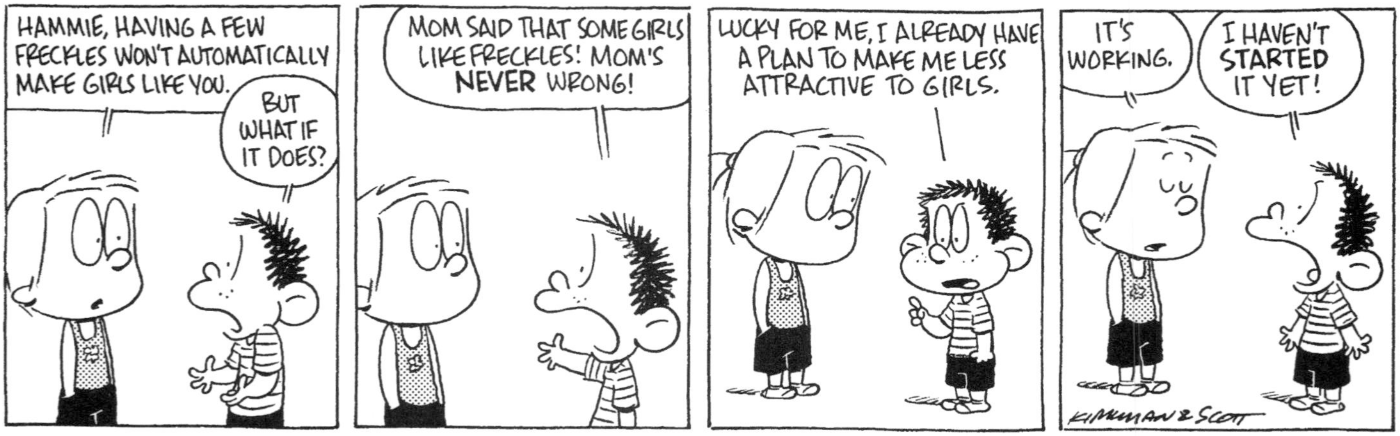
HAMMIE, HAVING A FEW FRECKLES WON'T AUTOMATICALLY MAKE GIRLS LIKE YOU.
BUT WHAT IF IT DOES?
MOM SAID THAT SOME GIRLS LIKE FRECKLES! MOM'S NEVER WRONG!
LUCKY FOR ME, I ALREADY HAVE A PLAN TO MAKE ME LESS ATTRACTIVE TO GIRLS.
IT'S WORKING.
I HAVEN'T STARTED IT YET!
KIRKMAN & SCOTT

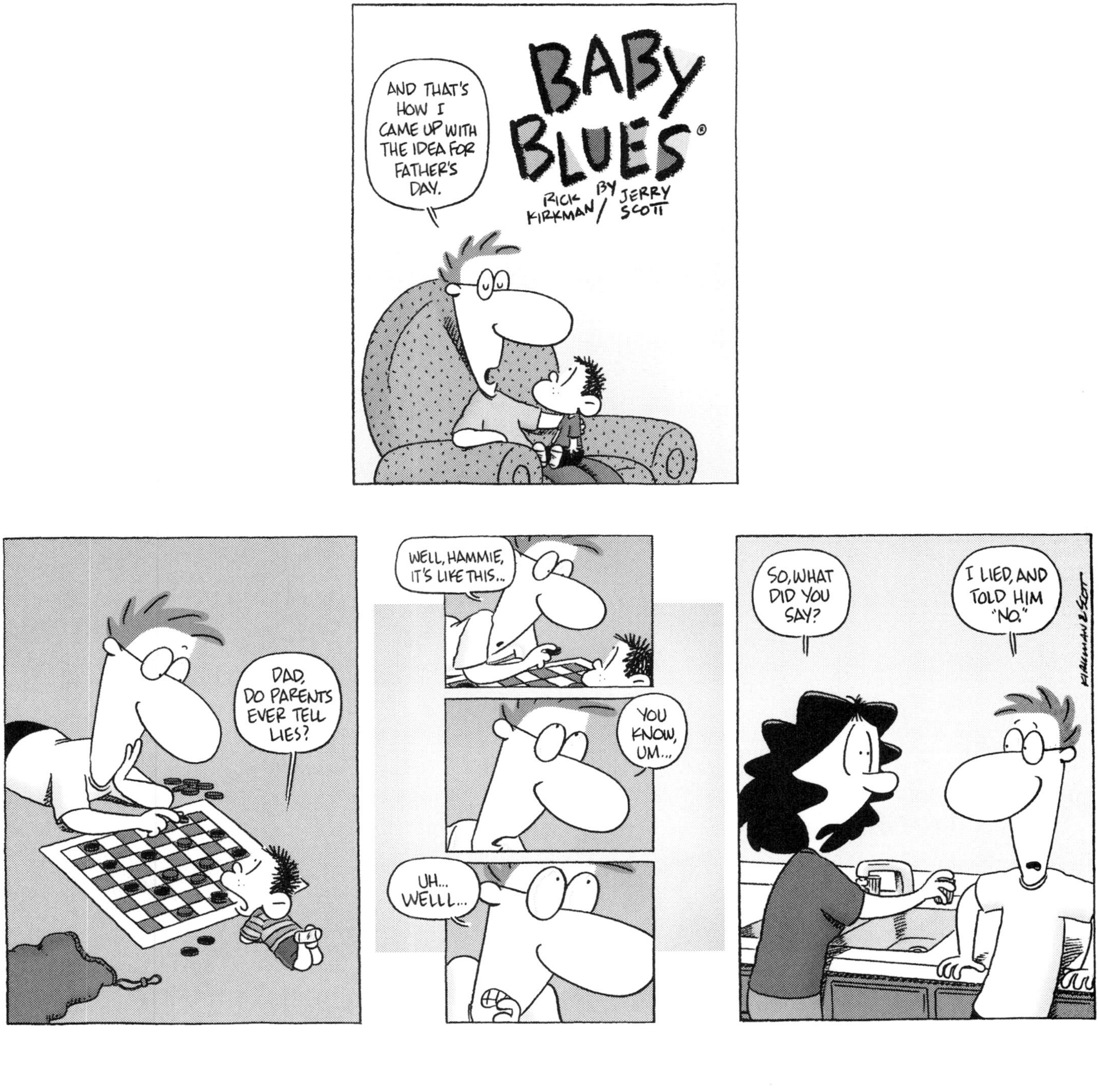
AND THAT'S HOW I CAME UP WITH THE IDEA FOR FATHER'S DAY.
BABY BLUES®
BY RICK KIRKMAN / JERRY SCOTT
DAD, DO PARENTS EVER TELL LIES?
WELL, HAMMIE, IT'S LIKE THIS...
YOU KNOW, UM...
UH... WELLL...
SO, WHAT DID YOU SAY?
I LIED, AND TOLD HIM "NO."

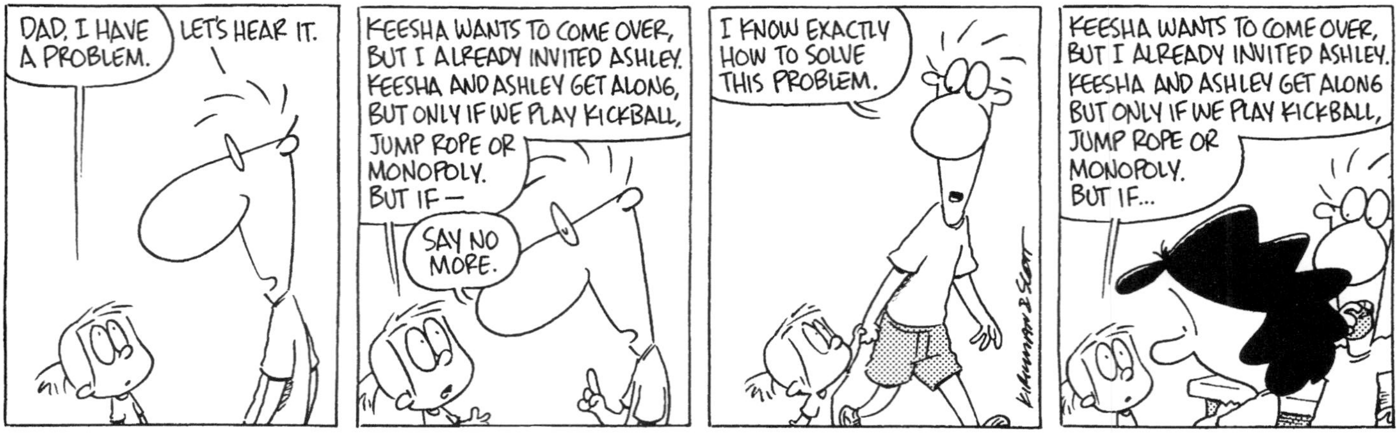
DAD, I HAVE A PROBLEM.
LET'S HEAR IT.
KEESHA WANTS TO COME OVER, BUT I ALREADY INVITED ASHLEY. KEESHA AND ASHLEY GET ALONG, BUT ONLY IF WE PLAY KICKBALL, JUMP ROPE OR MONOPOLY. BUT IF —
SAY NO MORE.
I KNOW EXACTLY HOW TO SOLVE THIS PROBLEM.
KEESHA WANTS TO COME OVER, BUT I ALREADY INVITED ASHLEY. KEESHA AND ASHLEY GET ALONG BUT ONLY IF WE PLAY KICKBALL, JUMP ROPE OR MONOPOLY. BUT IF...

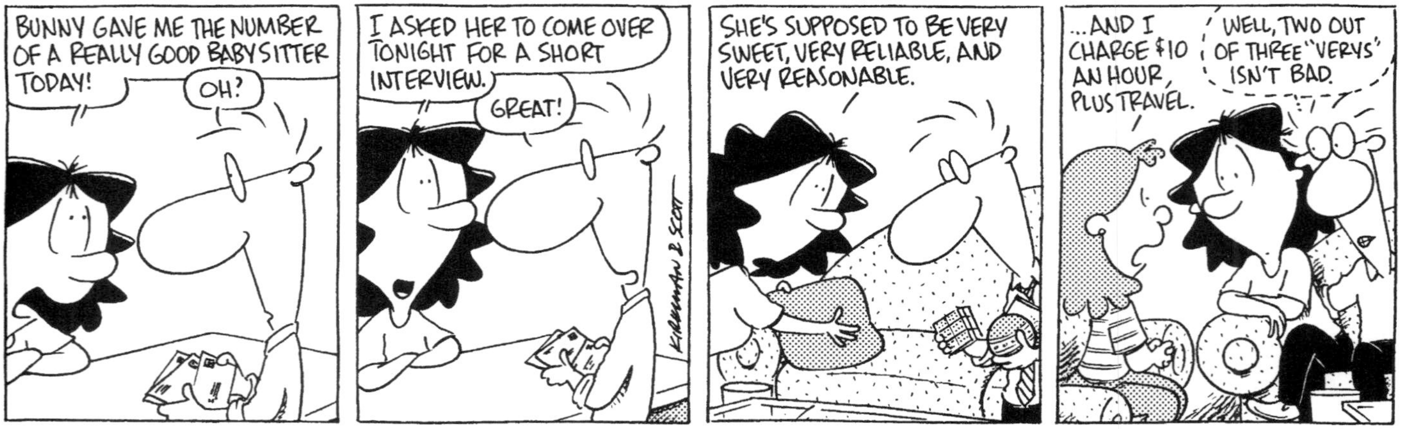
BUNNY GAVE ME THE NUMBER OF A REALLY GOOD BABYSITTER TODAY!
OH?
I ASKED HER TO COME OVER TONIGHT FOR A SHORT INTERVIEW.
GREAT!
SHE'S SUPPOSED TO BE VERY SWEET, VERY RELIABLE, AND VERY REASONABLE.
...AND I CHARGE $10 AN HOUR, PLUS TRAVEL.
WELL, TWO OUT OF THREE "VERYS" ISN'T BAD.

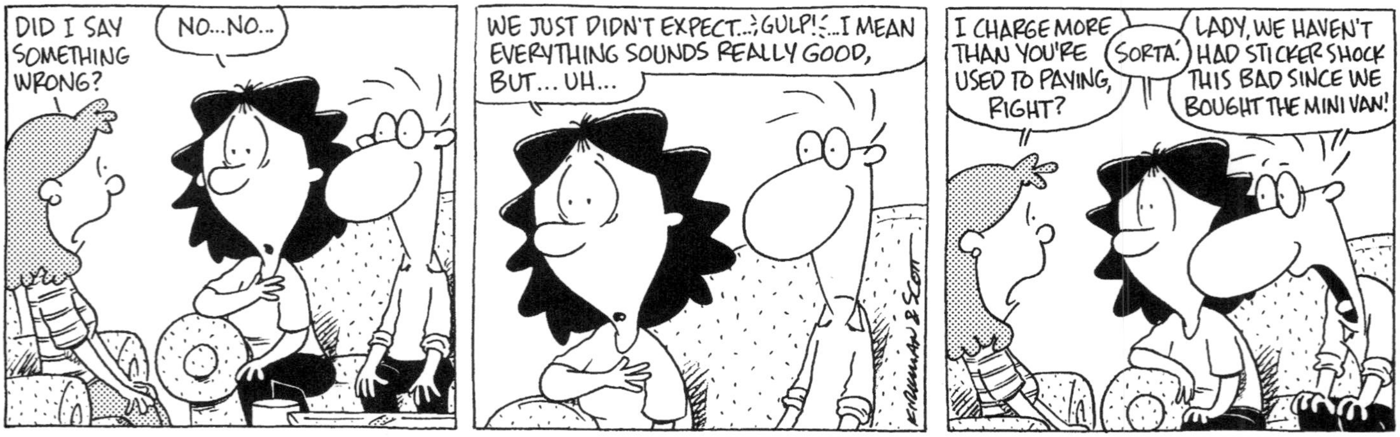
DID I SAY SOMETHING WRONG?
NO...NO...
WE JUST DIDN'T EXPECT...GULP!...I MEAN EVERYTHING SOUNDS REALLY GOOD, BUT... UH...
I CHARGE MORE THAN YOU'RE USED TO PAYING, RIGHT?
SORTA.
LADY, WE HAVEN'T HAD STICKER SHOCK THIS BAD SINCE WE BOUGHT THE MINI VAN!

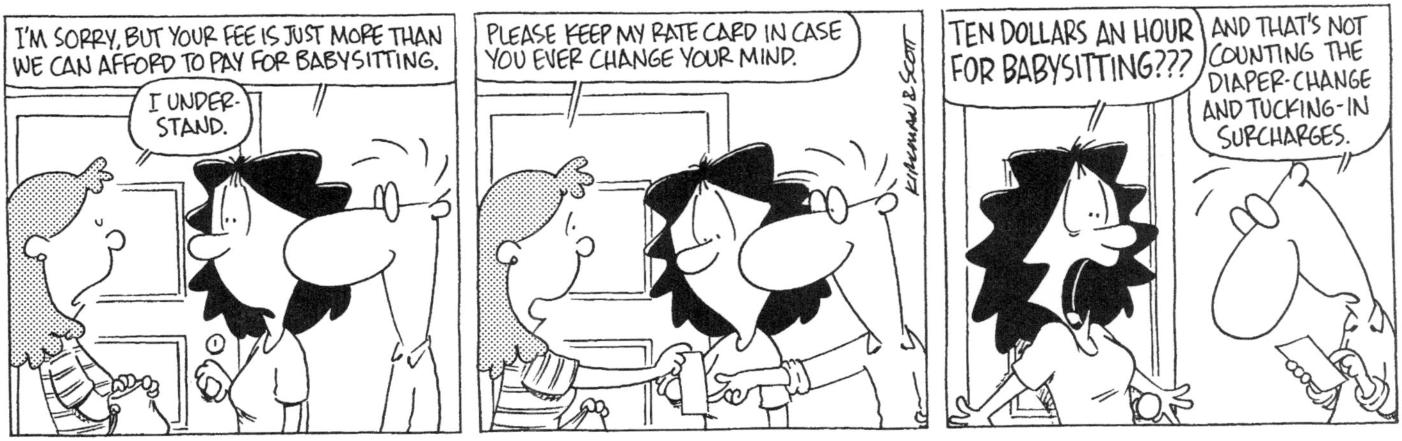
I'M SORRY, BUT YOUR FEE IS JUST MORE THAN WE CAN AFFORD TO PAY FOR BABYSITTING.
I UNDERSTAND.
PLEASE KEEP MY RATE CARD IN CASE YOU EVER CHANGE YOUR MIND.
KIRKMAN & SCOTT
TEN DOLLARS AN HOUR FOR BABYSITTING???
AND THAT'S NOT COUNTING THE DIAPER-CHANGE AND TUCKING-IN SURCHARGES.

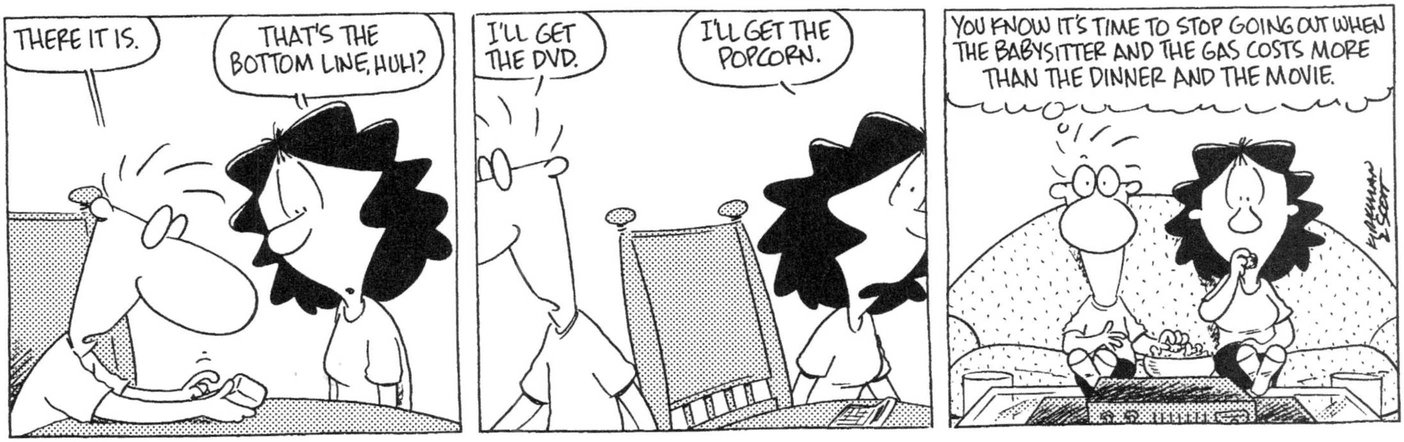
THERE IT IS.
THAT'S THE BOTTOM LINE, HUH?
I'LL GET THE DVD.
I'LL GET THE POPCORN.
YOU KNOW IT'S TIME TO STOP GOING OUT WHEN THE BABYSITTER AND THE GAS COSTS MORE THAN THE DINNER AND THE MOVIE.
KIRKMAN & SCOTT

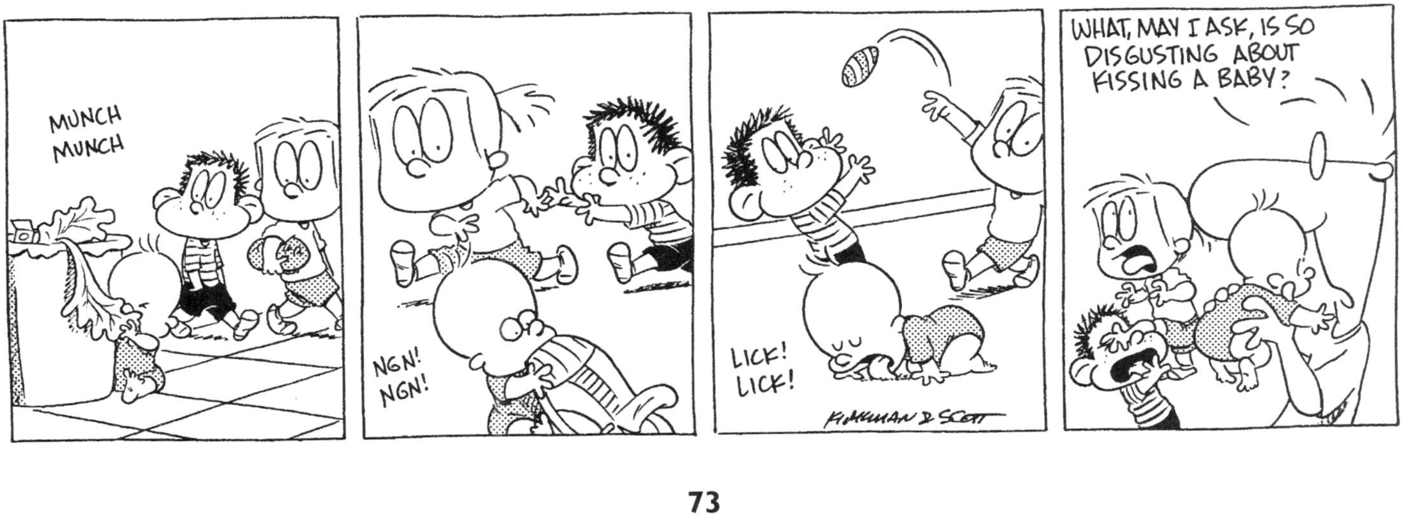
MUNCH MUNCH
NGN! NGN!
LICK! LICK!
KIRKMAN & SCOTT
WHAT, MAY I ASK, IS SO DISGUSTING ABOUT KISSING A BABY?

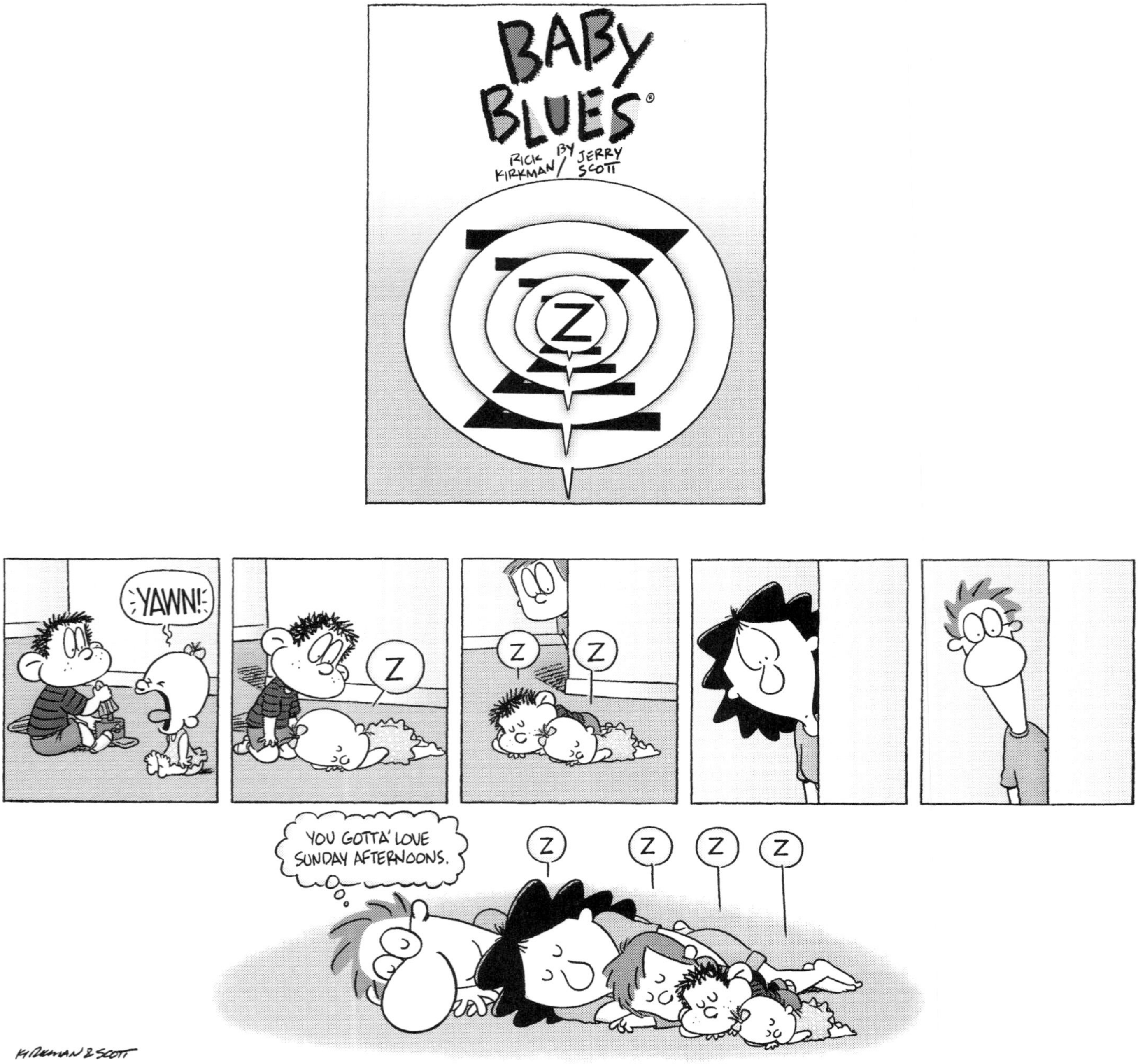
BABY BLUES®
BY RICK KIRKMAN / JERRY SCOTT
Z
YAWN!
Z
Z
Z
YOU GOTTA' LOVE SUNDAY AFTERNOONS.
Z
Z
Z
Z
KIRKMAN & SCOTT

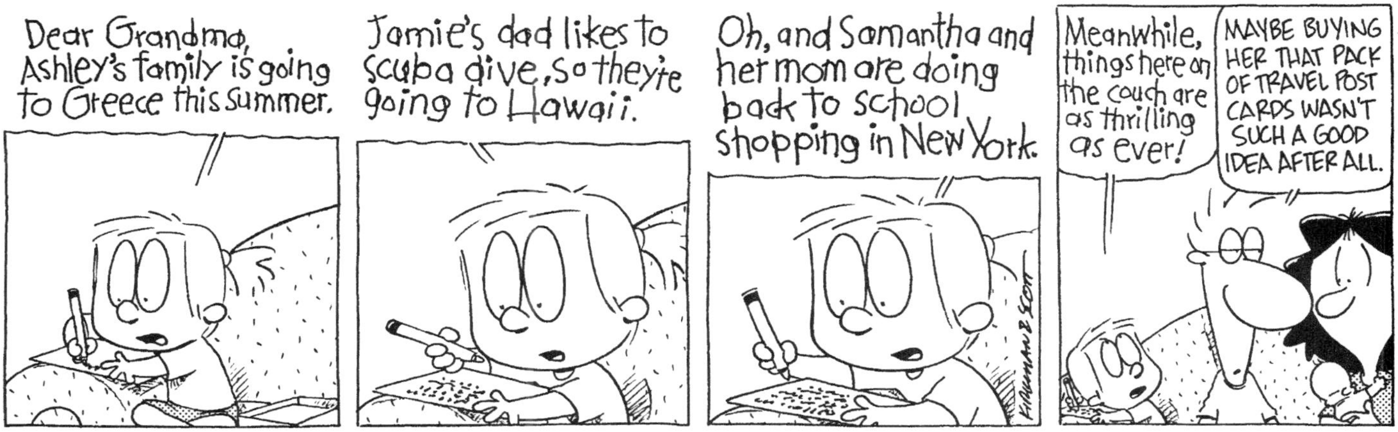
Dear Grandma,
Ashley's family is going to Greece this summer.
Jamie's dad likes to scuba dive, so they're going to Hawaii.
Oh, and Samantha and her mom are doing back to school shopping in New York.
Meanwhile, things here on the couch are as thrilling as ever!
MAYBE BUYING HER THAT PACK OF TRAVEL POST CARDS WASN'T SUCH A GOOD IDEA AFTER ALL.

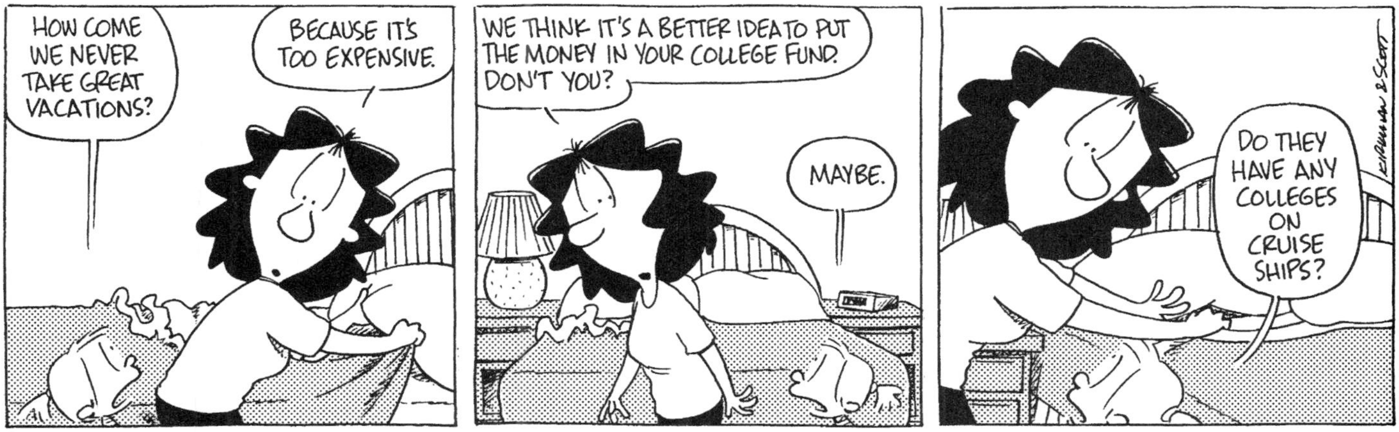
HOW COME WE NEVER TAKE GREAT VACATIONS?
BECAUSE IT'S TOO EXPENSIVE.
WE THINK IT'S A BETTER IDEA TO PUT THE MONEY IN YOUR COLLEGE FUND. DON'T YOU?
MAYBE.
DO THEY HAVE ANY COLLEGES ON CRUISE SHIPS?

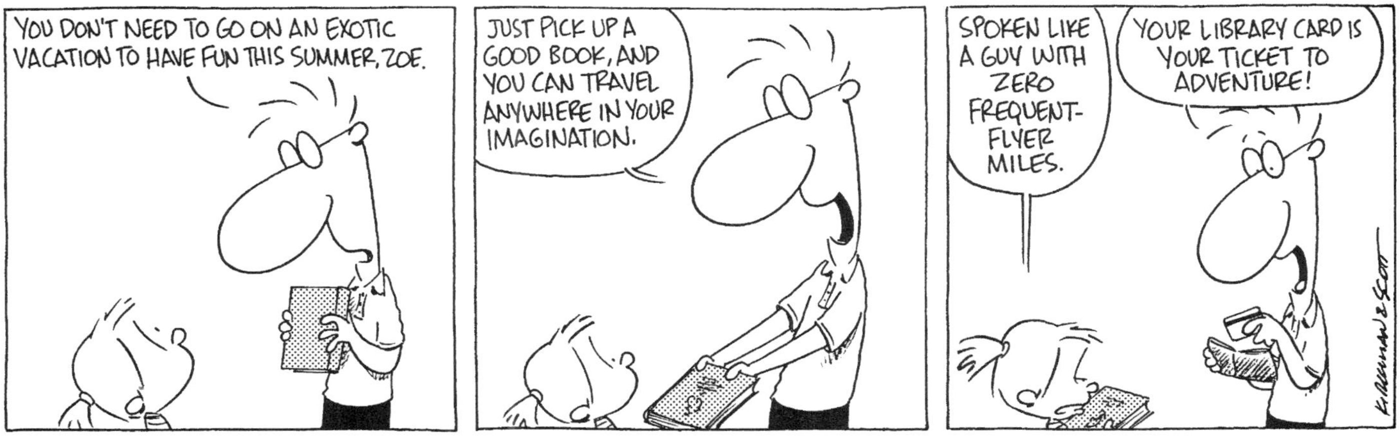
YOU DON'T NEED TO GO ON AN EXOTIC VACATION TO HAVE FUN THIS SUMMER, ZOE.
JUST PICK UP A GOOD BOOK, AND YOU CAN TRAVEL ANYWHERE IN YOUR IMAGINATION.
SPOKEN LIKE A GUY WITH ZERO FREQUENT-FLYER MILES.
YOUR LIBRARY CARD IS YOUR TICKET TO ADVENTURE!

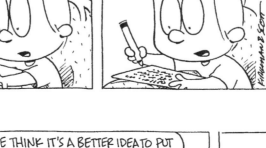

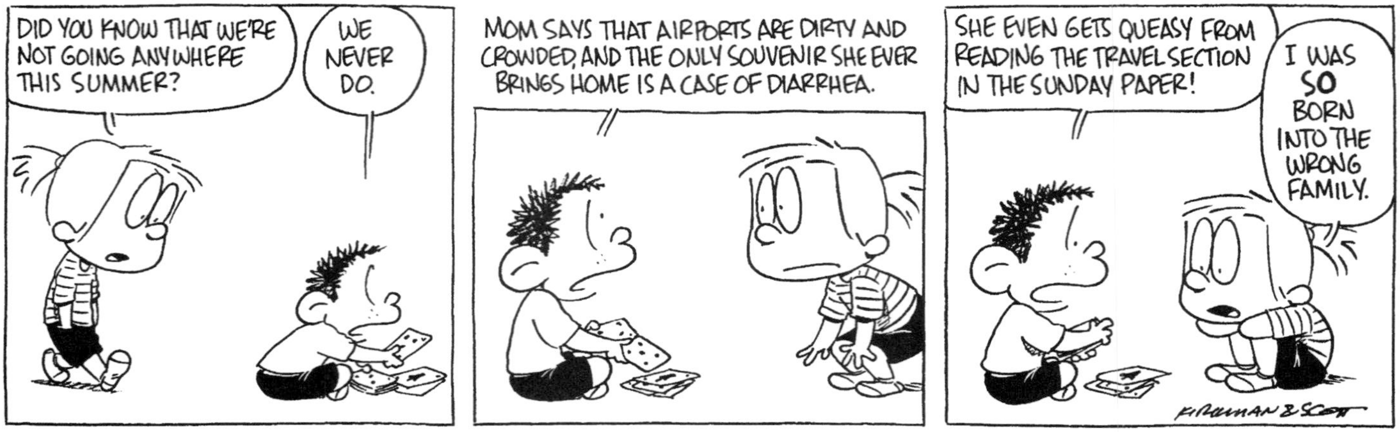
DID YOU KNOW THAT WE'RE NOT GOING ANYWHERE THIS SUMMER?
WE NEVER DO.
MOM SAYS THAT AIRPORTS ARE DIRTY AND CROWDED, AND THE ONLY SOUVENIR SHE EVER BRINGS HOME IS A CASE OF DIARRHEA.
SHE EVEN GETS QUEASY FROM READING THE TRAVEL SECTION IN THE SUNDAY PAPER!
I WAS SO BORN INTO THE WRONG FAMILY.
KIRKMAN & SCOTT

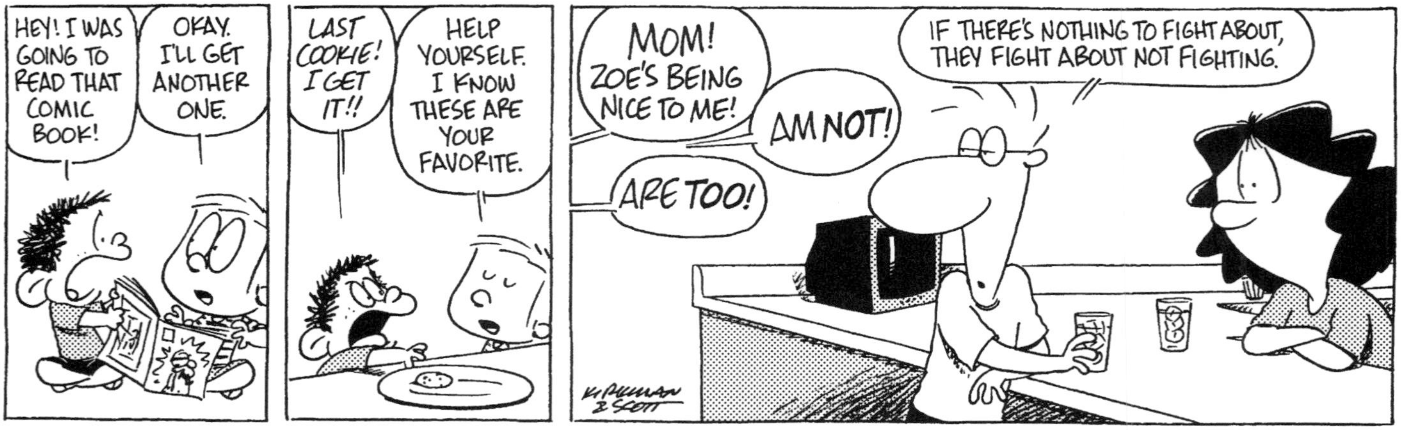
HEY! I WAS GOING TO READ THAT COMIC BOOK!
OKAY. I'LL GET ANOTHER ONE.
LAST COOKIE! I GET IT!!
HELP YOURSELF. I KNOW THESE ARE YOUR FAVORITE.
MOM! ZOE'S BEING NICE TO ME!
AM NOT!
ARE TOO!
IF THERE'S NOTHING TO FIGHT ABOUT, THEY FIGHT ABOUT NOT FIGHTING.
KIRKMAN & SCOTT

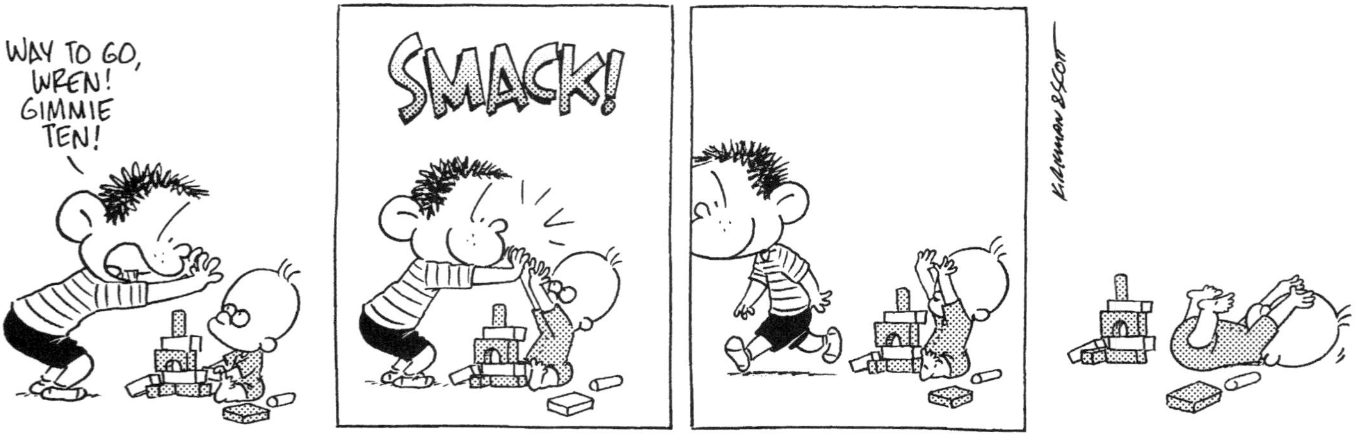
WAY TO GO, WREN! GIMMIE TEN!
SMACK!
KIRKMAN & SCOTT

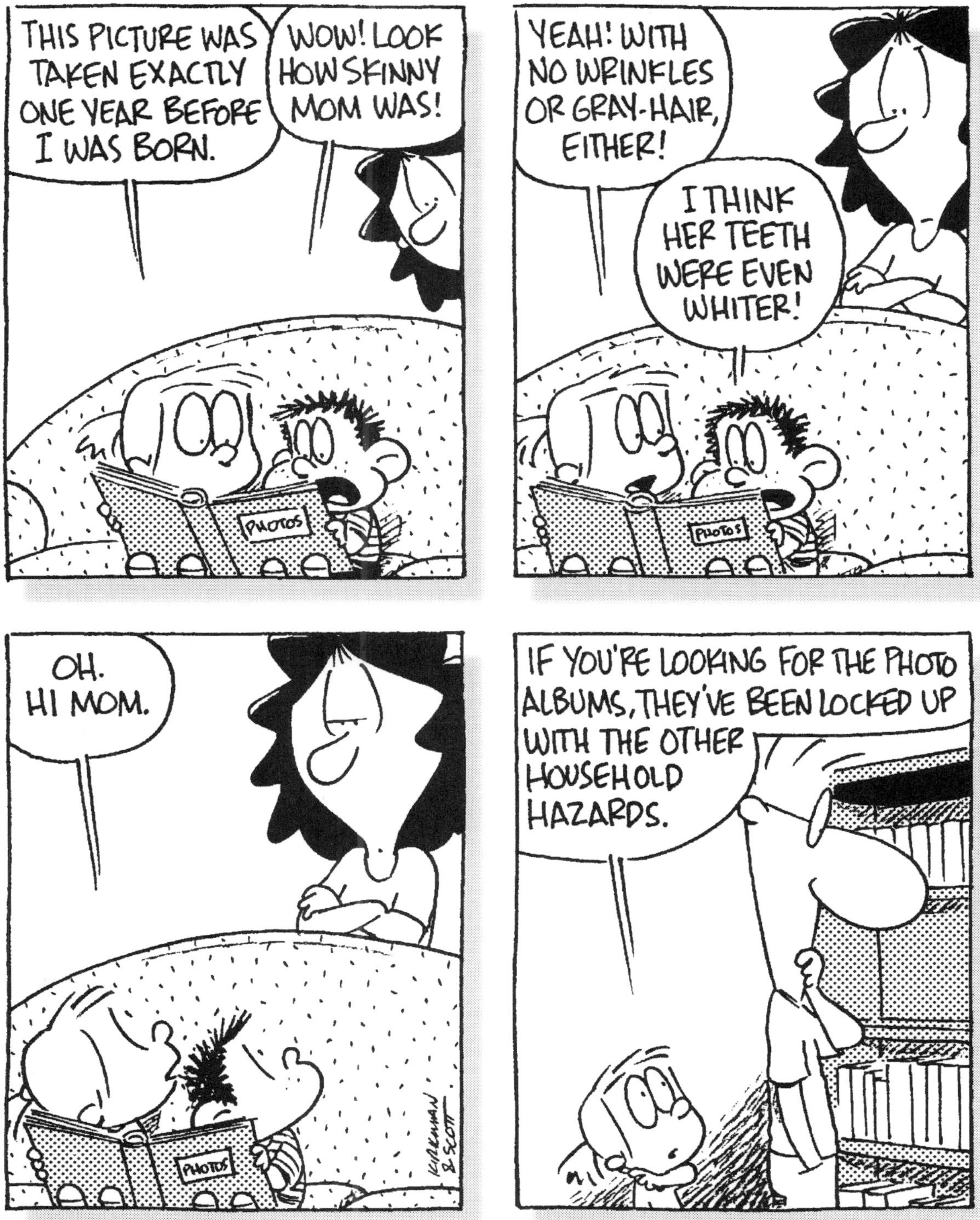
THIS PICTURE WAS TAKEN EXACTLY ONE YEAR BEFORE I WAS BORN.
WOW! LOOK HOW SKINNY MOM WAS!
PHOTOS
YEAH! WITH NO WRINKLES OR GRAY-HAIR, EITHER!
I THINK HER TEETH WERE EVEN WHITER!
PHOTOS
OH. HI MOM.
PHOTOS
KIRKMAN & SCOTT
IF YOU'RE LOOKING FOR THE PHOTO ALBUMS, THEY'VE BEEN LOCKED UP WITH THE OTHER HOUSEHOLD HAZARDS.

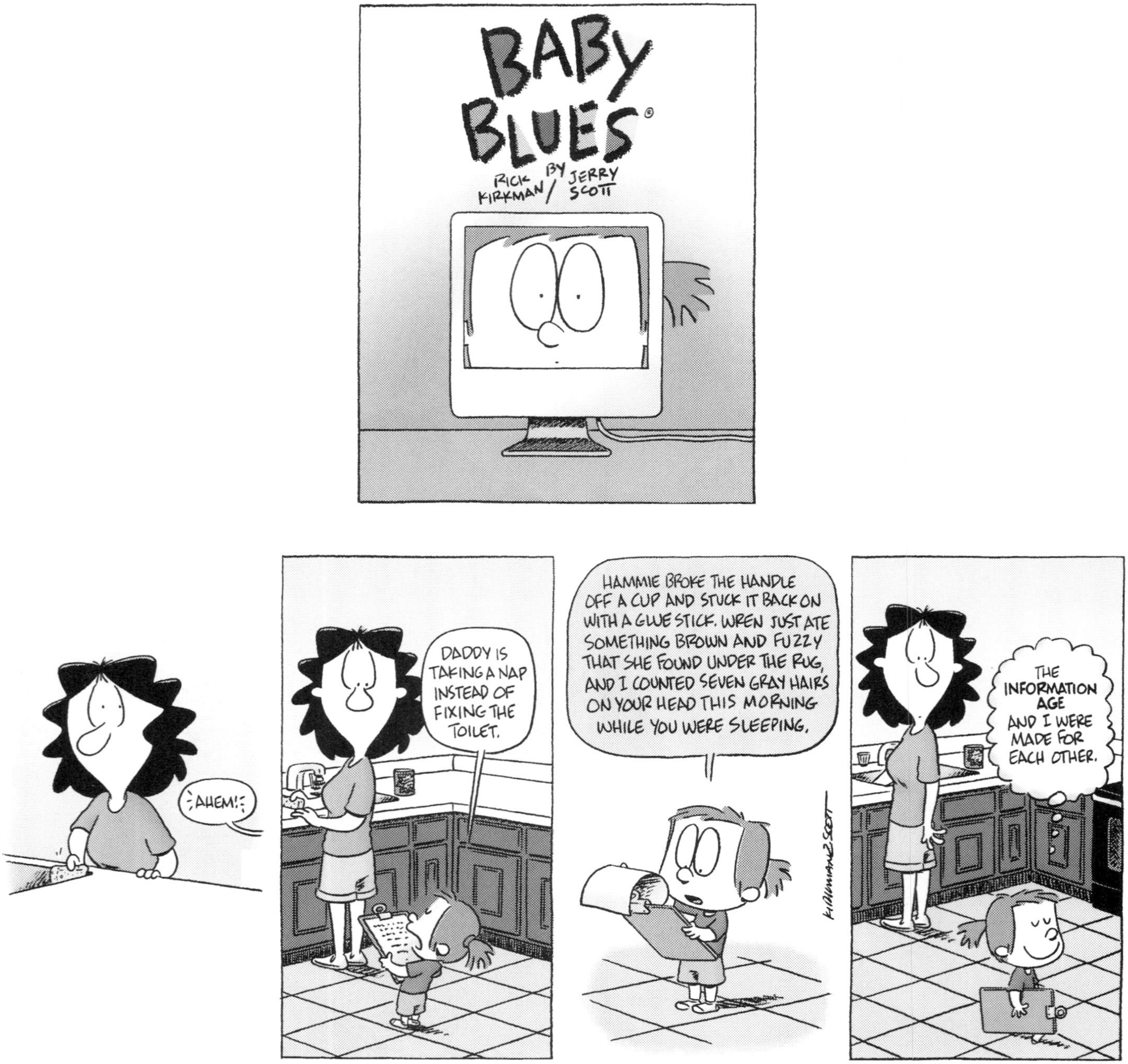
BABY BLUES®
BY RICK KIRKMAN / JERRY SCOTT
AHEM!
DADDY IS TAKING A NAP INSTEAD OF FIXING THE TOILET.
HAMMIE BROKE THE HANDLE OFF A CUP AND STUCK IT BACK ON WITH A GLUE STICK. WREN JUST ATE SOMETHING BROWN AND FUZZY THAT SHE FOUND UNDER THE RUG, AND I COUNTED SEVEN GRAY HAIRS ON YOUR HEAD THIS MORNING WHILE YOU WERE SLEEPING.
KIRKMAN & SCOTT
THE **INFORMATION AGE** AND I WERE MADE FOR EACH OTHER.

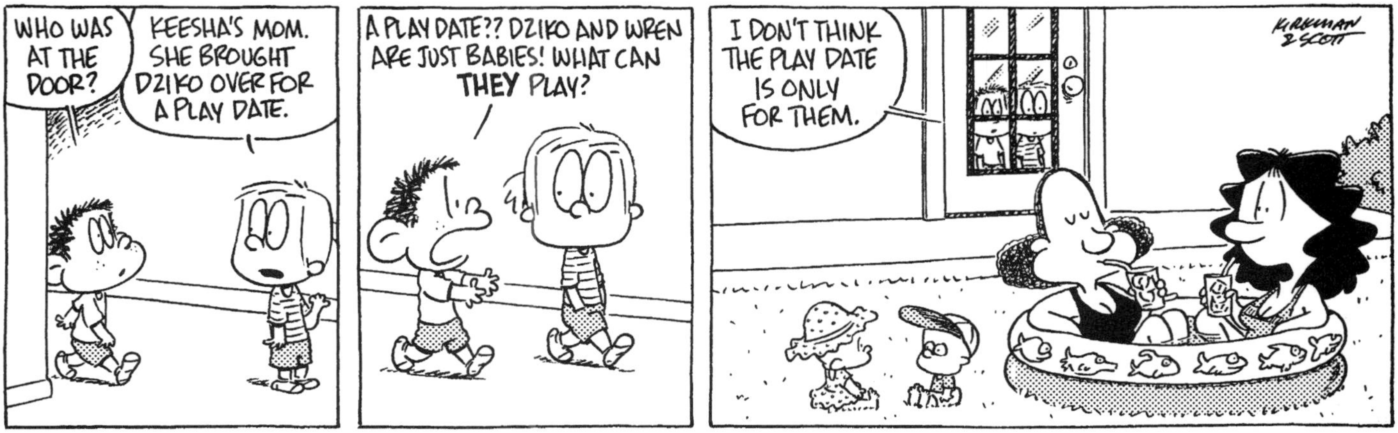
WHO WAS AT THE DOOR?
KEESHA'S MOM. SHE BROUGHT DZIKO OVER FOR A PLAY DATE.
A PLAY DATE?? DZIKO AND WREN ARE JUST BABIES! WHAT CAN THEY PLAY?
I DON'T THINK THE PLAY DATE IS ONLY FOR THEM.
KIRKMAN & SCOTT

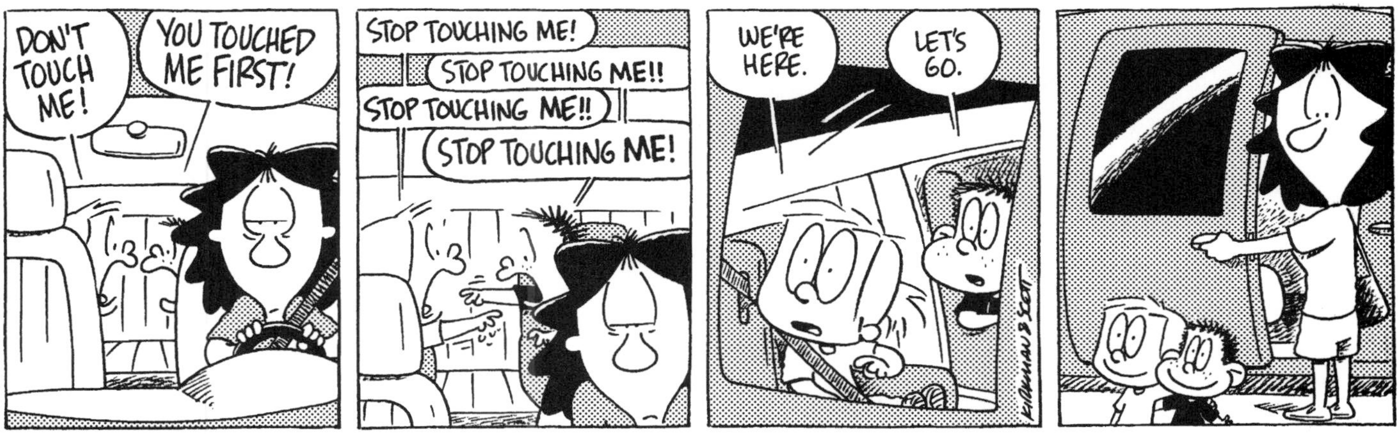
DON'T TOUCH ME!
YOU TOUCHED ME FIRST!
STOP TOUCHING ME!
STOP TOUCHING ME!!
STOP TOUCHING ME!!
STOP TOUCHING ME!
WE'RE HERE.
LET'S GO.
KIRKMAN & SCOTT

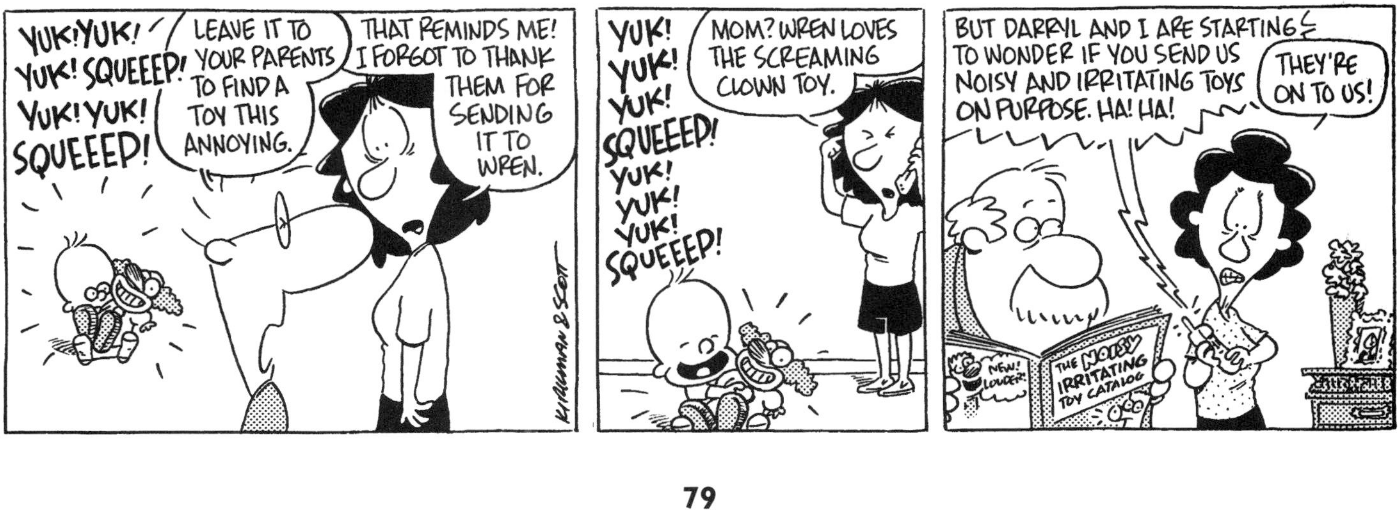
YUK! YUK! YUK! SQUEEEP! YUK! YUK! SQUEEEP!
LEAVE IT TO YOUR PARENTS TO FIND A TOY THIS ANNOYING.
THAT REMINDS ME! I FORGOT TO THANK THEM FOR SENDING IT TO WREN.
KIRKMAN & SCOTT
YUK! YUK! YUK! SQUEEEP! YUK! YUK! YUK! SQUEEEP!
MOM? WREN LOVES THE SCREAMING CLOWN TOY.
BUT DARRYL AND I ARE STARTING TO WONDER IF YOU SEND US NOISY AND IRRITATING TOYS ON PURPOSE. HA! HA!
THEY'RE ON TO US!
NEW! LOUDER!
THE NOISY IRRITATING TOY CATALOG

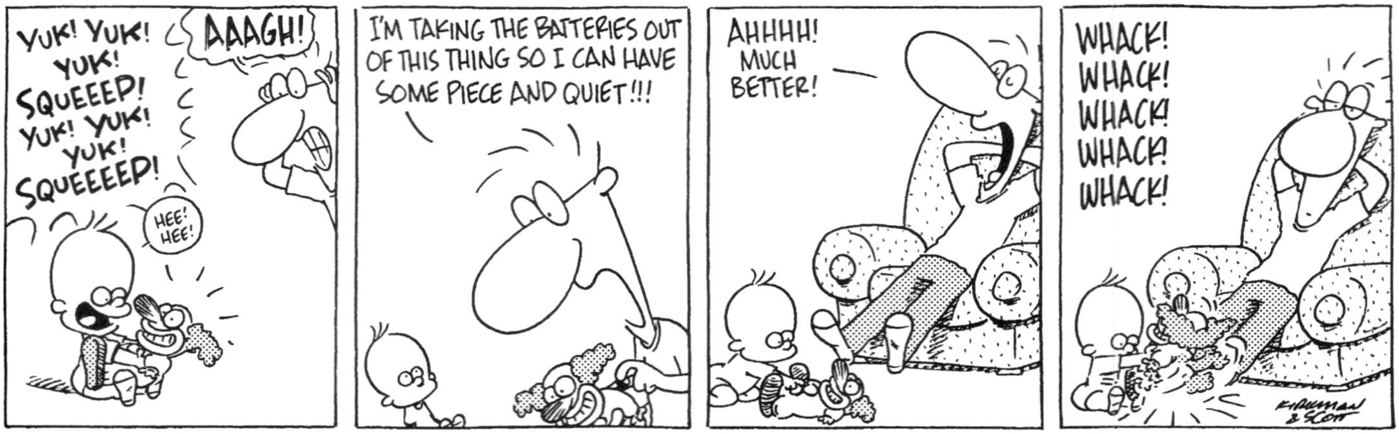
YUK! YUK! YUK! SQUEEEP! YUK! YUK! YUK! SQUEEEEP!
AAAGH!
HEE! HEE!
I'M TAKING THE BATTERIES OUT OF THIS THING SO I CAN HAVE SOME PIECE AND QUIET!!!
AHHHH! MUCH BETTER!
WHACK! WHACK! WHACK! WHACK! WHACK!

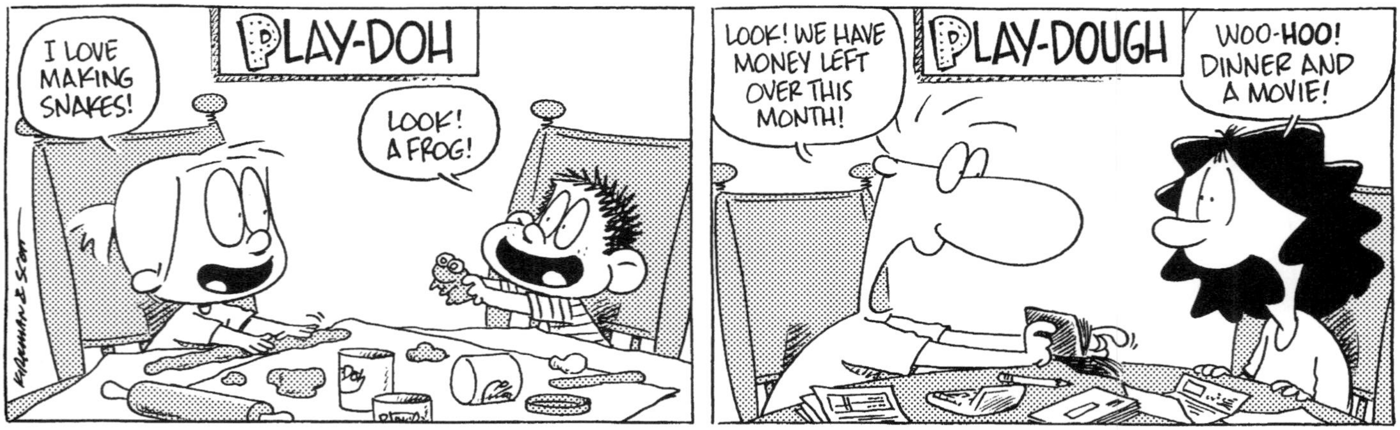
PLAY-DOH
I LOVE MAKING SNAKES!
LOOK! A FROG!
PLAY-DOUGH
LOOK! WE HAVE MONEY LEFT OVER THIS MONTH!
WOO-HOO! DINNER AND A MOVIE!

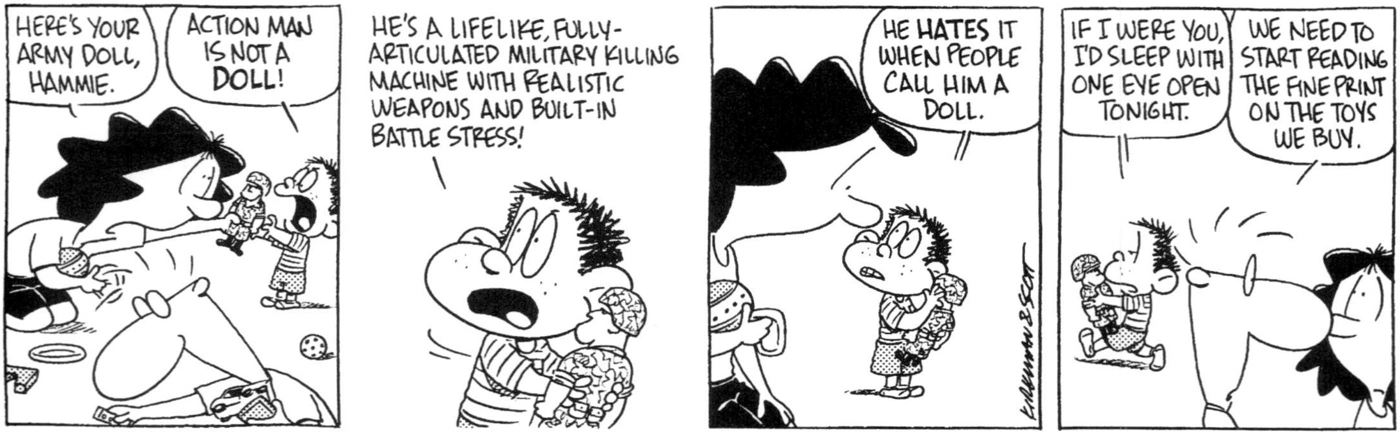
HERE'S YOUR ARMY DOLL, HAMMIE.
ACTION MAN IS NOT A DOLL!
HE'S A LIFELIKE, FULLY-ARTICULATED MILITARY KILLING MACHINE WITH REALISTIC WEAPONS AND BUILT-IN BATTLE STRESS!
HE HATES IT WHEN PEOPLE CALL HIM A DOLL.
IF I WERE YOU, I'D SLEEP WITH ONE EYE OPEN TONIGHT.
WE NEED TO START READING THE FINE PRINT ON THE TOYS WE BUY.

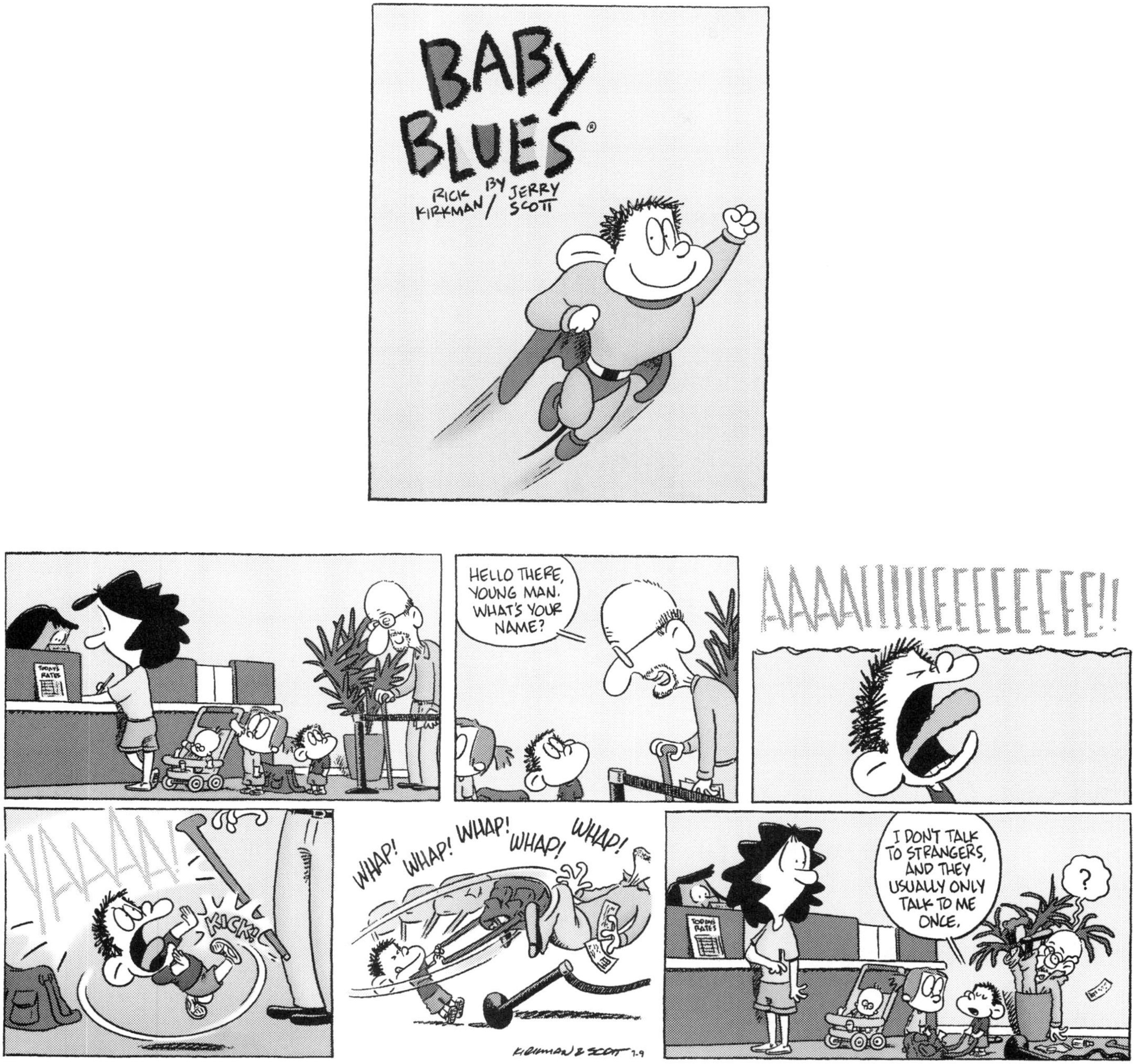

BABY BLUES®
BY RICK KIRKMAN / JERRY SCOTT
HELLO THERE, YOUNG MAN. WHAT'S YOUR NAME?
AAAAIIIIEEEEEEEE!!
YAAAAA!
KICK!
WHAP! WHAP! WHAP! WHAP! WHAP!
I DON'T TALK TO STRANGERS, AND THEY USUALLY ONLY TALK TO ME ONCE.
?
KIRKMAN & SCOTT

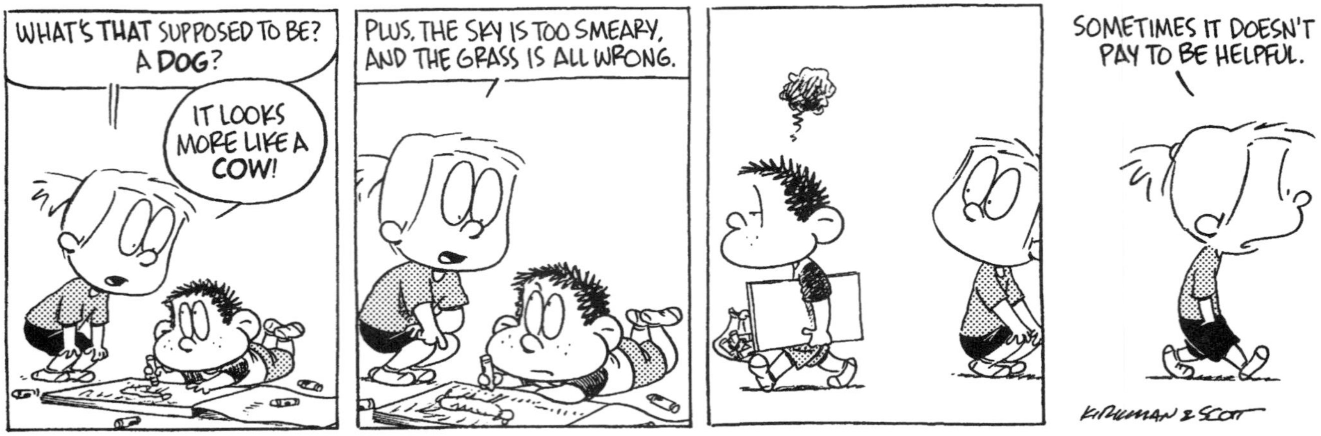

WHAT'S THAT SUPPOSED TO BE? A DOG?
IT LOOKS MORE LIKE A COW!
PLUS, THE SKY IS TOO SMEARY, AND THE GRASS IS ALL WRONG.
SOMETIMES IT DOESN'T PAY TO BE HELPFUL.
KIRKMAN & SCOTT

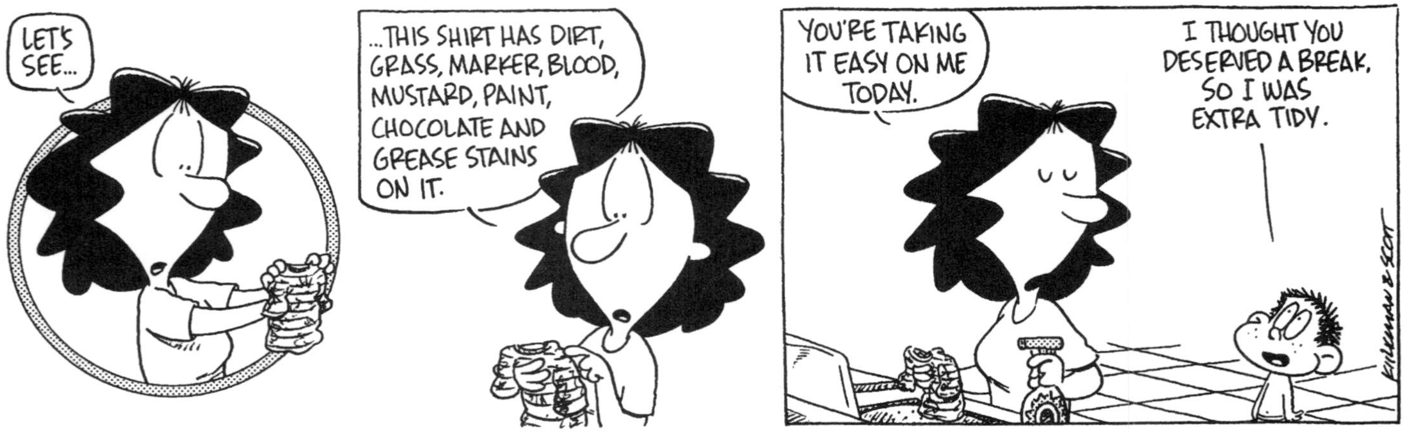

LET'S SEE...
...THIS SHIRT HAS DIRT, GRASS, MARKER, BLOOD, MUSTARD, PAINT, CHOCOLATE AND GREASE STAINS ON IT.
YOU'RE TAKING IT EASY ON ME TODAY.
I THOUGHT YOU DESERVED A BREAK, SO I WAS EXTRA TIDY.
KIRKMAN & SCOTT

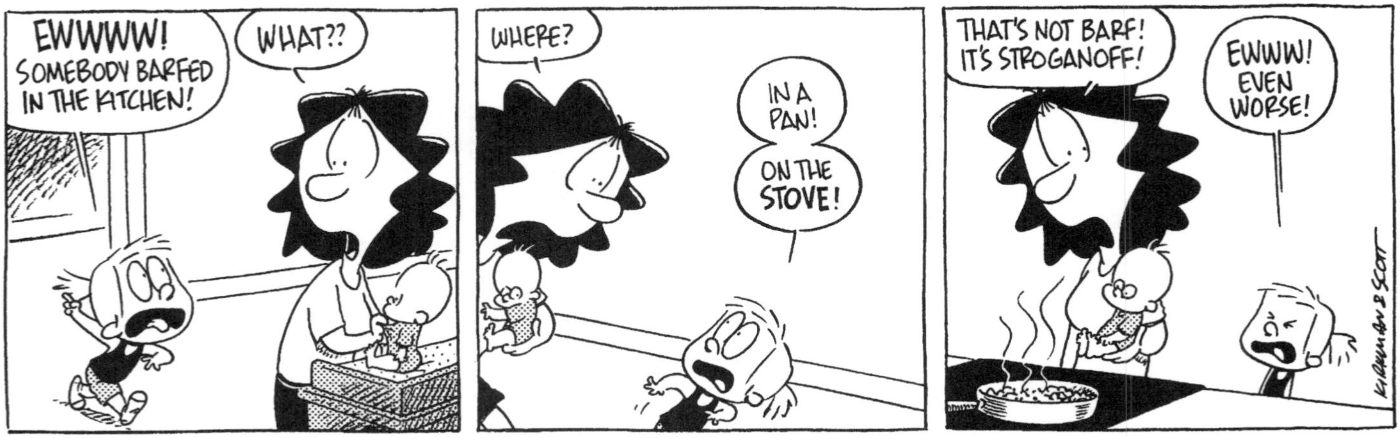

EWWWW! SOMEBODY BARFED IN THE KITCHEN!
WHAT??
WHERE?
IN A PAN!
ON THE STOVE!
THAT'S NOT BARF! IT'S STROGANOFF!
EWWW! EVEN WORSE!
KIRKMAN & SCOTT

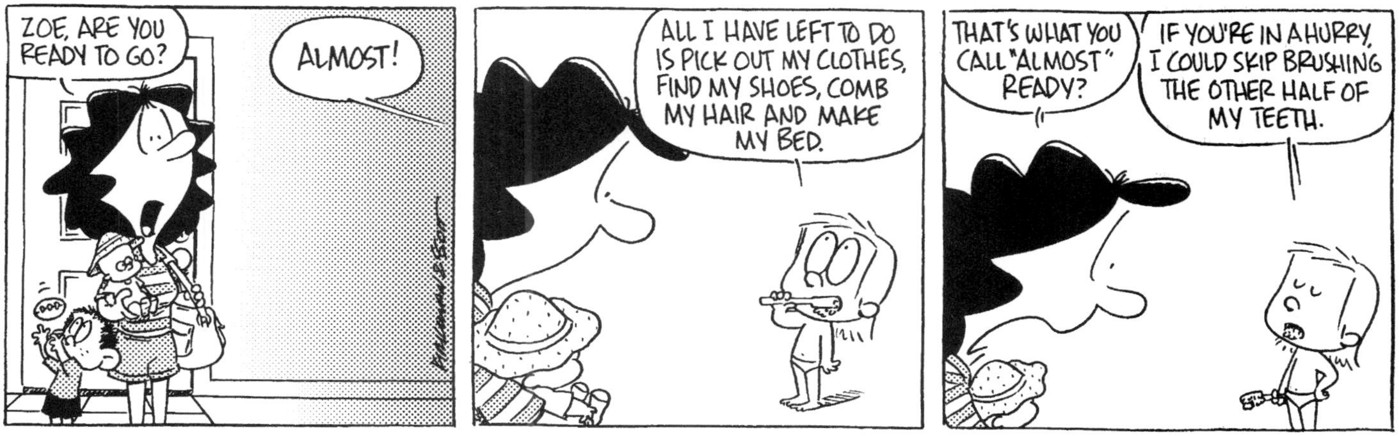
ZOE, ARE YOU READY TO GO?
ALMOST!
ALL I HAVE LEFT TO DO IS PICK OUT MY CLOTHES, FIND MY SHOES, COMB MY HAIR AND MAKE MY BED.
THAT'S WHAT YOU CALL "ALMOST" READY?
IF YOU'RE IN A HURRY, I COULD SKIP BRUSHING THE OTHER HALF OF MY TEETH.

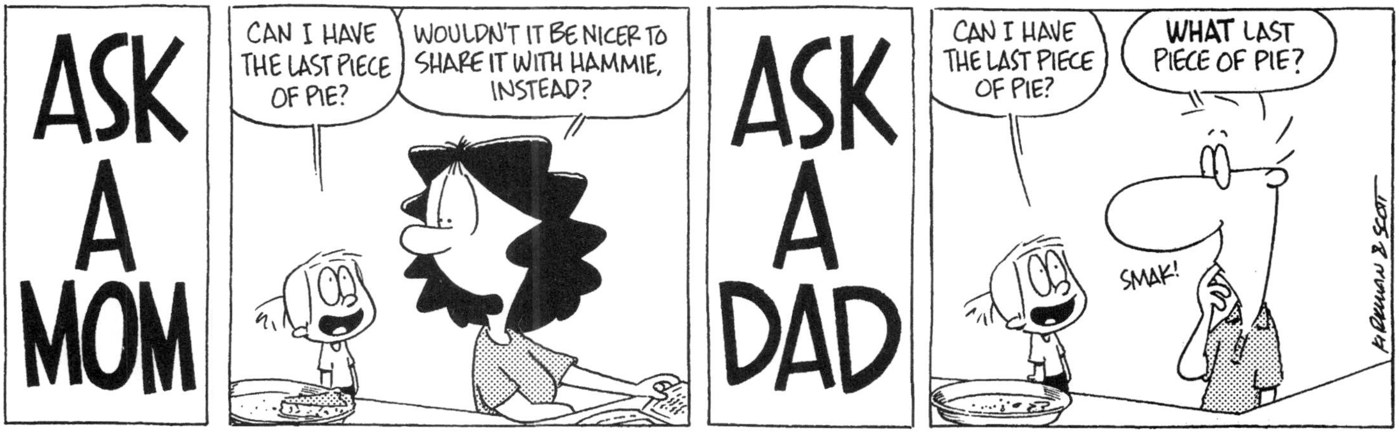
ASK A MOM
CAN I HAVE THE LAST PIECE OF PIE?
WOULDN'T IT BE NICER TO SHARE IT WITH HAMMIE, INSTEAD?
ASK A DAD
CAN I HAVE THE LAST PIECE OF PIE?
WHAT LAST PIECE OF PIE?
SMAK!

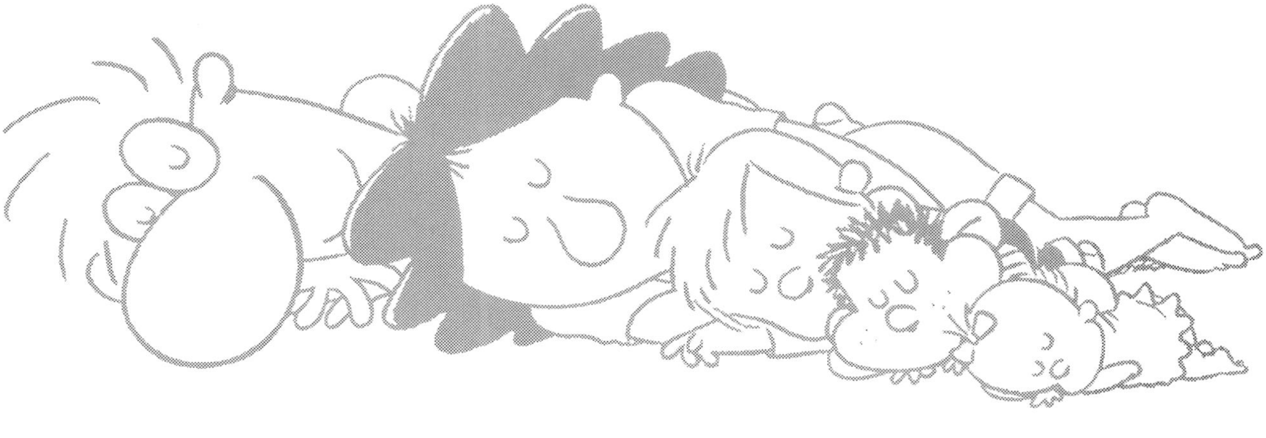

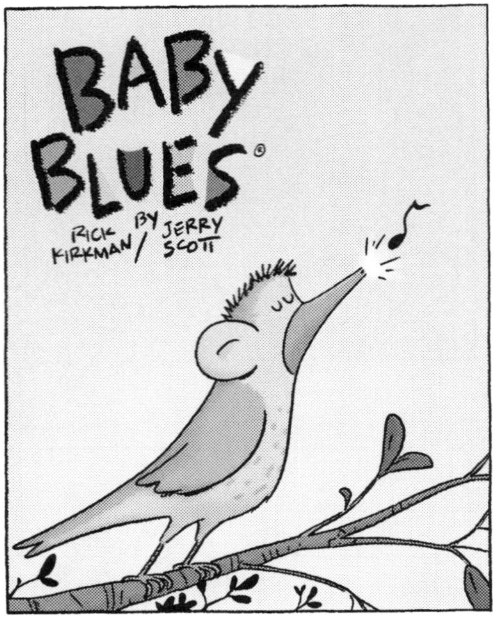
BABY BLUES®
BY RICK KIRKMAN / JERRY SCOTT

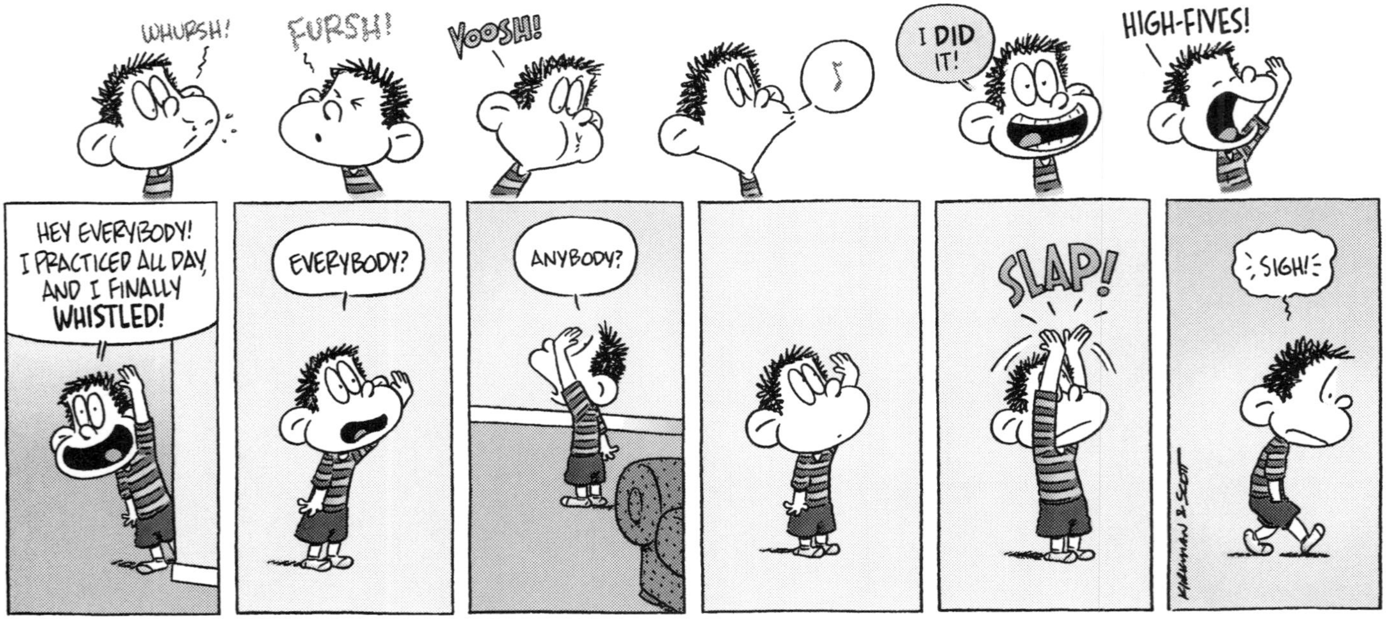
WHURSH!
FURSH!
VOOSH!
I DID IT!
HIGH-FIVES!
HEY EVERYBODY! I PRACTICED ALL DAY, AND I FINALLY WHISTLED!
EVERYBODY?
ANYBODY?
SLAP!
SIGH!
KIRKMAN & SCOTT

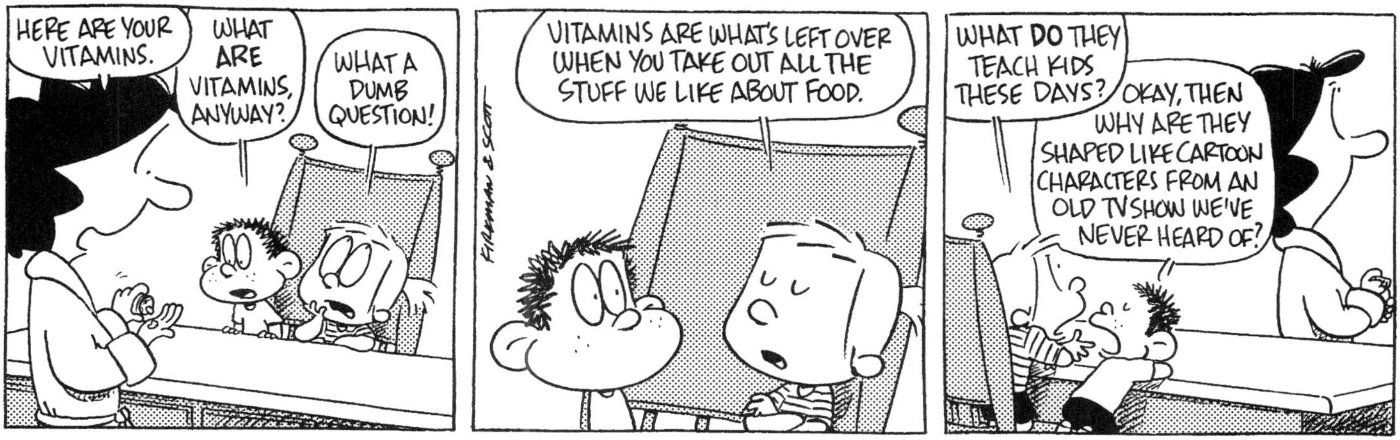
HERE ARE YOUR VITAMINS.
WHAT ARE VITAMINS, ANYWAY?
WHAT A DUMB QUESTION!
KIRKMAN & SCOTT
VITAMINS ARE WHAT'S LEFT OVER WHEN YOU TAKE OUT ALL THE STUFF WE LIKE ABOUT FOOD.
WHAT DO THEY TEACH KIDS THESE DAYS?
OKAY, THEN WHY ARE THEY SHAPED LIKE CARTOON CHARACTERS FROM AN OLD TV SHOW WE'VE NEVER HEARD OF?

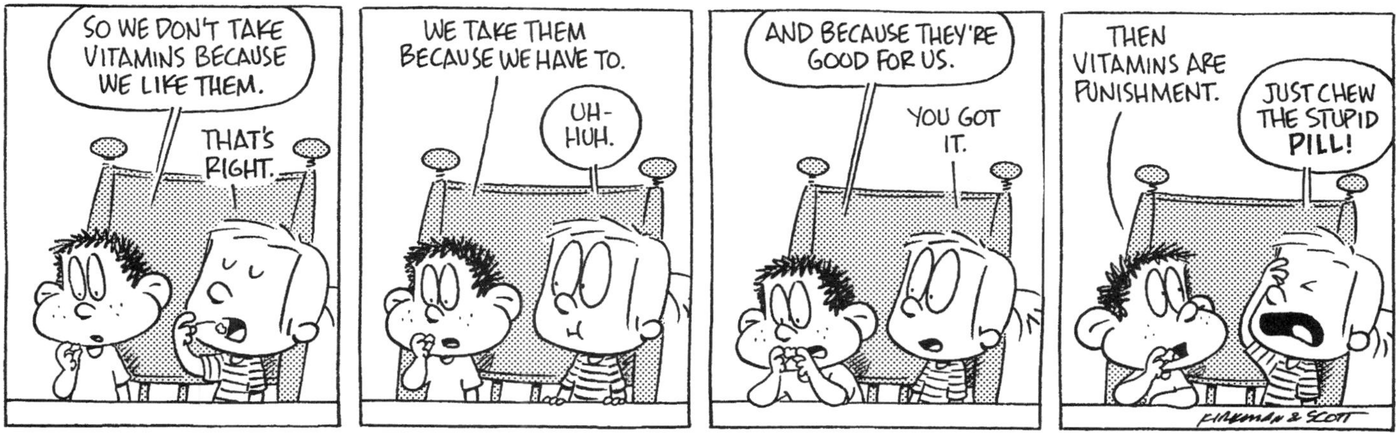
SO WE DON'T TAKE VITAMINS BECAUSE WE LIKE THEM.
THAT'S RIGHT.
WE TAKE THEM BECAUSE WE HAVE TO.
UH-HUH.
AND BECAUSE THEY'RE GOOD FOR US.
YOU GOT IT.
THEN VITAMINS ARE PUNISHMENT.
JUST CHEW THE STUPID PILL!
KIRKMAN & SCOTT

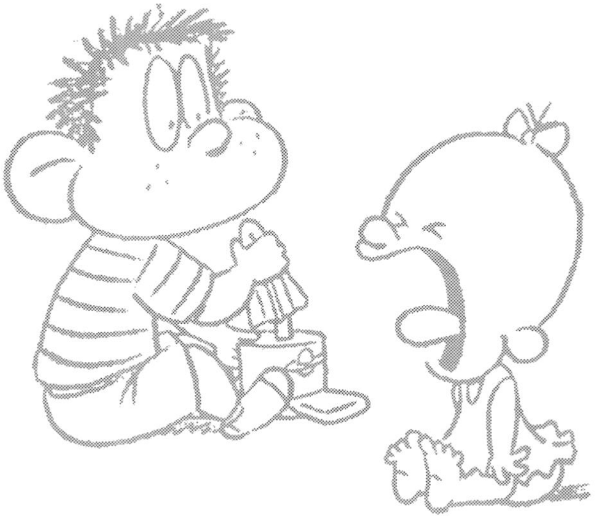

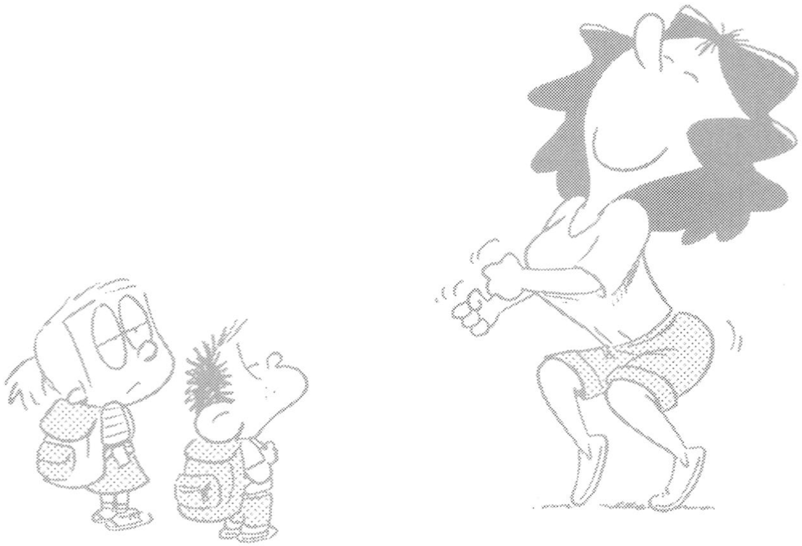

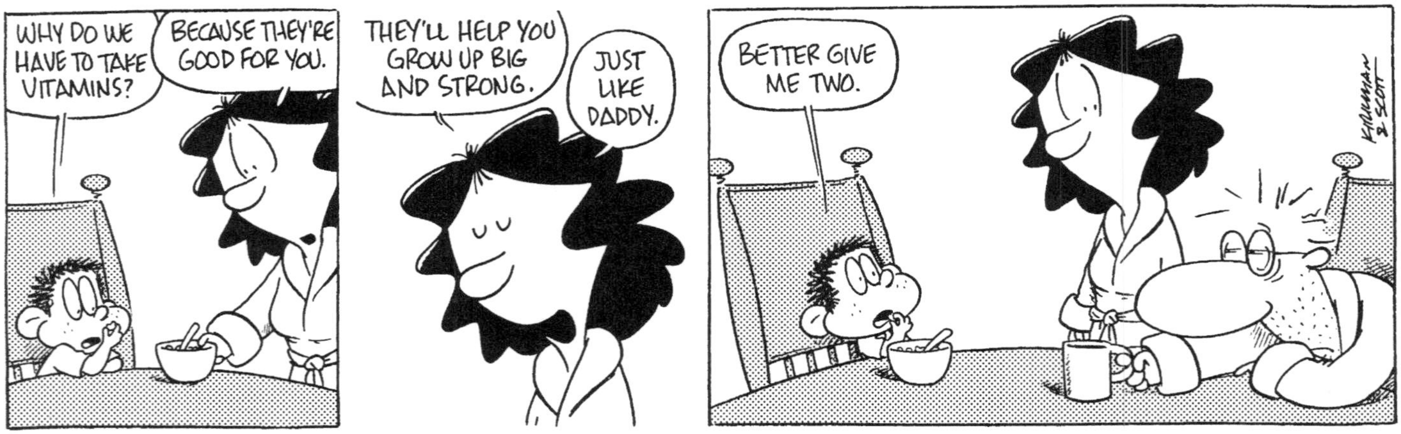

WHY DO WE HAVE TO TAKE VITAMINS?
BECAUSE THEY'RE GOOD FOR YOU.
THEY'LL HELP YOU GROW UP BIG AND STRONG.
JUST LIKE DADDY.
BETTER GIVE ME TWO.

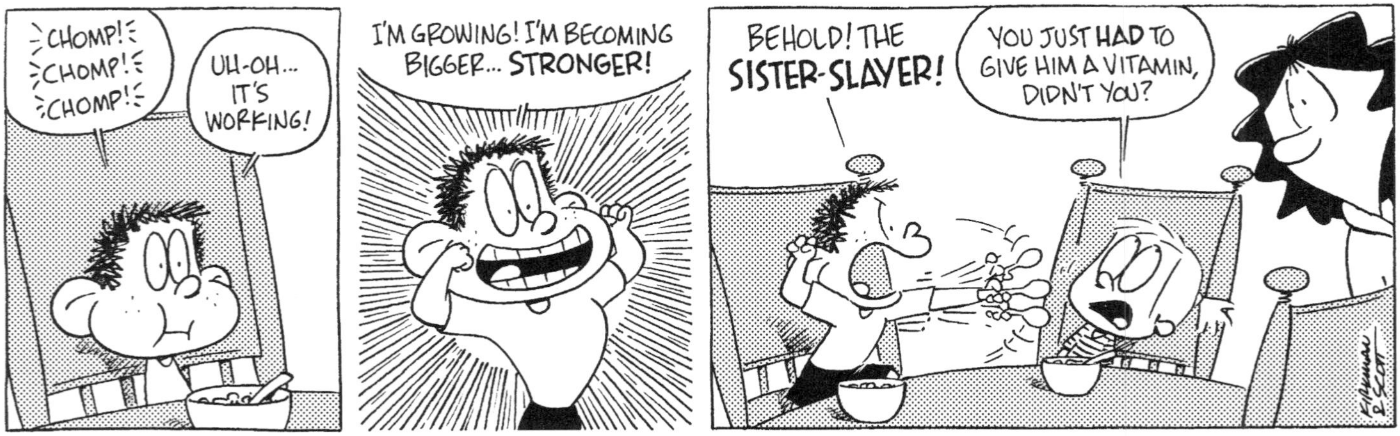

CHOMP! CHOMP! CHOMP!
UH-OH... IT'S WORKING!
I'M GROWING! I'M BECOMING BIGGER... **STRONGER!**
BEHOLD! THE **SISTER-SLAYER!**
YOU JUST **HAD** TO GIVE HIM A VITAMIN, DIDN'T YOU?

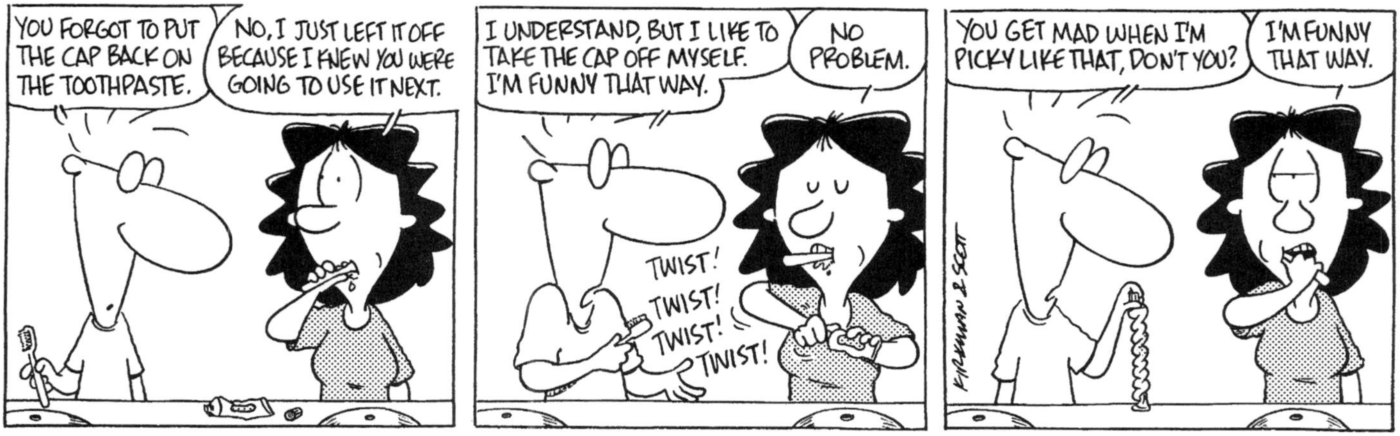
YOU FORGOT TO PUT THE CAP BACK ON THE TOOTHPASTE.
NO, I JUST LEFT IT OFF BECAUSE I KNEW YOU WERE GOING TO USE IT NEXT.
I UNDERSTAND, BUT I LIKE TO TAKE THE CAP OFF MYSELF. I'M FUNNY THAT WAY.
NO PROBLEM.
TWIST! TWIST! TWIST! TWIST!
YOU GET MAD WHEN I'M PICKY LIKE THAT, DON'T YOU?
I'M FUNNY THAT WAY.
KIRKMAN & SCOTT

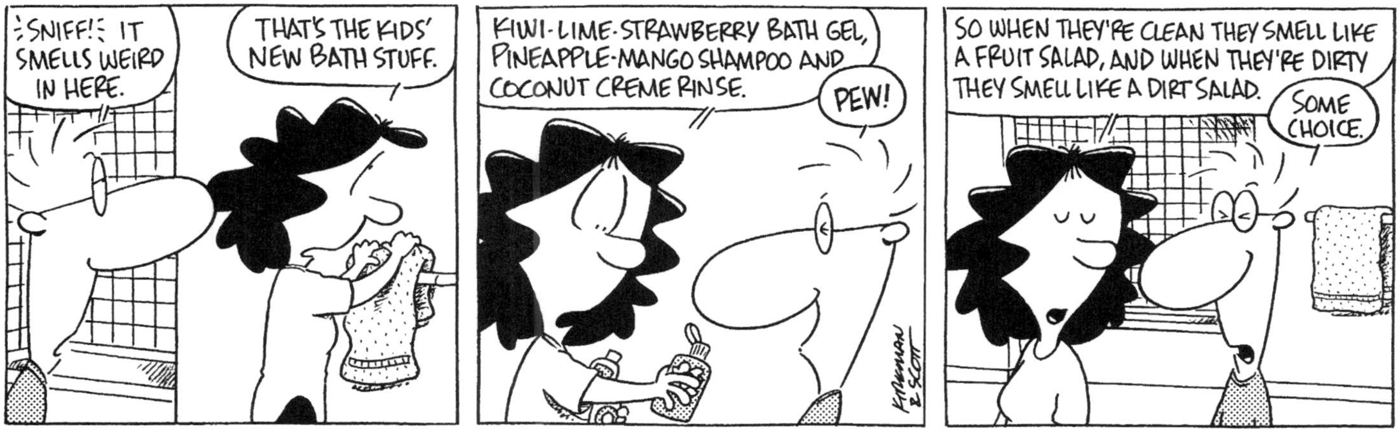
SNIFF! IT SMELLS WEIRD IN HERE.
THAT'S THE KIDS' NEW BATH STUFF.
KIWI-LIME-STRAWBERRY BATH GEL, PINEAPPLE-MANGO SHAMPOO AND COCONUT CREME RINSE.
PEW!
KIRKMAN & SCOTT
SO WHEN THEY'RE CLEAN THEY SMELL LIKE A FRUIT SALAD, AND WHEN THEY'RE DIRTY THEY SMELL LIKE A DIRT SALAD.
SOME CHOICE.

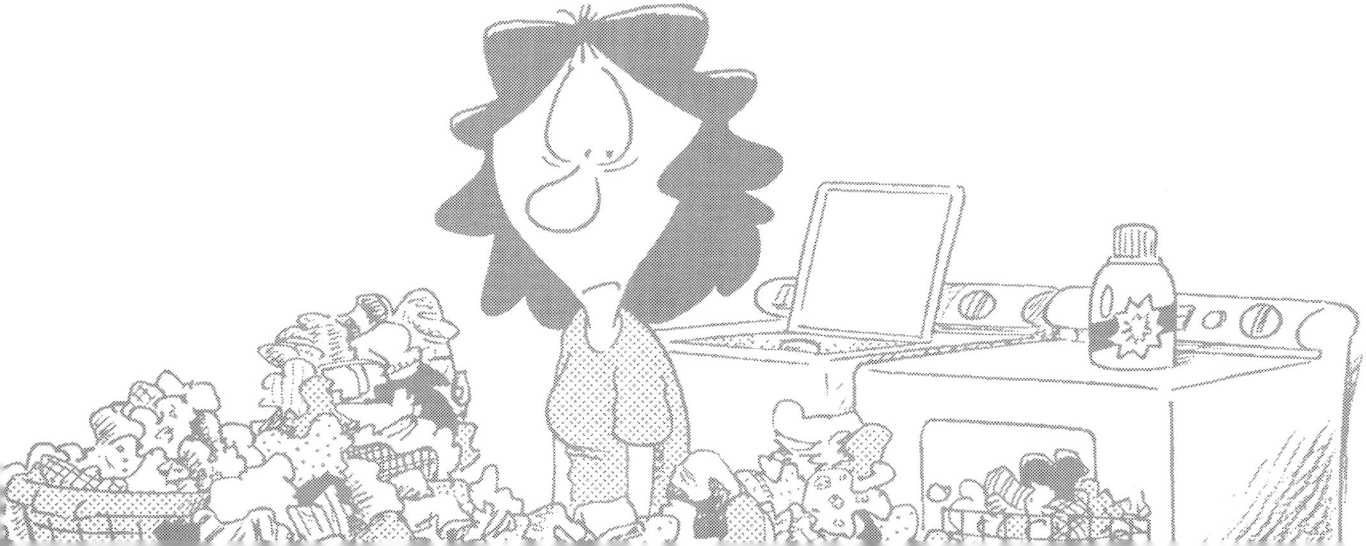

a BABY BLUES® Proverb

The grass is always greener on the knees of your kid's new white pants.

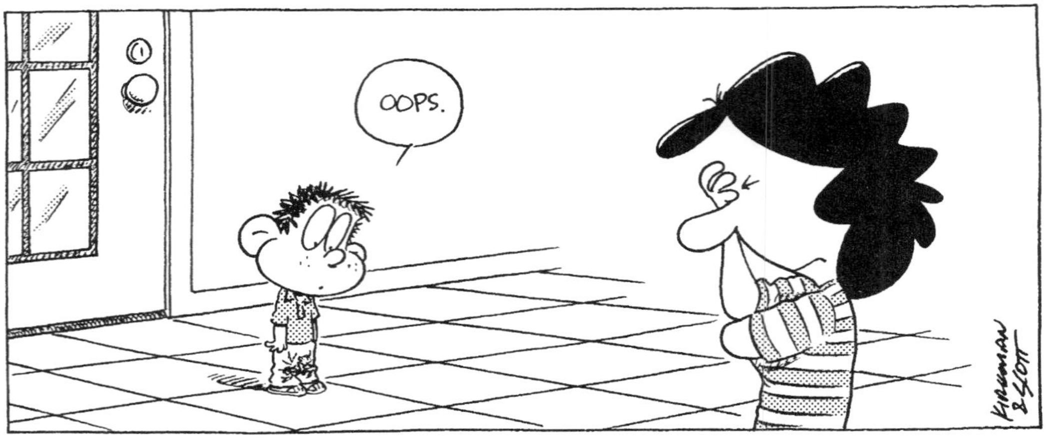
OOPS.

a BABY BLUES® Proverb

Give a child a fish, and he'll eat for a day. Teach a child to fish, and you'll end up with a hook in your ear lobe.

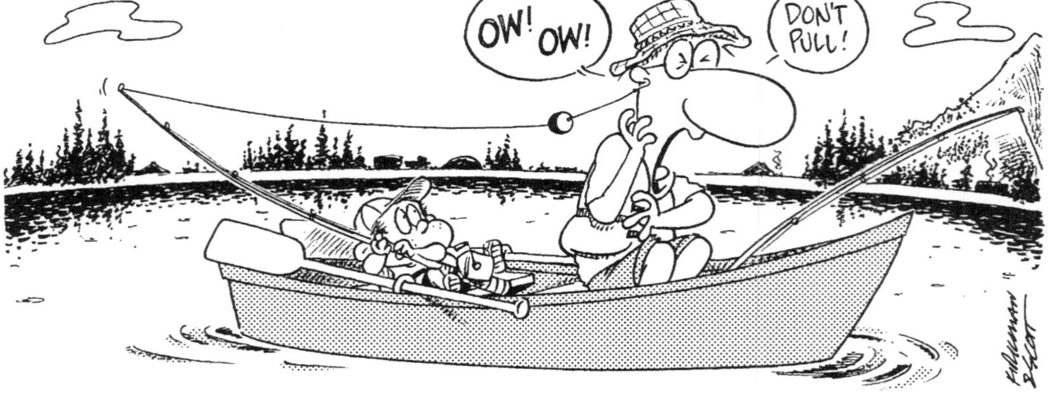
OW! OW!
DON'T PULL!

a BABY BLUES® Proverb

A bird in the hand is worth a $25 Polaroid.

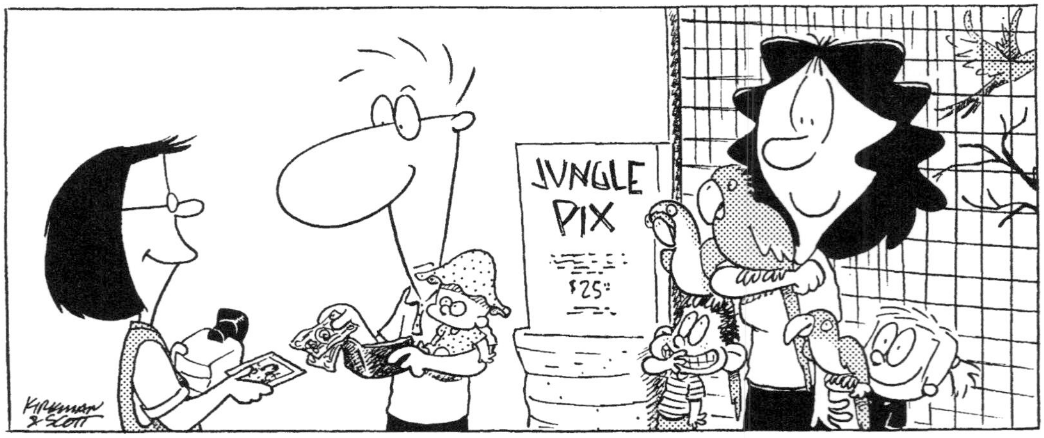
JUNGLE PIX
$25

a
BABY BLUES®
Proverb

Look out for number one.

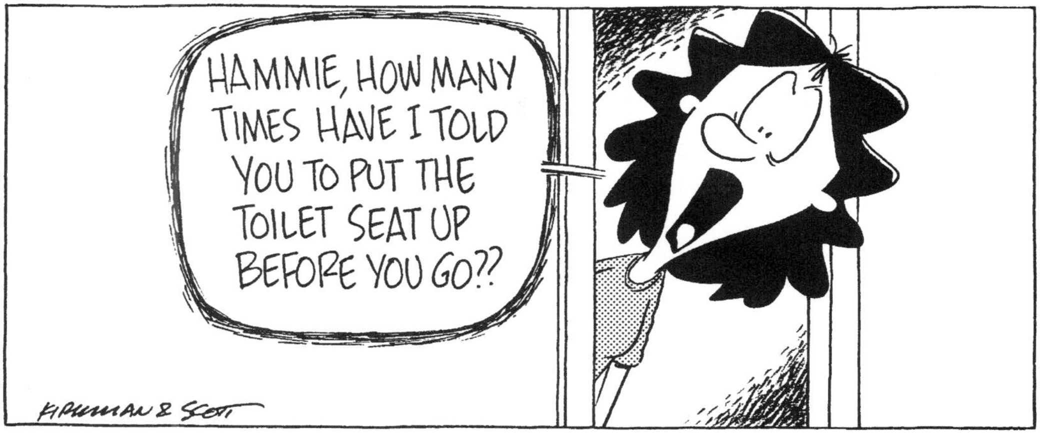
HAMMIE, HOW MANY TIMES HAVE I TOLD YOU TO PUT THE TOILET SEAT UP BEFORE YOU GO??

a
BABY BLUES®
Proverb

It's no use crying over spilled milk. Blame somebody else instead.

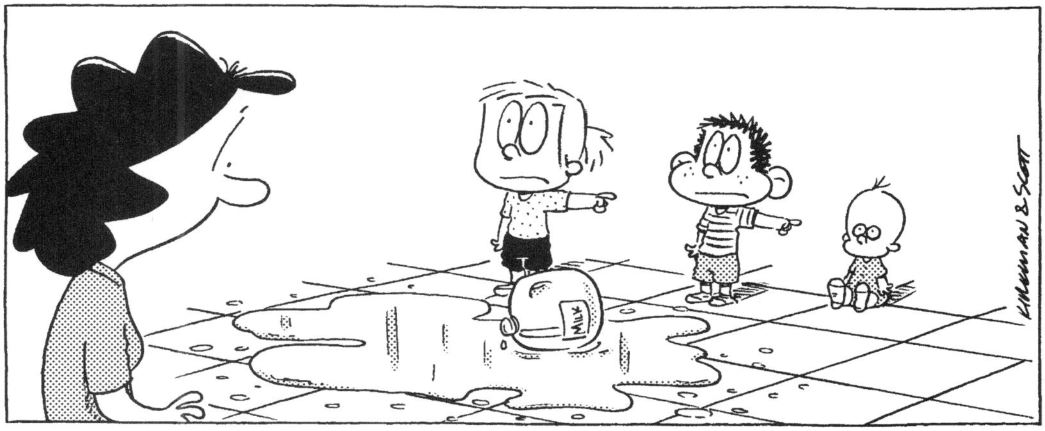
MILK

a
BABY BLUES®
Proverb

Nothing is certain but death and taxes.
And Laundry.

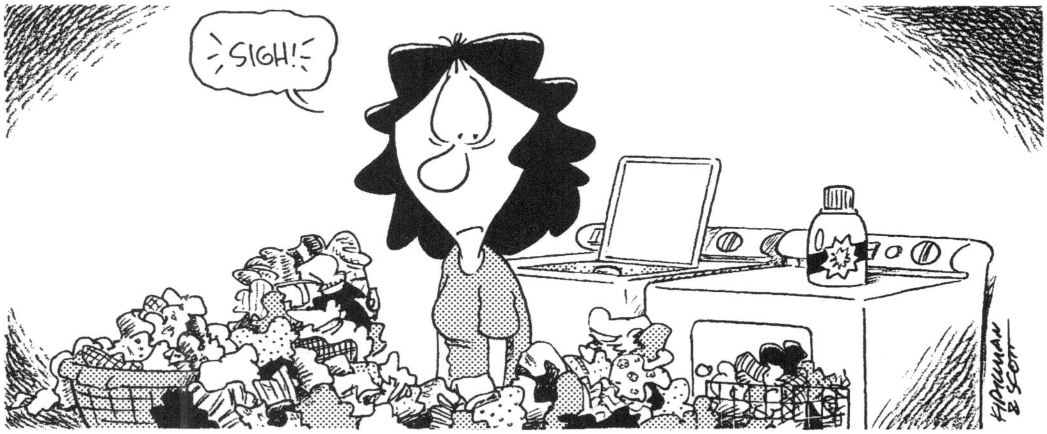
SIGH!

BABY BLUES®
BY RICK KIRKMAN & JERRY SCOTT

OKAY, READY?
WAIT!
JUST HOLD TH-
WHOOPS!
USE YOUR ELBOW!
I'M TRYING!
I CAN'T SEE!
GRUNT! WELL... JUST-
OW!
KIRKMAN & SCOTT

TODAY WE TRIMMED WREN'S FINGERNAILS.
IS THAT ALL?
IT'S ENOUGH.

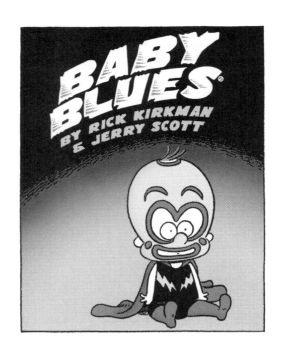

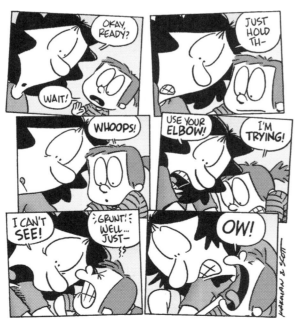

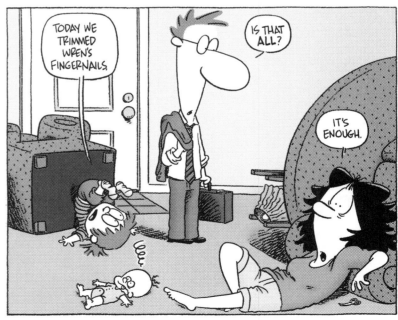

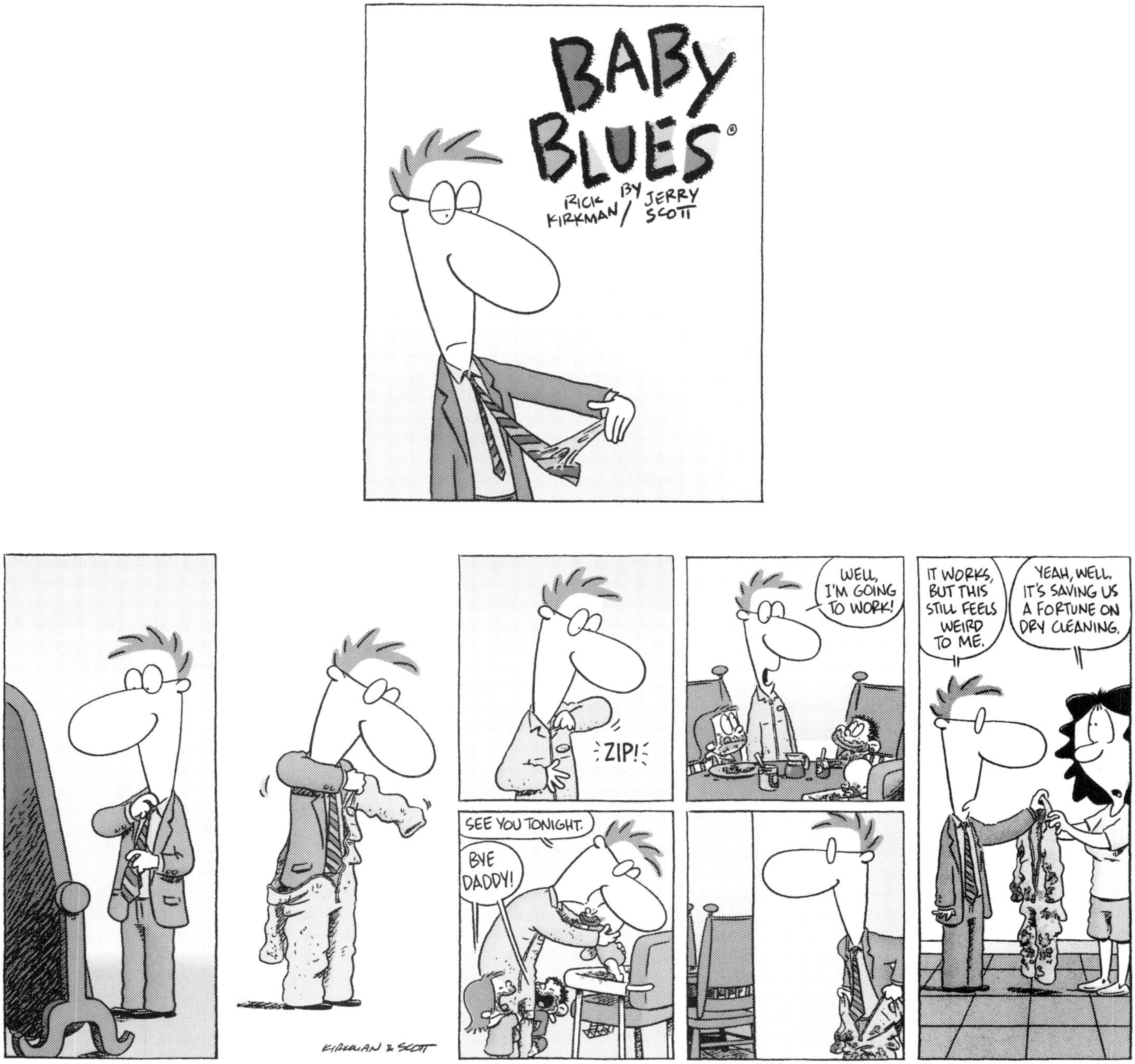
BABY BLUES®
BY RICK KIRKMAN / JERRY SCOTT
KIRKMAN & SCOTT
ZIP!
WELL, I'M GOING TO WORK!
SEE YOU TONIGHT.
BYE DADDY!
IT WORKS, BUT THIS STILL FEELS WEIRD TO ME.
YEAH, WELL. IT'S SAVING US A FORTUNE ON DRY CLEANING.

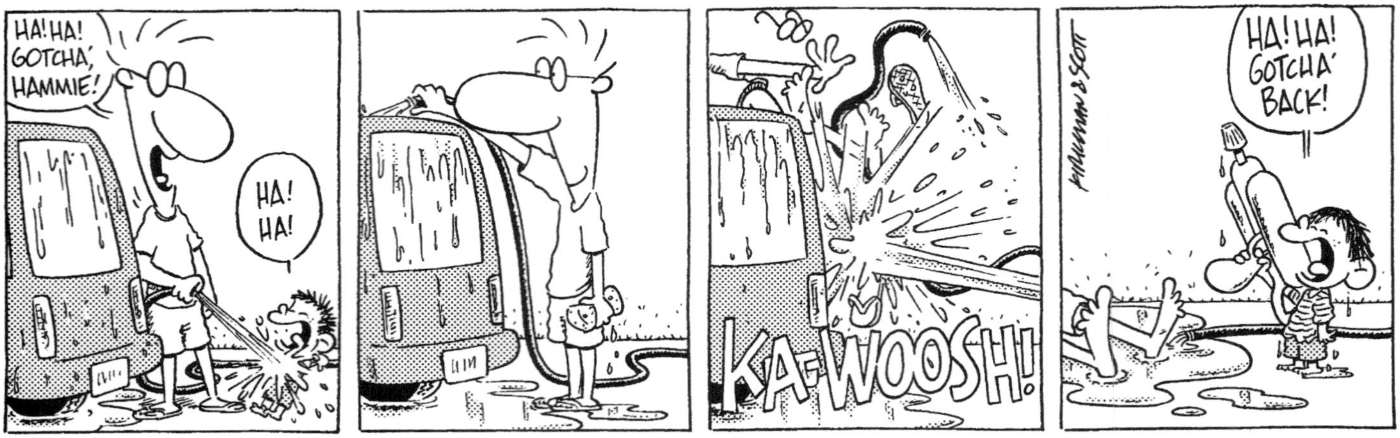
HA! HA! GOTCHA, HAMMIE!
HA! HA!
KA-WOOSH!
KIRKMAN & SCOTT
HA! HA! GOTCHA BACK!

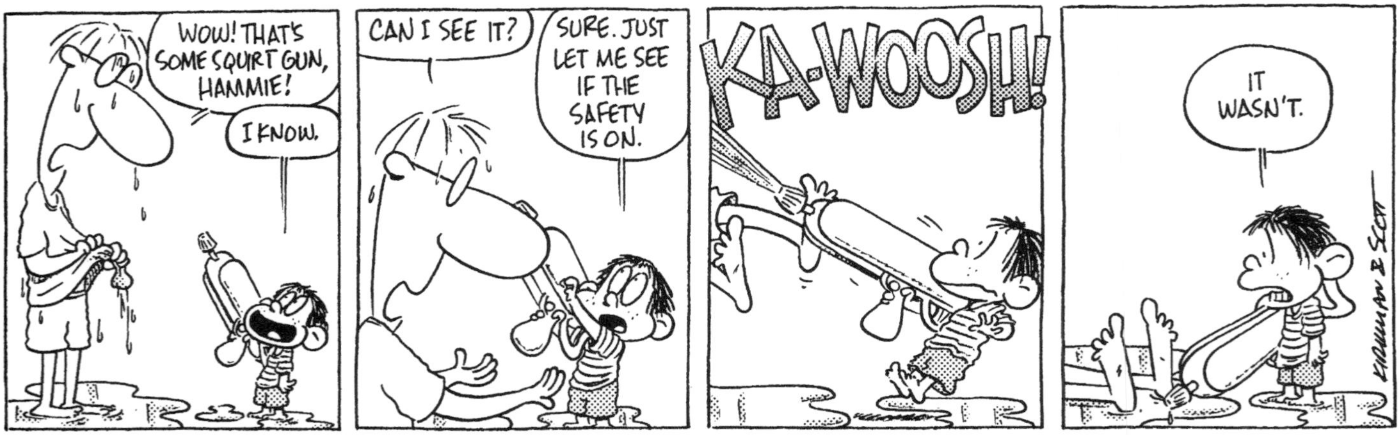
WOW! THAT'S SOME SQUIRT GUN, HAMMIE!
I KNOW.
CAN I SEE IT?
SURE. JUST LET ME SEE IF THE SAFETY IS ON.
KA-WOOSH!
IT WASN'T.
KIRKMAN & SCOTT

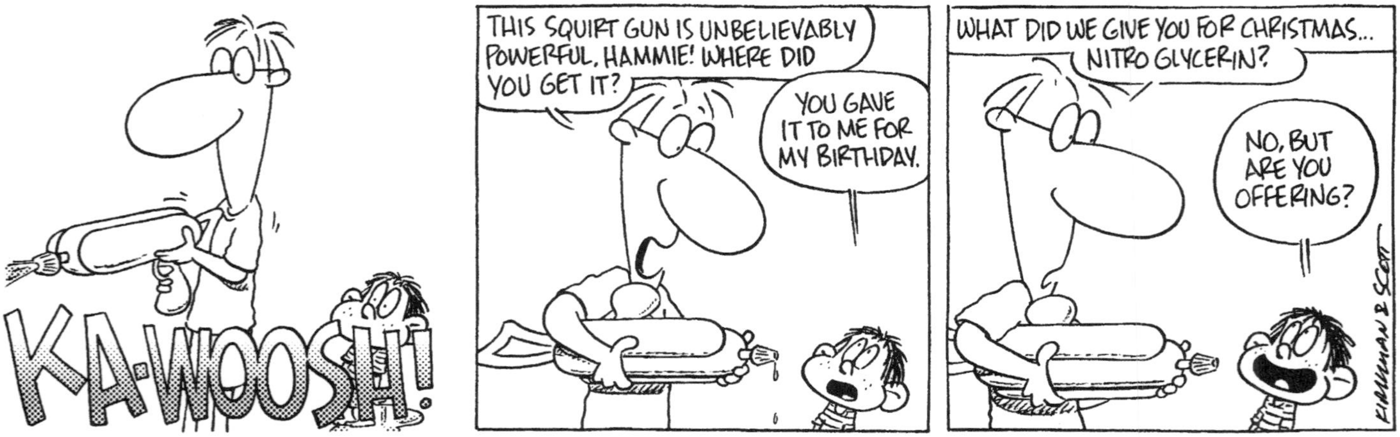
KA-WOOSH!
THIS SQUIRT GUN IS UNBELIEVABLY POWERFUL, HAMMIE! WHERE DID YOU GET IT?
YOU GAVE IT TO ME FOR MY BIRTHDAY.
WHAT DID WE GIVE YOU FOR CHRISTMAS... NITRO GLYCERIN?
NO, BUT ARE YOU OFFERING?
KIRKMAN & SCOTT

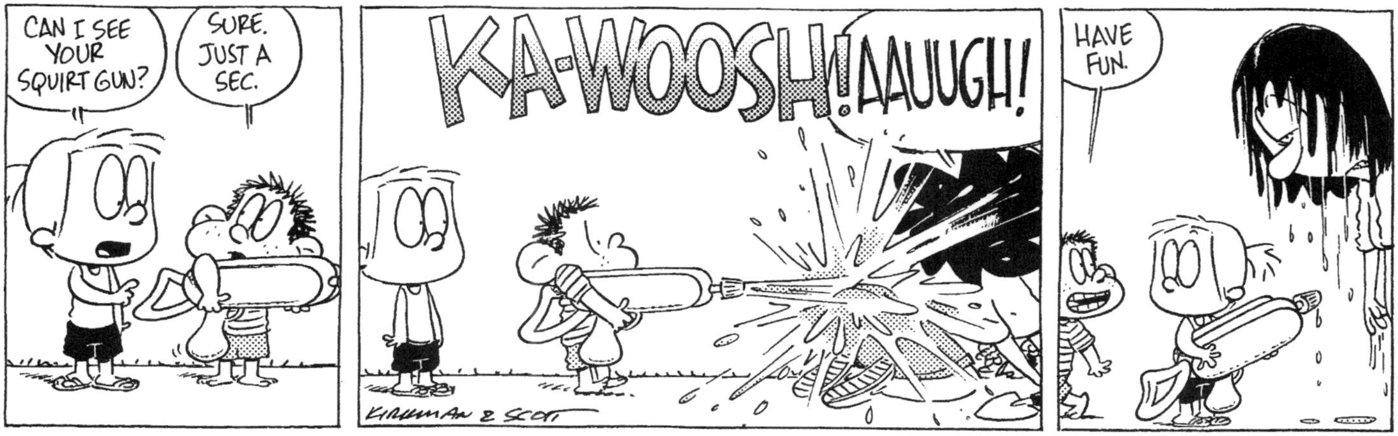
CAN I SEE YOUR SQUIRT GUN?
SURE. JUST A SEC.
KA-WOOSH!
AAUUGH!
KIRKMAN & SCOTT
HAVE FUN.

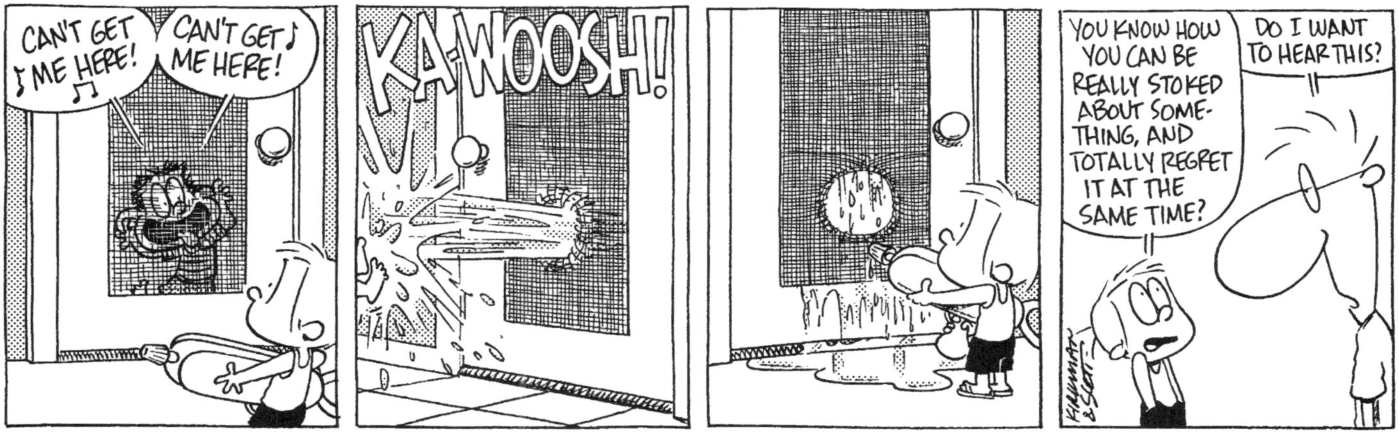
CAN'T GET ME HERE!
CAN'T GET ME HERE!
KA-WOOSH!
YOU KNOW HOW YOU CAN BE REALLY STOKED ABOUT SOMETHING, AND TOTALLY REGRET IT AT THE SAME TIME?
DO I WANT TO HEAR THIS?
KIRKMAN & SCOTT

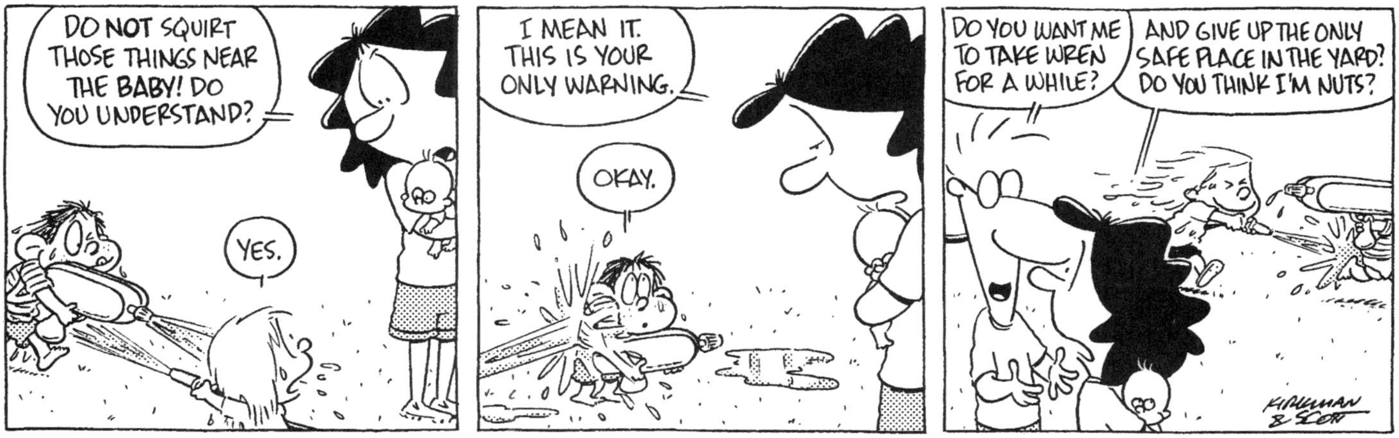
DO **NOT** SQUIRT THOSE THINGS NEAR THE **BABY**! DO YOU UNDERSTAND?
YES.
I MEAN IT. THIS IS YOUR ONLY WARNING.
OKAY.
DO YOU WANT ME TO TAKE WREN FOR A WHILE?
AND GIVE UP THE ONLY SAFE PLACE IN THE YARD? DO YOU THINK I'M NUTS?
KIRKMAN & SCOTT

B _ BY
BLU _ S

GUYS, I NEED TO TALK TO YOU ABOUT COOPERATION AND RESPECT.
BLAH BLAH
BLAH BLAH BLAH BLAH
BLAH BLAH BLAH BLAH BLAH
IT WAS FUNNY STUFF, BUT YOU GOT GREEDY WITH THE "HANGMAN" THING.
BLAH BLAH BLAH BLAH
BLAH BLAH BLAH BLAH BLAH...
BLAH BLAH BLAH BLAH BLAH

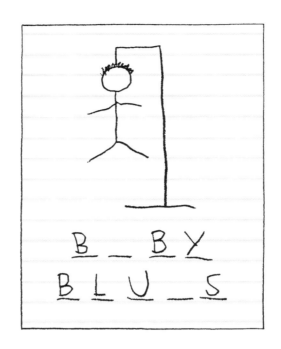

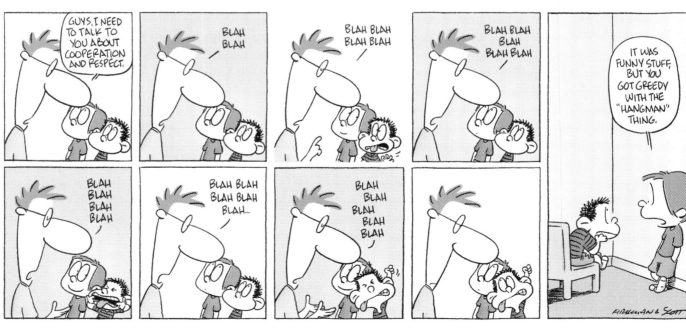

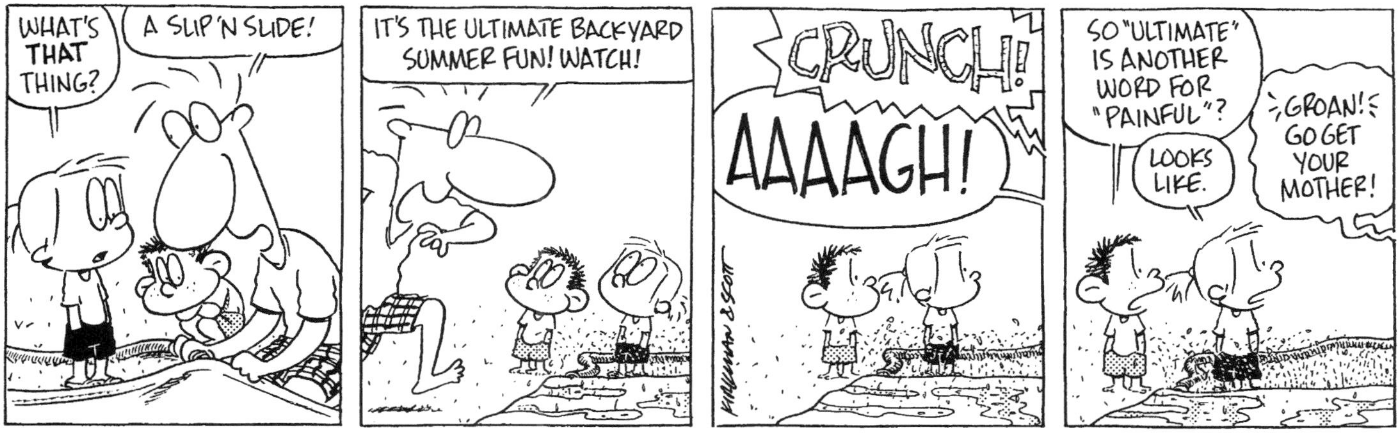
WHAT'S **THAT** THING?
A SLIP 'N SLIDE!
IT'S THE ULTIMATE BACKYARD SUMMER FUN! WATCH!
CRUNCH!
AAAAGH!
SO "ULTIMATE" IS ANOTHER WORD FOR "PAINFUL"?
LOOKS LIKE.
GROAN! GO GET YOUR MOTHER!

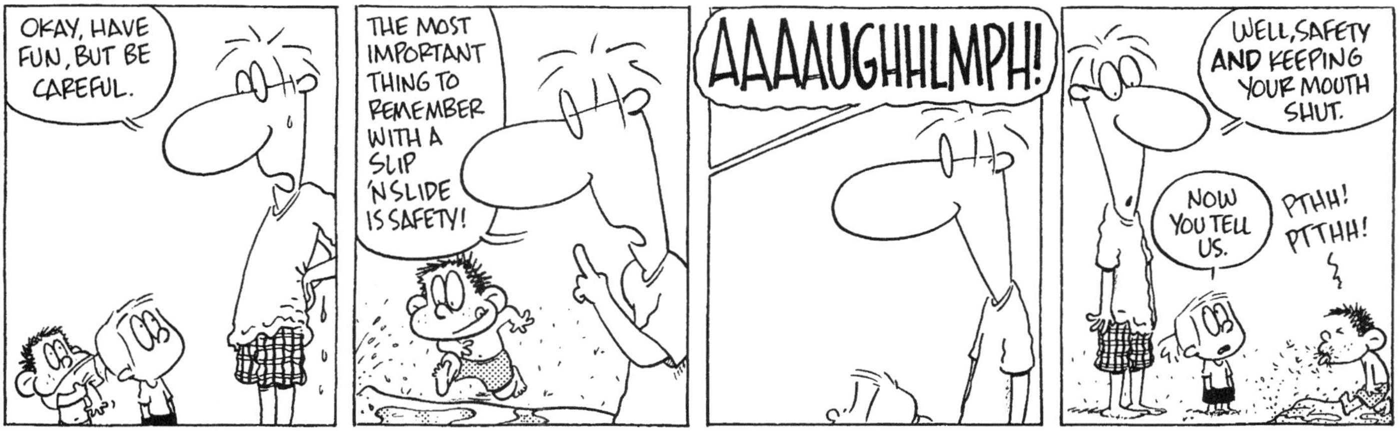
OKAY, HAVE FUN, BUT BE CAREFUL.
THE MOST IMPORTANT THING TO REMEMBER WITH A SLIP 'N SLIDE IS SAFETY!
AAAAUGHHLMPH!
WELL, SAFETY **AND** KEEPING YOUR MOUTH SHUT.
NOW YOU TELL US.
PTHH! PTTHH!

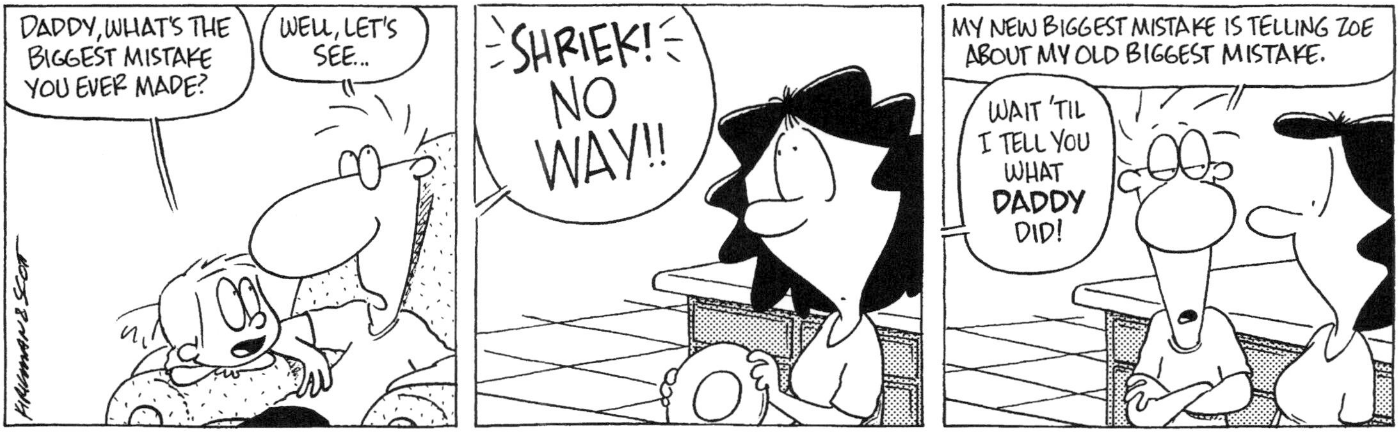
DADDY, WHAT'S THE BIGGEST MISTAKE YOU EVER MADE?
WELL, LET'S SEE...
SHRIEK! NO WAY!!
MY NEW BIGGEST MISTAKE IS TELLING ZOE ABOUT MY OLD BIGGEST MISTAKE.
WAIT 'TIL I TELL YOU WHAT **DADDY** DID!

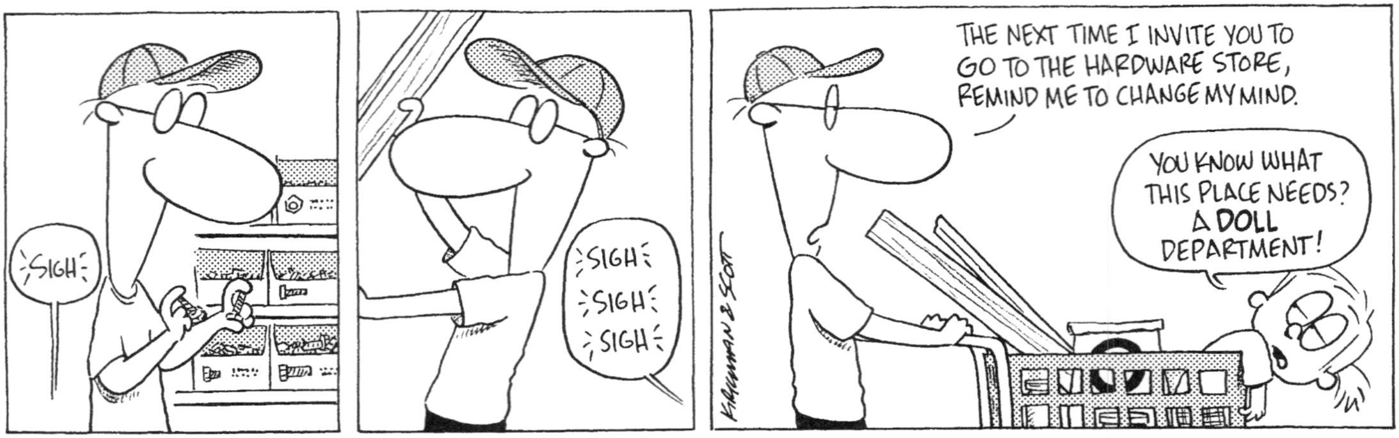
SIGH
SIGH SIGH SIGH
THE NEXT TIME I INVITE YOU TO GO TO THE HARDWARE STORE, REMIND ME TO CHANGE MY MIND.
YOU KNOW WHAT THIS PLACE NEEDS? A **DOLL** DEPARTMENT!
KIRKMAN & SCOTT

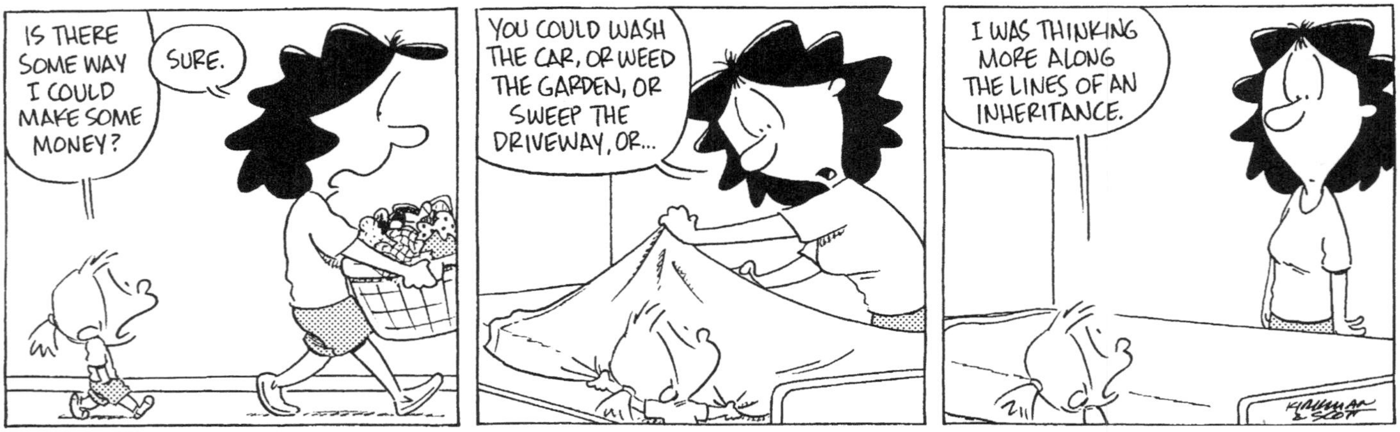
IS THERE SOME WAY I COULD MAKE SOME MONEY?
SURE.
YOU COULD WASH THE CAR, OR WEED THE GARDEN, OR SWEEP THE DRIVEWAY, OR...
I WAS THINKING MORE ALONG THE LINES OF AN INHERITANCE.
KIRKMAN & SCOTT

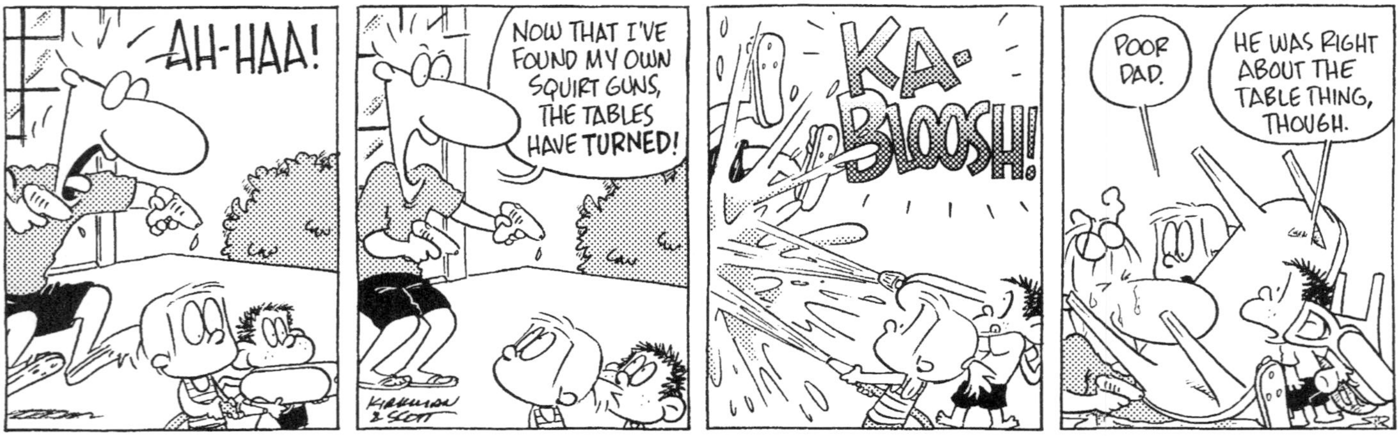
AH-HAA!
NOW THAT I'VE FOUND MY OWN SQUIRT GUNS, THE TABLES HAVE **TURNED**!
KIRKMAN & SCOTT
KA-BLOOSH!
POOR DAD.
HE WAS RIGHT ABOUT THE TABLE THING, THOUGH.

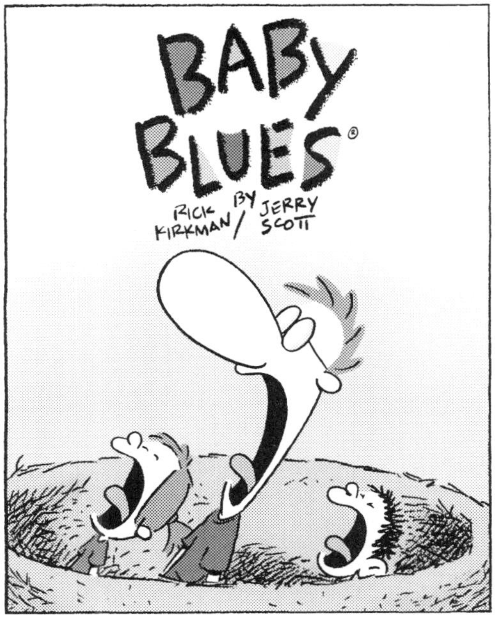
BABY BLUES®
BY
RICK KIRKMAN / JERRY SCOTT

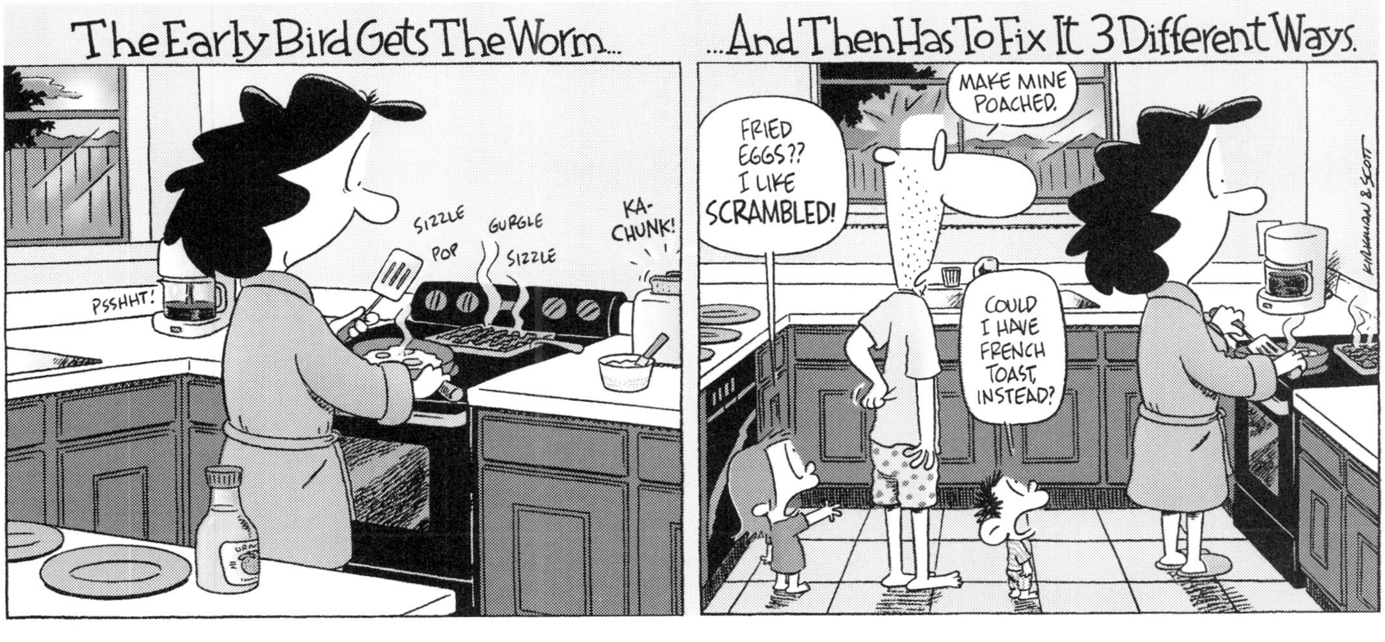
The Early Bird Gets The Worm...
...And Then Has To Fix It 3 Different Ways.
PSSHHT!
SIZZLE
POP
GURGLE
SIZZLE
KA-CHUNK!
FRIED EGGS?? I LIKE SCRAMBLED!
MAKE MINE POACHED.
COULD I HAVE FRENCH TOAST, INSTEAD?
KIRKMAN & SCOTT

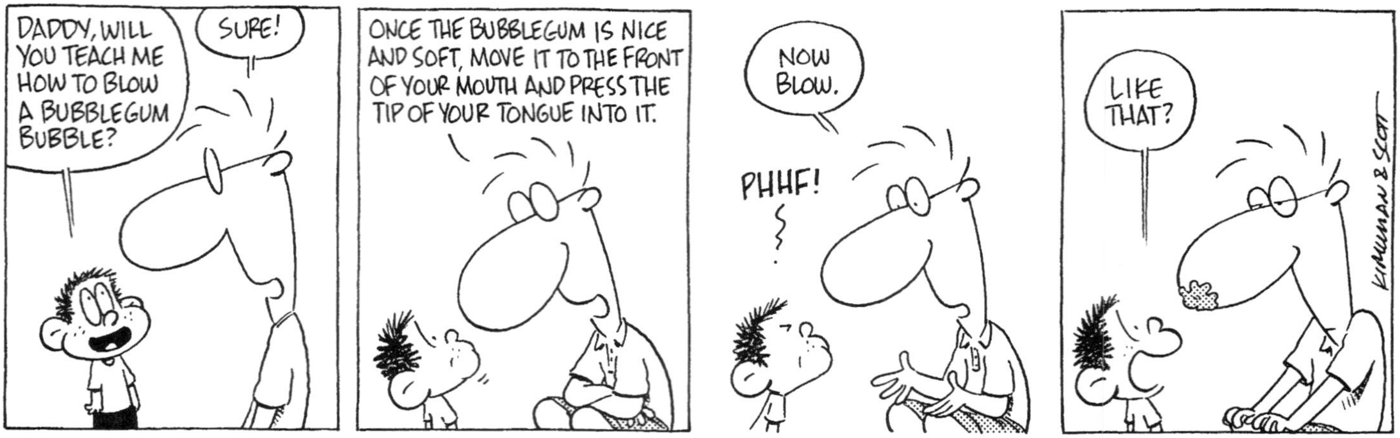
DADDY, WILL YOU TEACH ME HOW TO BLOW A BUBBLEGUM BUBBLE?
SURE!
ONCE THE BUBBLEGUM IS NICE AND SOFT, MOVE IT TO THE FRONT OF YOUR MOUTH AND PRESS THE TIP OF YOUR TONGUE INTO IT.
NOW BLOW.
PHHF!
LIKE THAT?
KIRKMAN & SCOTT

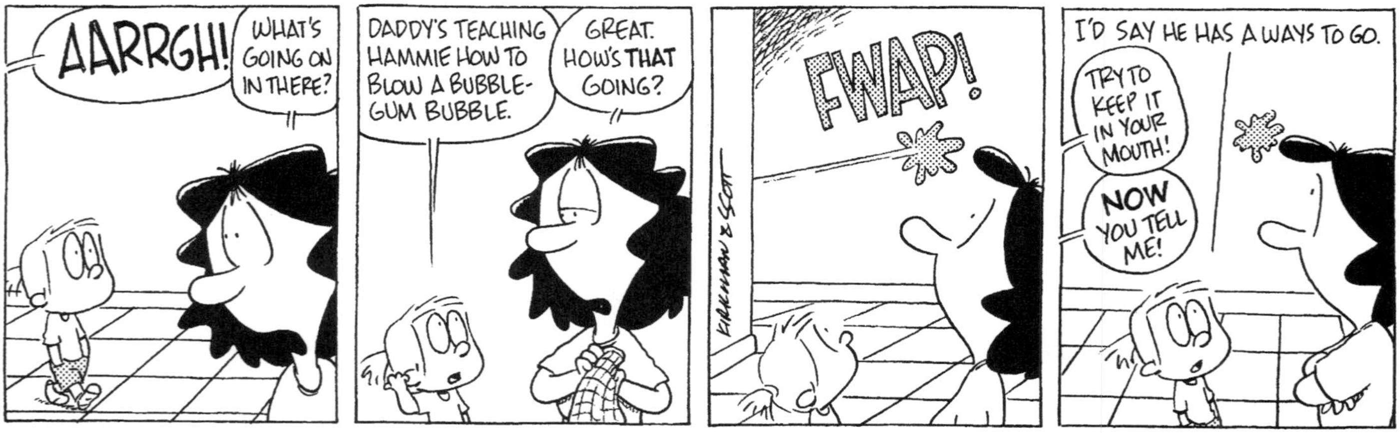
AARRGH!
WHAT'S GOING ON IN THERE?
DADDY'S TEACHING HAMMIE HOW TO BLOW A BUBBLE-GUM BUBBLE.
GREAT. HOW'S THAT GOING?
KIRKMAN & SCOTT
FWAP!
I'D SAY HE HAS A WAYS TO GO.
TRY TO KEEP IT IN YOUR MOUTH!
NOW YOU TELL ME!

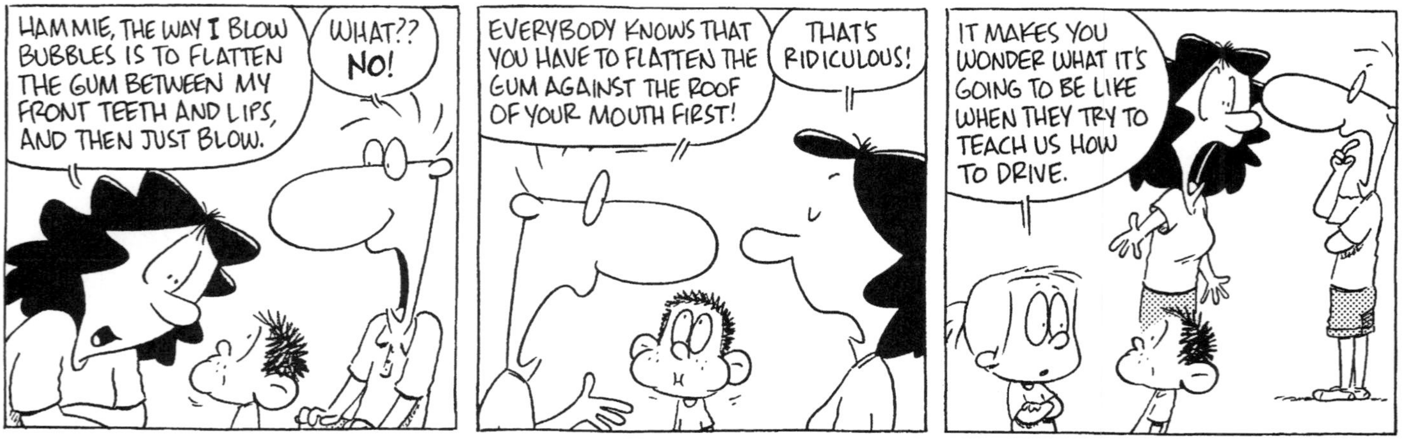
HAMMIE, THE WAY I BLOW BUBBLES IS TO FLATTEN THE GUM BETWEEN MY FRONT TEETH AND LIPS, AND THEN JUST BLOW.
WHAT?? NO!
EVERYBODY KNOWS THAT YOU HAVE TO FLATTEN THE GUM AGAINST THE ROOF OF YOUR MOUTH FIRST!
THAT'S RIDICULOUS!
IT MAKES YOU WONDER WHAT IT'S GOING TO BE LIKE WHEN THEY TRY TO TEACH US HOW TO DRIVE.

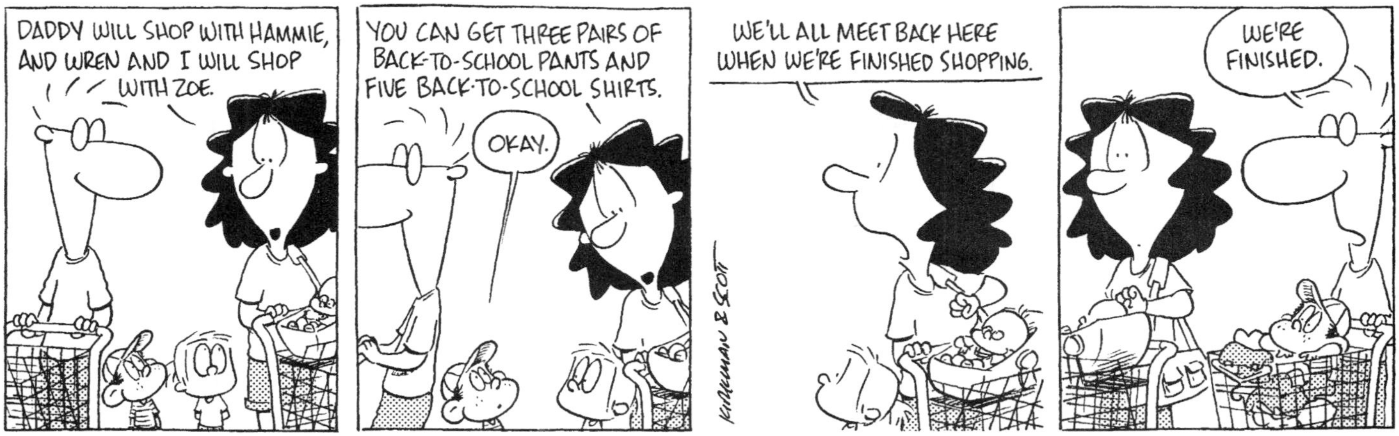
DADDY WILL SHOP WITH HAMMIE, AND WREN AND I WILL SHOP WITH ZOE.
YOU CAN GET THREE PAIRS OF BACK-TO-SCHOOL PANTS AND FIVE BACK-TO-SCHOOL SHIRTS.
OKAY.
KIRKMAN & SCOTT
WE'LL ALL MEET BACK HERE WHEN WE'RE FINISHED SHOPPING.
WE'RE FINISHED.

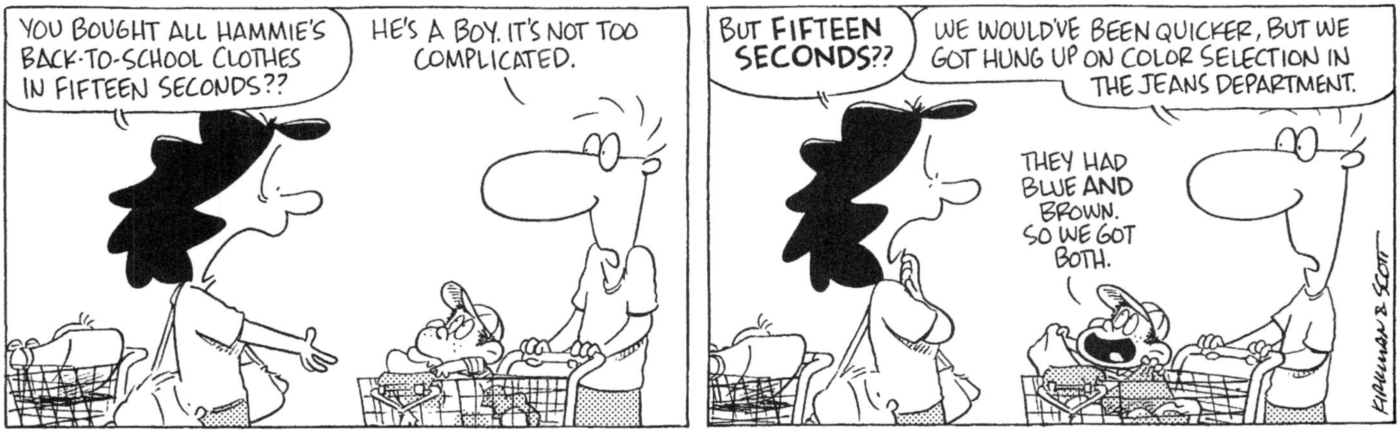
YOU BOUGHT ALL HAMMIE'S BACK-TO-SCHOOL CLOTHES IN FIFTEEN SECONDS??
HE'S A BOY. IT'S NOT TOO COMPLICATED.
BUT **FIFTEEN SECONDS**??
WE WOULD'VE BEEN QUICKER, BUT WE GOT HUNG UP ON COLOR SELECTION IN THE JEANS DEPARTMENT.
THEY HAD BLUE **AND** BROWN. SO WE GOT BOTH.
KIRKMAN & SCOTT

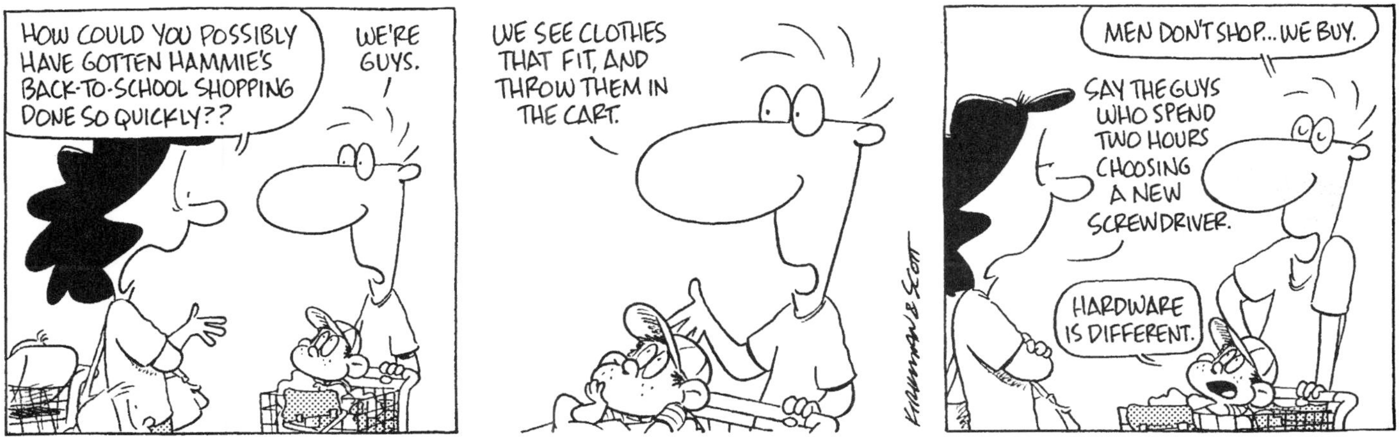
HOW COULD YOU POSSIBLY HAVE GOTTEN HAMMIE'S BACK-TO-SCHOOL SHOPPING DONE SO QUICKLY??
WE'RE GUYS.
WE SEE CLOTHES THAT FIT, AND THROW THEM IN THE CART.
KIRKMAN & SCOTT
MEN DON'T SHOP... WE BUY.
SAY THE GUYS WHO SPEND TWO HOURS CHOOSING A NEW SCREWDRIVER.
HARDWARE IS DIFFERENT.

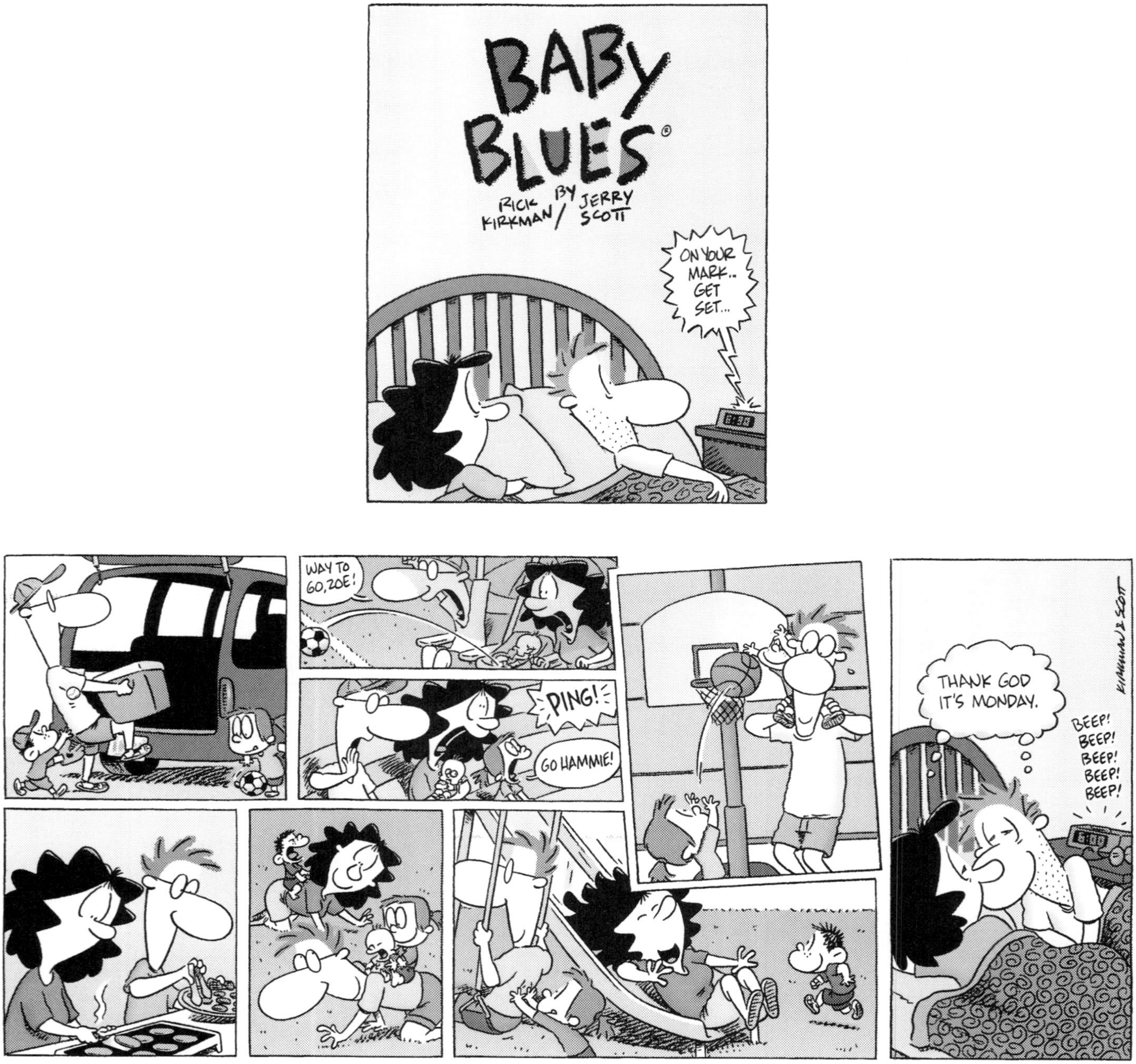
BABY BLUES®
BY RICK KIRKMAN / JERRY SCOTT
ON YOUR MARK.. GET SET...
WAY TO GO, ZOE!
PING!
GO HAMMIE!
THANK GOD IT'S MONDAY.
BEEP! BEEP! BEEP! BEEP! BEEP!
KIRKMAN & SCOTT

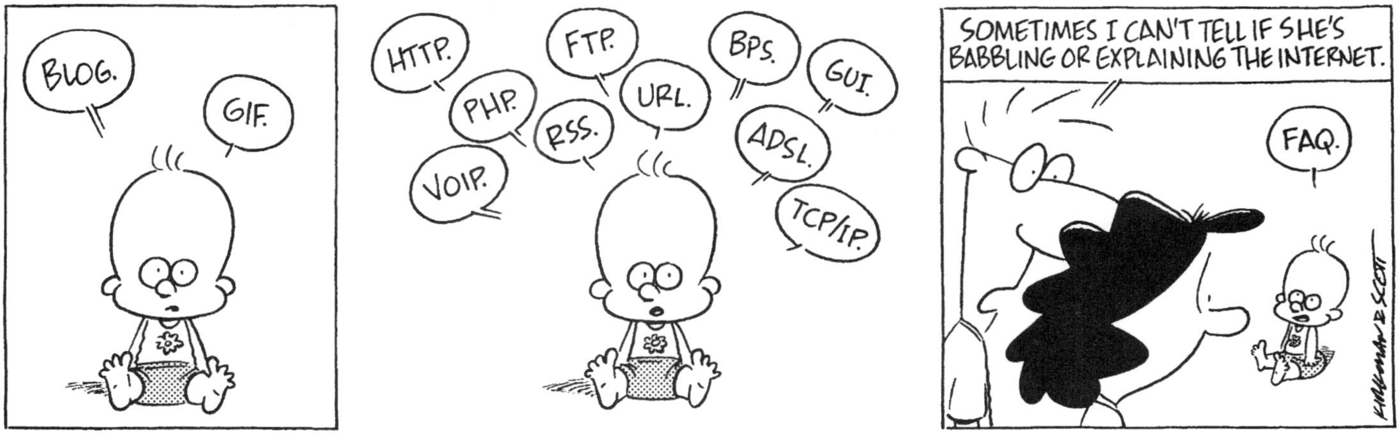
BLOG.
GIF.
HTTP.
PHP.
VOIP.
FTP.
RSS.
URL.
BPS.
GUI.
ADSL.
TCP/IP.
SOMETIMES I CAN'T TELL IF SHE'S BABBLING OR EXPLAINING THE INTERNET.
FAQ.

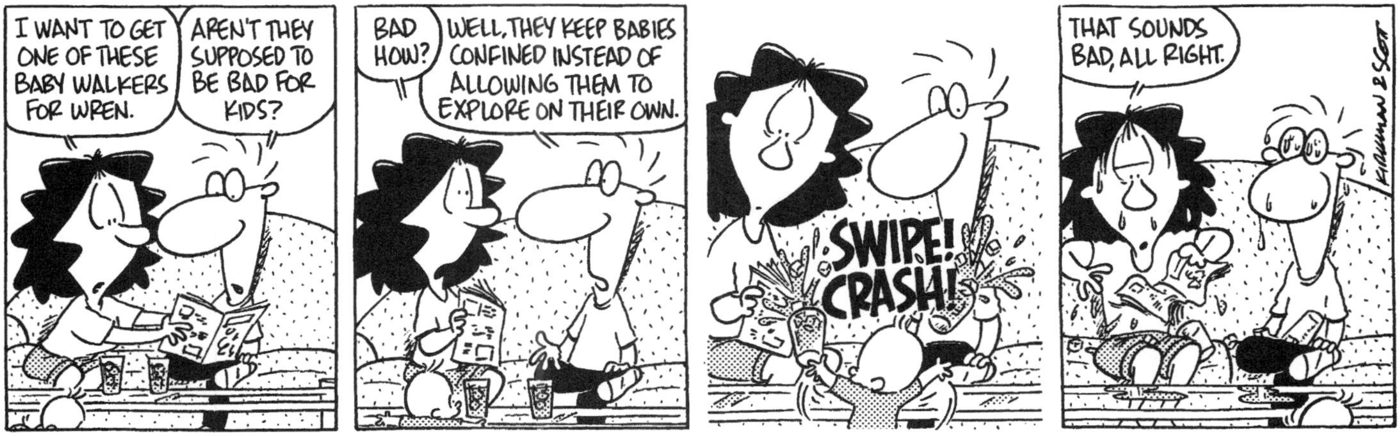
I WANT TO GET ONE OF THESE BABY WALKERS FOR WREN.
AREN'T THEY SUPPOSED TO BE BAD FOR KIDS?
BAD HOW?
WELL, THEY KEEP BABIES CONFINED INSTEAD OF ALLOWING THEM TO EXPLORE ON THEIR OWN.
SWIPE! CRASH!
THAT SOUNDS BAD, ALL RIGHT.

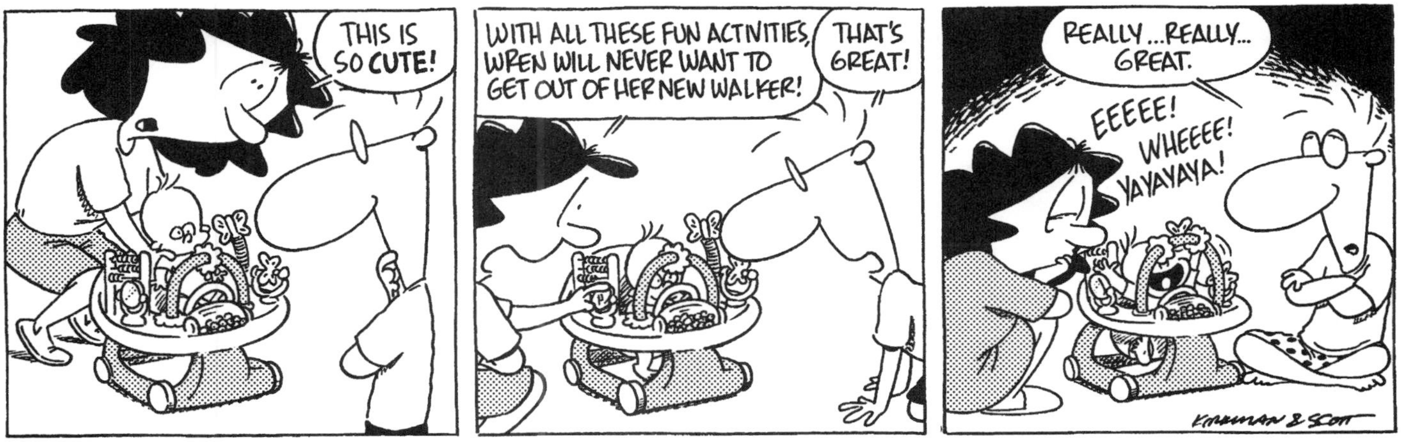
THIS IS SO CUTE!
WITH ALL THESE FUN ACTIVITIES, WREN WILL NEVER WANT TO GET OUT OF HER NEW WALKER!
THAT'S GREAT!
REALLY ...REALLY... GREAT.
EEEEE!
WHEEEE!
YAYAYAYA!

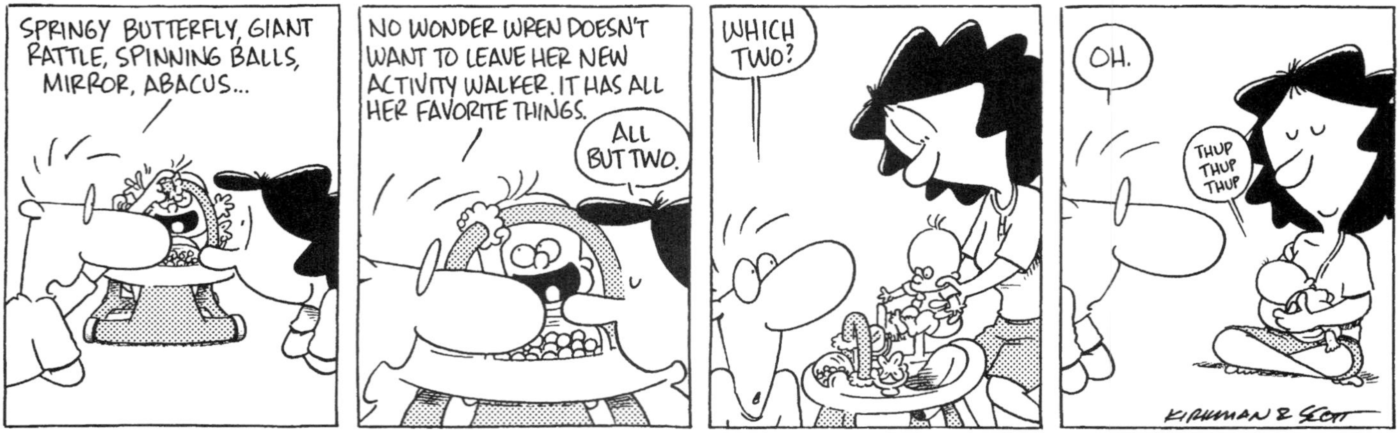
SPRINGY BUTTERFLY, GIANT RATTLE, SPINNING BALLS, MIRROR, ABACUS...
NO WONDER WREN DOESN'T WANT TO LEAVE HER NEW ACTIVITY WALKER. IT HAS ALL HER FAVORITE THINGS.
ALL BUT TWO.
WHICH TWO?
OH.
THUP THUP THUP
KIRKMAN & SCOTT

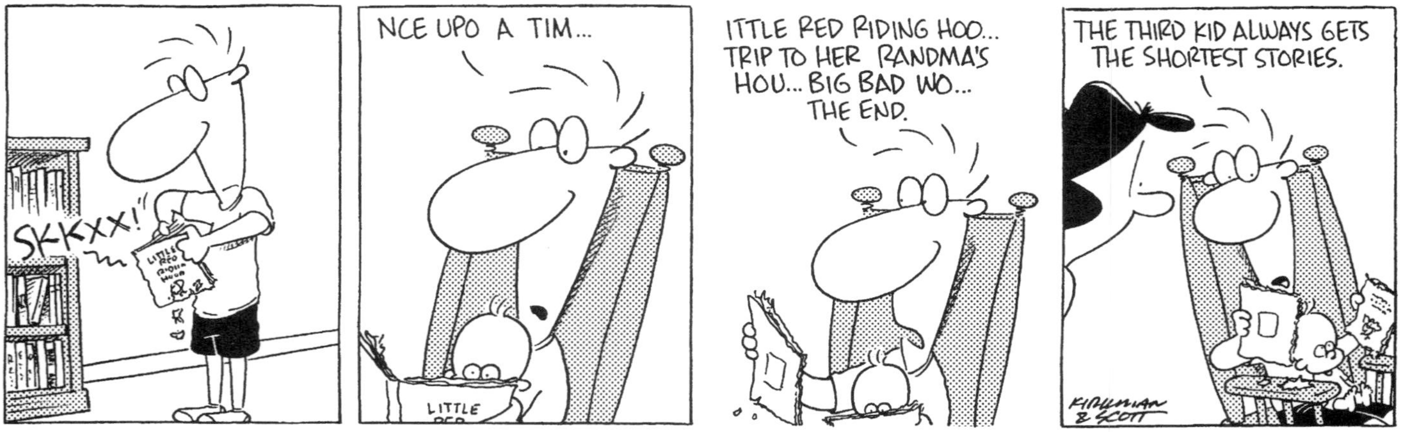
SKKXX!
NCE UPO A TIM...
ITTLE RED RIDING HOO... TRIP TO HER RANDMA'S HOU... BIG BAD WO... THE END.
THE THIRD KID ALWAYS GETS THE SHORTEST STORIES.
KIRKMAN & SCOTT

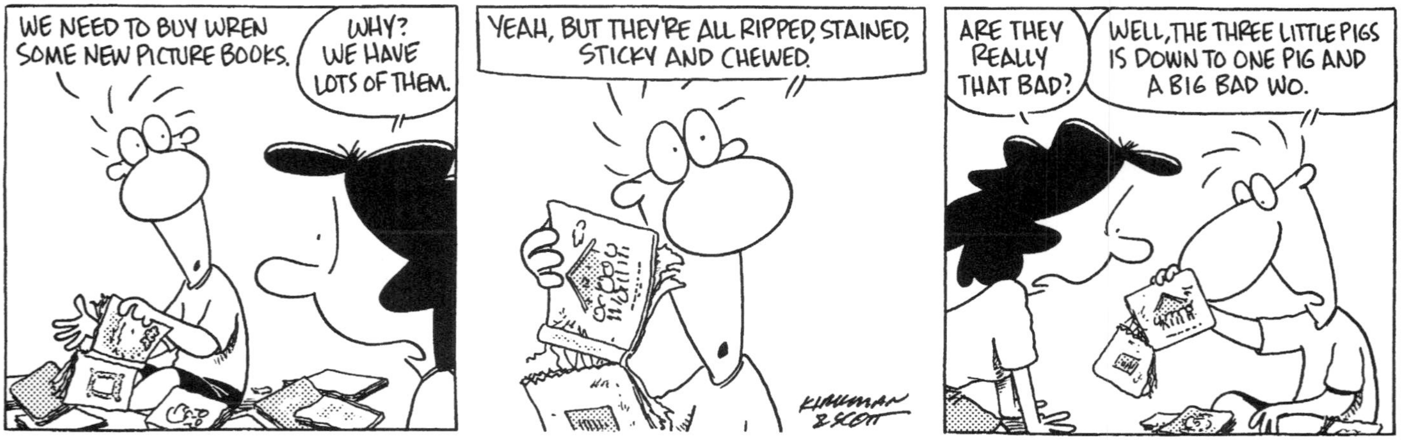
WE NEED TO BUY WREN SOME NEW PICTURE BOOKS.
WHY? WE HAVE LOTS OF THEM.
YEAH, BUT THEY'RE ALL RIPPED, STAINED, STICKY AND CHEWED.
KIRKMAN & SCOTT
ARE THEY REALLY THAT BAD?
WELL, THE THREE LITTLE PIGS IS DOWN TO ONE PIG AND A BIG BAD WO.

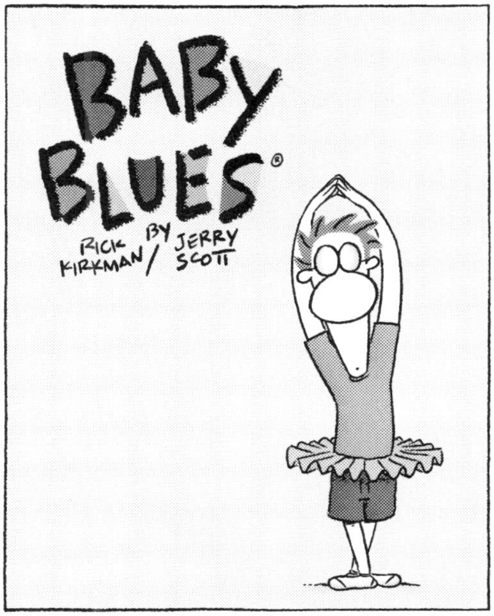
BABY BLUES®
BY
RICK KIRKMAN / JERRY SCOTT

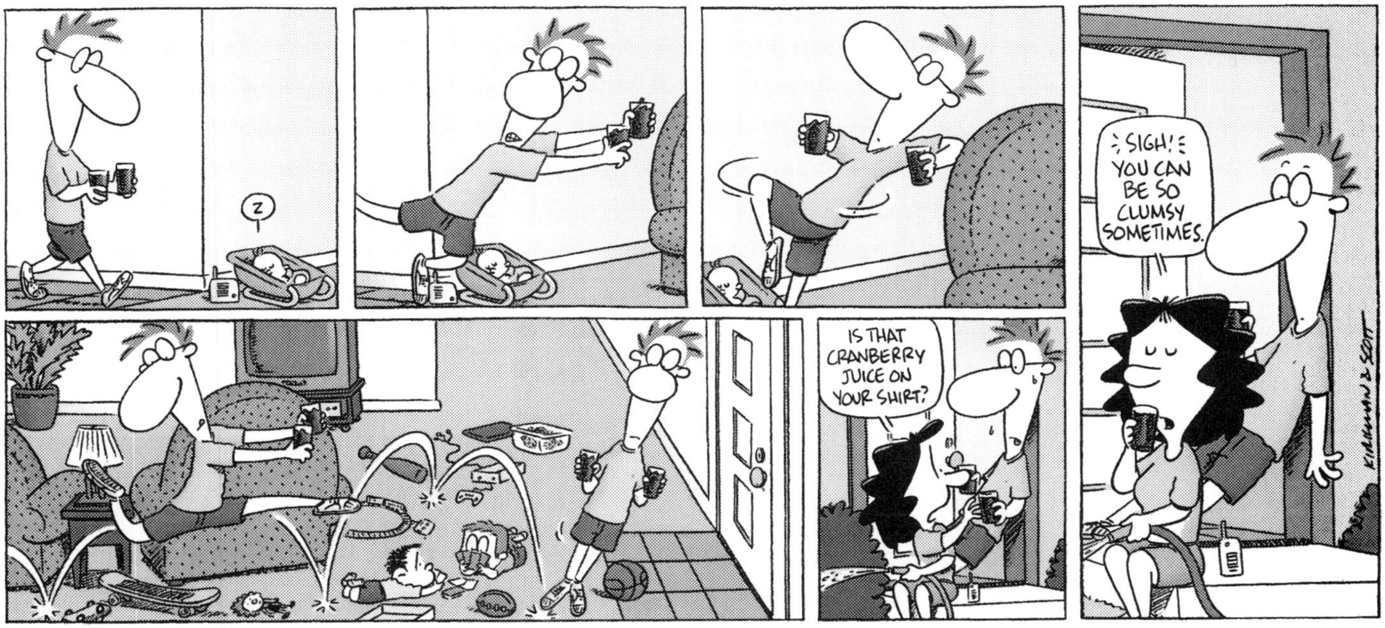
Z
IS THAT CRANBERRY JUICE ON YOUR SHIRT?
SIGH! YOU CAN BE SO CLUMSY SOMETIMES.
KIRKMAN & SCOTT

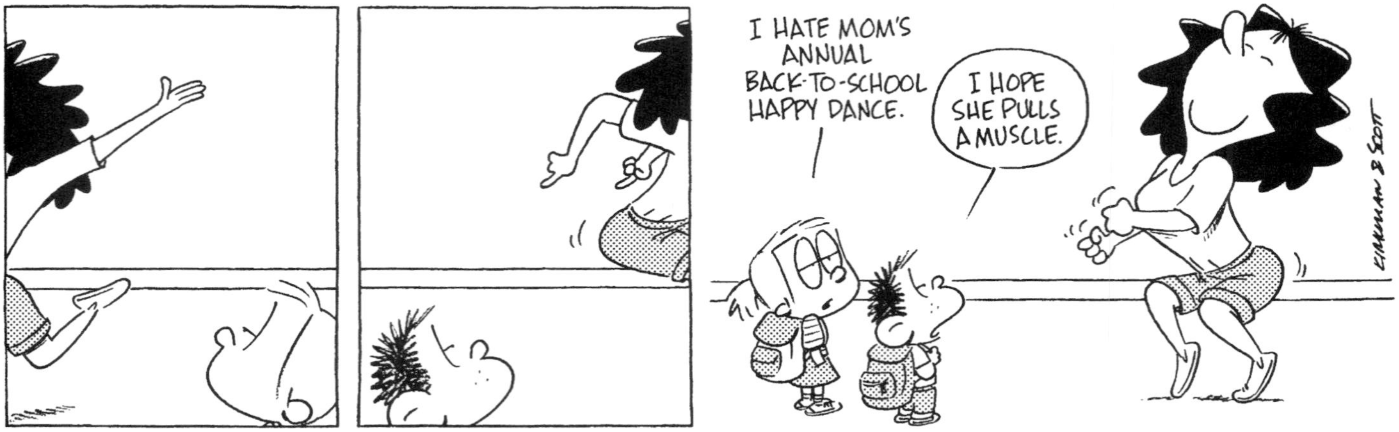
I HATE MOM'S ANNUAL BACK-TO-SCHOOL HAPPY DANCE.
I HOPE SHE PULLS A MUSCLE.
KIRKMAN & SCOTT

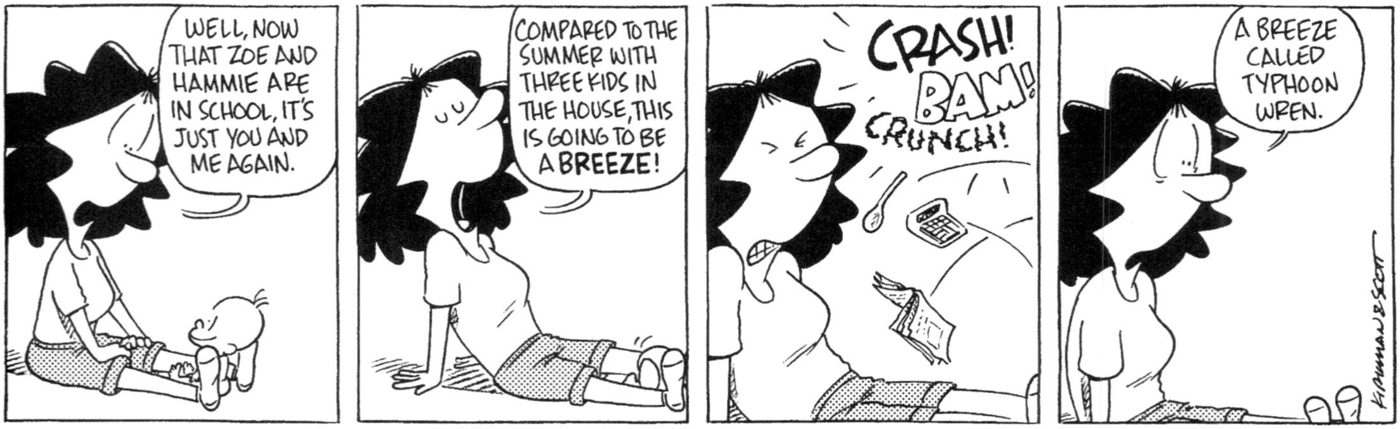
WELL, NOW THAT ZOE AND HAMMIE ARE IN SCHOOL, IT'S JUST YOU AND ME AGAIN.
COMPARED TO THE SUMMER WITH THREE KIDS IN THE HOUSE, THIS IS GOING TO BE A **BREEZE**!
CRASH!
BAM!
CRUNCH!
A BREEZE CALLED TYPHOON WREN.
KIRKMAN & SCOTT

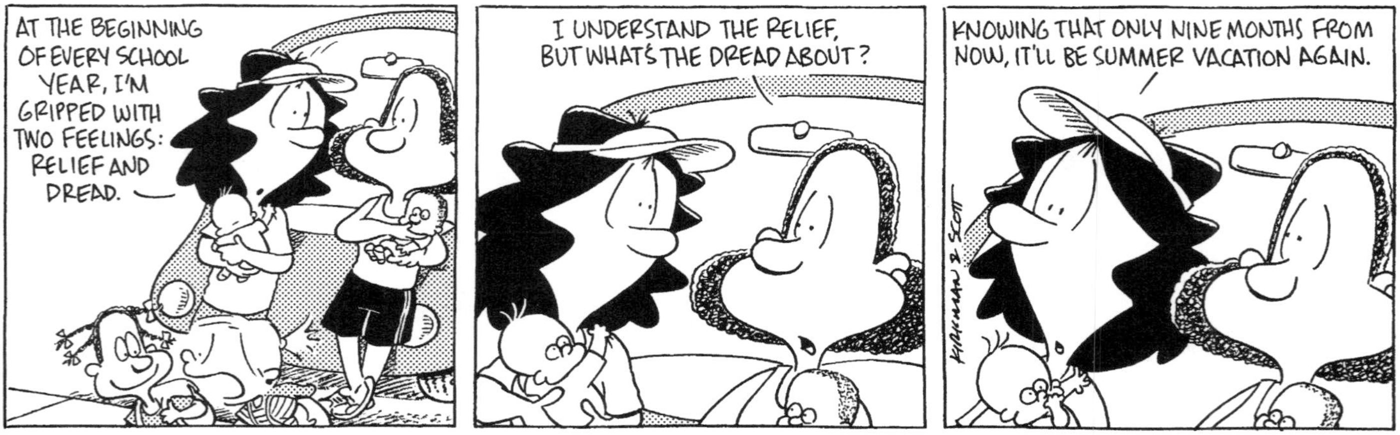
AT THE BEGINNING OF EVERY SCHOOL YEAR, I'M GRIPPED WITH TWO FEELINGS: RELIEF AND DREAD.
I UNDERSTAND THE RELIEF, BUT WHAT'S THE DREAD ABOUT?
KIRKMAN & SCOTT
KNOWING THAT ONLY NINE MONTHS FROM NOW, IT'LL BE SUMMER VACATION AGAIN.

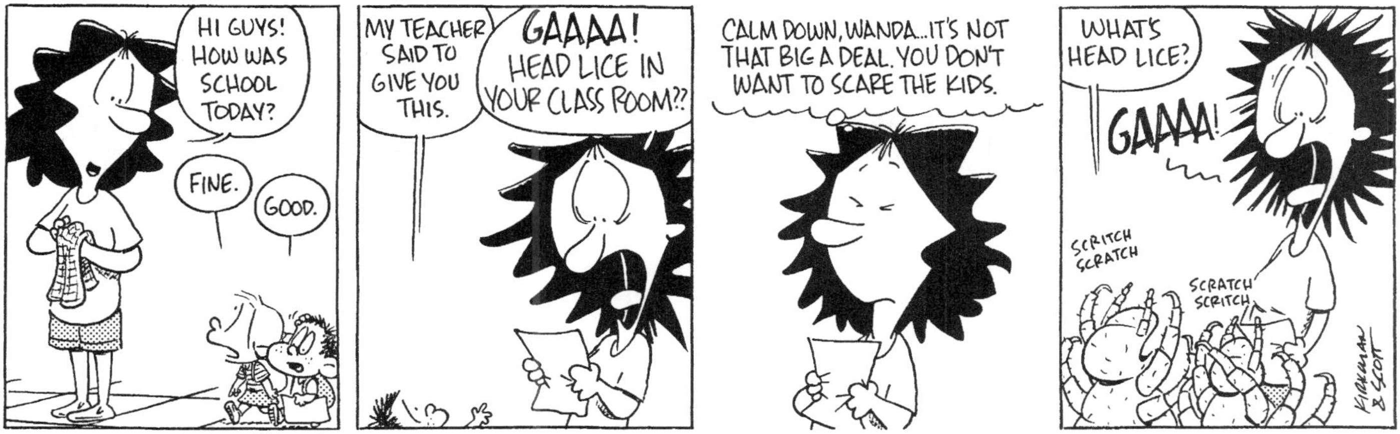
HI GUYS! HOW WAS SCHOOL TODAY?
FINE.
GOOD.
MY TEACHER SAID TO GIVE YOU THIS.
GAAAA! HEAD LICE IN YOUR CLASS ROOM??
CALM DOWN, WANDA...IT'S NOT THAT BIG A DEAL. YOU DON'T WANT TO SCARE THE KIDS.
WHAT'S HEAD LICE?
GAAAA!
SCRITCH SCRATCH
SCRATCH SCRITCH
KIRKMAN & SCOTT

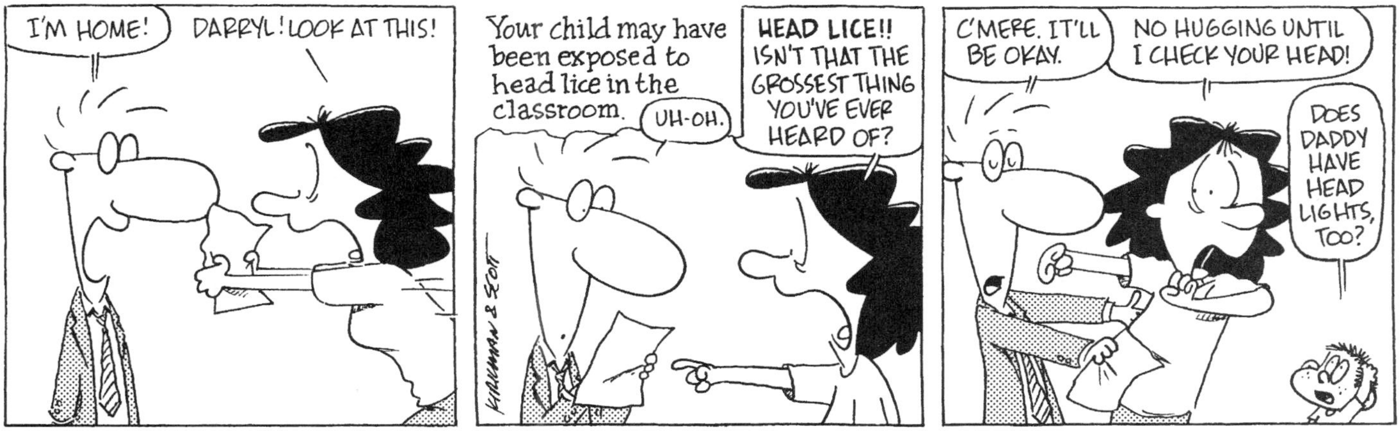
I'M HOME!
DARRYL! LOOK AT THIS!
Your child may have been exposed to head lice in the classroom.
UH-OH.
HEAD LICE!! ISN'T THAT THE GROSSEST THING YOU'VE EVER HEARD OF?
KIRKMAN & SCOTT
C'MERE. IT'LL BE OKAY.
NO HUGGING UNTIL I CHECK YOUR HEAD!
DOES DADDY HAVE HEAD LIGHTS, TOO?

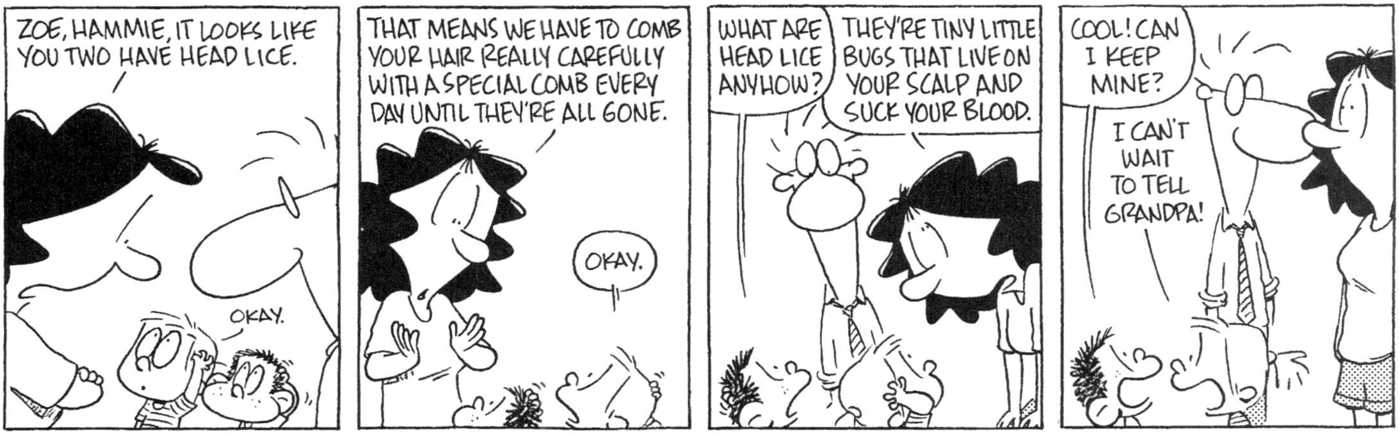
ZOE, HAMMIE, IT LOOKS LIKE YOU TWO HAVE HEAD LICE.
OKAY.
THAT MEANS WE HAVE TO COMB YOUR HAIR REALLY CAREFULLY WITH A SPECIAL COMB EVERY DAY UNTIL THEY'RE ALL GONE.
OKAY.
WHAT ARE HEAD LICE ANYHOW?
THEY'RE TINY LITTLE BUGS THAT LIVE ON YOUR SCALP AND SUCK YOUR BLOOD.
COOL! CAN I KEEP MINE?
I CAN'T WAIT TO TELL GRANDPA!

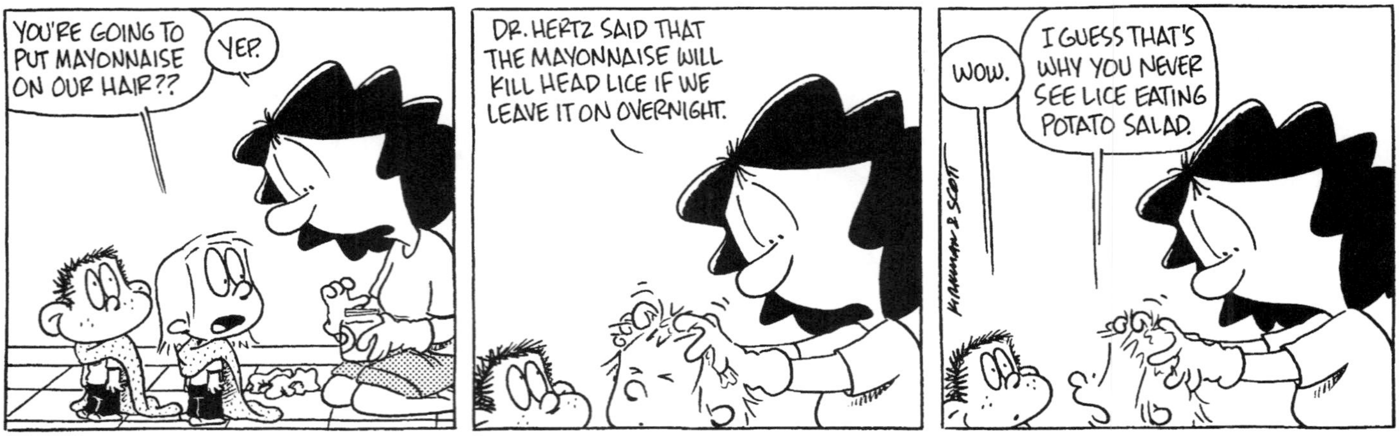
YOU'RE GOING TO PUT MAYONNAISE ON OUR HAIR??
YEP.
DR. HERTZ SAID THAT THE MAYONNAISE WILL KILL HEAD LICE IF WE LEAVE IT ON OVERNIGHT.
WOW.
I GUESS THAT'S WHY YOU NEVER SEE LICE EATING POTATO SALAD.

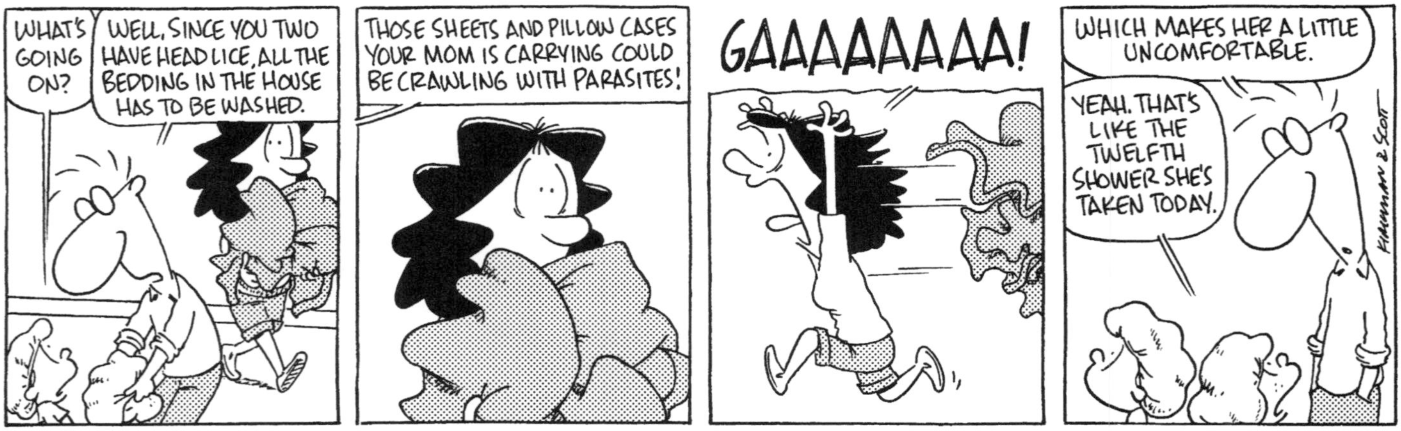
WHAT'S GOING ON?
WELL, SINCE YOU TWO HAVE HEAD LICE, ALL THE BEDDING IN THE HOUSE HAS TO BE WASHED.
THOSE SHEETS AND PILLOW CASES YOUR MOM IS CARRYING COULD BE CRAWLING WITH PARASITES!
GAAAAAAAA!
WHICH MAKES HER A LITTLE UNCOMFORTABLE.
YEAH. THAT'S LIKE THE TWELFTH SHOWER SHE'S TAKEN TODAY.

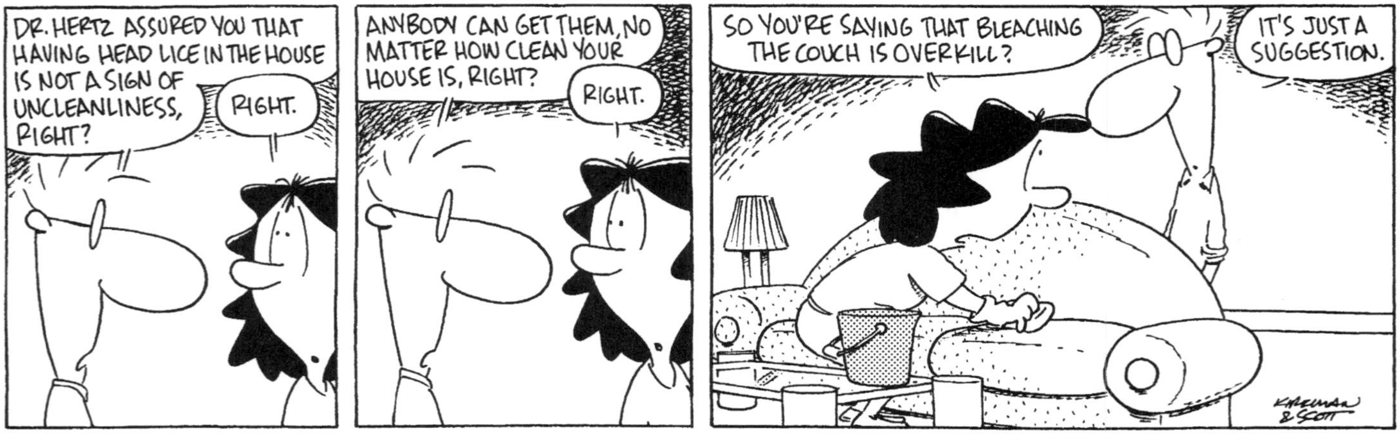
DR. HERTZ ASSURED YOU THAT HAVING HEAD LICE IN THE HOUSE IS NOT A SIGN OF UNCLEANLINESS, RIGHT?
RIGHT.
ANYBODY CAN GET THEM, NO MATTER HOW CLEAN YOUR HOUSE IS, RIGHT?
RIGHT.
SO YOU'RE SAYING THAT BLEACHING THE COUCH IS OVERKILL?
IT'S JUST A SUGGESTION.

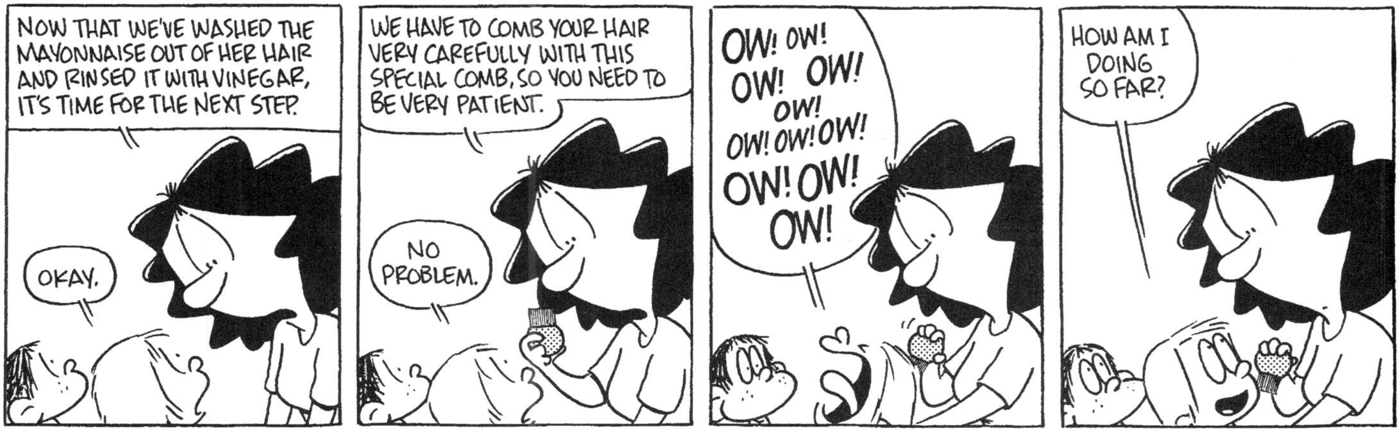
NOW THAT WE'VE WASHED THE MAYONNAISE OUT OF HER HAIR AND RINSED IT WITH VINEGAR, IT'S TIME FOR THE NEXT STEP.
OKAY.
WE HAVE TO COMB YOUR HAIR VERY CAREFULLY WITH THIS SPECIAL COMB, SO YOU NEED TO BE VERY PATIENT.
NO PROBLEM.
OW! OW! OW! OW! OW! OW! OW! OW! OW! OW! OW!
HOW AM I DOING SO FAR?

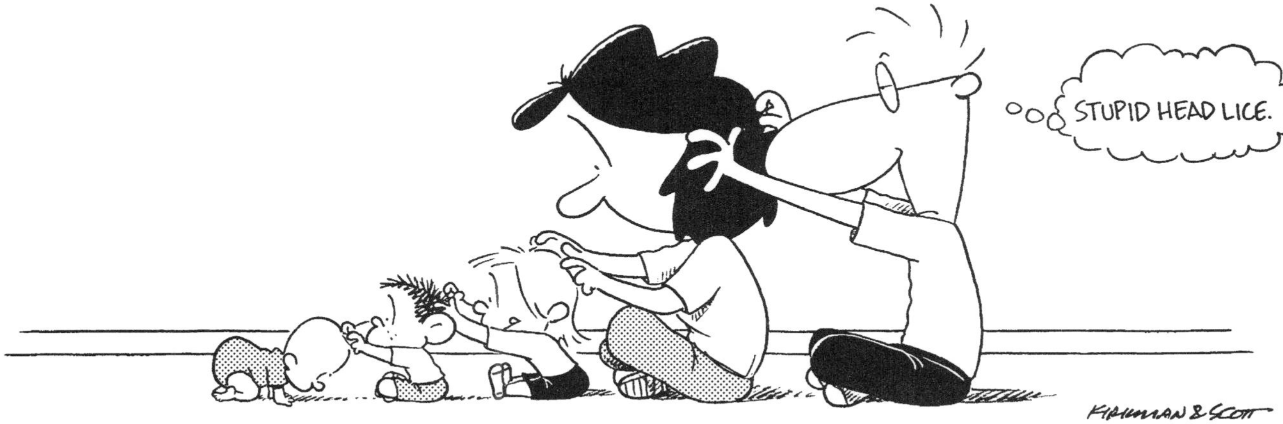
STUPID HEAD LICE.
KIRKMAN & SCOTT

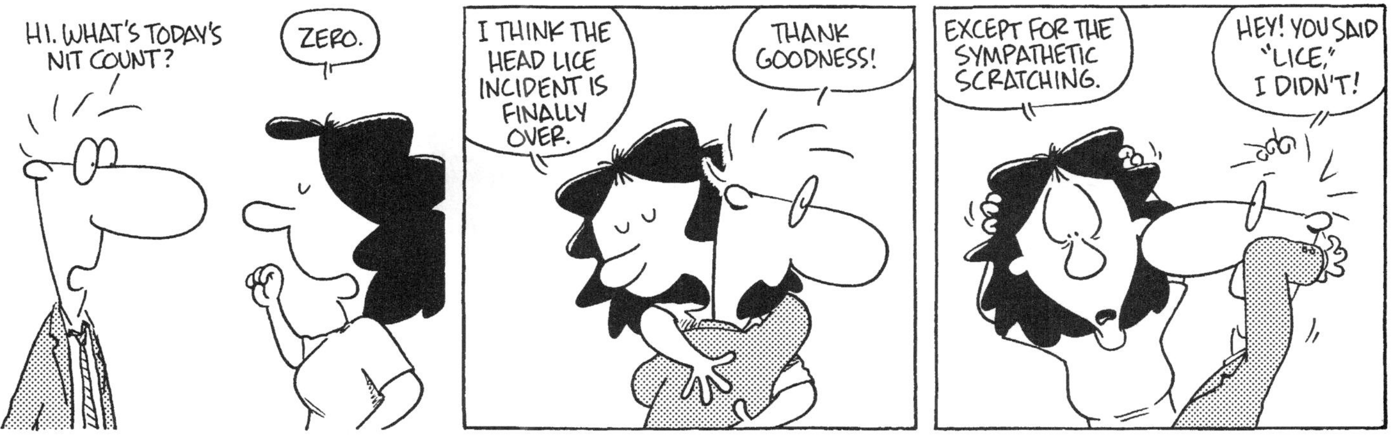
HI. WHAT'S TODAY'S NIT COUNT?
ZERO.
I THINK THE HEAD LICE INCIDENT IS FINALLY OVER.
THANK GOODNESS!
EXCEPT FOR THE SYMPATHETIC SCRATCHING.
HEY! YOU SAID "LICE," I DIDN'T!

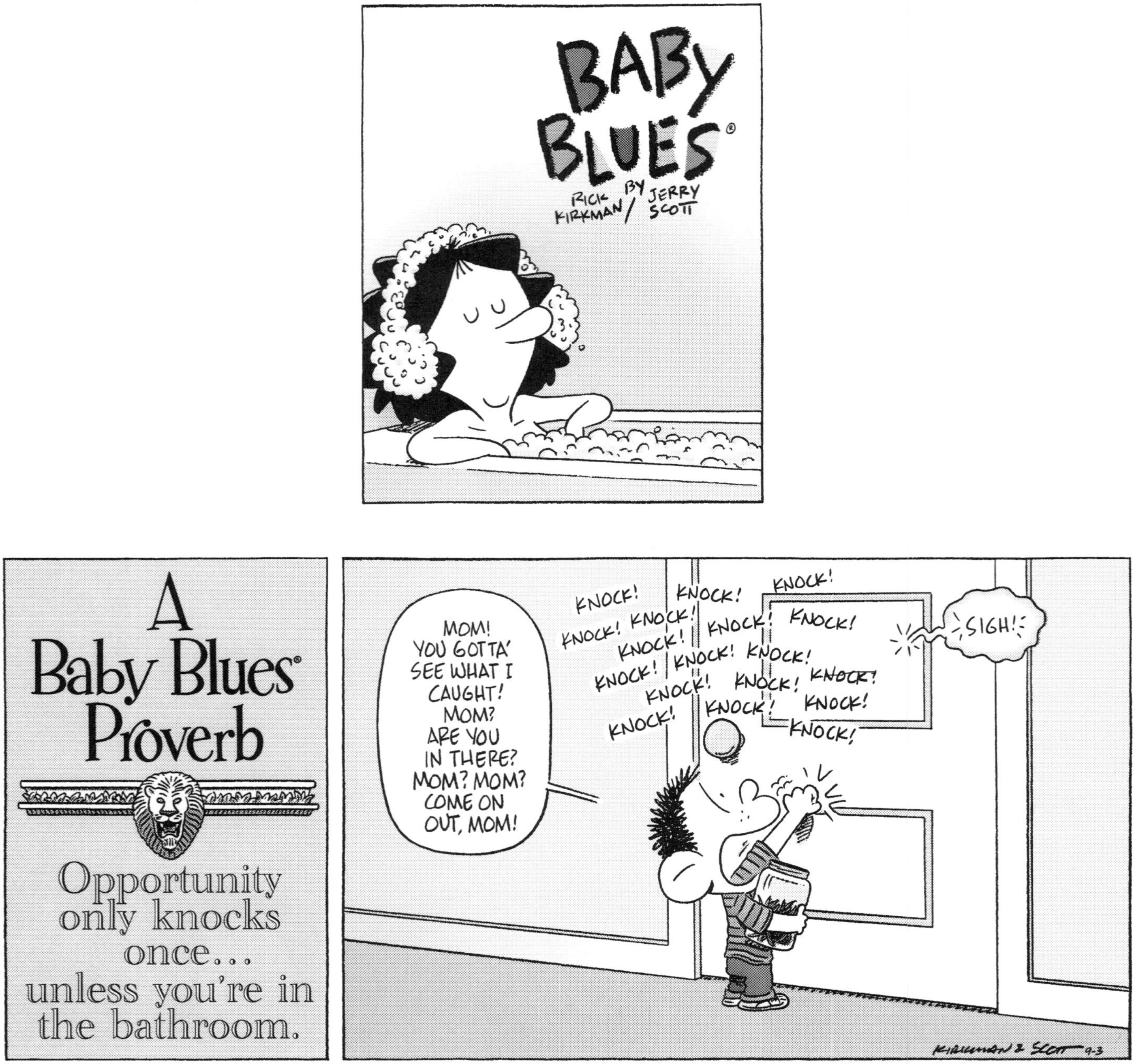
BABY BLUES®
BY RICK KIRKMAN / JERRY SCOTT
A Baby Blues® Proverb
Opportunity only knocks once... unless you're in the bathroom.
MOM! YOU GOTTA' SEE WHAT I CAUGHT! MOM? ARE YOU IN THERE? MOM? MOM? COME ON OUT, MOM!
KNOCK! KNOCK! KNOCK! KNOCK! KNOCK! KNOCK! KNOCK! KNOCK! KNOCK! KNOCK! KNOCK! KNOCK! KNOCK! KNOCK! KNOCK! KNOCK! KNOCK! KNOCK!
SIGH!
KIRKMAN & SCOTT 9-3

BABY BLUES®
BY RICK KIRKMAN / JERRY SCOTT

What is mankind's greatest invention?
THAT'S EASY. IT'S THE CHAIR.
THAT'S THE STUPIDEST THING I'VE EVER HEARD!
THERE'S THE WHEEL, THE CAR, THE AIRPLANE, THE TELEPHONE, THE COMPUTER, THE INTERNET, MEDICINE...
AND YOU PICK THE CHAIR??
THAT'S RIGHT.
BECAUSE...
...WITHOUT THE CHAIR...
...YOU DON'T GET THE COOKIES...
MUNCH! MUNCH! MUNCH!
3. The Chair
KIRKMAN & SCOTT

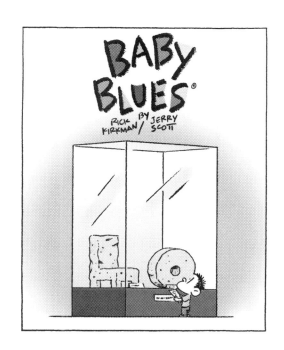

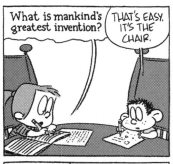

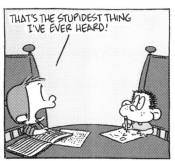

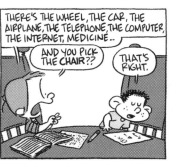

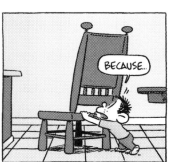

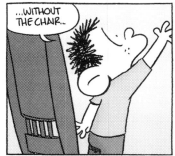

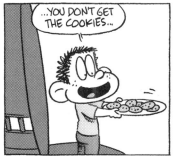

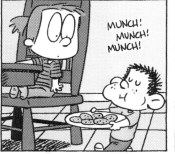

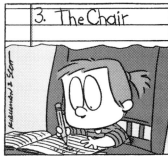

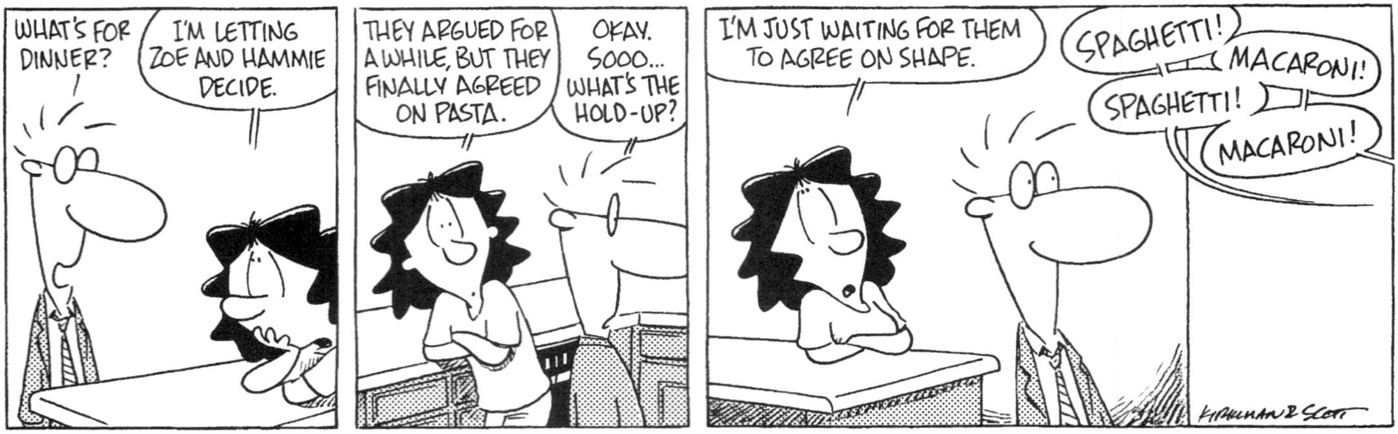

WHAT'S FOR DINNER?
I'M LETTING ZOE AND HAMMIE DECIDE.
THEY ARGUED FOR A WHILE, BUT THEY FINALLY AGREED ON PASTA.
OKAY. SOOO... WHAT'S THE HOLD-UP?
I'M JUST WAITING FOR THEM TO AGREE ON SHAPE.
SPAGHETTI!
MACARONI!
SPAGHETTI!
MACARONI!
KIRKMAN & SCOTT

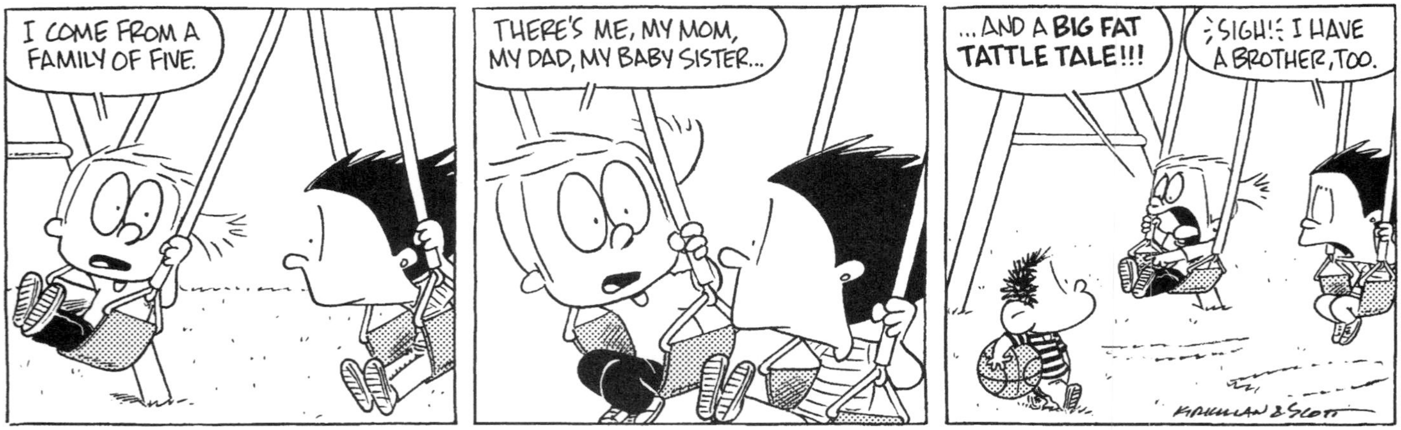

I COME FROM A FAMILY OF FIVE.
THERE'S ME, MY MOM, MY DAD, MY BABY SISTER...
...AND A **BIG FAT TATTLE TALE**!!!
SIGH! I HAVE A BROTHER, TOO.
KIRKMAN & SCOTT

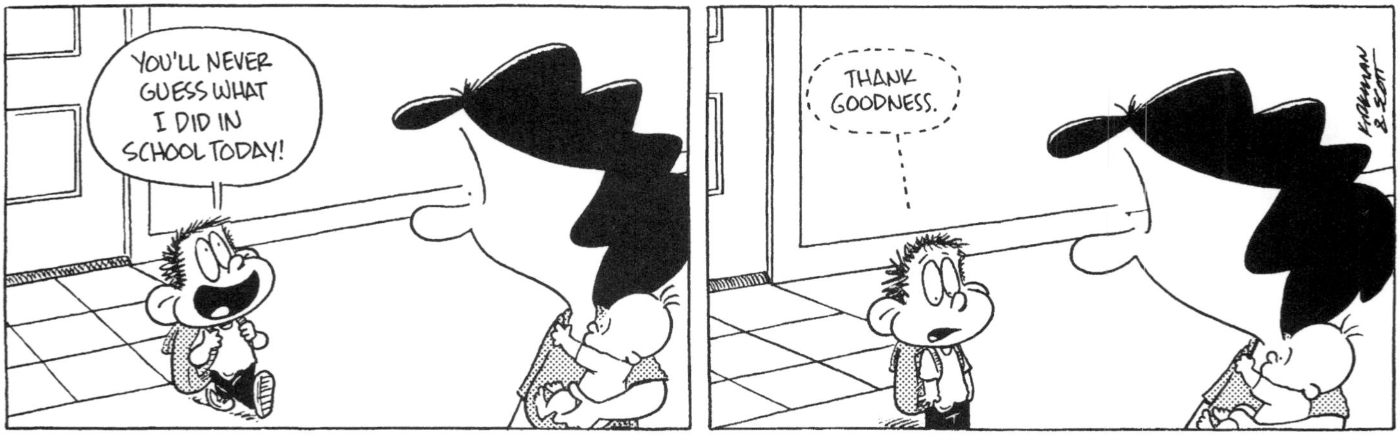

YOU'LL NEVER GUESS WHAT I DID IN SCHOOL TODAY!
THANK GOODNESS.
KIRKMAN & SCOTT

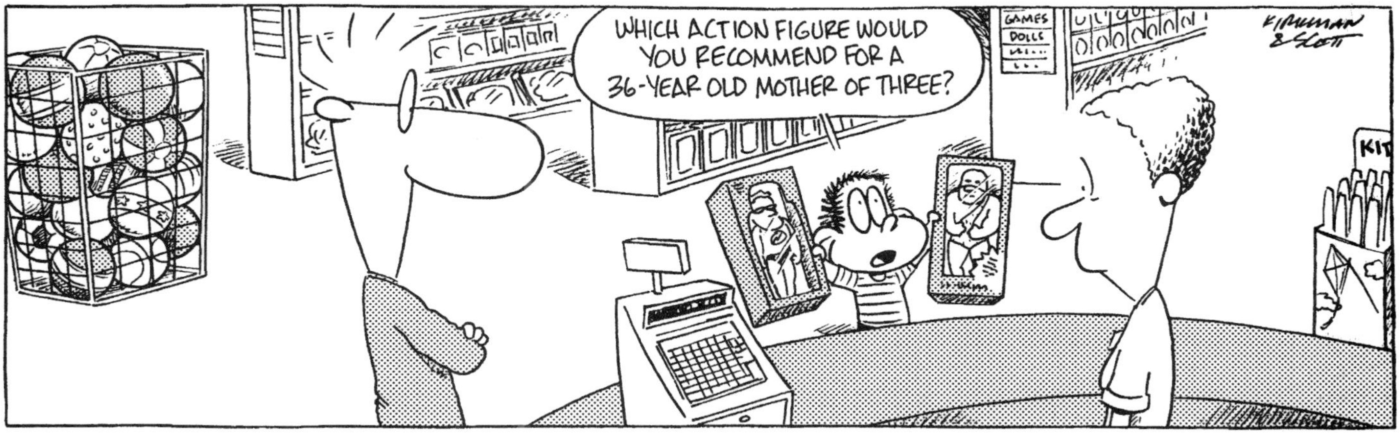
KIRKMAN & SCOTT
GAMES
DOLLS
WHICH ACTION FIGURE WOULD YOU RECOMMEND FOR A 36-YEAR OLD MOTHER OF THREE?

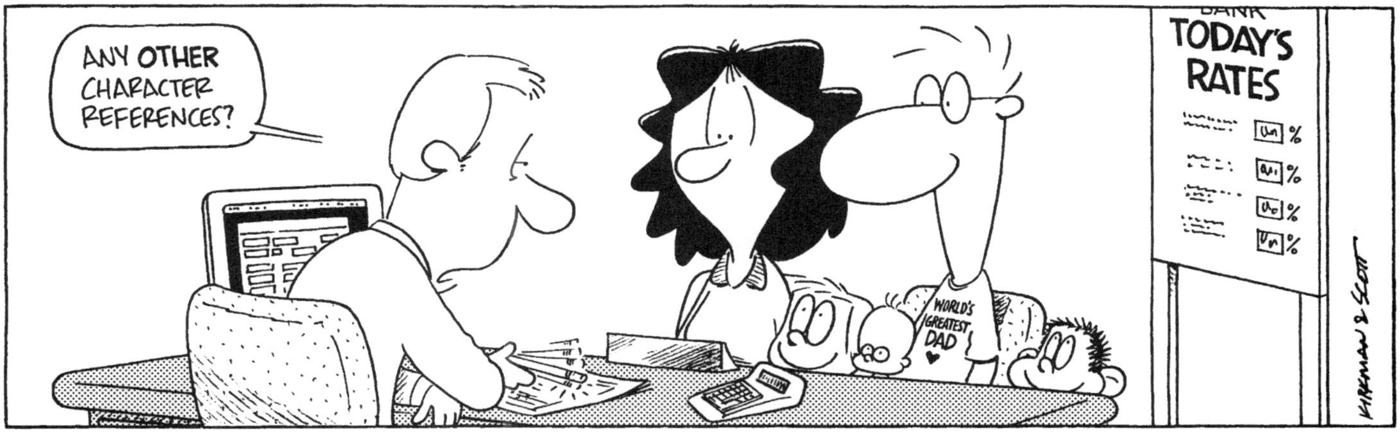
ANY **OTHER** CHARACTER REFERENCES?
TODAY'S RATES
WORLD'S GREATEST DAD
KIRKMAN & SCOTT

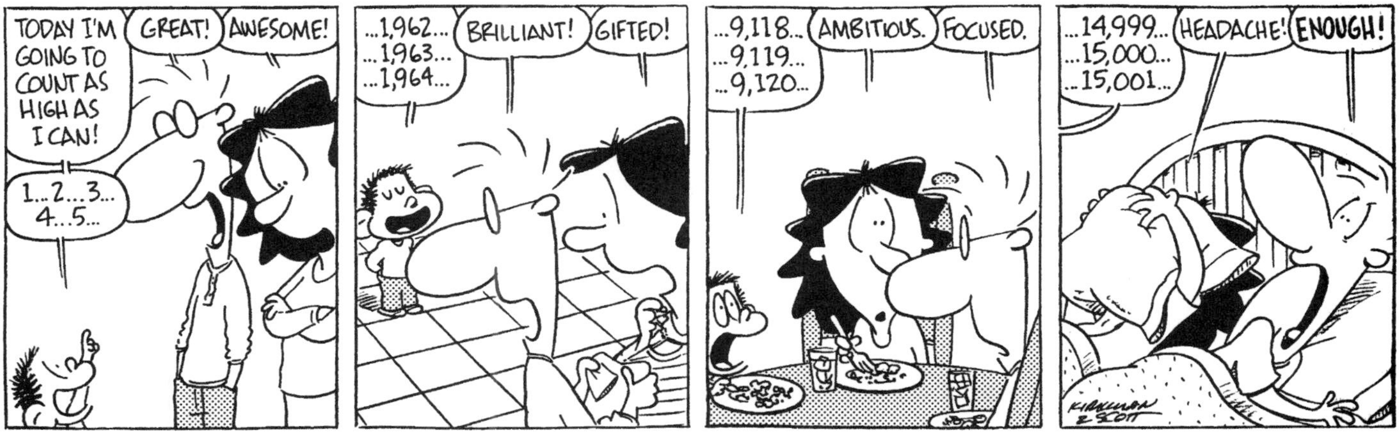
TODAY I'M GOING TO COUNT AS HIGH AS I CAN!
1...2...3... 4...5...
GREAT!
AWESOME!
...1,962... ...1,963... ...1,964...
BRILLIANT!
GIFTED!
...9,118... ...9,119... ...9,120...
AMBITIOUS.
FOCUSED.
...14,999... ...15,000... ...15,001...
HEADACHE!
ENOUGH!
KIRKMAN & SCOTT

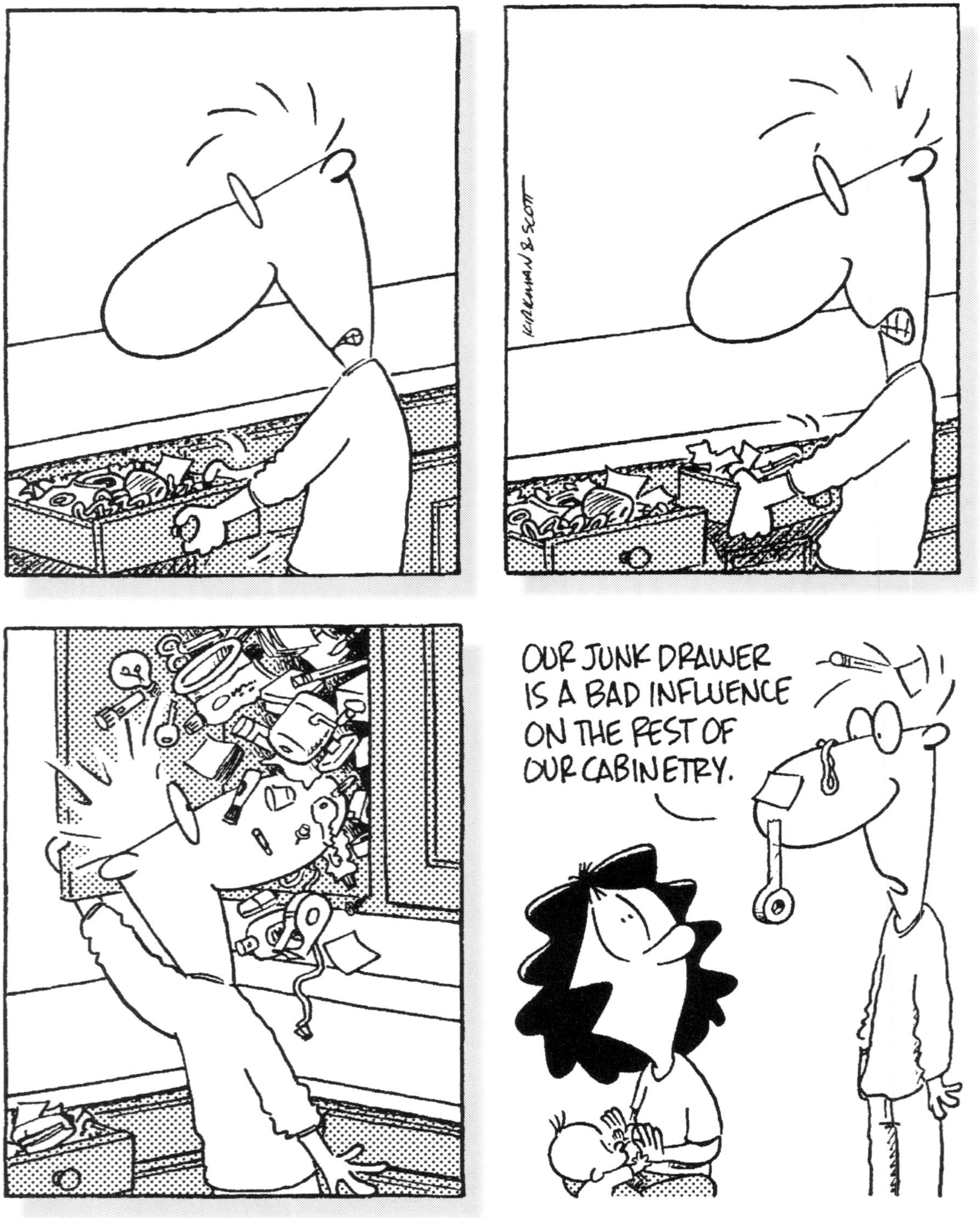
KIRKMAN & SCOTT
OUR JUNK DRAWER IS A BAD INFLUENCE ON THE REST OF OUR CABINETRY.

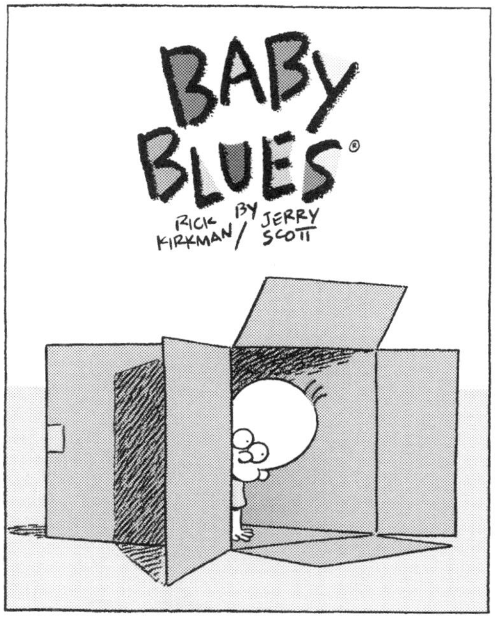
BABY BLUES®
BY RICK KIRKMAN / JERRY SCOTT

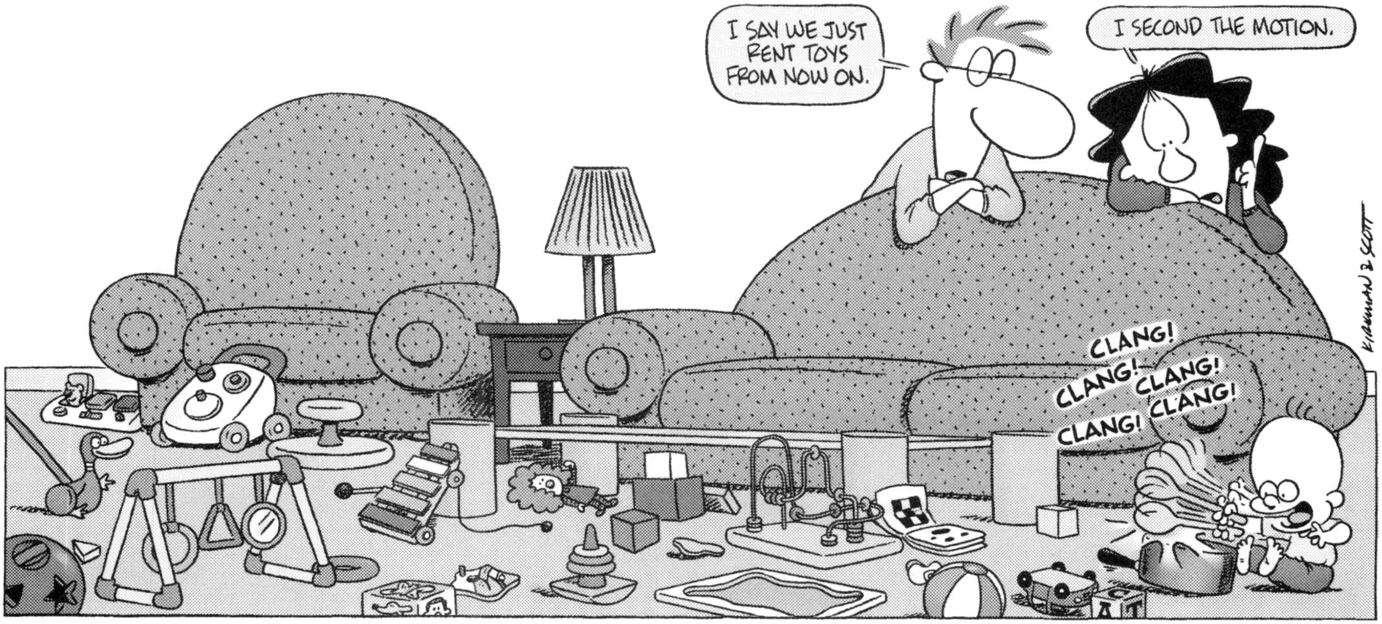
I SAY WE JUST RENT TOYS FROM NOW ON.
I SECOND THE MOTION.
CLANG! CLANG! CLANG! CLANG! CLANG!
KIRKMAN & SCOTT

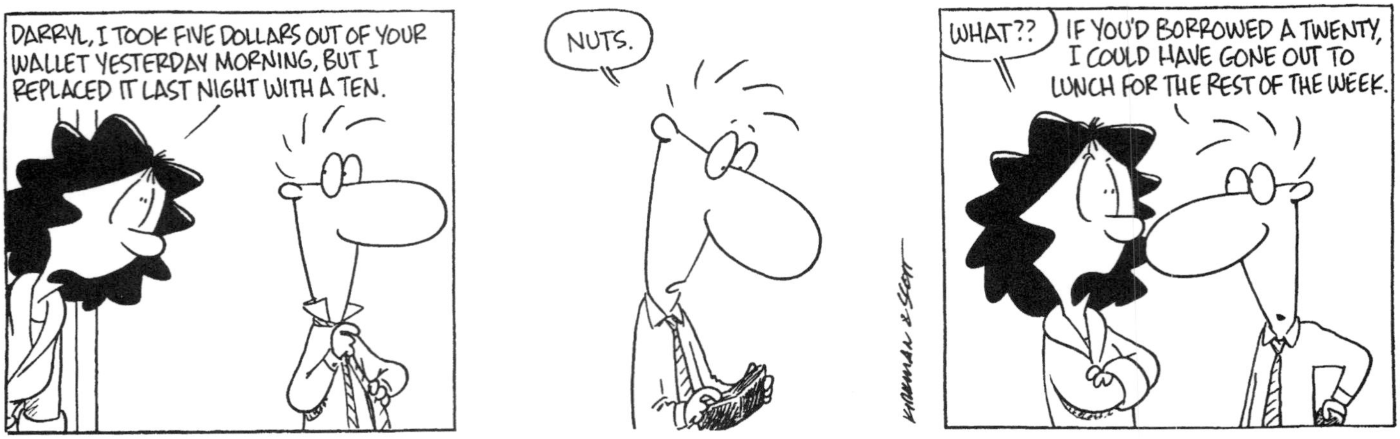
DARRYL, I TOOK FIVE DOLLARS OUT OF YOUR WALLET YESTERDAY MORNING, BUT I REPLACED IT LAST NIGHT WITH A TEN.
NUTS.
WHAT??
IF YOU'D BORROWED A TWENTY, I COULD HAVE GONE OUT TO LUNCH FOR THE REST OF THE WEEK.
KIRKMAN & SCOTT

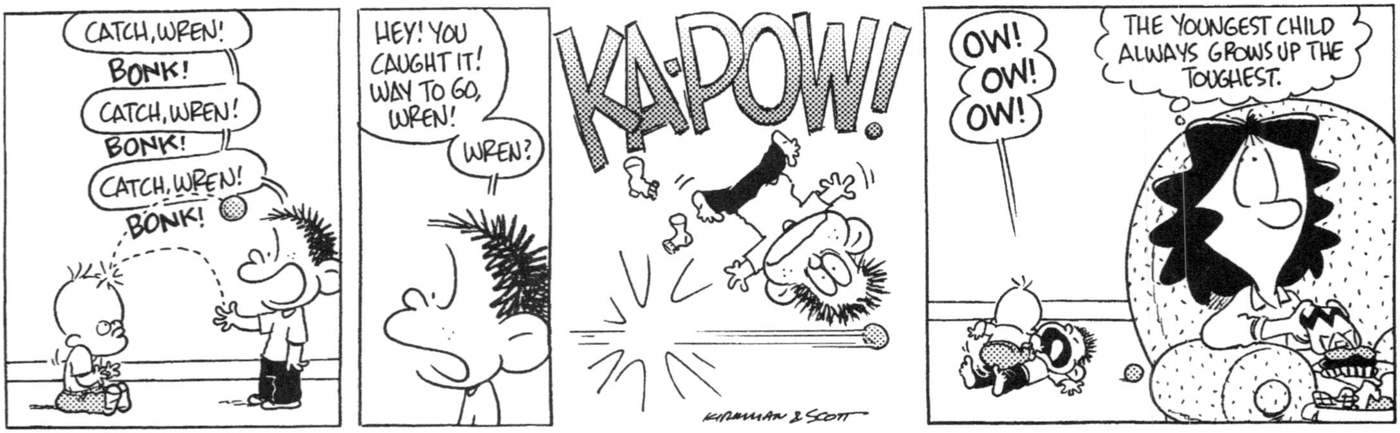
CATCH, WREN!
BONK!
CATCH, WREN!
BONK!
CATCH, WREN!
BONK!
HEY! YOU CAUGHT IT! WAY TO GO, WREN!
WREN?
KA-POW!
KIRKMAN & SCOTT
OW! OW! OW!
THE YOUNGEST CHILD ALWAYS GROWS UP THE TOUGHEST.

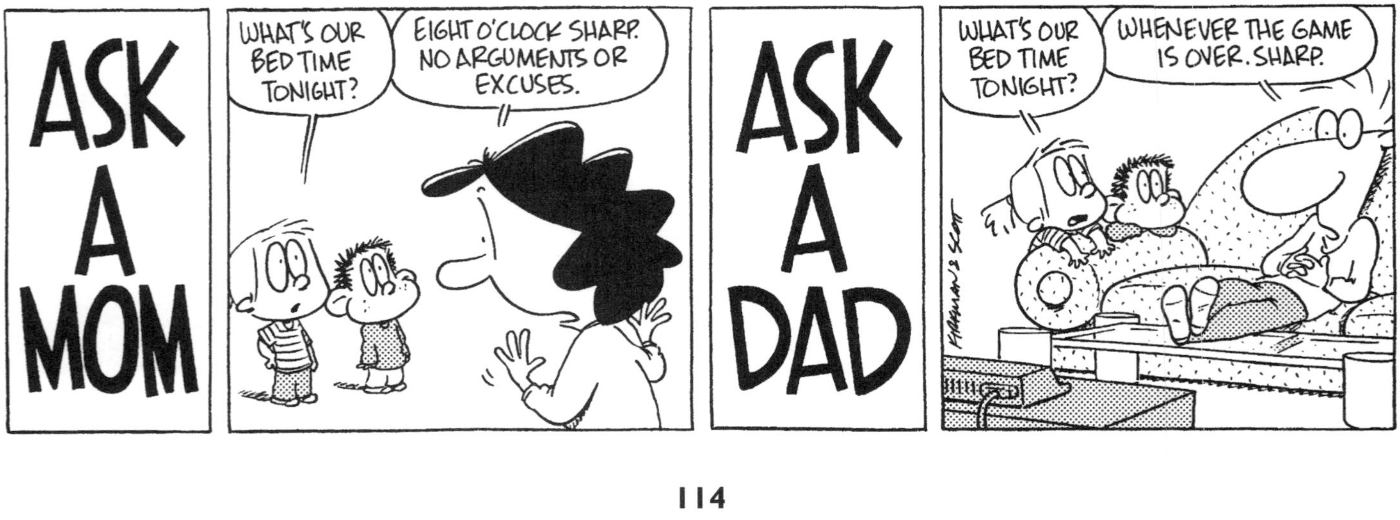
ASK A MOM
WHAT'S OUR BED TIME TONIGHT?
EIGHT O'CLOCK SHARP. NO ARGUMENTS OR EXCUSES.
ASK A DAD
WHAT'S OUR BED TIME TONIGHT?
WHENEVER THE GAME IS OVER. SHARP.
KIRKMAN & SCOTT

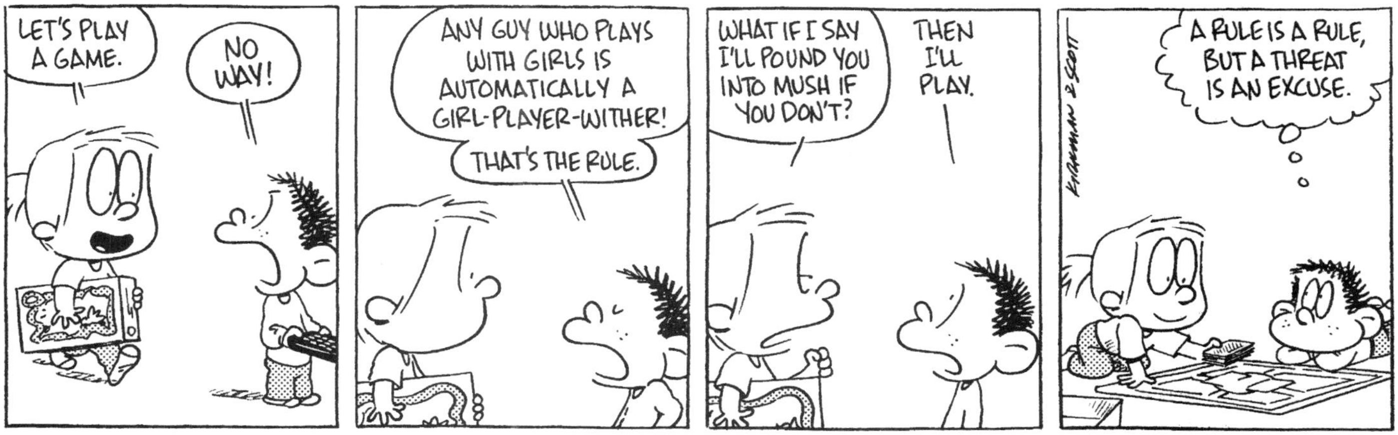
LET'S PLAY A GAME.
NO WAY!
ANY GUY WHO PLAYS WITH GIRLS IS AUTOMATICALLY A GIRL-PLAYER-WITHER!
THAT'S THE RULE.
WHAT IF I SAY I'LL POUND YOU INTO MUSH IF YOU DON'T?
THEN I'LL PLAY.
A RULE IS A RULE, BUT A THREAT IS AN EXCUSE.
KIRKMAN & SCOTT

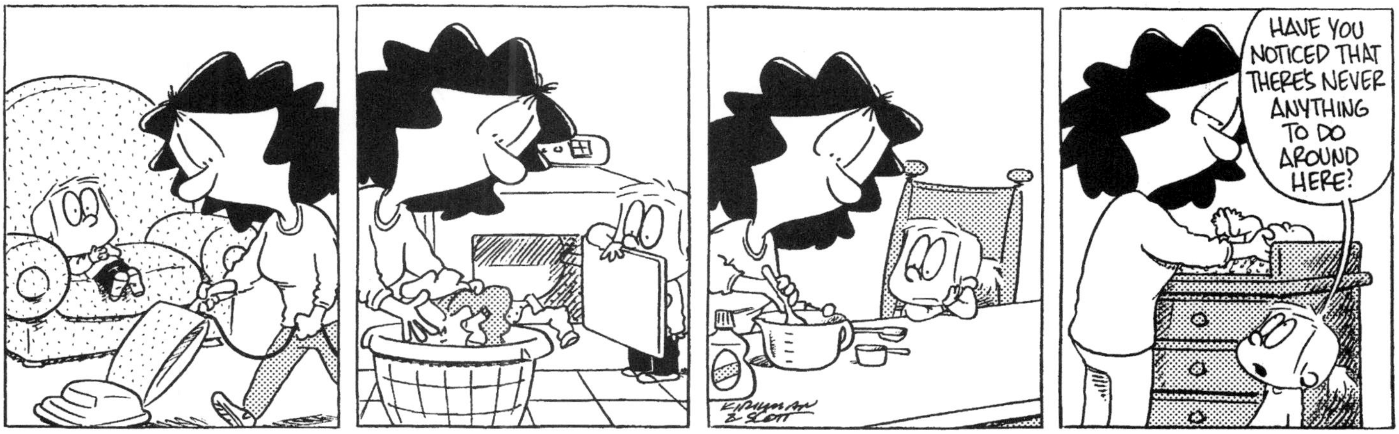
KIRKMAN & SCOTT
HAVE YOU NOTICED THAT THERE'S NEVER ANYTHING TO DO AROUND HERE?

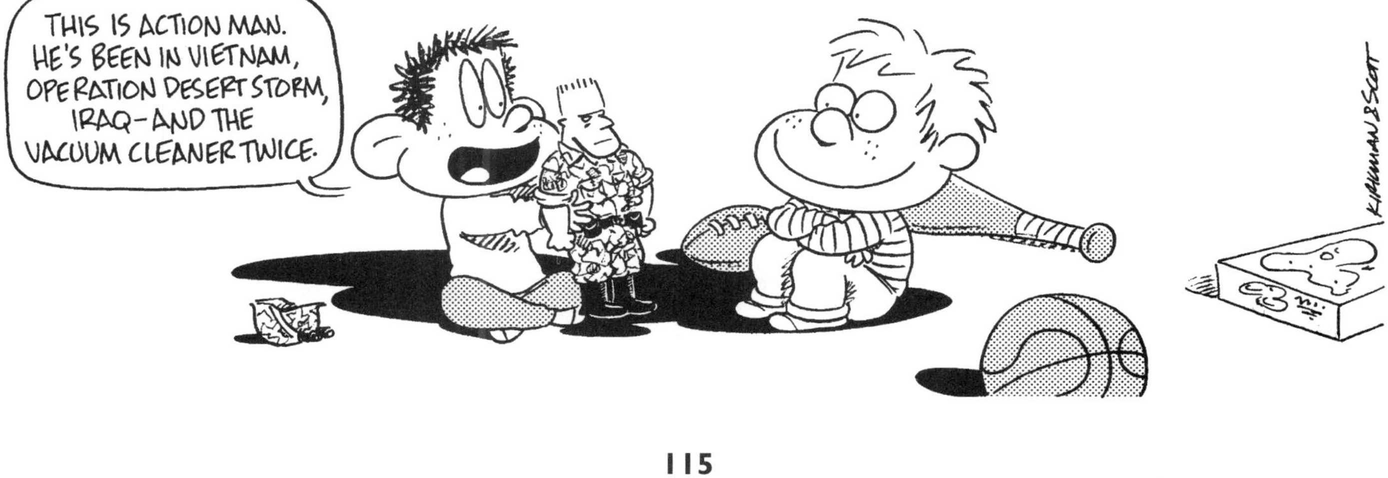
THIS IS ACTION MAN. HE'S BEEN IN VIETNAM, OPERATION DESERT STORM, IRAQ—AND THE VACUUM CLEANER TWICE.
KIRKMAN & SCOTT

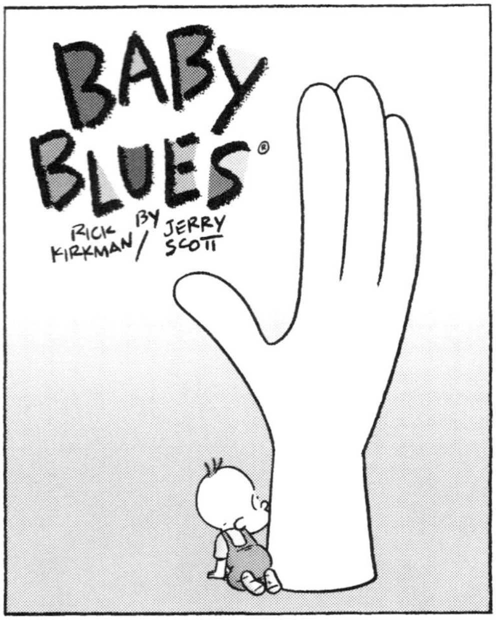
BABY BLUES®
BY RICK KIRKMAN / JERRY SCOTT

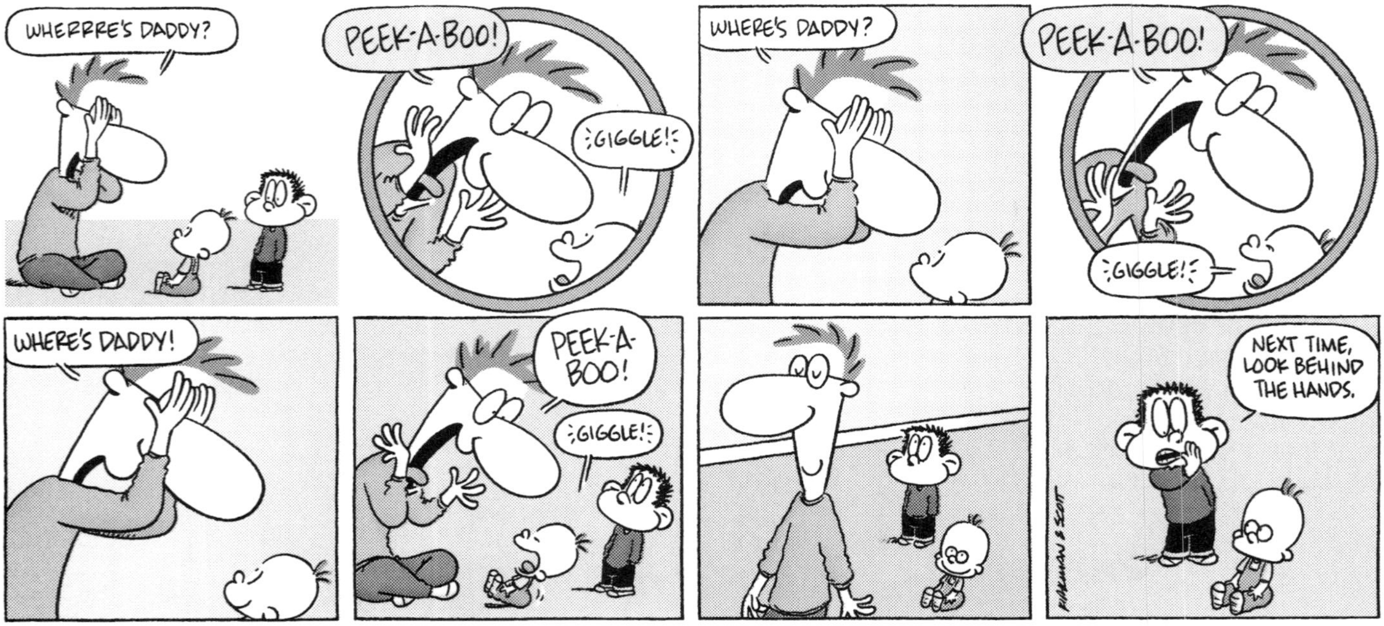
WHERRRE'S DADDY?
PEEK-A-BOO!
GIGGLE!
WHERE'S DADDY?
PEEK-A-BOO!
GIGGLE!
WHERE'S DADDY!
PEEK-A-BOO!
GIGGLE!
KIRKMAN & SCOTT
NEXT TIME, LOOK BEHIND THE HANDS.

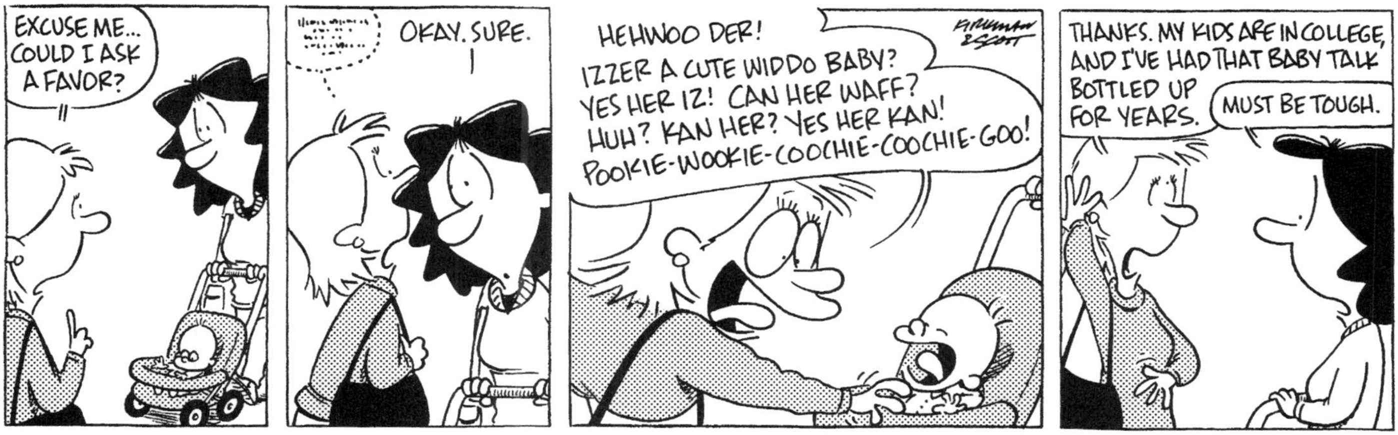
EXCUSE ME... COULD I ASK A FAVOR?
OKAY. SURE.
HEHWOO DER!
IZZER A CUTE WIDDO BABY? YES HER IZ! CAN HER WAFF? HUH? KAN HER? YES HER KAN! POOKIE-WOOKIE-COOCHIE-COOCHIE-GOO!
THANKS. MY KIDS ARE IN COLLEGE, AND I'VE HAD THAT BABY TALK BOTTLED UP FOR YEARS.
MUST BE TOUGH.

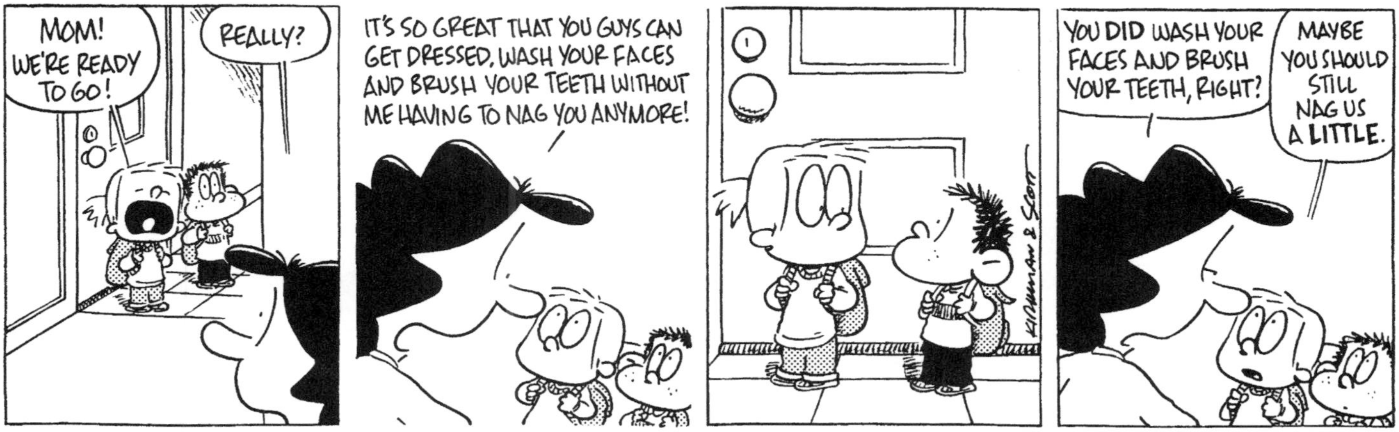
MOM! WE'RE READY TO GO!
REALLY?
IT'S SO GREAT THAT YOU GUYS CAN GET DRESSED, WASH YOUR FACES AND BRUSH YOUR TEETH WITHOUT ME HAVING TO NAG YOU ANYMORE!
YOU DID WASH YOUR FACES AND BRUSH YOUR TEETH, RIGHT?
MAYBE YOU SHOULD STILL NAG US A LITTLE.

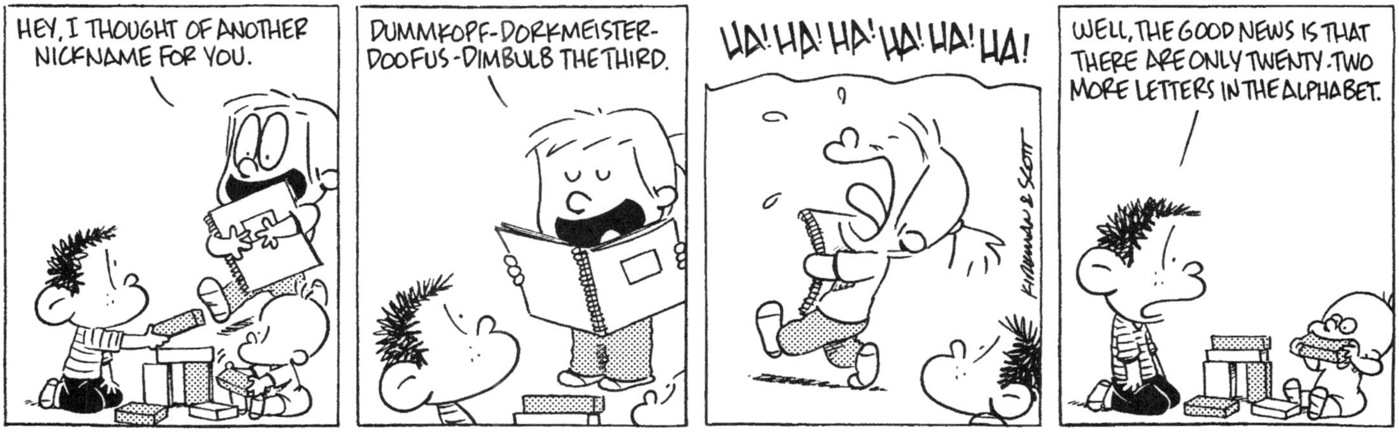
HEY, I THOUGHT OF ANOTHER NICKNAME FOR YOU.
DUMMKOPF-DORKMEISTER-DOOFUS-DIMBULB THE THIRD.
HA! HA! HA! HA! HA! HA!
WELL, THE GOOD NEWS IS THAT THERE ARE ONLY TWENTY-TWO MORE LETTERS IN THE ALPHABET.

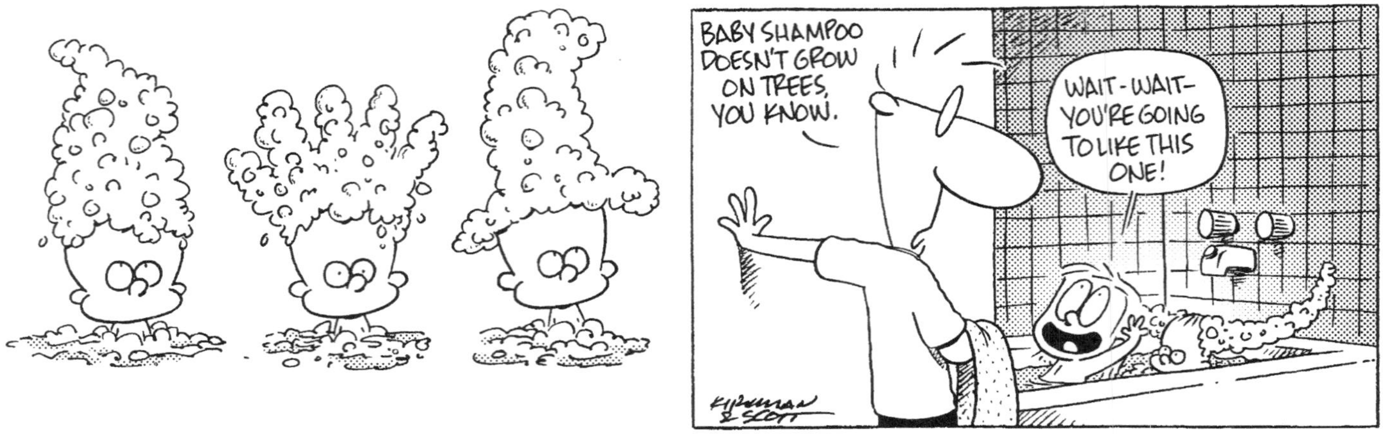
BABY SHAMPOO DOESN'T GROW ON TREES, YOU KNOW.
WAIT-WAIT-YOU'RE GOING TO LIKE THIS ONE!

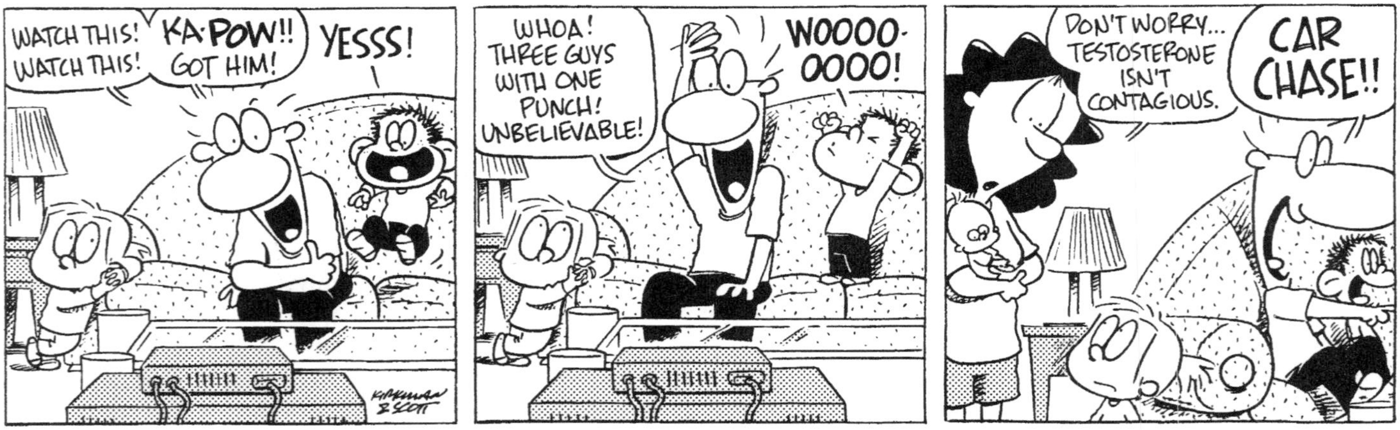
WATCH THIS! WATCH THIS!
KA-POW!! GOT HIM!
YESSS!
WHOA! THREE GUYS WITH ONE PUNCH! UNBELIEVABLE!
WOOOO-OOOO!
DON'T WORRY... TESTOSTERONE ISN'T CONTAGIOUS.
CAR CHASE!!

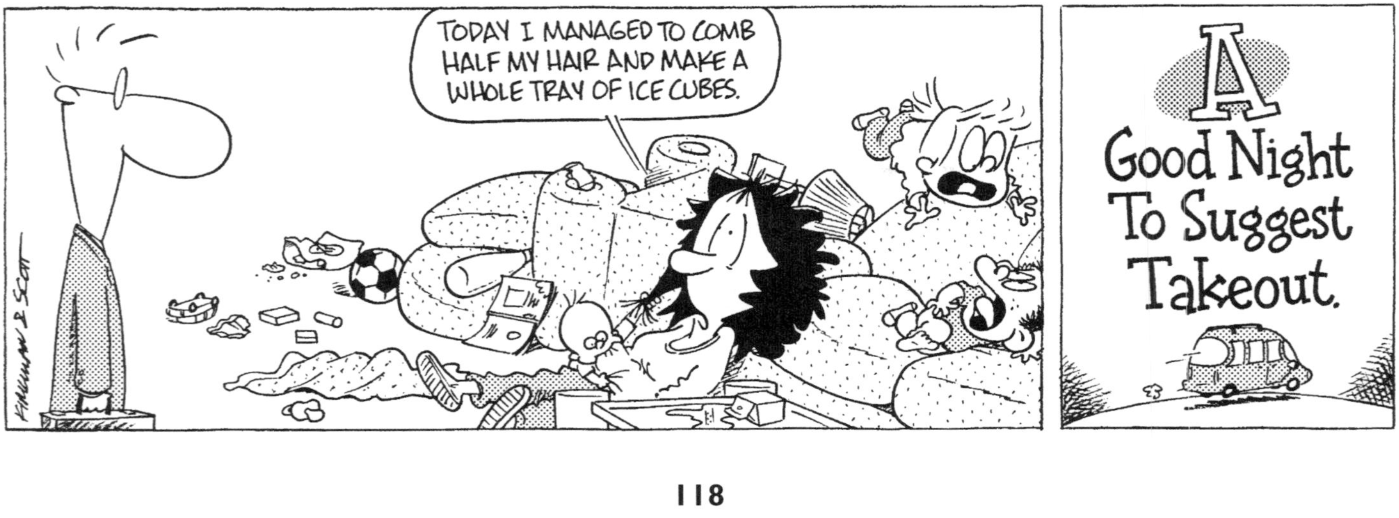
TODAY I MANAGED TO COMB HALF MY HAIR AND MAKE A WHOLE TRAY OF ICE CUBES.
A Good Night To Suggest Takeout.

BABY BLUES®
BY RICK KIRKMAN / JERRY SCOTT
YOU
ME

WAAAAAAAA!
MY TURN.
WAAAAAAAA!
ZZZZZZZ
WAAAAAAAAA!
ZZZ
Zz WHA-?
IT'S ALL RIGHT. I ALREADY HANDLED IT.
REALLY?
THAT STILL COUNTS AS A TURN FOR ME, THOUGH. RIGHT?
KIRKMAN & SCOTT

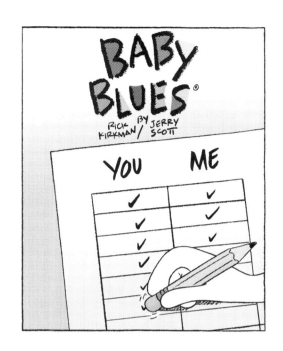

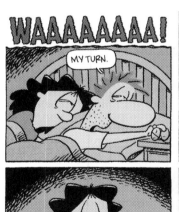

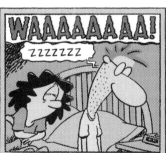

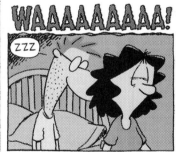

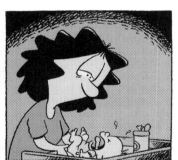

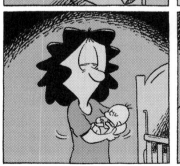

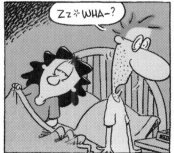

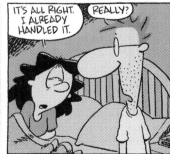

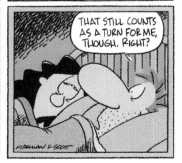

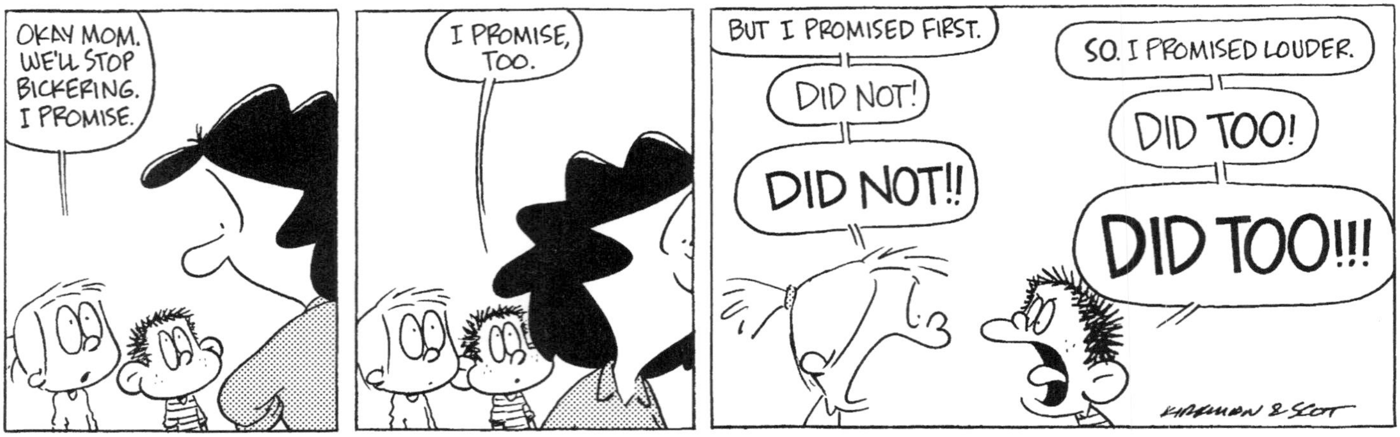
OKAY MOM. WE'LL STOP BICKERING. I PROMISE.
I PROMISE, TOO.
BUT I PROMISED FIRST.
DID NOT!
DID NOT!!
SO. I PROMISED LOUDER.
DID TOO!
DID TOO!!!
KIRKMAN & SCOTT

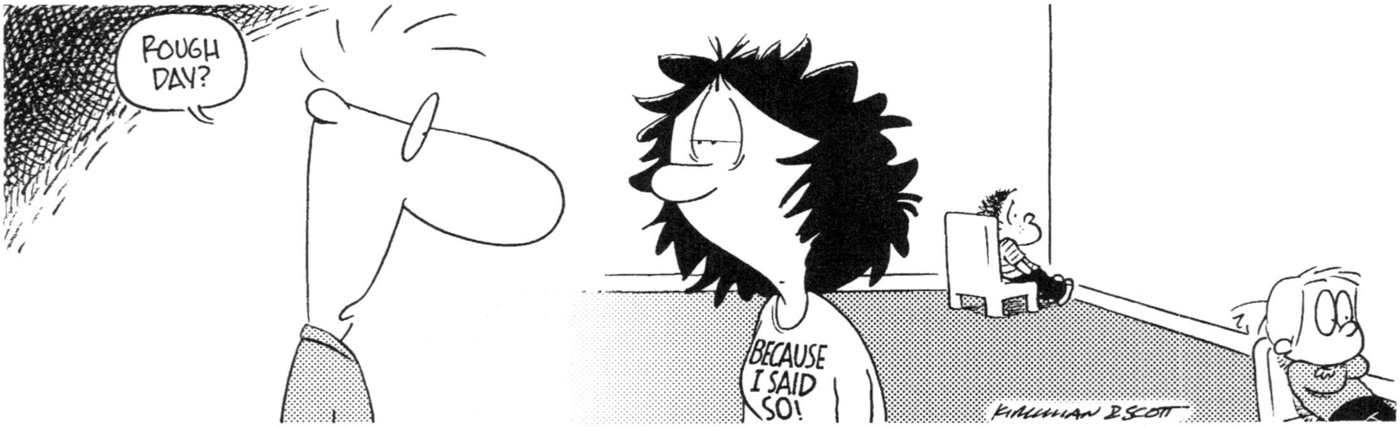
ROUGH DAY?
BECAUSE I SAID SO!
KIRKMAN & SCOTT

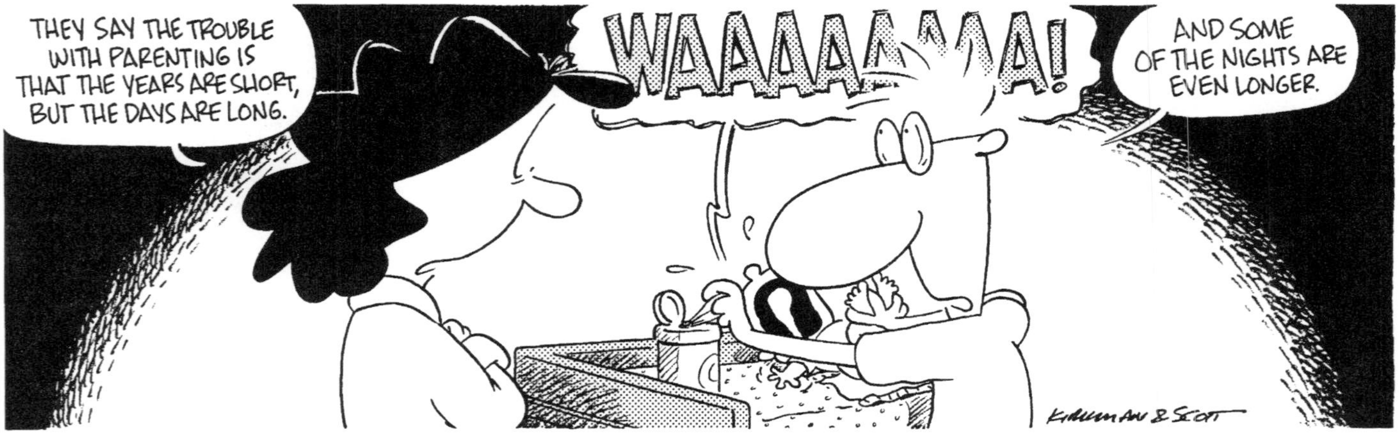
THEY SAY THE TROUBLE WITH PARENTING IS THAT THE YEARS ARE SHORT, BUT THE DAYS ARE LONG.
WAAAAAAAA!
AND SOME OF THE NIGHTS ARE EVEN LONGER.
KIRKMAN & SCOTT

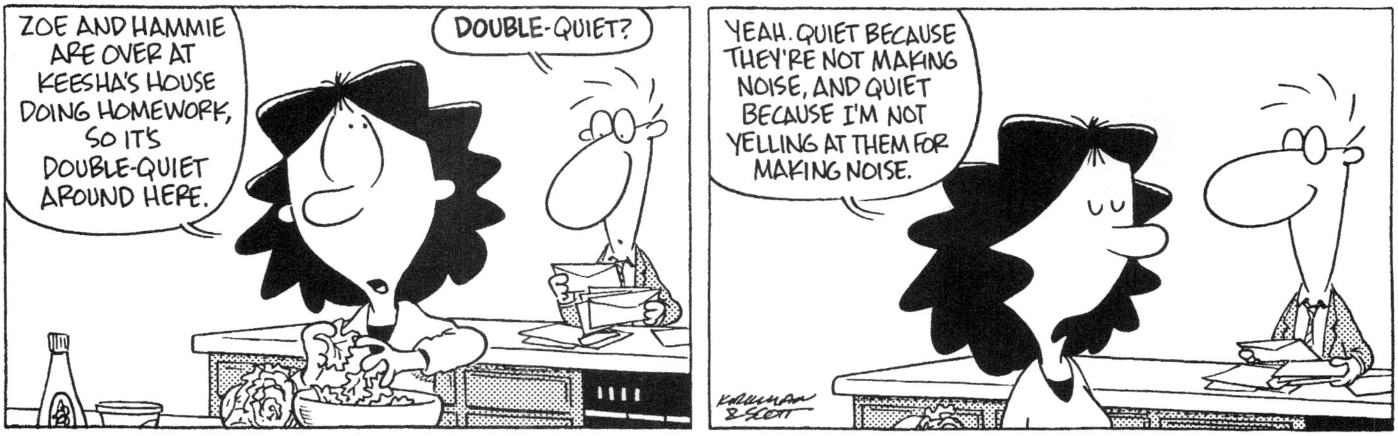
ZOE AND HAMMIE ARE OVER AT KEESHA'S HOUSE DOING HOMEWORK, SO IT'S DOUBLE-QUIET AROUND HERE.
DOUBLE-QUIET?
YEAH. QUIET BECAUSE THEY'RE NOT MAKING NOISE, AND QUIET BECAUSE I'M NOT YELLING AT THEM FOR MAKING NOISE.

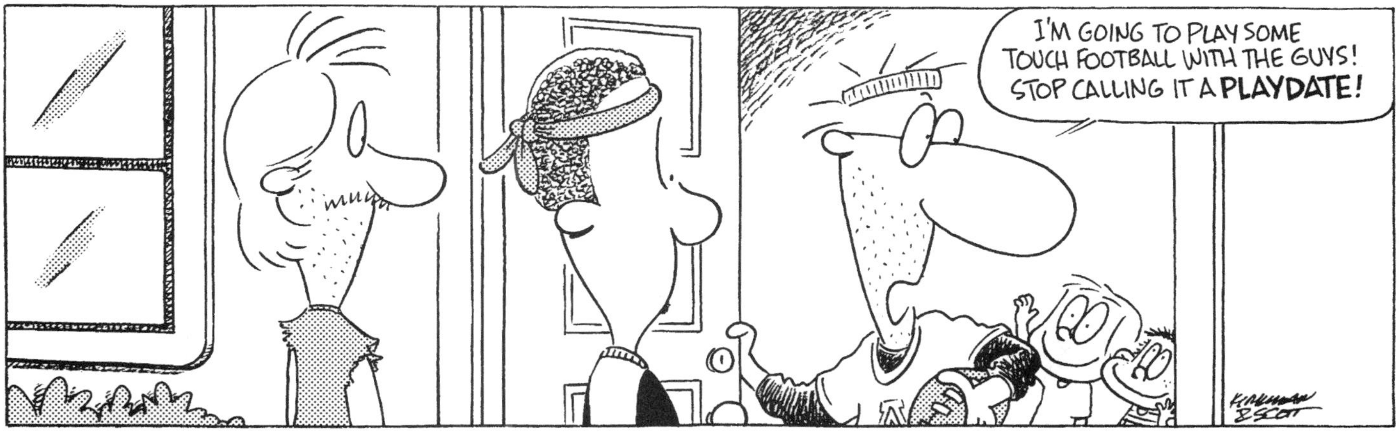
I'M GOING TO PLAY SOME TOUCH FOOTBALL WITH THE GUYS! STOP CALLING IT A **PLAYDATE**!

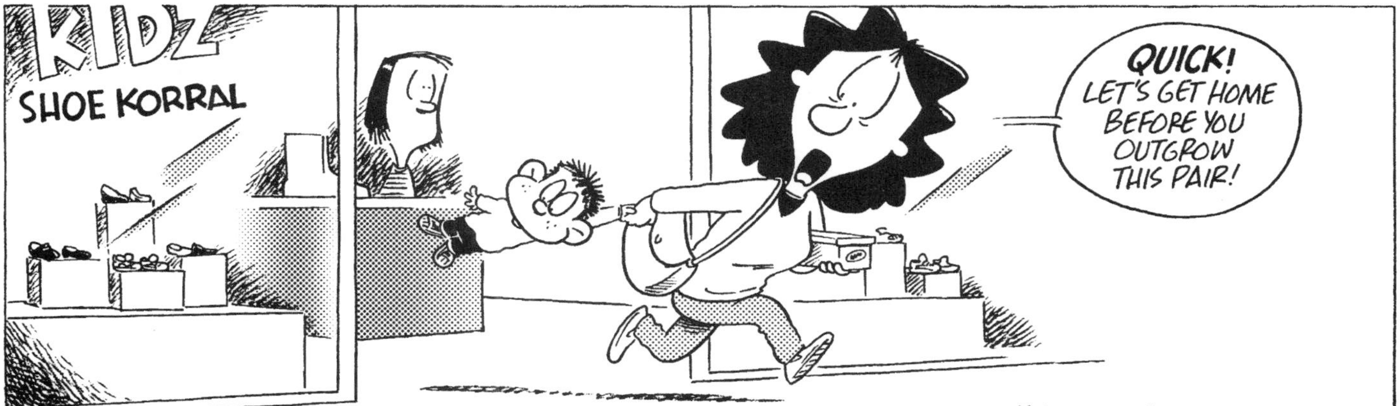
KIDZ
SHOE KORRAL
QUICK! LET'S GET HOME BEFORE YOU OUTGROW THIS PAIR!

BABY BLUES

CARPOOL
GROCERY STORE
DRY CLEANER
WHEW!
I'M HOME!
MALL
CARPOOL
LIBRARY
JUST BE GLAD YOU DON'T HAVE TO COMMUTE.

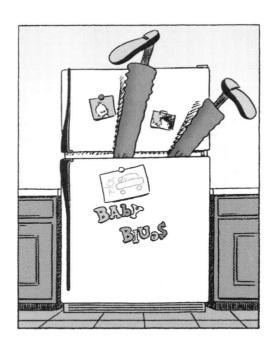

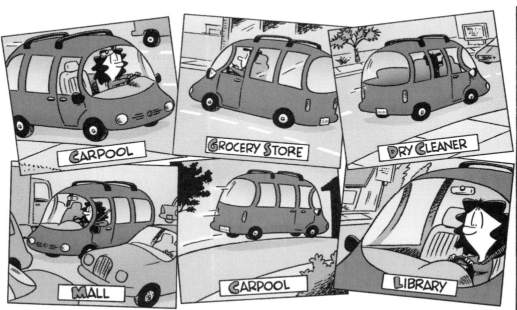

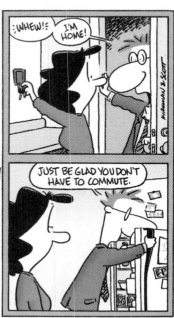

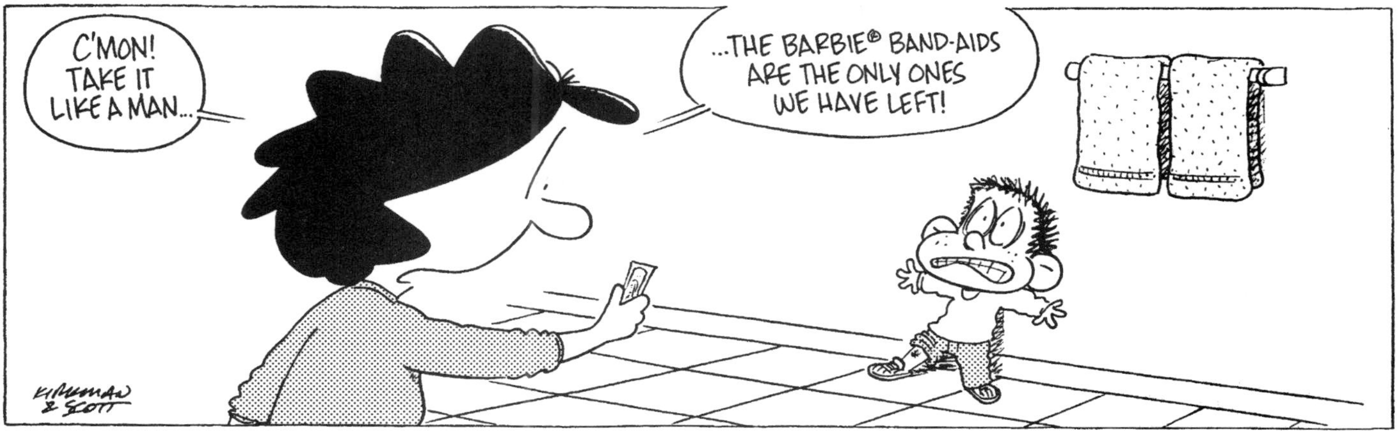
C'MON! TAKE IT LIKE A MAN...
...THE BARBIE® BAND-AIDS ARE THE ONLY ONES WE HAVE LEFT!
KIRKMAN & SCOTT

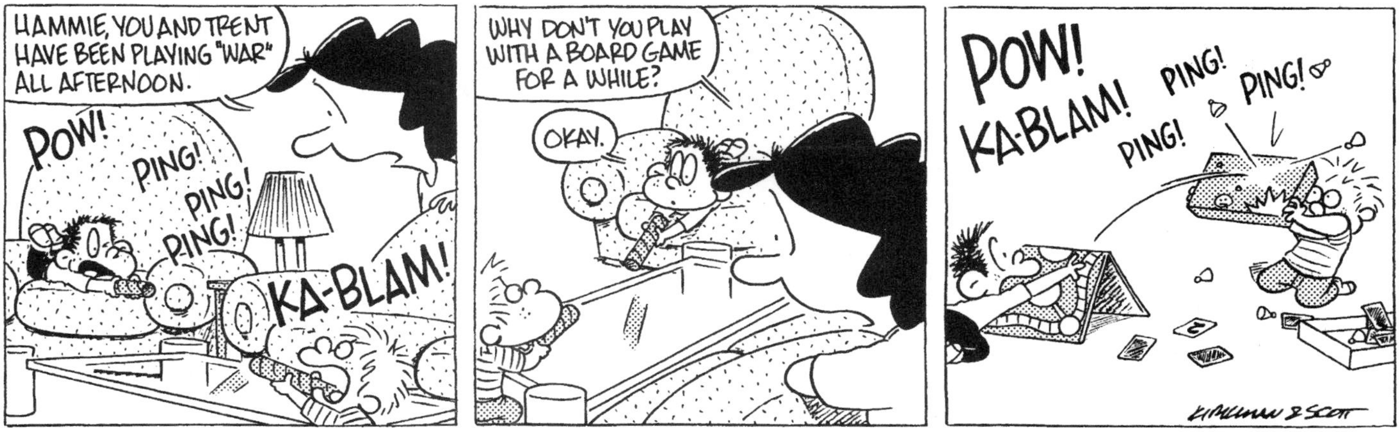
HAMMIE, YOU AND TRENT HAVE BEEN PLAYING "WAR" ALL AFTERNOON.
POW!
PING!
PING!
PING!
KA-BLAM!
WHY DON'T YOU PLAY WITH A BOARD GAME FOR A WHILE?
OKAY.
POW!
KA-BLAM!
PING!
PING!
PING!
KIRKMAN & SCOTT

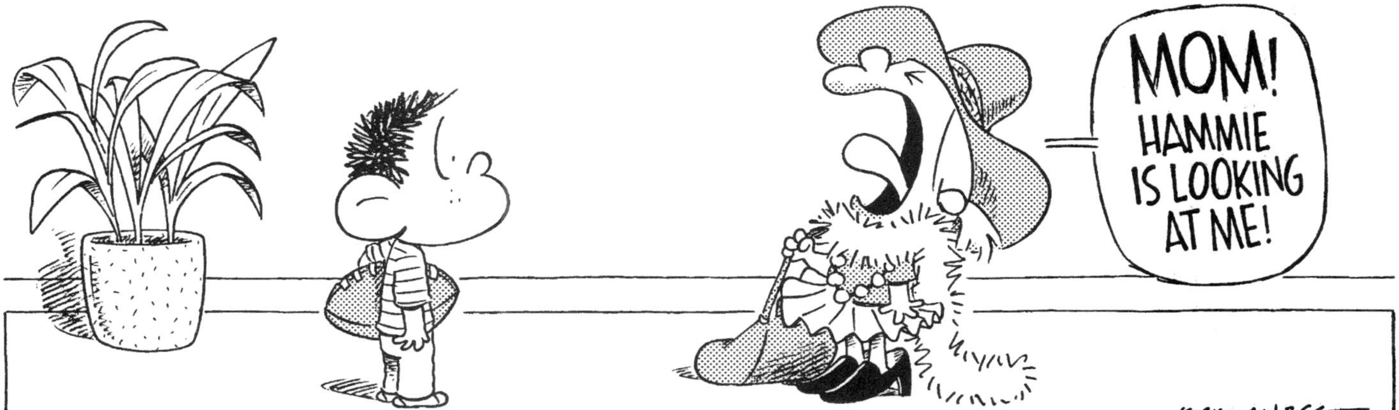
MOM! HAMMIE IS LOOKING AT ME!
KIRKMAN & SCOTT

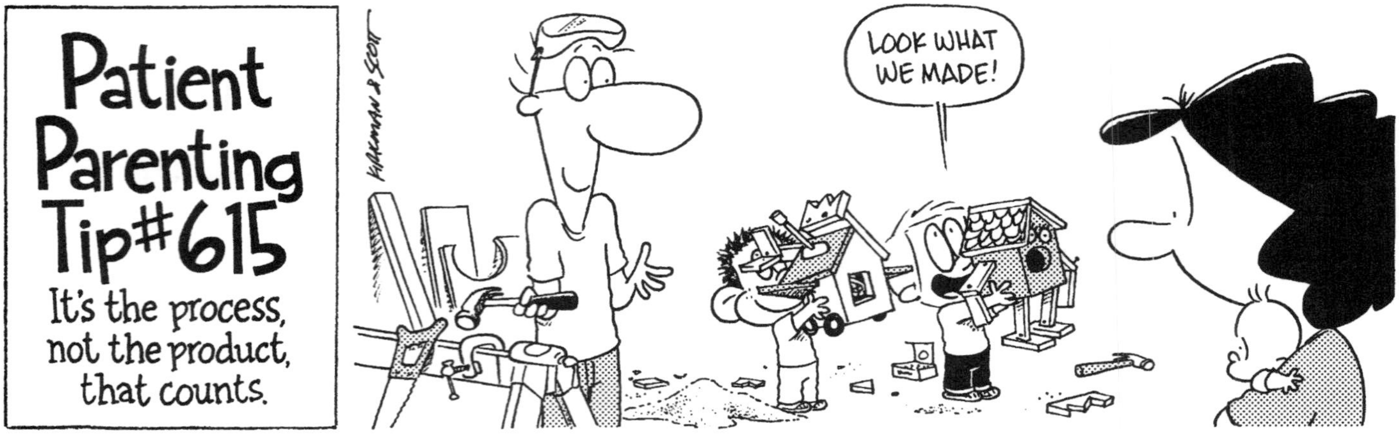
Patient Parenting Tip #615
It's the process, not the product, that counts.
KIRKMAN & SCOTT
LOOK WHAT WE MADE!

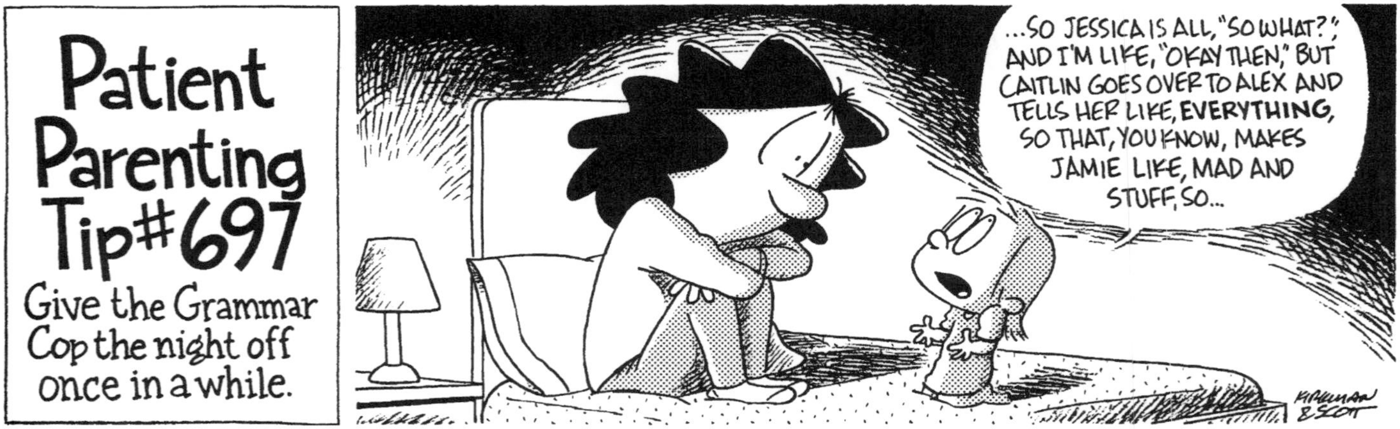
Patient Parenting Tip #697
Give the Grammar Cop the night off once in a while.
...SO JESSICA IS ALL, "SO WHAT?," AND I'M LIKE, "OKAY THEN," BUT CAITLIN GOES OVER TO ALEX AND TELLS HER LIKE, **EVERYTHING**, SO THAT, YOU KNOW, MAKES JAMIE LIKE, MAD AND STUFF, SO...
KIRKMAN & SCOTT

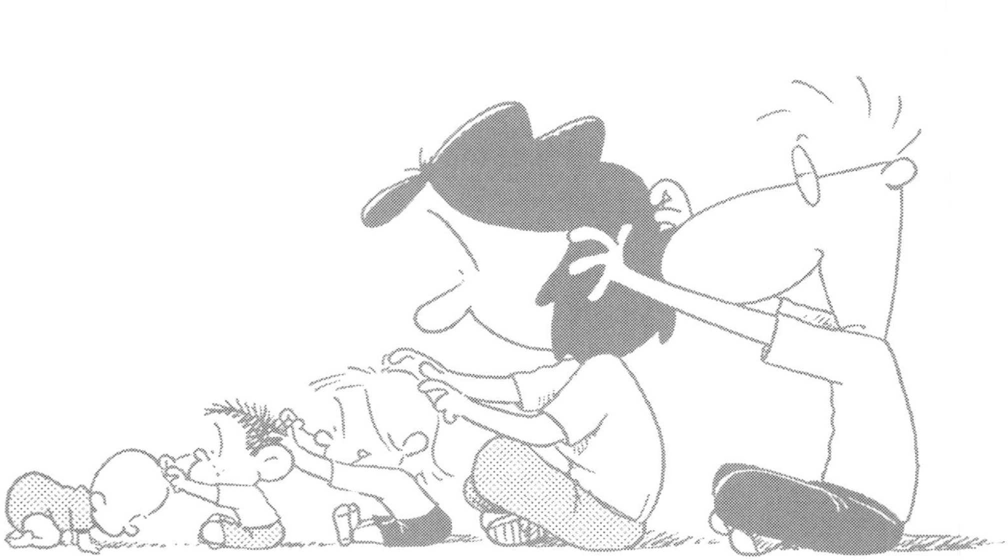

BABY BLUES®
BY RICK KIRKMAN / JERRY SCOTT

LOOK AT YOU! ARE YOU TRYING TO STAND UP LIKE A BIG GIRL?
WAIT... WREN... DON'T-
MOMMY'S HANDS ARE FULL, WREN! JUST WAIT! DON'T PULL ON MY PANTS LIKE TH-A-A-A-A-A-O-O-OH BOY.
SIGH! WELL, I GUESS SOMEDAY THIS WILL SEEM FUNNY...
...TO ME.
HA! HA! HA! HAR! HA! HA! HA!

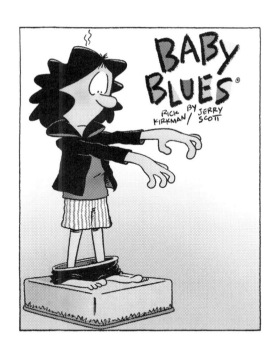

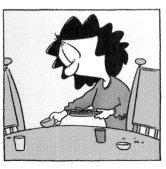

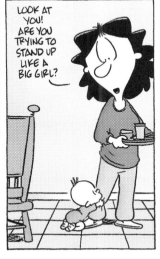

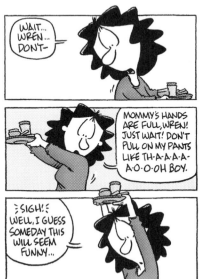

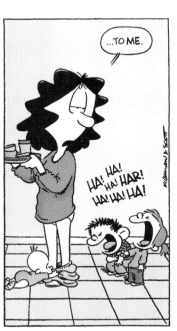

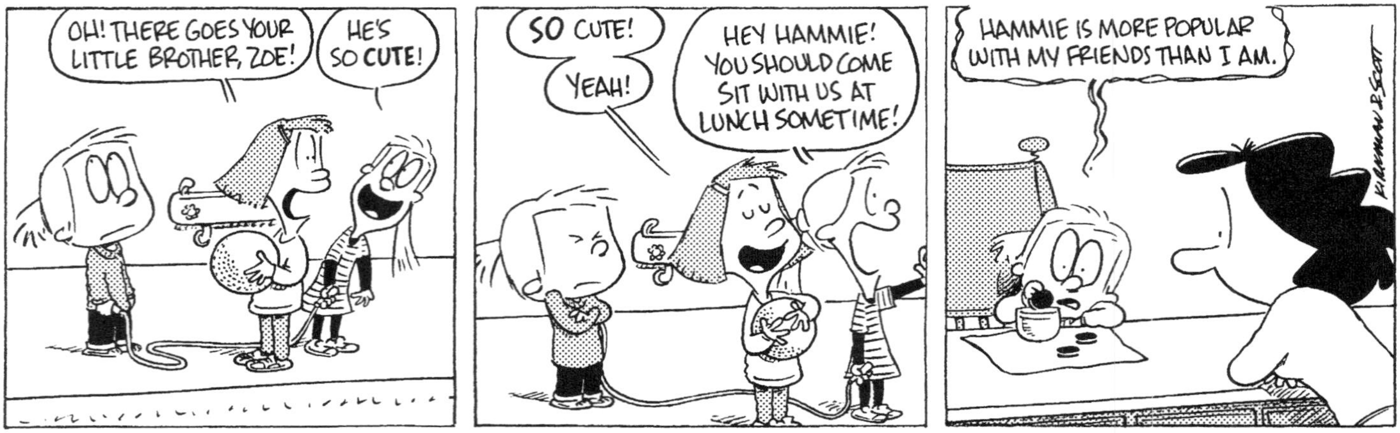
OH! THERE GOES YOUR LITTLE BROTHER, ZOE!
HE'S SO CUTE!
SO CUTE!
YEAH!
HEY HAMMIE! YOU SHOULD COME SIT WITH US AT LUNCH SOMETIME!
HAMMIE IS MORE POPULAR WITH MY FRIENDS THAN I AM.

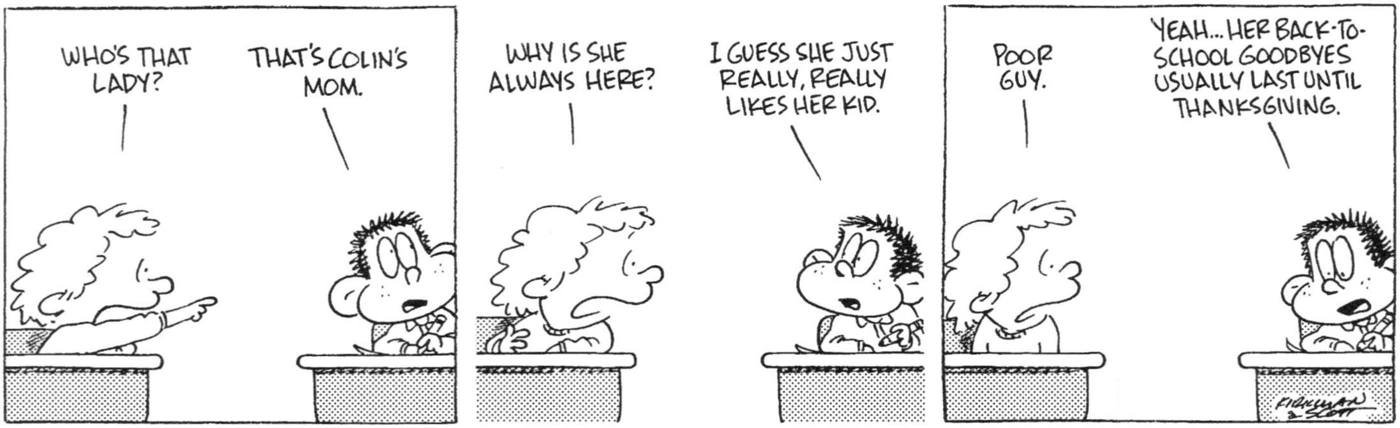
WHO'S THAT LADY?
THAT'S COLIN'S MOM.
WHY IS SHE ALWAYS HERE?
I GUESS SHE JUST REALLY, REALLY LIKES HER KID.
POOR GUY.
YEAH... HER BACK-TO-SCHOOL GOODBYES USUALLY LAST UNTIL THANKSGIVING.

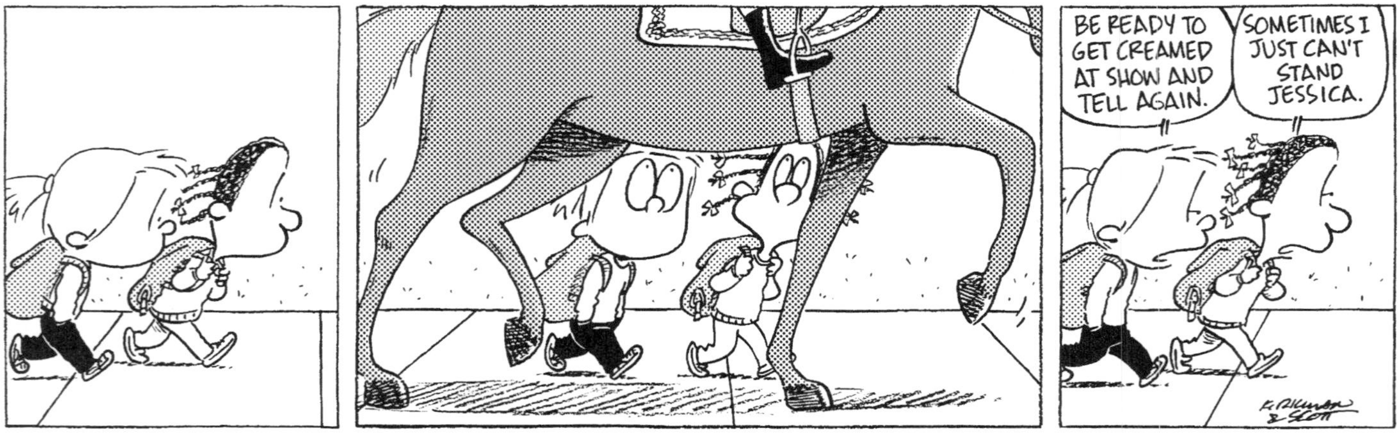
BE READY TO GET CREAMED AT SHOW AND TELL AGAIN.
SOMETIMES I JUST CAN'T STAND JESSICA.

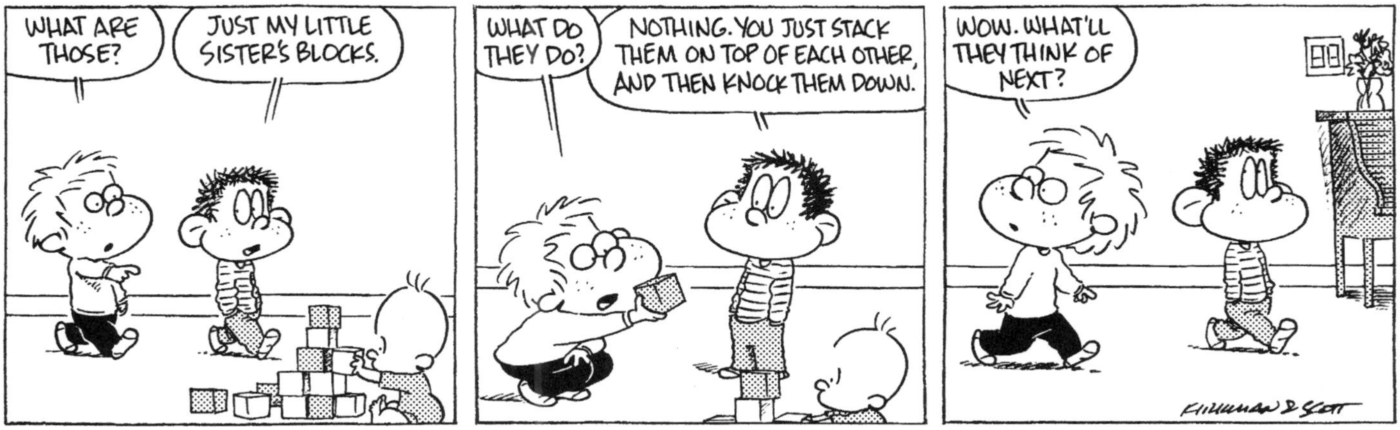
WHAT ARE THOSE?
JUST MY LITTLE SISTER'S BLOCKS.
WHAT DO THEY DO?
NOTHING. YOU JUST STACK THEM ON TOP OF EACH OTHER, AND THEN KNOCK THEM DOWN.
WOW. WHAT'LL THEY THINK OF NEXT?

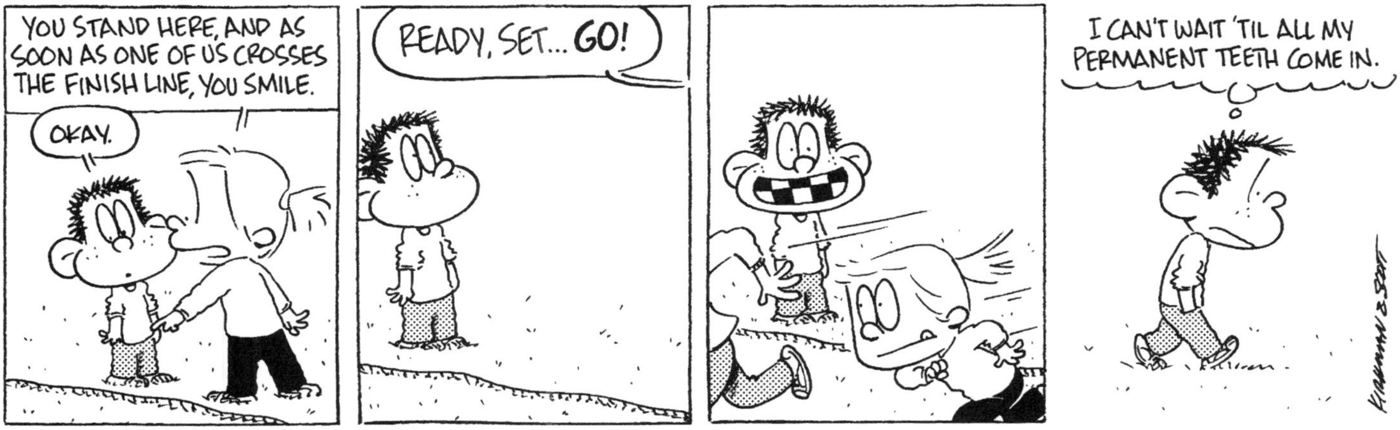
YOU STAND HERE, AND AS SOON AS ONE OF US CROSSES THE FINISH LINE, YOU SMILE.
OKAY.
READY, SET... GO!
I CAN'T WAIT 'TIL ALL MY PERMANENT TEETH COME IN.

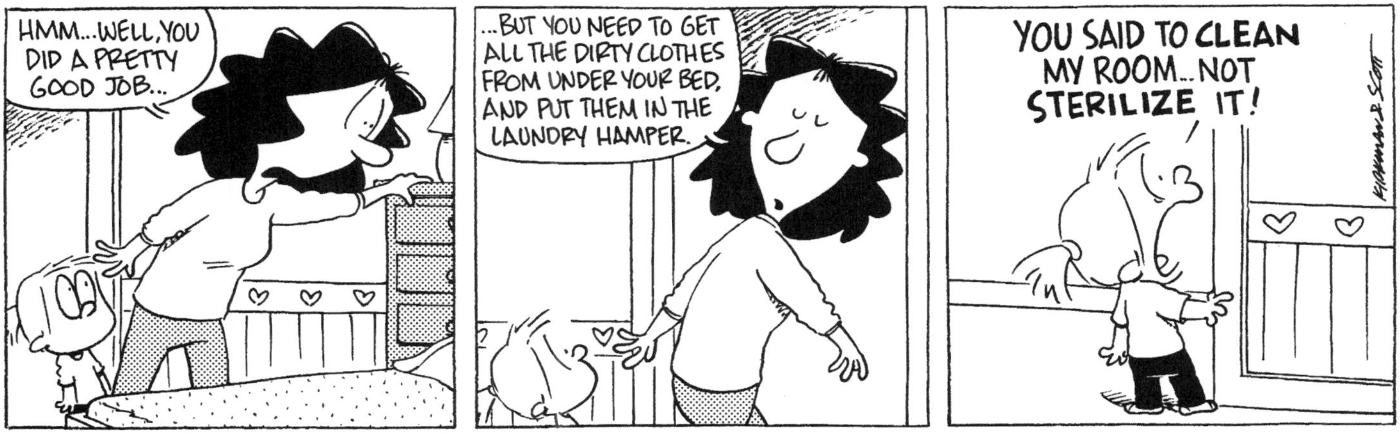
HMM...WELL, YOU DID A PRETTY GOOD JOB...
...BUT YOU NEED TO GET ALL THE DIRTY CLOTHES FROM UNDER YOUR BED, AND PUT THEM IN THE LAUNDRY HAMPER.
YOU SAID TO CLEAN MY ROOM...NOT STERILIZE IT!

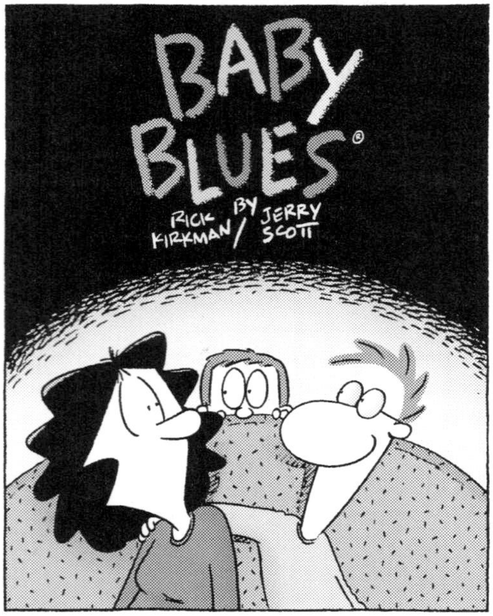
BABY BLUES®
RICK KIRKMAN / BY JERRY SCOTT

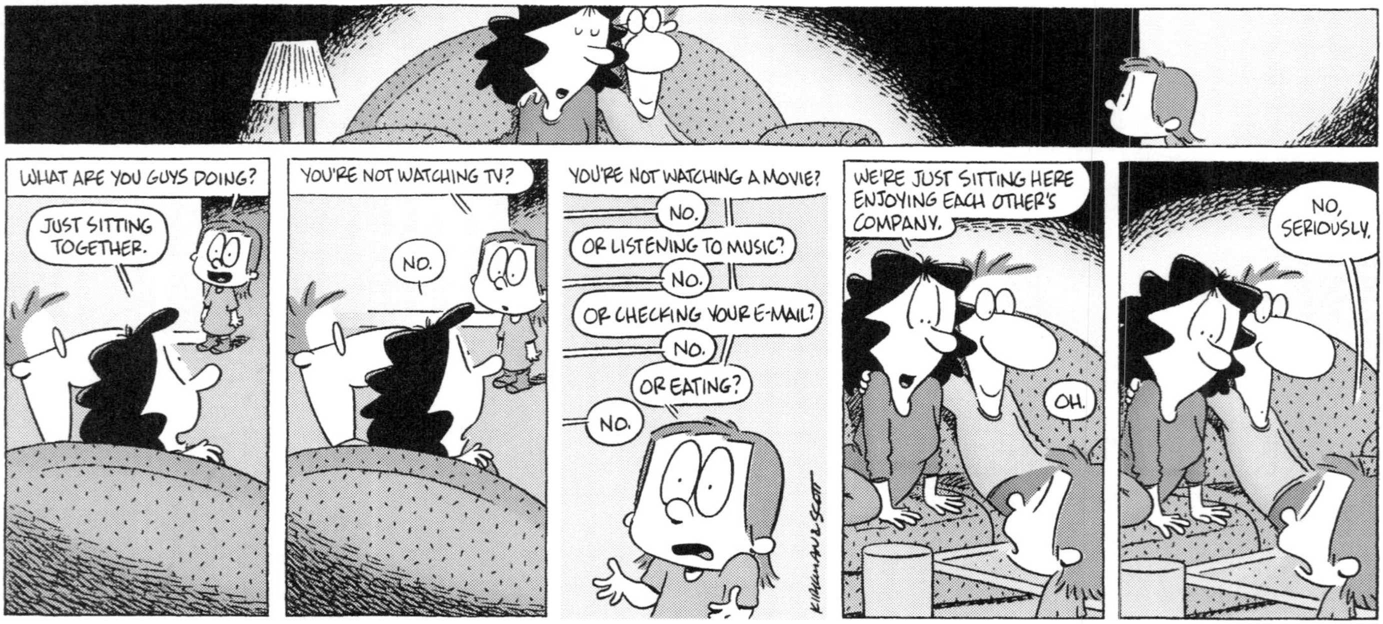
WHAT ARE YOU GUYS DOING?
JUST SITTING TOGETHER.
YOU'RE NOT WATCHING TV?
NO.
YOU'RE NOT WATCHING A MOVIE?
NO.
OR LISTENING TO MUSIC?
NO.
OR CHECKING YOUR E-MAIL?
NO.
OR EATING?
NO.
KIRKMAN & SCOTT
WE'RE JUST SITTING HERE ENJOYING EACH OTHER'S COMPANY.
OH.
NO, SERIOUSLY.